FamilyCircle®

Quick & Easy COOKING

Meredith® Consumer Marketing
Des Moines, Iowa

Family Circle® Quick & Easy Cooking

Meredith® Corporation Consumer Marketing
Vice President, Consumer Marketing: David Ball
Consumer Product Marketing Director: Steve Swanson
Consumer Product Marketing Manager: Wendy Merical
Business Manager: Todd Voss
Associate Director, Production: Douglas M. Johnston

Waterbury Publications, Inc.
Editorial Director: Lisa Kingsley
Associate Editor: Tricia Laning
Creative Director: Ken Carlson
Associate Design Director: Doug Samuelson
Contributing Recipe Editor: Mary Williams
Contributing Copy Editors: Terri Fredrickson, Gretchen Kauffman, Margaret Smith
Contributing Indexer: Elizabeth T. Parson

Family Circle® Magazine
Editor in Chief: Linda Fears
Creative Director: Karmen Lizzul
Food Director: Regina Ragone, M.S., R.D.
Senior Food Editor: Julie Miltenberger
Associate Food Editor: Michael Tyrell
Assistant Food Editor: Cindy Heller
Editorial Assistant: Allison Baker

Meredith Publishing Group
President: Jack Griffin
Executive Vice President: Andy Sareyan
Vice President, Manufacturing: Bruce Heston

Meredith Corporation
Chairman of the Board: William T. Kerr
President and Chief Executive Officer: Stephen M. Lacy

In Memoriam: E.T. Meredith III (1933–2003)

No matter the day and whatever the season,

nothing is as satisfying as sitting down to a fresh, home-cooked meal. It's a far less expensive and a more healthful alternative to eating out or hitting the drive-through—and it just feels good to know that you've made something delicious and nourishing for your family.

The fast pace of life can leave little time or energy to cook—but there's a way around that. The recipes in *Quick & Easy Cooking* were created for busy cooks who want to feed their families well. With a handful of easy-to-find ingredients, simple preparation, and short start-to-finish times, most of them can be on the table in 30 minutes or less from the time you walk in the door.

And simple doesn't mean boring. With more than 450 recipes for family-pleasing pastas, quick-to-grill meats, warming soups and stews, crisp and healthful salads, and fix-and-forget slow cooker meals, you can eat something wonderful and different every night of the week—and know that there's a dish to please every taste, season, mood, and occasion.

The recipes in this book may be easy to make, but there are a few things you can do to make your meal planning as efficient as possible. Take a little time on the weekend to thumb through the book and select recipes for the upcoming week. Set a menu for each night, make a grocery list, and do the shopping.

When "What's for dinner?" is the question, you can answer with confidence—and get an enthusiastic "Yum!" in response.

Because health and time-saving features are paramount these days, look for the following icons throughout the book:

Healthy: A "healthy" icon means that the recipe meets certain calorie, fat, and sodium guidelines. See page 336 for more information.

One Pan: A "one pan" icon means that the recipe uses a single pan in its preparation, and that translates to easy cleanup.

Layered Turkey Enchiladas, **page 106**

Bean and Potato Chowder, **page 151**

Lamb Chops with Tomatoes, **page 210**

Fresh Strawberry Fool, **page 323**

Table of Contents

Steak with Sweet Potato-Mango Chutney, **page 14**

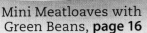
Mini Meatloaves with Green Beans, **page 16**

Pork and Potatoes with Tomato Relish, **page 34**

Herbed Lamb Steak Salad, **page 56**

Meaty Main Dishes

Whether you broil juicy steaks, sauté simple stir-fries, or combine chops with pasta and veggies, these hearty beef, pork, and lamb dishes will satisfy even the most robust appetites.

Herbed Steaks with Horseradish ▢one

Make quick herbed mayonnaise by stirring horseradish, Dijon mustard, and snipped fresh herbs, such as basil, parsley, chives, and/or dill, into regular or light mayo.

Start to Finish: 20 minutes **Makes:** 4 servings

- 2 **12- to 14-ounce beef top loin steaks, 1 inch thick**
  Salt and ground black pepper
- 2 **tablespoons prepared horseradish**
- 1 **tablespoon Dijon-style mustard**
- 2 **teaspoons snipped fresh Italian (flat-leaf) parsley**
- 1 **teaspoon snipped fresh thyme**
  Broiled cherry tomatoes (optional)
  Broiled sweet pepper strips (optional)
  Herbed mayonnaise (optional)
  Fresh thyme sprigs (optional)

1. Preheat broiler. Trim fat from steaks. Lightly sprinkle steaks with salt and black pepper. Place steaks on the unheated rack of a broiler pan. Broil 3 to 4 inches from heat for 7 minutes. Meanwhile, in a small bowl, combine horseradish, mustard, parsley, and thyme.

2. Turn steaks. Broil for 8 to 9 minutes more for medium (160°F). The last 1 minute of broiling, spread steaks with horseradish mixture. If desired, serve with tomatoes, peppers, and herbed mayonnaise; garnish with fresh thyme sprigs.

Per serving: 284 cal., 15 g total fat (6 g sat. fat), 84 mg chol., 351 mg sodium, 1 g carbo., 0 g fiber, 33 g pro.

Wine-Balsamic Glazed Steak

While the steak and sauce are cooking, sauté sliced zucchini and sweet red pepper strips to serve as a fresh, colorful side.

Start to Finish: 30 minutes **Makes:** 4 servings

- 2 **teaspoons cooking oil**
- 1 **pound boneless beef top loin or top sirloin steak, cut 1/2 to 3/4 inch thick**
- 3 **cloves garlic, minced**
- 1/8 **teaspoon crushed red pepper**
- 3/4 **cup dry red wine**
- 2 **cups sliced fresh mushrooms**
- 3 **tablespoons balsamic vinegar**
- 2 **tablespoons soy sauce**
- 4 **teaspoons honey**
- 2 **tablespoons butter**

1. In a large skillet, heat oil over medium-high heat until very hot. Add steak(s). Reduce heat to medium and cook for 10 to 13 minutes or to desired doneness, turning meat occasionally. If meat browns too quickly, reduce heat to medium-low. Transfer meat to platter; keep warm.

2. Add garlic and red pepper to skillet; cook for 10 seconds. Remove skillet from heat. Carefully add wine. Return to heat. Boil, uncovered, about 5 minutes or until most of the liquid is evaporated. Add mushrooms, vinegar, soy sauce, and honey; return to simmer. Cook and stir about 4 minutes or until mushrooms are tender. Stir in butter until melted. Spoon over steak(s).

Per serving: 377 cal., 21 g total fat (9 g sat. fat), 82 mg chol., 588 mg sodium, 12 g carbo., 0 g fiber, 27 g pro.

Beef Tenderloin with Peppercorns

This elegant and luxurious entrée is supersimple to make—perfect for entertaining.

Start to Finish: 20 minutes **Makes:** 4 servings

- 4 **4- to 5-ounce beef tenderloin steaks, 1 inch thick**
- 4 **teaspoons cracked black peppercorns**
- 3 **tablespoons butter or margarine**
- 2 **teaspoons all-purpose flour**
- 1/8 **teaspoon salt**
- 1/8 **teaspoon ground black pepper**
- 2/3 **cup half-and-half, light cream, or milk**
- 2 **tablespoons horseradish mustard**
  Cracked peppercorns (optional)

1. Trim fat from steaks. Rub both sides of steaks with cracked peppercorns. In a large skillet, melt 2 tablespoons of the butter over medium-high heat. Add steaks; reduce heat to medium. Cook for 10 to 13 minutes for medium rare (145°F) to medium (160°F), turning once halfway through cooking. Transfer steaks to a serving platter; keep warm.

2. Meanwhile, for sauce, in a small saucepan, melt remaining 1 tablespoon butter. Stir in flour, salt, and ground pepper. Add half-and-half. Cook and stir until thickened and bubbly. Stir in mustard. Spoon sauce over the steaks. If desired, sprinkle with additional cracked peppercorns.

Per serving: 317 cal., 22 g total fat (11 g sat. fat), 96 mg chol., 303 mg sodium, 5 g carbo., 1 g fiber, 26 g pro.

Beef Tenderloin with Peppercorns

Flat Iron Steak with BBQ Beans

The flat iron steak is a relatively new cut of meat that has become all the rage on restaurant menus—and for good reason. It's a tender, inexpensive cut that has deep, rich flavor. Supposedly, it's named for its similarity in appearance to the old-fashioned flat metal irons. It's cooked on a grill pan here, but it's perfect for the outdoor grill too.

Start to Finish: 20 minutes **Makes:** 4 servings

- 2 **boneless beef chuck top blade (flat iron) steaks, halved (1 to 1¼ pounds)**
- 2 **teaspoons fajita seasoning**
- 1 **15-ounce can black beans, rinsed and drained**
- ⅓ **cup bottled barbecue sauce**
- 2 **to 3 medium tomatoes, sliced**
  Corn bread (optional)
  Pickled jalapeño peppers, (optional) (see tip, page 22)

1. Grease a large grill pan. Preheat grill pan over medium-high heat. Trim fat from steaks. Sprinkle steaks with fajita seasoning. On grill pan, grill steaks for 8 to 12 minutes for medium rare (145°F) or 12 to 15 minutes for medium (160°F), turning once halfway through grilling.

2. Meanwhile, in a medium microwave-safe bowl, stir together beans and barbecue sauce. Cover loosely with plastic wrap. Microwave on 100% power (high) for 3 minutes, stirring once.

3. Arrange steaks, beans, and sliced tomatoes on plates. If desired, serve with corn bread and top with pickled jalapeño slices.

Per serving: 272 cal., 8 g total fat (2 g sat. fat), 67 mg chol., 667 mg sodium, 25 g carbo., 6 g fiber, 29 g pro.

Flank Steak with Parsley and Lemon ♥ 🔲

The parsley-lemon-garlic mixture that brightens the flavor of this simple steak is similar to gremolata—the traditional accompaniment to osso buco, the rich Italian dish of braised veal shanks.

Start to Finish: 20 minutes **Makes:** 4 servings

- 1¼ **to 1½ pounds beef flank steak**
  Salt and ground black pepper
- 4 **teaspoons olive oil**
- ¼ **teaspoon finely shredded lemon peel**
- 1 **tablespoon fresh lemon juice**
- 1 **tablespoon chopped fresh parsley**
- 1 **clove garlic, chopped**
- ¼ **teaspoon salt**
- ¼ **teaspoon freshly ground black pepper**
  Boiled small round red potatoes (optional)

1. Preheat broiler. Trim fat from steak. Lightly sprinkle both sides of steak with salt and pepper. Place steak on the unheated rack of a broiler pan. Broil 4 to 5 inches from heat for 15 to 18 minutes or until medium doneness (160°F). Cover and let stand for 5 minutes.

2. Meanwhile, in a small bowl, sir together olive oil, lemon peel, lemon juice, parsley, garlic, ¼ teaspoon salt, and ¼ teaspoon pepper.

3. Thinly slice steak diagonally across the grain. Transfer to a serving platter; spoon parsley-lemon-garlic mixture on steak. If desired, serve with boiled new potatoes.

Per serving: 263 cal., 14 g total fat (5 g sat. fat), 57 mg chol., 367 mg sodium, 1 g carbo., 0 g fiber, 30 g pro.

Flank Steak
with Parsley and Lemon

Spinach-Stuffed Flank Steak ♥ [one]

It takes a little time to flatten the steak and roll and cut the spirals, and the effort is well worth it. The steaks look great and hold a yummy filling of dried tomatoes, spinach, Parmesan cheese, and fresh basil.

Start to Finish: 30 minutes **Makes:** 4 servings

- ¼ **cup dried tomatoes (not oil-packed)**
- 1 **pound beef flank steak or top round steak**
- ⅛ **teaspoon salt**
- ⅛ **teaspoon ground black pepper**
- 1 **10-ounce package frozen chopped spinach, thawed and well drained**
- 2 **tablespoons grated Parmesan cheese**
- 2 **tablespoons snipped fresh basil**
  Cooked polenta (optional)

1. In a small bowl, soak dried tomatoes in enough hot water to cover for 10 minutes. Drain. Snip into small pieces.

2. Meanwhile, trim fat from steak. Score both sides of steak in a diamond pattern by making shallow diagonal cuts at 1-inch intervals. Place meat between two pieces of plastic wrap. Working from center to edges, pound with flat side of a meat mallet to a 12×8-inch rectangle. Discard plastic wrap. Sprinkle meat with the salt and pepper.

3. Spread spinach over the steak. Sprinkle with the softened tomatoes, Parmesan cheese, and basil. Roll up the steak from a short side. Secure with wooden toothpicks at 1-inch intervals, starting ½ inch from an end. Cut between the toothpicks into eight 1-inch slices.

4. Preheat broiler. Place slices, cut sides down, on unheated rack of a broiler pan. Broil 3 to 4 inches from heat for 12 to 16 minutes for medium doneness (160°F). Remove toothpicks. If desired, serve with cooked polenta.

Per serving: 213 cal., 9 g total fat (4 g sat. fat), 47 mg chol., 303 mg sodium, 5 g carbo., 3 g fiber, 28 g pro.

Spinach-Stuffed Flank Steak

Jerk Steaks with Zucchini Salad and Couscous

Look for hot and spicy Jamaican jerk sauce—a fragrant and flavorful combination of allspice, chiles, garlic, and thyme—in the condiment or specialty aisle of your supermarket.

Start to Finish: 30 minutes **Makes:** 4 servings

- 2 **tablespoons olive oil**
- ½ **cup chopped onion (1 medium)**
- 2 **cloves garlic, minced**
- ½ **teaspoon salt**
- 1 **teaspoon curry powder**
- 1 **10- to 12-ounce package quick-cooking couscous**
- 1 **teaspoon olive oil**
- 4 **beef cube steaks (1¼ pounds)**
- ½ **teaspoon salt**
- ⅓ **cup prepared Jamaican jerk sauce**
- 2 **tablespoons olive oil**
- ⅓ **cup snipped fresh mint**
- 1½ **teaspoons finely shredded lemon peel**
- 1 **teaspoon salt**
- ¼ **teaspoon freshly ground black pepper**
- 3 **medium zucchini (1½ pounds), cubed**
  Fresh mint sprigs (optional)
  Lemon wedges (optional)

1. For couscous, in a medium saucepan, heat 2 tablespoons olive oil over medium heat. Cook onion, garlic, and the ½ teaspoon salt in hot oil about 6 minutes or until onion is tender. Add curry powder; cook for 30 seconds more. Stir in couscous and the amount of boiling water specified in the package directions. Remove from heat; cover and set aside.

2. Meanwhile, for the steaks, heat a large grill pan over medium-high heat; brush with the 1 teaspoon olive oil. Sprinkle steaks with ½ teaspoon salt; transfer to grill pan. Brush tops of steaks with half the jerk sauce; cook for 2 to 3 minutes. Turn; brush steaks with remaining jerk sauce and cook for 2 to 3 minutes more for medium-rare doneness (145°F).

3. For zucchini salad, in a large bowl, combine 2 tablespoons olive oil, the mint, lemon peel, the 1 teaspoon salt, and the pepper. Add zucchini and toss to coat.

4. Fluff couscous with a fork. Divide couscous and zucchini salad among 4 serving plates. Top couscous with steaks. If desired, garnish with mint sprigs and lemon wedges.

Per serving: 681 cal., 24 g total fat (5 g sat. fat), 81 mg chol., 1,157 mg sodium, 70 g carbo., 6 g fiber, 45 g pro.

Sautéed Sirloin and Mushrooms ♥

Use a variety of mushrooms in this recipe: button, cremini, or portobello. Buying them sliced saves time.

Start to Finish: 30 minutes **Makes:** 4 servings

1	to 1¼ **pounds boneless beef top sirloin steak, ¾ inch thick**
¾	**teaspoon cracked black pepper**
1	**tablespoon butter or margarine**
¾	**cup beef broth**
1	**tablespoon teriyaki sauce, soy sauce, or hoisin sauce**
1¾	**cups packaged sliced fresh mushrooms**
1	**small onion, cut into very thin wedges**

1. Trim fat from steak. Cut steak in four serving-size portions. Sprinkle both sides of steaks with cracked pepper; pat pepper into meat with fingers. In a large skillet, melt butter over medium-high heat. Add steaks; reduce heat to medium. Cook steaks for 9 to 11 minutes for medium rare (145°F) to medium (160°F). Remove steaks from skillet, reserving drippings; cover steaks to keep warm.

2. Carefully add beef broth and teriyaki sauce to drippings in skillet. Cook until bubbly, stirring to scrape browned bits. Stir in mushrooms and onion. Cook, uncovered, over medium heat for 8 to 10 minutes or until most of the liquid has evaporated. Transfer steaks to dinner plates; top with mushroom mixture.

Per serving: 191 cal., 8 g total fat (3 g sat. fat), 62 mg chol., 403 mg sodium, 3 g carbo., 1 g fiber, 26 g pro.

Sautéed Sirloin and Mushrooms

Blackened Skirt Steak

A few simple add-ins turn canned sweet potatoes into a yummy side dish for this crusty steak. Use more or less cayenne, depending on your taste.

Start to Finish: 20 minutes **Makes:** 4 servings

- 1 **pound beef plate skirt steak or flank steak**
- 1 **tablespoon coarsely ground black pepper**
- 1 **teaspoon garlic salt**
- 1 **teaspoon paprika**
- 1 **teaspoon dried onion flakes**
- 2 **tablespoons vegetable oil**
- 2 **16-ounce cans sweet potatoes in light syrup**
- 3 **tablespoons butter or margarine**
- 1/2 **teaspoon garlic salt**
- 1/4 **teaspoon cayenne pepper**

1. Trim fat from steak. In a small bowl, combine black pepper, 1 teaspoon garlic salt, paprika, and dried onion flakes. Brush steak with 1 tablespoon of the oil. Rub pepper mixture on both sides of steak.

2. In a large nonstick skillet, heat the remaining 1 tablespoon oil over medium-high heat. Add steak; cook for 4 minutes for medium rare (145°F), turning once halfway through cooking. Remove from heat.

3. Meanwhile, for mashed sweet potatoes, drain sweet potatoes, reserving 1/2 cup liquid. In a medium saucepan, combine sweet potatoes and reserved liquid. Heat over medium-high heat, uncovered, about 5 minutes or until heated through. Add butter, 1/2 teaspoon garlic salt, and cayenne pepper. Beat until smooth.

4. Thinly slice the steak across the grain and divide among 4 plates. Serve with mashed sweet potatoes.

Per serving: 534 cal., 26 g total fat (15 g sat. fat), 79 mg chol., 782 mg sodium, 49 g carbo., 6 g fiber, 25 g pro.

Steak with Sautéed Onions

Onion marmalade is a sweet-savory relish made with caramelized sweet red or yellow onions and ingredients such as balsamic vinegar, brown sugar, raisins, pine nuts, herbs, and spices. If you can't find it, a couple dollops of orange marmalade will do just fine.

Start to Finish: 25 minutes **Makes:** 6 servings

- 6 **4-ounce beef tenderloin steaks, 1 inch thick**
- 1/4 **teaspoon salt**
- 1/4 **teaspoon ground black pepper**
- 2 **tablespoons butter or margarine**
- 1 **small red onion, cut in 6 wedges**
- 2 **cloves garlic, minced**
- 1 **teaspoon dried basil, crushed**
- 1/2 **teaspoon dried oregano, crushed**
- 2 **tablespoons whipping cream**
- 2 **tablespoons onion marmalade or orange marmalade**

1. Sprinkle meat with salt and pepper. In a large skillet, melt butter over medium heat. Add onion and garlic. Cook and stir for 6 to 8 minutes or until onion is tender but not brown. Remove onion from skillet.

2. Increase heat to medium-high. Add steaks to skillet; cook for 10 to 13 minutes for medium rare (145°F) to medium (160°F), turning and sprinkling meat with basil and oregano halfway through cooking.

3. Remove meat from skillet; place on serving platter. Return onions to skillet. Heat through. Remove skillet from heat. Stir in whipping cream. Spoon cream over steaks. Top each steak with 1 tablespoon onion marmalade, then divide cooked onions evenly among the steaks.

Per serving: 271 cal., 13 g total fat (4 g sat. fat), 63 mg chol., 110 mg sodium, 14 g carbo., 0 g fiber, 24 g pro.

Steak with Sweet Potato-Mango Chutney ♥

Mango chutney makes a tasty sandwich spread. Try it on a grilled Muenster, Swiss, or Havarti sandwich. Or put a spoon or two on soft cheese to spread on crackers.

Start to Finish: 20 minutes **Makes:** 4 servings

- 1 **large sweet potato, peeled and diced (12 ounces)**
- 4 **6-ounce boneless beef eye round steaks, 3/4 inch thick**
  Salt
  Steak seasoning blend
- 1/3 **cup mango chutney**
- 1/4 **cup dried cranberries**
  Fresh rosemary sprigs (optional)

1. In a medium saucepan, cook sweet potato, covered, in lightly salted boiling water for 8 to 10 minutes or until tender; drain and keep warm.

2. Meanwhile, trim fat from steaks. Lightly season steaks with salt and steak seasoning blend. Heat a large nonstick skillet over medium-high heat. Add steaks to skillet; reduce heat to medium. Cook for 8 to 10 minutes for medium rare (145°F) or to desired doneness. If meat browns too quickly, reduce heat to medium-low. Transfer to serving plates; cover to keep warm.

3. Add sweet potato to skillet; cook and stir for 2 minutes. Add chutney and cranberries to skillet. Stir gently to heat through. Season to taste with additional salt and steak seasoning. Serve with steaks. If desired, garnish with fresh rosemary.

Per serving: 344 cal., 5 g total fat (2 g sat. fat), 70 mg chol., 418 mg sodium, 32 g carbo., 4 g fiber, 40 g pro.

Steak with Sweet Potato-Mango Chutney

Curry Pepper Steak with Sweet Potatoes

Pepper steak takes a turn to the East with flavorings of curry, ginger, and ground red pepper.

Start to Finish: 30 minutes **Makes:** 4 servings

- **3** tablespoons vegetable oil
- **1** pound beef top round steak, cut in thin bite-size strips
- **1¼** teaspoons salt
- **2** green sweet peppers, cored, seeded, and cut in ½-inch strips
- **2** sweet potatoes (1 pound), peeled, quartered lengthwise, and sliced crosswise ¼ inch thick
- **1** large onion, thinly sliced
- **½** teaspoon curry powder
- **¼** teaspoon ground ginger
- **⅛** teaspoon cayenne pepper
- **½** cup water

1. In a large skillet, heat 2 tablespoons of the oil over medium-high heat. Sprinkle meat with ¼ teaspoon of the salt. Add meat to skillet; cook and stir about 3 minutes or to desired doneness. Remove meat from skillet; cover to keep warm.

2. Add remaining 1 tablespoon oil to skillet; add sweet peppers, sweet potatoes, and onion; cook for 6 minutes, stirring frequently. Add curry, ginger, cayenne pepper, and remaining 1 teaspoon salt; cook for 2 minutes. Add water; cover and cook 6 minutes or until sweet potatoes are tender, stirring occasionally. Add meat; heat through.

Per serving: 375 cal., 15 g total fat (2 g sat. fat), 71 mg chol., 793 mg sodium, 31 g carbo., 4 g fiber, 29 g pro.

Curry Pepper Steak with Sweet Potatoes

Mini Meatloaves with Green Beans

Making miniature meatloaves means this comfort food cooks quickly—in about 15 minutes. Traditional sizes of meatloaf take an hour or more.

Start to Finish: 22 minutes **Oven:** 450°F
Makes: 4 servings

- **1** egg, lightly beaten
- **1** cup purchased pasta sauce
- **½** cup fine dry bread crumbs
- **2** tablespoons fresh basil leaves, coarsely chopped
- **¼** teaspoon salt
- **1** pound lean ground beef
- **1** cup shredded mozzarella cheese (4 ounces)
- **1** 12-ounce package fresh green beans, trimmed
- **1** tablespoon olive oil
  Crushed red pepper (optional)

1. Preheat oven to 450°F. In a large bowl, combine egg, ½ cup of the pasta sauce, the bread crumbs, basil, and the salt. Add beef and half the cheese; mix well. Divide beef mixture in four equal portions. Shape each portion in a 5½×2-inch oval. Place on a 15×10×1-inch baking pan. Spoon remaining pasta sauce on the loaves. Bake about 15 minutes or until internal temperature registers 160°F. Sprinkle with remaining cheese and bake for 1 to 2 minutes more or until cheese is melted.

2. Meanwhile, in a medium saucepan, cook green beans in boiling lightly salted water for 10 minutes. Drain; toss with 1 tablespoon olive oil and, if desired, crushed red pepper. Serve beans with meat loaves.

Per serving: 496 cal., 29 g total fat (12 g sat. fat), 145 mg chol., 742 mg sodium, 25 g carbo., 5 g fiber, 34 g pro.

Quick Tip Fine dry bread crumbs from the grocery store are convenient and handy to keep in your pantry. However, if you run out, you can easily make them. Arrange a single layer of bread slices on a baking sheet and toast in a 300°F oven until the bread is dry and lightly browned. Cool, then process in a food processor or blender to the texture you like. Use whole wheat or rye bread for different taste and texture—or season by adding salt, pepper, dried herbs, and finely grated Parmesan cheese.

Beef and Asparagus Sauté

The sweetest, tenderest asparagus is in the market during spring. Look for slender stalks that have closed, dry (not soggy) tips.

Start to Finish: 20 minutes **Makes:** 4 servings

- **12 ounces fresh asparagus**
- **2 teaspoons olive oil**
- **1 pound beef strips for stir-fry (top round)**
  Salt and ground black pepper
- **¹/₂ cup packaged shredded carrots (1 medium carrot)**
- **1 teaspoon dried herbes de Provence, crushed**
- **¹/₂ cup dry Marsala**
- **¹/₄ teaspoon finely shredded lemon peel**

1. Snap off and discard woody bases from asparagus. Bias-slice asparagus in 2-inch pieces; set aside.

2. In a large nonstick skillet, heat 1 teaspoon of the olive oil over medium-high heat. Add half the meat to hot oil. Sprinkle with salt and pepper. Cook and stir for 3 minutes. Remove meat from skillet. Repeat with the remaining 1 teaspoon oil and remaining meat.

3. Return all the meat to the skillet. Add asparagus, carrots, and herbes de Provence; cook and stir for 2 minutes more. Add Marsala and lemon peel; reduce heat. Cook for 3 to 5 minutes more or until beef is desired doneness and asparagus is crisp-tender.

Per serving: 327 cal., 7 g total fat (2 g sat. fat), 69 mg chol., 209 mg sodium, 29 g carbo., 2 g fiber, 28 g pro.

Cube Steaks with Tomato-Mushroom Sauce

Cubed steak, an economical but slightly tough cut of meat, is tenderized at the meat counter. Brown it first for good flavor and crust. Cooking it for 30 minutes in liquid (canned tomatoes and cream of mushroom soup for this recipe) makes the meat moist and tender.

Prep: 15 minutes **Cook:** 30 minutes **Makes:** 4 servings

- **2 tablespoons vegetable oil**
- **4 4-ounce beef cube steaks**
- **1 cup sliced fresh mushrooms**
- **¹/₂ cup chopped onion (1 medium)**
- **1 clove garlic, minced**
- **1 14.5-ounce can diced tomatoes with basil, garlic, and oregano, undrained**
- **1 10.75-ounce can reduced-fat and reduced-sodium condensed cream of mushroom soup**
- **3 cups hot cooked noodles**

1. In an extra-large skillet, heat oil over medium-high heat. Add steaks; cook until browned on both sides, turning once. Remove steaks from skillet. Add mushrooms, onion, and garlic to skillet and cook until onion is tender.

2. Stir in undrained tomatoes and soup. Return steaks to skillet, turning to coat with sauce. Bring to boiling; reduce heat. Simmer, covered, about 30 minutes or until meat is tender. Serve with noodles.

Per serving: 468 cal., 15 g total fat (3 g sat. fat), 108 mg chol., 916 mg sodium, 48 g carbo., 2 g fiber, 34 g pro.

Stir-Fried Beef and Noodles

Add complex Asian flavor to this dish by substituting ¼ teaspoon five-spice power for the ginger. Five-spice powder is an aromatic blend of ground cinnamon, cloves, star anise, fennel, and Szechwan pepper.

Start to Finish: 30 minutes **Makes:** 3 servings

1	**3-ounce package beef-flavor ramen noodles**
8	**ounces beef sirloin steak, ¾ inch thick**
1	**tablespoon vegetable oil**
½	**cup thinly sliced carrot (1 medium)**
½	**cup bias-sliced celery (1 stalk)**
1	**6-ounce package frozen pea pods, thawed**
¼	**cup water**
1	**tablespoon snipped fresh parsley**
2	**teaspoons teriyaki sauce**
½	**teaspoon ground ginger**
¼	**teaspoon crushed red pepper (optional)**

1. Cook ramen noodles following package directions, except drain noodles and reserve the seasoning package.

2. Meanwhile, trim fat from the steak. Cut the steak in thin bite-size strips; set aside.

3. Pour oil into a wok or large skillet. (Add more oil as necessary during cooking.) Heat over medium-high heat. Add carrot and celery. Stir-fry for 2 to 3 minutes or until crisp-tender. Remove the vegetables from the wok.

4. Add the steak strips to the hot wok. Stir-fry for 2 to 3 minutes or to desired doneness. Return carrot and celery to the wok. Stir in noodles, reserved seasoning package, pea pods, water, parsley, teriyaki sauce, ginger, and, if desired, crushed red pepper. Cook over medium heat until heated through, stirring occasionally.

Per serving: 621 cal., 30 g total fat (3 g sat. fat), 50 mg chol., 1,724 mg sodium, 61 g carbo., 2 g fiber, 30 g pro.

Quick Tip It's easier to eat ramen noodles when they're slightly broken. Before opening the package, gently break the noodles in a few places by lightly pressing or twisting the package.

Stir-Fried Beef and Noodles

Spicy Beef-Noodle Bowl

Spicy Beef-Noodle Bowl 🍜

Bottled peanut sauce adds authentic Thai flavor to this one-pot meal. For crunch, sprinkle chopped roasted peanuts, if you like.

Start to Finish: 20 minutes **Makes:** 4 servings

1	tablespoon vegetable oil
1	pound boneless beef sirloin steak, cut in thin bite-size strips
2	14-ounce cans reduced-sodium beef broth
1/3	cup bottled peanut sauce
1 1/2	cups medium egg noodles (3 ounces)
2	cups broccoli florets
1/4	cup bias-sliced green onions (2) (optional)

1. In a Dutch oven, heat oil over medium-high heat. Add beef strips; cook until browned.

2. Add beef broth and peanut sauce to meat in Dutch oven; bring to boiling. Stir in noodles; reduce heat. Simmer, uncovered, for 4 minutes, stirring occasionally. Add broccoli; return to boiling. Reduce heat; simmer, uncovered, for 3 to 4 minutes more or just until noodles are tender, stirring occasionally.

3. Divide beef and noodle mixture among 4 bowls. If desired, sprinkle with green onions.

Per serving: 316 cal., 12 g total fat (3 g sat. fat), 60 mg chol., 762 mg sodium, 18 g carbo., 2 g fiber, 31 g pro.

Beef Paprikash

This rich, creamy dish is ideal on a cold fall or winter evening. Be careful not to let the sauce simmer after you add the sour cream or it will curdle.

Start to Finish: 30 minutes **Makes:** 6 servings

2	tablespoons vegetable oil
1 1/2	pounds beef strips for stir-fry (top round)
1	teaspoon salt
1/2	teaspoon ground black pepper
2	medium onions, sliced
1	8-ounce package sliced mushrooms
3	cups beef broth
1	8-ounce container sour cream
3	tablespoons paprika
2	tablespoons Dijon-style mustard
2	tablespoons tomato paste
1/2	teaspoon dried thyme
1	12-ounce package egg noodles, cooked following package directions, kept warm

1. In a large skillet, heat 1 tablespoon of the oil over medium-high heat. (Add more oil as necessary during cooking.) Sprinkle beef with 1/2 teaspoon of the salt and 1/8 teaspoon of the pepper. In batches, add beef to skillet; cook and stir for 2 to 3 minutes or to desired doneness. Remove beef strips to a plate and keep warm.

2. Add 1 tablespoon oil to the skillet; heat. Add onions; cook over high heat 5 minutes, stirring frequently. Add mushrooms; cook 6 to 7 minutes or until heated through.

3. Meanwhile, in a small bowl, whisk together 1 cup of the broth, sour cream, paprika, and mustard until smooth.

4. Add the remaining 2 cups broth, the tomato paste, thyme, and the remaining 1/2 teaspoon salt and remaining pepper to the onion mixture in skillet. Bring to simmering, stirring to combine. Stir in the sour cream mixture and the reserved beef strips. Gently heat through for about 3 minutes, stirring occasionally. Do not let mixture come to simmering.

5. Place hot noodles in a large bowl. Pour the beef mixture over; gently stir to combine. Tent with aluminum foil; let stand 5 minutes before serving to absorb sauce.

Per serving: 523 cal., 22 g total fat (7 g sat. fat), 133 mg chol., 1,100 mg sodium, 43 g carbo., 4 g fiber, 38 g pro.

Thai Beef with Couscous

Purchased Thai green curry does double duty here—to flavor the meat and the coconut-flavored couscous.

Start to Finish: 15 minutes **Makes:** 4 servings

1	tablespoon green curry paste
1	pound beef plate skirt steak or flank steak, cut crosswise in 4 pieces
3/4	teaspoon salt
1 1/2	teaspoons vegetable oil
1/2	teaspoon green curry paste
1	cup coconut milk
1	cup water
1/2	teaspoon salt
1	10-ounce package couscous
1	10-ounce package frozen peas, thawed
2	tablespoons snipped fresh cilantro
	Fresh cilantro leaves (optional)

1. Rub the 1 tablespoon curry paste onto both sides of the steak; sprinkle with salt. In an extra-large skillet, heat 1/2 teaspoon of the oil over medium-high heat. Add steak; cook for 6 to 8 minutes for medium rare (145°F), turning once halfway through cooking.

2. Meanwhile, in a 2-quart saucepan, heat the remaining 1 teaspoon oil over medium heat. Add 1/2 teaspoon curry paste; cook, stirring, for 30 seconds. Add coconut milk, water, and salt; bring to boiling. Stir in couscous. Cover and remove from heat; let stand for 5 minutes. Fluff couscous with a fork. Stir in peas and snipped cilantro; cover and let stand for 1 minute more.

3. Thinly slice steak. Divide steak and couscous among 4 serving plates. If desired, garnish with cilantro leaves.

Per serving: 615 cal., 25 g total fat (14 g sat. fat), 44 mg chol., 1,051 mg sodium, 67 g carbo., 6 g fiber, 30 g pro.

Hot-and-Sour Thai Beef Salad ♥ 🄌

Many Asian dishes, like this one, are notable for perfect balance—sweet and sour flavors, hot and cool temperatures, and crunchy and soft textures.

Start to Finish: 30 minutes **Makes:** 4 servings

- 1 **large yellow, red, or green sweet pepper, cut in bite-size strips**
- ½ **a medium cucumber, cut in bite-size strips (1 cup)**
- ¼ **cup fresh lime juice**
- 3 **tablespoons reduced-sodium soy sauce**
- 2 **tablespoons packed brown sugar**
- 1 **tablespoon grated fresh ginger or ½ teaspoon ground ginger**
- 1 **tablespoon snipped fresh basil or 1 teaspoon dried basil, crushed**
- 1½ **teaspoons snipped fresh mint or 1 teaspoon dried mint, crushed**
- 12 **ounces beef top sirloin steak**
   Nonstick cooking spray
- 1 **clove garlic, minced**
- 1 **jalapeño pepper, seeded and minced (see tip, below)**
- 4 **cups packaged mixed greens**

1. In a medium bowl, combine sweet pepper and cucumber. For dressing, in a small bowl, stir together lime juice, soy sauce, brown sugar, ground ginger (if using), basil, and mint. Set aside.

2. Trim fat from beef. Cut beef in thin bite-size strips. Coat a wok or large skillet with cooking spray. Heat over medium heat. Add garlic, jalapeño pepper, and fresh ginger (if using). Cook and stir for 30 seconds. Add beef strips; cook and stir for 3 to 4 minutes or to desired doneness. Remove beef mixture from wok. Add to vegetable mixture. Toss gently.

3. Add dressing to wok. Bring to boiling; boil, stirring, for 30 seconds. Remove from heat.

4. Divide greens among 4 dinner plates. Spoon beef mixture over the greens. Drizzle hot dressing over all. Serve immediately.

Per serving: 219 cal., 8 g total fat (3 g sat. fat), 57 mg chol., 468 mg sodium, 15 g carbo., 1 g fiber, 22 g pro.

Spicy Beef and Noodle Salad

Let the steak rest for 5 to 10 minutes before slicing it to allow the flavorful juices to absorb into the meat rather than coat the cutting board.

Start to Finish: 20 minutes **Makes:** 4 servings

- 1 **pound beef flank steak**
- 1 **tablespoon soy sauce**
- 8 **ounces rice noodles**
- 1 **medium English cucumber**
- 1 **cup packaged fresh julienned carrots**
- ½ **cup Asian sweet chili sauce**
- ½ **cup water**
   Fresh cilantro leaves (optional)

1. Preheat broiler. Trim fat from steak. Brush steak with soy sauce. Place steak on the rack of an unheated broiler pan. Broil 4 to 5 inches from heat for 15 to 18 minutes or to desired doneness (160°F for medium), turning once halfway through broiling. Thinly slice beef across the grain.

2. Meanwhile, cook noodles following package directions; drain in colander. Rinse with cold water; drain again.

3. Slice cucumber crosswise in three sections. Using a vegetable peeler, cut lengthwise ribbons from sections.

4. In a small bowl, combine chili sauce and water. Divide steak, noodles, cucumber ribbons, and carrots among 4 bowls. Drizzle with chili sauce mixture. If desired, sprinkle with cilantro.

Per serving: 477 cal., 9 g total fat (4 g sat. fat), 40 mg chol., 839 mg sodium, 70 g carbo., 3 g fiber, 27 g pro.

Quick Tip Because hot chile peppers, such as jalapeños, contain volatile oils that can burn your skin and eyes, avoid direct contact with chiles as much as possible. When working with chile peppers, wear plastic or rubber gloves. If your bare hands do touch the chile peppers, wash your hands well with soap and water.

Hot-and-Sour Thai Beef Salad

Mexican Beef and Veggies ♥

Top this veggie-packed dish with a sprinkling of Cotija cheese—a flavorful, low-fat Mexican cheese that's similar to feta.

Start to Finish: 30 minutes. **Makes:** 4 to 6 servings

12	ounces lean ground beef
1	medium (1¼ pounds) butternut squash, peeled, seeded, and cubed (about 3 cups)
2	cloves garlic, minced
1	teaspoon ground cumin
½	teaspoon salt
⅛	teaspoon ground cinnamon
1	14.5-ounce can diced tomatoes
1	medium zucchini, halved lengthwise and sliced ¼ inch thick
¼	cup water
¼	cup chopped fresh cilantro
2	to 3 cups hot cooked white or brown rice
	Bottled hot pepper sauce (optional)

1. In a large skillet, cook ground beef, squash, garlic, cumin, salt, and cinnamon over medium heat until beef is no longer pink. Drain off fat.

2. Stir in undrained tomatoes; bring to boiling; reduce heat. Simmer, covered, about 8 minutes or just until squash is tender. Stir in zucchini and the water. Simmer, covered, about 4 minutes more or until zucchini is tender. Stir in cilantro. Serve over hot cooked rice. If desired, season to taste with bottled hot pepper sauce.

Per serving: 313 cal., 9 g total fat (3 g sat. fat), 54 mg chol., 504 mg sodium, 39 g carbo., 3 g fiber, 20 g pro.

Zippy Beef, Mac, and Cheese

This hearty dish calls for a light, fresh side: Arrange peeled, sectioned oranges and strips of crunchy jicama on lettuce and drizzle with a citrus vinaigrette.

Start to Finish: 30 minutes **Makes:** 4 servings

6	ounces dried elbow macaroni or corkscrew macaroni (about 1½ cups)
12	ounces lean ground beef, pork, or uncooked turkey
1	15-ounce can tomato sauce
1	14.5-ounce can stewed tomatoes or Mexican-style stewed tomatoes
4	ounces American or sharp American cheese, cut in small cubes
1	tablespoon chili powder
	Finely shredded or grated Parmesan cheese (optional)

1. In a 3-quart saucepan, cook macaroni following package directions. Drain in colander. Return macaroni to saucepan; keep warm.

2. Meanwhile, in a large skillet, cook ground meat over medium heat until browned. Drain off fat.

3. Stir ground meat, tomato sauce, undrained tomatoes, the 4 ounces cheese, and chili powder into cooked macaroni. Cook and stir over medium heat for 6 to 8 minutes or until heated through. If desired, sprinkle servings with Parmesan cheese.

Per serving: 587 cal., 25 g total fat (13 g sat. fat), 93 mg chol., 1,665 mg sodium, 49 g carbo., 3 g fiber, 40 g pro.

Zippy Beef, Mac, and Cheese

Beef and Broccoli Stir-Fry

This recipe uses only half of the Stir-Fry Sauce. Store the rest in the refrigerator up to 2 weeks and you'll be ready for another quick-fix meal.

Start to Finish: 30 minutes **Makes:** 4 servings

Quick-cooking brown rice
1 tablespoon vegetable oil
1 pound beef strips for stir-fry (top round)
3 teaspoons cornstarch
1 teaspoon vegetable oil
1 sweet onion, halved and sliced
2 cloves garlic, minced
1/4 to 1/2 teaspoon crushed red pepper
1 8-ounce package fresh broccoli florets
1/2 cup Stir-Fry Sauce
1/2 cup chicken broth
1 bunch watercress (3 cups)

1. Cook brown rice following package directions for 4 servings.

2. Meanwhile, in a large skillet or wok, heat the 1 tablespoon oil over medium-high heat. In a medium bowl, toss beef with 2 teaspoons of the cornstarch. Add beef to skillet. Cook and stir for 1 to 2 minutes or to desired doneness. With a slotted spoon, transfer beef to clean bowl.

3. Add the 1 teaspoon oil to skillet. Add onion, garlic, and crushed red pepper; cook and stir for 30 seconds. Stir in broccoli and the 1/2 cup Stir-Fry Sauce. In a small bowl, stir together chicken broth and the remaining 1 teaspoon cornstarch; add to skillet. Cook about 5 minutes or until broccoli is tender, stirring occasionally.

4. Return beef to skillet; add watercress. Cook and stir for 1 minute more. Serve with brown rice.

Stir-Fry Sauce: In a jar with a tight-fitting lid, combine 1 cup reduced-sodium soy sauce, 1/3 cup dry sherry, 4 teaspoons grated fresh ginger, and 2 teaspoons sugar. Stir until sugar is dissolved. Refrigerate up to 2 weeks. Shake before using.

Per serving: 476 cal., 15 g total fat (4 g sat. fat), 46 mg chol., 2,530 mg sodium, 43 g carbo., 4 g fiber, 35 g pro.

Quick Tip If you don't have the time or ingredients to make the Stir-Fry Sauce, substitute 1/2 cup bottled stir-fry sauce. Use classic stir-fry sauce if you like mild, Szechwan if you like spicy (or 1/4 cup of each).

Beef-Sesame Noodles

Dark sesame oil is made from toasted sesame seeds. Because toasting the seeds intensifies the flavor, just a bit makes a big impact.

Prep: 15 minutes **Makes:** 4 servings

1/2 cup reduced-sodium beef broth
1/3 cup soy sauce
2 tablespoons balsamic vinegar
1 tablespoon grated fresh ginger
2 teaspoons dark sesame oil
1/4 teaspoon sugar
1 9-ounce package frozen sugar snap peas, thawed and drained
8 ounces thinly sliced deli roast beef, cut in 3×1-inch strips
4 ounces mushrooms, quartered
1 cup cherry tomatoes, halved
2 5-ounce packages Japanese curly noodles or 12 ounces capellini pasta

1. In a large bowl, combine beef broth, soy sauce, vinegar, ginger, sesame oil, and sugar. Add peas, beef, mushrooms, and tomatoes; toss to combine.

2. In a large saucepan, bring 5 quarts water to boiling. Stir in noodles; cover and remove from heat for 4 to 5 minutes or until tender. Drain noodles. Place on a serving platter or 4 plates. Top with beef mixture.

Per serving: 423 cal., 5 g total fat (1 g sat. fat), 6 g fiber, 26 mg chol., 3,403 mg sodium, 67 g carbo., 6 g fiber, 25 g pro.

Oriental Beef and Broccoli Salad ♥

Serve this healthful salad with rice crackers and iced green tea.

Start to Finish: 20 minutes **Makes:** 4 servings

12 ounces beef sirloin steak
2/3 cup bottled ginger vinaigrette salad dressing
3 cups fresh broccoli florets
8 cups torn mixed greens
1 medium red sweet pepper, cut in bite-size strips

1. Trim fat from steak. Thinly slice across the grain into bite-size strips; set aside. In a wok or extra-large skillet, heat 2 tablespoons of the salad dressing over medium-high heat. Add broccoli; cook and stir for 3 minutes. Add meat to wok. Cook and stir 2 to 3 minutes or until meat is slightly pink in center. Remove meat and broccoli from wok.

2. In a large bowl, combine greens, sweet pepper, meat strips, and broccoli. Drizzle with remaining salad dressing; toss to coat.

Per serving: 237 cal., 9 g total fat (2 g sat. fat), 60 mg chol., 468 mg sodium, 17 g carbo., 4 g fiber, 22 g pro.

Herb-Garlic Beef Roast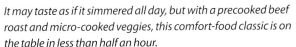

It may taste as if it simmered all day, but with a precooked beef roast and micro-cooked veggies, this comfort-food classic is on the table in less than half an hour.

Start to Finish: 20 minutes **Makes:** 4 servings

1	**17-ounce package refrigerated cooked beef roast au jus**
1	**pound small round red potatoes**
3	**medium carrots**
1	**tablespoon vegetable oil**
	Freshly ground black pepper
3	**tablespoons snipped fresh Italian (flat-leaf) parsley**
3	**to 6 cloves garlic, minced**
1	**tablespoon finely shredded lemon peel**

1. In a large skillet, heat beef roast, covered, over medium heat for 10 minutes. Uncover and simmer about 5 minutes more or until juices are slightly reduced.

2. Meanwhile, quarter potatoes. Peel and diagonally slice carrots in ¾-inch pieces. Place vegetables in a microwave-safe dish. Drizzle with oil and sprinkle with pepper; toss to coat. Lightly cover with lid or plastic wrap. Microwave on 100% power (high) about 10 minutes or until tender.

3. For herb-garlic mixture, in a small bowl, combine parsley, garlic, and lemon peel. To serve, stir vegetables into skillet with beef and juices. Divide among 4 dishes. Sprinkle with herb-garlic mixture.

Per serving: 311 cal., 12 g total fat (5 g sat. fat), 64 mg chol., 465 mg sodium, 28 g carbo., 4 g fiber, 25 g pro.

Quick Tip Peeling garlic can be a tedious job—especially when you're in a hurry. Here's how to make quick work of it: Lay each clove on a cutting board. Lay the flat side of a chef's knife on top of the clove. With your other hand, give the top of the knife blade a sharp rap to slightly crush the clove. The papery skin will come right off.

Beef Patties au Poivre

Beef Patties au Poivre

With elements—peppercorns, cream, and brandy—of the French classic steak au poivre, this budget-friendly recipe calls for beef patties instead of steak.

Start to Finish: 25 minutes **Makes:** 4 servings

- 1 **tablespoon green peppercorns in brine, drained**
- 1 **tablespoon butter**
- ¼ **cup frozen chopped onion, thawed**
- 2 **tablespoons brandy**
- 2 **tablespoons all-purpose flour**
- 1 **cup beef broth**
- ¼ **cup whipping cream**
- 4 **4-ounce purchased uncooked beef patties**
- ½ **teaspoon salt**
- ¼ **teaspoon ground black pepper**
- 4 **hamburger buns (optional)**
  Seasoned french-fried potatoes (optional)

1. On a clean work surface, crush half the peppercorns with the back of a spoon.

2. For sauce, in a small saucepan, melt butter over medium heat. Add onion and all the peppercorns; cook for 4 to 5 minutes or until browned. Carefully add brandy. Cook for 30 seconds, stirring to scrape up any browned bits from the bottom of the pan with a wooden spoon. Stir in flour; cook and stir for 2 minutes. Add beef broth; cook and stir until thickened and bubbly. Reduce heat; cook for 2 to 3 minutes. Add whipping cream; cook and stir for 1 to 2 minutes. Remove from heat; cover sauce to keep warm.

3. Heat a large nonstick skillet over medium heat. Sprinkle beef patties with salt and pepper. Add patties to skillet; cook for 1 to 2 minutes on each side or until an instant-read thermometer inserted in centers registers 160°F.

4. If desired, serve patties on buns with sauce and seasoned fries.

Per serving: 322 cal., 22 g total fat (11 g sat. fat), 106 mg chol., 644 mg sodium, 4 g carbo., 0 g fiber, 24 g pro.

Micro-Bake Moussaka

Make this hearty Greek casserole in just 30 minutes, using a microwave oven. Broil the eggplant for a beautiful and delicious brown crust before layering with the other ingredients.

Start to Finish: 30 minutes **Makes:** 6 servings

- 1 **pound eggplant, sliced ¼ inch thick**
- 1 **tablespoon olive oil**
   Salt and ground black pepper
- 1 **pound lean ground beef**
- 1 **cup chopped onion (1 large)**
- 1 **clove garlic, minced**
- ½ **teaspoon salt**
- ¼ **teaspoon ground black pepper**
- ⅛ **teaspoon ground cinnamon**
- 2 **tablespoons water**
- 2 **tablespoons snipped fresh parsley**
- 1 **tablespoon tomato paste**
- 1 **egg yolk**
- 1 **8-ounce container sour cream**
- 3 **tablespoons freshly grated Parmesan cheese**
   Dash ground nutmeg

1. Place broiler pan with rack in oven 4 inches from heat. Preheat broiler. Brush eggplant with oil and sprinkle lightly with salt and pepper. Arrange eggplant on ot broiler pan; broil for 4 to 5 minutes each side or until browned.

2. Meanwhile, in a microwave-safe bowl, combine ground beef, onion, garlic, the ½ teaspoon salt, the ¼ teaspoon pepper, and the cinnamon. Microwave, uncovered, on 100% power (high) for 3 minutes; stir. Microwave for 2 to 3 minutes more or until beef is cooked through. Pour off drippings. Stir in water, parsley, and tomato paste.

3. In a small bowl, combine egg yolk, sour cream, and Parmesan cheese. Grease a shallow microwave-safe and broilerproof 1½-quart casserole. Layer half the eggplant in dish, then meat mixture and remaining eggplant. Spread sour cream mixture; sprinkle with nutmeg. Cover and microwave on 100% power (high) for 4 minutes. Broil 4 inches from heat about 2 minutes or until top is browned and set.

Per serving: 305 cal., 23 g total fat (10 g sat. fat), 108 mg chol., 435 mg sodium, 8 g carbo., 3 g fiber, 17g pro

Quick Tip) Keep cut carrots, celery, radishes, and sweet pepper slices in a container of water in the refrigerator. They'll stay crisp—and you'll have something fresh and crunchy (and healthful) to serve as sides to simple meals.

Italian Pizza Burgers

These supersimple burgers will please the pizza fans in your family.

Start to Finish: 30 minutes **Makes:** 4 burgers

- 4 **4-ounce uncooked beef patties**
- 4 **¾-inch slices sourdough bread**
- 1 **cup mushroom pasta sauce**
- 1 **cup shredded provolone or mozzarella cheese (4 ounces)**
- 2 **tablespoons thinly sliced fresh basil**

1. Preheat broiler. Place beef patties on the unheated rack of a broiler pan. Broil 3 to 4 inches from heat for 10 to 12 minutes or until an instant-read thermometer inserted in centers registers 160°F, turning once halfway through broiling. Add the bread slices to the broiler pan the last 2 to 3 minutes of broiling; turn once to toast evenly.

2. Meanwhile, in a medium saucepan, heat pasta sauce over medium heat until heated through, stirring occasionally. Place 1 patty on each bread slice. Spoon pasta sauce over patties; sprinkle with cheese. Broil for 1 to 2 minutes more or until cheese is melted. Top with basil.

Per burger: 504 cal., 30 g total fat (13 g sat. fat), 96 mg chol., 815 mg sodium, 27 g carbo., 2 g fiber, 30 g pro.

Italian Pizza Burgers

Sicilian Pasta with Meat Sauce

Sicilians like a little sweet with meat, which explains the raisins and a hint of cinnamon in this hearty meat sauce. Watch pine nuts carefully when you toast them—they burn easily.

Start to Finish: 30 minutes **Makes:** 6 servings

- 2 teaspoons olive oil
- 1 cup finely chopped onion (1 large)
- 2 teaspoons bottled minced garlic
- 1 teaspoon ground cumin
- ¹/₂ teaspoon ground cinnamon
- 1 pound lean ground beef
- 1 teaspoon salt
- ¹/₂ teaspoon freshly ground black pepper
- 1 28-ounce can whole tomatoes, undrained
- ¹/₃ cup raisins
- 2 tablespoons tomato paste
- 1 pound dried tubetti, anelletti (ring shape), or corkscrew pasta, cooked following package directions
- ¹/₄ cup snipped fresh Italian (flat-leaf) parsley
- ¹/₄ cup pine nuts (pignoli) or almonds, toasted

1. In a large skillet, heat olive oil over medium-high heat. Add onion; cook about 5 minutes or until softened. Stir in garlic, cumin, and cinnamon; cook for 30 seconds. Add beef, salt, and pepper; cook about 5 minutes or until beef is browned.

2. Stir in undrained tomatoes, raisins, and tomato paste. Bring to boiling, breaking up tomatoes with a spoon; reduce heat. Simmer, uncovered, for 10 minutes.

3. Toss beef mixture with pasta and parsley. Sprinkle with pine nuts.

Per serving: 562 cal., 18 g total fat (5 g sat. fat), 51 mg chol., 679 mg sodium, 73 g carbo., 5 g fiber, 27 g pro.

Main-Dish Spanish Rice ♥ ▣

If you don't have leftover roast beef in the refrigerator, stop by the deli counter for sandwich-style roast beef. It works well here; the meat is simply stirred into a rice-bean-salsa mixture that's rolled up in flour tortillas.

Start to Finish: 15 minutes **Oven:** 350°F
Makes: 6 servings

- 1 14.5-ounce can Mexican-style stewed tomatoes, cut up
- ³/₄ cup quick-cooking brown rice
- ²/₃ cup water
- ¹/₂ teaspoon sugar
- ¹/₄ teaspoon garlic powder
- ¹/₈ teaspoon ground black pepper
- 1 15-ounce can black beans, rinsed and drained
- ¹/₂ pound thinly sliced cooked beef, cut in strips
- ¹/₂ cup prepared salsa
- 12 7-inch flour tortillas
  Plain yogurt (optional)
  Sliced green onions (optional)

1. Preheat oven to 350°F. In a large skillet, stir together undrained tomatoes, rice, water, sugar, garlic powder, and pepper. Bring to boiling; reduce heat. Simmer, covered, for 12 to 14 minutes or until rice is tender. Stir in beans, beef, and salsa; heat through.

2. Meanwhile, wrap tortillas in foil; heat in oven for 10 minutes.

3. To serve, spoon rice mixture onto warm tortillas; roll up. If desired, top with yogurt and green onions.

Per serving: 348 cal., 8 g total fat (2 g sat. fat), 22 mg chol., 714 mg sodium, 53 g carbo., 6 g fiber, 19 g pro.

Potato-Topped Beef Bowl ▣

Enjoy shepherd's pie on the fly with these quick-to-make bowls of ground beef, vegetables, and mashed potatoes. It's hearty pub fare in a fraction of the time and every bit as yummy.

Start to Finish: 20 minutes **Makes:** 4 servings

- 1 pound lean ground beef
- 1 16-ounce package frozen mixed vegetables
- 1 8-ounce package shredded cheddar cheese (2 cups)
- ¹/₄ cup snipped fresh Italian (flat-leaf) parsley
- ¹/₄ teaspoon salt
- ¹/₈ teaspoon ground black pepper
- 2 cups instant mashed potato flakes
- 2 cups boiling water
- 2 tablespoons butter or margarine, melted
  Salt and ground black pepper

1. Preheat broiler. In an extra-large skillet, cook ground beef over medium-high heat until browned; drain off fat. Stir in frozen vegetables. Cook until heated through, stirring occasionally. Stir in half the cheese, half the parsley, the ¹/₄ teaspoon salt, and the ¹/₈ teaspoon pepper.

2. Meanwhile, in a large bowl, combine potato flakes, boiling water, and 1 tablespoon of the butter. Stir until smooth. Season with salt and pepper to taste; set aside.

3. Divide beef mixture among four 16-ounce broiler-safe dishes. Top with potatoes; sprinkle with remaining cheese. Broil 3 inches from heat for 2 to 3 minutes or until cheese is melted. Drizzle with the remaining 1 tablespoon melted butter; sprinkle with the remaining parsley.

Per serving: 677 cal., 42 g total fat (22 g sat. fat), 152 mg chol., 693 mg sodium, 35 g carbo., 5 g fiber, 41 g pro.

Potato-Topped Beef Bowl

Beef and Bok Choy ♥ 🔲

To toast sesame seeds, spread them in an even layer in a heavy skillet and heat over medium heat, shaking the pan often, until they're a deep golden color—about 3 to 5 minutes. Watch closely to prevent them from burning.

Start to Finish: 20 minutes **Makes:** 4 servings

- 2 **teaspoons dark sesame oil**
- 12 **ounces beef sirloin steak, cut in thin bite-size strips**
- 1 **to 2 teaspoons red chile pepper paste**
- 1½ **pounds bok choy, sliced (about 6 cups)**
- 2 **cloves garlic, minced**
- 1 **tablespoon reduced-sodium soy sauce**
- 2 **teaspoons toasted sesame seeds**

1. In a large skillet, heat 1 teaspoon of the sesame oil over medium-high heat. Add beef strips and chile paste; cook and stir about 3 minutes or until beef is desired doneness. Remove beef with a slotted spoon, reserving liquid in skillet; cover beef to keep warm.

2. Add the remaining 1 teaspoon sesame oil to skillet. Add bok choy and garlic; cook and stir over medium-high heat for 2 to 3 minutes or until bok choy is crisp-tender. Transfer to serving dishes. Top with beef mixture. Drizzle with soy sauce and sprinkle with toasted sesame seeds.

Per serving: 179 cal., 9 g total fat (2 g sat. fat), 52 mg chol., 2/1 mg sodium, 4 g carbo., 1 g fiber, 20 g pro.

Beef and Bok Choy

Burgers with Dill Sauce 🔲

A cool, crunchy, creamy sauce tops these lean burgers that have only 3 grams of carbohydrate per serving.

Start to Finish: 30 minutes **Makes:** 4 burgers

- ¼ **cup finely chopped onion**
- ¼ **cup snipped fresh parsley**
- 1 **tablespoon minced garlic (6 cloves)**
- ½ **teaspoon kosher salt**
- 1 **pound lean ground beef or lamb**
- ¼ **cup light sour cream or plain low-fat yogurt**
- 2 **tablespoons mayonnaise**
- 1 **tablespoon Dijon-style mustard or whole-grain brown mustard**
- 1 **teaspoon snipped fresh dill or ¼ teaspoon dried dill**
- 1 **teaspoon balsamic vinegar**
- ¼ **cup chopped, seeded cucumber**

1. Preheat broiler. In a large mixing bowl, combine onion, parsley, garlic, and salt. Add meat; mix well. Shape into four ¾-inch-thick patties.

2. Place patties on the unheated rack of a broiler pan. Broil 3 to 4 inches from the heat for 12 to 14 minutes or until an instant-read thermometer inserted in centers registers 160°F, turning once halfway through broiling.

3. Meanwhile, for sauce, in a small bowl, combine sour cream, mayonnaise, mustard, dill, and balsamic vinegar. Stir in cucumber. Spoon sauce over burgers.

Per burger: 304 cal., 22 g total fat (8 g sat. fat), 82 mg chol., 491 mg sodium, 3 g carbo., 0 g fiber, 23 g pro.

Quick Tip You don't have to use kosher salt in this recipe—you can certainly use regular table salt—but kosher salt has a nice, flaky texture and fresh taste (from a lack of additives) that appeal to many cooks. Look for kosher salt in the spice or kosher section of your supermarket.

Burgers with Dill Sauce

Pork Chops with Dried Cranberries and Port ♥ 🔲

Keep the chops warm on a platter by loosely tenting them with foil while you make the sauce. Don't put them in a hot oven because they'll dry out.

Start to Finish: 25 minutes **Makes:** 4 servings

- 4   boneless pork top loin chops, ¾ inch thick
-     Salt and ground black pepper
- 2   teaspoons olive oil or vegetable oil
- ⅓   cup chopped shallots
- ¼   teaspoon dried thyme, crushed
- ½   cup port wine
- ⅓   cup chicken broth
- ¼   cup dried cranberries
-     Steamed green beans (optional)

1. Trim fat from chops. Sprinkle chops with salt and pepper. In a large skillet, heat oil over medium heat. Add chops; cook in hot oil for 8 to 12 minutes or until temperature registers 160°F, turning once halfway through cooking. Remove chops, reserving drippings in skillet. Keep chops warm.

2. Add shallots and thyme to reserved drippings in skillet. Cook and stir for 1 minute. Carefully stir port, chicken broth, and cranberries into skillet. Bring to boiling. Boil, uncovered, about 3 minutes or until sauce is reduced by half. Return chops to skillet, turning to coat with sauce. If desired, serve with steamed green beans.

Per serving: 388 cal., 10 g total fat (3 g sat. fat), 83 mg chol., 230 mg sodium, 31 g carbo., 2 g fiber, 34 g pro.

Pork and Potatoes with Tomato Relish 🔲

This dish tastes best made with ripe summer tomatoes. Serve it with a crisp green salad and crusty bread to soak up the juices.

Start to Finish: 20 minutes **Makes:** 4 servings

- 1   24-ounce package refrigerated mashed potatoes
- 4   boneless pork loin chops, ¾ inch thick
-     Salt and ground black pepper
- 2   tablespoons olive oil or vegetable oil
- 1   large red onion, quartered and sliced (2 cups)
- 2   medium tomatoes, cut in thin wedges
- ¼   cup bottled red wine vinaigrette salad dressing

1. Prepare mashed potatoes following microwave package directions.

2. Meanwhile, trim fat from chops. Sprinkle chops lightly with salt and pepper. In an extra-large skillet, heat oil over medium-high heat. Add chops; cook for 3 minutes. Turn chops; add onion to skillet. Cook about 10 minutes more or until temperature registers 160°F, turning chops to brown evenly and stirring onion occasionally. Remove chops to serving plates; keep warm.

3. For tomato relish, add tomatoes and vinaigrette to skillet; cook and stir for 1 minute more. Serve chops with mashed potatoes and tomato relish. Season with cracked black pepper.

Per serving: 433 cal., 20 g total fat (3 g sat. fat), 62 mg chol., 624 mg sodium, 32 g carbo., 3 g fiber, 31 g pro.

Pork Chops with Dried Cranberries and Port

Peach-Sauced Pork

Pork pairs well with fruit, such as apples in the fall and peaches in the summer. By using canned peaches, you can enjoy this quick-to-fix dish any time of year.

Start to Finish: 30 minutes **Makes:** 4 servings

12	**ounces pork tenderloin**
	Nonstick cooking spray
1	**16-ounce can peach slices in light syrup**
¼	**cup water**
1½	**teaspoons cornstarch**
¼	**teaspoon salt**
⅛	**teaspoon ground allspice**
	Hot cooked rice (optional)
	Snipped fresh parsley (optional)
	Lemon peel strips (optional)

1. Trim fat from pork. Cut pork crosswise in 16 slices, each about ½ inch thick. Place each pork slice between 2 pieces of plastic wrap. Using the flat side of a meat mallet, lightly pound pork to ¼-inch thickness, working from the center to the edges. Discard plastic wrap.

2. Coat a large skillet with cooking spray. Heat skillet over medium heat. Cook half the pork in the hot skillet for 4 to 6 minutes or until tender and juices run clear, turning once halfway through cooking. Remove pork from skillet; cover to keep warm. Repeat with remaining pork. Carefully wipe skillet with a paper towel.

3. Meanwhile, drain peaches, reserving ½ cup syrup. Set peaches aside. In a small bowl, stir together the reserved syrup, the water, cornstarch, salt, and allspice. Add syrup mixture to skillet. Cook and stir until thickened and bubbly. Cook and stir for 2 minutes more. Return the pork and peaches to skillet; heat through.

4. If desired, serve over hot cooked rice and garnish with parsley and lemon peel.

Per serving: 174 cal., 3 g total fat (1 g sat. fat), 60 mg chol., 183 mg sodium, 17 g carbo., 1 g fiber, 19 g pro.

Pork Chops with Caramelized Onions ♥

Superjuicy sweet onion varieties, such as Vidalia, Walla Walla, and Maui, are the best choices for this dish. The high sugar content makes them ideal for caramelizing.

Start to Finish: 30 minutes **Makes:** 4 servings

2	**tablespoons all-purpose flour**
4	**boneless pork loin chops, ¾ inch thick (about 1 pound)**
2	**tablespoons butter**
2	**large onions, cut in ½-inch wedges**
2	**cloves garlic, minced**
1	**teaspoon snipped fresh rosemary**
¼	**teaspoon salt (optional)**
¼	**teaspoon ground black pepper**
⅓	**cup dry white wine or beef broth**
⅓	**cup beef broth**

1. Place flour in a shallow dish. Trim fat from pork chops. Dip chops in flour, coating both sides. In a large heavy skillet, melt butter over medium-high heat; add chops and

brown on both sides. Remove chops from skillet; cover to keep warm. Reduce heat to medium. Add onion, garlic, rosemary, salt (if desired), and pepper to skillet. Cook, covered, for 5 minutes, stirring twice. Uncover and cook for 5 minutes more or until onions are browned, stirring occasionally.

2. Carefully add wine to skillet; boil gently until wine is reduced by half. Stir in beef broth. Return chops to skillet. Simmer, covered, for 8 to 10 minutes more or until temperature registers 160°F. Transfer chops to a serving platter; cover to keep warm.

3. For sauce, gently boil juices and onions for 2 to 4 minutes or until slightly thickened, stirring constantly. Spoon onions and sauce over chops.

Per serving: 265 cal., 12 g total fat (6 g sat. fat), 78 mg chol., 174 mg sodium, 9 g carbo., 1 g fiber, 26 g pro.

Mexican Skillet Dinner

If you can't find chorizo—a highly spiced, coarsely ground pork sausage—at your supermarket, look at a Hispanic market. It can vary in degree of spiciness, so ask the butcher about each variety. Many markets sell both mild and spicy versions.

Start to Finish: 25 minutes **Makes:** 6 servings

12 ounces chorizo or pork sausage
2 cups frozen whole kernel corn
1 14.5-ounce can diced tomatoes, undrained
1 cup uncooked instant rice
½ cup water
2 teaspoons chili powder
½ teaspoon ground cumin
1 15-ounce can pinto beans, rinsed and drained
¾ cup shredded Mexican-blend cheese or Colby and Monterey Jack cheese (3 ounces)

1. Remove casing from sausage, if present. In a large skillet, cook sausage over medium heat for 10 to 15 minutes or until browned. Drain off fat and set aside.

2. Add corn, undrained tomatoes, uncooked rice, water, chili powder, and cumin to skillet. Bring to boiling; reduce heat. Simmer, covered, for 5 minutes or until liquid is absorbed and rice is tender. Stir in beans and cooked sausage; heat through. Sprinkle with cheese. Cover and let stand for 2 to 3 minutes or until cheese is slightly melted.

Per serving: 230 cal., 27 g total fat (11 g sat. fat), 13 mg chol., 585 mg sodium, 38 g carbo., 5 g fiber, 23 g pro.

Ginger-Sesame Stir-Fry

Delightfully chewy cellophane noodles—also called bean thread or glass noodles because of their translucence—are made from mung bean starch. Most Asian markets carry them.

Start to Finish: 30 minutes **Makes:** 4 servings

1 tablespoon vegetable oil
1 small onion, cut in thin wedges
2 cloves garlic, minced (1 teaspoon)
8 ounces boneless pork loin, cut in bite-size strips, or cubed firm tofu
½ cup thinly bias-sliced carrot (1 medium)
1½ cups fresh snow pea pods
1 tablespoon sesame seeds
2 tablespoons reduced-sodium soy sauce
1 tablespoon grated fresh ginger
1 teaspoon dark sesame oil
¼ to ½ teaspoon crushed red pepper
¼ cup bottled plum sauce
¼ cup water
2 to 3 cups hot cooked cellophane noodles, rice vermicelli noodles, or rice
Snipped fresh cilantro and chopped roasted cashews (optional)

1. In a wok or large skillet, heat oil over medium-high heat. Add onion and garlic. Cook and stir for 2 minutes. Add pork or tofu and carrot; cook and stir for 2 minutes more. Add snow peas and sesame seeds; cook and stir for 3 minutes. Add soy sauce, ginger, sesame oil, and crushed red pepper. Cook and stir for 1 minute more. Stir in plum sauce and water; heat through. Serve over noodles. If desired, top with cilantro and cashews.

Per serving: 319 cal., 10 g total fat (2 g sat. fat), 31 mg chol., 444 mg sodium, 43 g carbo., 3 g fiber, 15 g pro

Ginger-Sesame Stir-Fry

Balsamic Pork Chops ♥ [one]

Serve these chops with green beans and hot cooked orzo tossed with butter and freshly grated Parmesan cheese.

Start to Finish: 25 minutes **Makes:** 4 servings

- 2 **teaspoons olive oil**
- 4 **pork loin chops, 1 inch thick (1½ pounds)**
  Salt and ground black pepper
- ¼ **cup minced shallots**
- ½ **cup chicken broth**
- ¼ **cup balsamic vinegar**
- ¼ **teaspoon dried thyme, crushed**
- 1 **tablespoon butter or margarine**

1. In a large skillet, heat oil over medium-high heat. Trim fat from pork chops. Sprinkle chops with salt and pepper. Cook chops in hot oil about 10 minutes or until temperature registers 160°F, turning chops once halfway through cooking. Transfer chops to a serving platter; cover to keep warm.

2. For sauce, add shallots to drippings in skillet; cook and stir for 1 minute. Add chicken broth, vinegar, and thyme. Cook and stir over high heat for 5 minutes. Remove from heat; stir in butter. Pour sauce over chops.

Per serving: 274 cal., 13 g total fat (5 g sat. fat), 91 mg chol., 306 mg sodium, 5 g carbo., 0 g fiber, 31 g pro.

Pork Medallions with Cherry Sauce ♥ [one]

Making thin, quick-cooking medallions from slices of pork tenderloin is easy. Press meat firmly with the heel of your hand.

Start to Finish: 20 minutes **Makes:** 4 servings

- 1 **pound pork tenderloin**
  Salt and freshly ground black pepper
  Nonstick cooking spray
- ¾ **cup cranberry juice or apple juice**
- 2 **teaspoons spicy brown mustard**
- 1 **teaspoon cornstarch**
- 1 **cup sweet cherries (such as Rainier or Bing), halved and pitted, or 1 cup frozen pitted dark sweet cherries, thawed**

1. Trim fat from pork. Cut pork crosswise in 1-inch slices. Place each slice between two pieces of plastic wrap. With the heel of your hand, press each slice in a ½-inch-thick medallion. Discard plastic wrap. Sprinkle pork lightly with salt and pepper.

2. Coat a large unheated nonstick skillet with cooking spray. Heat skillet over medium-high heat. Add pork; cook for 6 minutes or until pork is slightly pink in center and juices run clear, turning once. Transfer pork to a serving platter; keep warm.

3. For cherry sauce, combine cranberry juice, mustard, and cornstarch; add to skillet. Cook and stir until thickened and bubbly. Cook and stir for 2 minutes more. Stir cherries into juice mixture in skillet. Serve sauce over pork.

Per serving: 197 cal., 5 g total fat (2 g sat. fat), 81 mg chol., 127 mg sodium, 12 g carbo., 0 g fiber, 26 g pro.

Balsamic Pork and Dumplings

Reducing the balsamic vinegar by half intensifies flavor for a luxurious, almost syrupy quality that coats the pork beautifully.

Start to Finish: 20 minutes **Makes:** 4 servings

- 1 **16.9-ounce package frozen potato-and-onion-filled pierogi (potato dumplings)**
- 12 **ounces green and/or wax beans, trimmed (3 cups)**
- 1 **pound pork tenderloin**
  Salt and ground black pepper
- 2 **tablespoons olive oil**
- ½ **cup balsamic vinegar**
- 2 **teaspoons snipped fresh rosemary (optional)**

1. Cook pierogi and beans in boiling water following package directions. Drain pierogi and beans; divide among 4 plates.

2. Meanwhile, trim fat from pork. Cut pork crosswise in ½-inch medallions. Gently flatten pork slices by hand to ¼-inch thickness; lightly sprinkle with salt and pepper. In a large skillet, heat oil over medium heat. Add pork; cook for 2 to 3 minutes each side or until pork is slightly pink in center and juices run clear. Transfer pork to serving plates with pierogi and beans.

3. Drain fat from skillet. Add balsamic vinegar to hot skillet. Cook, uncovered, about 1 minute or until reduced by half. Drizzle over pork, pierogi, and beans. If desired, sprinkle with rosemary.

Per serving: 419 cal., 11 g total fat (2 g sat. fat), 79 mg chol., 636 mg sodium, 47 g carbo., 4 g fiber, 30 g pro.

Quick Tip Pierogi are Polish and Russian dumplings filled with meat, cheese, mashed potatoes, mushrooms, cabbage, other vegetables, or sweet fillings. As with other types of stuffed pasta or dough pockets (such as ravioli), pierogi are done when they float to the top of the pot.

Whole Wheat Pasta
with Pork and Potatoes

Whole Wheat Pasta with Pork and Potatoes

It may seem like carb overload to have potatoes in a pasta dish, but Italians quite often enjoy the combination of "pasta e patate." They also put potatoes on pizza.

Prep: 20 minutes **Cook:** 15 minutes **Makes:** 4 servings

- 1 **20-ounce package refrigerated red-skin potato wedges or 1¼ pounds tiny new potatoes, halved or quartered**
- 8 **ounces dried whole wheat or whole grain pasta (any shape)**
- 12 **ounces lean boneless pork, cut in thin bite-size strips**
   Salt and ground black pepper
- 2 **tablespoons olive oil**
- 3 **cloves garlic, minced**
- ¾ **cup chopped onion**
- 1¼ **cups frozen peas, thawed**
- ¼ **cup pitted kalamata olives, quartered**
- ¾ **cup chicken broth**
- ¼ **cup dry white wine or chicken broth**
- 3 **tablespoons assorted snipped fresh herbs (such as basil, thyme, oregano, and/or parsley)**
- ¼ **teaspoon salt**
- ¼ **teaspoon ground black pepper**
- ½ **cup finely shredded Parmesan cheese (2 ounces)**
   Lemon wedges (optional)

1. If using fresh potatoes, cook, covered, in lightly salted boiling water for 10 minutes; drain. Set aside.

2. Cook pasta following package directions. Drain. Return pasta to hot saucepan; cover and keep warm.

3. Meanwhile, trim fat from pork. Sprinkle pork with salt and pepper. In a large skillet, heat olive oil over medium heat. (Add more oil as necessary during cooking.) Add garlic; cook for 30 seconds. Add pork. Cook and stir over medium-high heat for 3 to 4 minutes or until pork is browned. Remove pork from skillet. Add onions to skillet. Cook about 3 minutes or until tender. Add potatoes, peas, olives, chicken broth, wine, 2 tablespoons of the snipped herbs, the salt, and the pepper. Bring to boiling; reduce heat. Cook, uncovered, about 3 minutes or until potatoes and peas are tender.

4. Transfer potato mixture to the pan with pasta. Add pork. Gently toss to mix; heat through. Transfer mixture to a warm serving platter. Top with Parmesan cheese and the remaining 1 tablespoon snipped herbs. If desired, squeeze lemon on pasta. Serve immediately.

Per serving: 643 cal., 19 g total fat (5 g sat. fat), 60 mg chol., 1,026 mg sodium, 77 g carbo., 8 g fiber, 37 g pro.

Breaded Pork with Cabbage and Kale

Kale is available washed, chopped, and bagged in some supermarkets. If you buy fresh and wash it yourself, cut out and discard the tough rib in the center of each leaf before chopping the leaves.

Start to Finish: 20 minutes **Oven:** 250°F
Makes: 4 servings

- 1¼ **pounds center-cut pork loin, cut in 4 slices**
- 2 **cups corn bread stuffing mix, crushed**
- 2 **tablespoons olive oil**
- 2 **cups sliced red cabbage**
- 6 **cups coarsely chopped kale**
- ⅓ **cup balsamic vinegar**
   Salt and ground black pepper

1. Preheat oven to 250°F. Place each pork slice between two pieces of plastic wrap. Using the flat side of a meat mallet, lightly pound pork to ¼-inch thickness. Place stuffing mix in shallow dish; coat pork with stuffing mix.

2. In an extra-large skillet, heat 1 tablespoon of the olive oil over medium-high heat. Cook two of the pork slices for 2 to 3 minutes each side or until crisp, golden, and cooked through. Transfer to baking sheet; keep warm in oven. Repeat with remaining oil and pork.

3. Wipe skillet with paper towels. Add cabbage. Cook and stir until cabbage is crisp-tender. Add kale and vinegar; cook just until wilted. Lightly sprinkle with salt and pepper. Serve with pork.

Per serving: 394 cal., 14 g total fat (2 g sat. fat), 78 mg chol., 769 mg sodium, 35 g carbo., 4 g fiber, 32 g pro.

Breaded Pork with Cabbage and Kale

Sausage, Beans, and Greens

Sausage, Beans, and Greens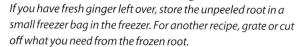

Escarole, a vitamin-loaded relative of endive, has a delicious, almost nutty flavor. Serve it as a salad green or cooked. When sautéed in olive oil and garlic, it's a tasty side dish.

Start to Finish: 25 minutes **Makes:** 4 servings

8	ounces hot or mild fresh Italian sausage links, bias-sliced in ¹⁄₂-inch pieces
¹⁄₂	cup chopped onion (1 medium)
2	19-ounce cans white kidney (cannellini) beans, rinsed and drained
2	cups coarsely chopped escarole or spinach
³⁄₄	cup reduced-sodium chicken broth
¹⁄₄	cup dry white wine or reduced-sodium chicken broth
2	tablespoons snipped fresh thyme or 1 teaspoon dried thyme, crushed
¹⁄₄	cup finely shredded Parmesan cheese (optional)

1. In a large saucepan, cook sausage and onion over medium heat about 5 minutes or until onion is tender. Drain off fat.

2. Add beans, escarole, chicken broth, wine, and thyme to sausage mixture in skillet. Bring to boiling; reduce heat. Simmer, covered, for 5 minutes. Ladle into serving bowls. If desired, sprinkle with Parmesan cheese.

Per serving: 397 cal., 14 g total fat (5 g sat. fat), 38 mg chol., 993 mg sodium, 41 g carbo., 12 g fiber, 20 g pro.

Thai Pork Stir-Fry ♥

If you have fresh ginger left over, store the unpeeled root in a small freezer bag in the freezer. For another recipe, grate or cut off what you need from the frozen root.

Start to Finish: 30 minutes **Makes:** 6 servings

2	tablespoons olive oil
1	tablespoon reduced-sodium soy sauce
¹⁄₂	teaspoon garlic powder
¹⁄₂	teaspoon finely chopped fresh ginger or ¹⁄₄ teaspoon ground ginger
¹⁄₂	teaspoon ground black pepper
¹⁄₂	teaspoon ground cardamom
¹⁄₂	teaspoon chili powder
1¹⁄₂	pounds pork loin, cut in bite-size strips
2	cups broccoli florets
1	cup cauliflower florets
1	cup thinly sliced carrots (2 medium)
2	tablespoons white vinegar
1	tablespoon curry powder
2	cups hot cooked brown rice

1. In an extra-large skillet, combine olive oil, soy sauce, garlic powder, ginger, pepper, cardamom, and chili powder. Add half the pork; cook and stir over medium-high heat for 3 minutes. Using a slotted spoon, remove pork from skillet. Repeat with the remaining pork. Return all of the pork to the skillet.

2. Add broccoli, cauliflower, carrots, vinegar, and curry powder to pork mixture. Bring to boiling; reduce heat. Simmer, covered, for 3 to 5 minutes or until vegetables are crisp-tender, stirring occasionally.

3. Serve pork and vegetables over brown rice.

Per serving: 301 cal., 11 g total fat (3 g sat. fat), 71 mg chol., 206 mg sodium, 21 g carbo., 3 g fiber, 28 g pro.

Thai Pork Stir-Fry

Kielbasa and Orzo

Kielbasa and Orzo [one]

Any variety of kielbasa works here. To reduce fat and calories, use one made with turkey.

Start to Finish: 16 minutes **Makes:** 4 servings

- 1 **tablespoon vegetable oil**
- 1 **pound cooked kielbasa, halved lengthwise and cut in 2-inch pieces**
- 1 **cup dried orzo (rosamarina)**
- 1 **14-ounce can beef broth**
- ½ **cup water**
- 1 **teaspoon dried Italian seasoning, crushed**
- 2½ **cups zucchini, halved lengthwise and coarsely chopped (2 medium)**
- ⅓ **cup 1-inch pieces green onions and/or finely chopped red sweet pepper (optional)**
  Salt and ground black pepper

1. In a large skillet, heat oil over medium-high heat. Cook kielbasa in hot oil about 2 minutes or until browned. Stir in orzo. Cook and stir for 1 minute.

2. Stir in beef broth, water, and Italian seasoning. Bring to boiling; reduce heat. Simmer, covered, about 8 minutes or until orzo is tender, adding the zucchini the last 4 minutes of cooking and stirring occasionally.

3. If desired, stir in green onion and sweet pepper. Season to taste with salt and pepper.

Per serving: 467 cal., 24 g total fat (8 g sat. fat), 79 mg chol., 1,630 mg sodium, 40 g carbo., 3 g fiber, 23 g pro.

Apricot Pork and Garlicky Green Beans ♥

Enjoy this dish during peak apricot season—generally from early May to the end of June.

Start to Finish: 20 minutes **Makes:** 4 servings

- 1 **tablespoon olive oil**
- 4 **pork rib chops, ½ inch thick**
  Salt and ground black pepper
- 4 **apricots, pitted and cut in wedges**
- 2 **tablespoons honey**
- 3 **cloves garlic, sliced**
- 1 **pound green beans, trimmed**
- ¼ **cup water**

1. In an extra-large nonstick skillet, heat olive oil over medium-high heat; reduce heat to medium. Trim fat from chops. Sprinkle chops lightly with salt and pepper. Add chops to skillet; cook for 5 minutes, turning once. Add apricots, honey, and garlic to skillet. Cook, covered, for 5 to 7 minutes or until apricots are tender and pork is slightly pink in center.

2. Meanwhile, in a 2-quart microwave-safe casserole dish, combine beans and the water. Microwave, covered, on

100% (high) power about 6 minutes or until beans are crisp-tender, stirring once; drain.

3. Transfer pork, apricots, and beans to a serving platter. Spoon juices from skillet over beans.

Per serving: 295 cal., 14 g total fat (4 g sat. fat), 57 mg chol., 207 mg sodium, 20 g carbo., 4 g fiber, 22 g pro.

Cuban Fried Rice

This island-inspired dish covers all the flavor bases: salty ham, sweet pineapple, spicy jalapeño, and a fresh squeeze of tart lime.

Start to Finish: 20 minutes **Makes:** 4 servings

- 1 **fresh pineapple, peeled, packed in juice**
- 1 **tablespoon olive oil**
- 1 **14.8-ounce pouch cooked long grain rice**
- 12 **ounces cooked ham, coarsely chopped**
- 1 **cup chopped or sliced sweet pepper (1 large)**
- 1 **jalapeño pepper, sliced (see tip, page 22)**
- ½ **a 15-ounce can black beans, rinsed and drained (¾ cup)**
  Lime wedges

1. Remove pineapple from container, reserving juice. Cut pineapple in ¾-inch slices; discard core if present. In an extra-large skillet, heat oil over medium-high heat. Add pineapple slices; cook for 3 to 4 minutes or until pineapple begins to brown. Divide pineapple among 4 plates.

2. Meanwhile, prepare rice following package directions.

3. Add ham, sweet pepper, and jalapeño pepper to skillet; cook for 3 minutes, stirring occasionally. Add beans and rice. Cook about 3 minutes or until heated through, stirring occasionally. Stir in reserved pineapple juice. Serve with lime wedges.

Per serving: 375 cal., 9 g total fat (1 g sat. fat), 38 mg chol., 1,549 mg sodium, 58 g carbo., 6 g fiber, 24 g pro.

Cuban Fried Rice

Pork Chops Provençal

Pork Chops Provençal

Adding wine to the pan and scraping up the browned bits left by the pork chops is called deglazing. The drippings and brown bits add great flavor to the sauce.

Prep: 15 minutes **Cook:** 14 minutes **Makes:** 4 servings

- 8 **ounces orzo (rosamarina)**
- 1 **tablespoon olive oil**
- 4 **boneless pork chops, ³⁄₄ inch thick**
- ¹⁄₈ **teaspoon salt**
- ¹⁄₄ **teaspoon ground black pepper**
- 1 **cup dry white wine**
- 2 **cloves garlic, minced**
- 3 **plum tomatoes, seeded and chopped**
- 1 **tablespoon grainy Dijon-style mustard**
- ¹⁄₃ **cup pitted and coarsely chopped niçoise olives**
- 1 **tablespoon capers**
- 2 **tablespoons snipped fresh parsley**

1. Cook orzo following package directions.

2. In a large nonstick skillet, heat oil over medium-high heat. Trim fat from pork chops. Sprinkle chops with salt and pepper. Add chops to skillet; reduce heat to medium. Cook for 8 to 12 minutes or until temperature registers (160°F), turning once halfway through cooking. Transfer chops to a plate; cover to keep warm.

3. For sauce, add wine and garlic to skillet, stirring to scrape up browned bits. Cook over medium heat for 3 minutes. Stir in tomatoes, mustard, olives, and capers. Cook for 3 minutes, stirring occasionally. Stir in parsley. To serve, spoon sauce over chops. Serve orzo on the side.

Per serving: 583 cal., 19 g total fat (4 g sat. fat), 78 mg chol., 468 mg sodium, 51 g carbo., 4 g fiber, 39 g pro.

Asian-Glazed Pork

Broccoli slaw mix is a great convenience product—super-healthful, all natural, and versatile. Here it adds crunch, color, and nutrition to this teriyaki-style dish.

Start to Finish: 20 minutes **Makes:** 4 servings

- 4 **ounces dried angel hair pasta**
- 4 **boneless pork loin chops, ³⁄₄ inch thick**
   Salt and ground black pepper
- 4 **tablespoons orange marmalade**
- 2 **cups packaged shredded broccoli (broccoli slaw mix)**
- 2 **tablespoons bottled teriyaki sauce**

1. Cook pasta following package directions.

2. Preheat broiler. Trim fat from chops. Place chops on the unheated rack of a broiler pan. Sprinkle chops lightly with salt and pepper. Broil chops, 3 to 4 inches from heat, for 5 minutes. Turn chops. Broil for 4 to 6 minutes more or until done (160°F), brushing with 2 tablespoons of the marmalade the last 3 to 4 minutes of broiling.

3. Meanwhile, drain pasta. Toss the hot pasta with shredded broccoli, teriyaki sauce, and the remaining 2 tablespoons marmalade. Divide pasta mixture among 4 plates; top each with a chop.

Per serving: 353 cal., 10 g total fat (3 g sat. fat), 73 mg chol., 592 mg sodium, 38 g carbo., 2 g fiber, 27 g pro.

Cajun Pork with Spicy Beans

Give this dish as much zing as you like, depending on the barbecue sauce. Serve it with a side of corn bread.

Prep: 10 minutes **Cook:** 14 minutes **Makes:** 4 servings

- 4 **boneless pork chops (about 1¼ pounds)**
- 2 **teaspoons Cajun seasoning**
- 1 **tablespoon olive oil**
- ¾ **cup chopped red sweet pepper (1 medium)**
- ½ **cup chopped red onion (1 medium)**
- 1 **19-ounce can black beans, drained (do not rinse)**
- 1 **8-ounce can no-salt-added whole kernel corn, drained**
- 2 **tablespoons bottled barbecue sauce**

1. Trim fat from chops. Sprinkle 1 teaspoon Cajun seasoning on both sides of chops. In a large nonstick skillet, heat olive oil over medium heat. Add chops; cook for 3 minutes. Turn. Add sweet pepper and onion around chops. Cook, covered, about 7 minutes or until pork is almost cooked in center.

2. Stir in the remaining 1 teaspoon Cajun seasoning; cook for 1 minute. Add black beans, corn, and barbecue sauce; simmer for 2 to 3 minutes or until heated through.

Per serving: 386 cal., 13 g total fat (4 g sat. fat), 78 mg chol., 761 mg sodium, 34 g carbo., 8 g fiber, 38 g pro.

Maple Pork and Apples

Pure maple syrup costs more than imitation, but the taste difference is significant. Use it when flavor really counts. Sprinkle the finished dish with chopped toasted pecans, if you like.

Start to Finish: 20 minutes **Makes:** 4 servings

- 4 **pork loin chops, ½ inch thick**
  Salt and ground black pepper
- 2 **tablespoons butter or margarine**
- 12 **baby carrots with tops (not baby-cut carrots), halved lengthwise**
- 1 **medium apple, sliced crosswise and seeds removed**
- ⅓ **cup pure maple syrup**

1. Trim fat from chops. Sprinkle chops lightly with salt and pepper. In a large skillet, melt butter over medium heat; add chops. Brown for 2 minutes, turning once. Reduce heat to medium-low. Add carrots, apple slices, and maple syrup. Simmer, covered, about 8 minutes or until chops are done (160°F).

2. Using a slotted spoon, transfer chops, carrots, and apples to platter. Bring syrup mixture to boiling. Boil gently, uncovered, for 1 to 2 minutes or until thickened. Pour over chops.

Per serving: 451 cal., 19 g total fat (8 g sat. fat), 124 mg chol., 447 mg sodium, 25 g carbo., 1 g fiber, 44 g pro.

Maple Pork and Apples

Wilted Cabbage and Brats

Wilted Cabbage and Brats

Pan-frying the cabbage wedges browns the edges. Use a cooking apple, such as Granny Smith, Jonathan, Fuji, or Braeburn (not Red Delicious), that will hold its shape.

Start to Finish: 20 minutes **Makes:** 4 servings

- 2 tablespoons olive oil
- 1/2 a 2-pound head napa cabbage, cut in 4 wedges, leaving the core intact to hold wedges together
- 14 to 16 ounces cooked smoked bratwurst links, halved diagonally
- 2 small apples, cored and cut in thin wedges
- 1/4 cup water
- 2 tablespoons Dijon-style mustard
- 1/2 cup sour cream or light sour cream
- 1 tablespoon snipped fresh sage
  Fresh sage leaves (optional)

1. In an extra-large skillet, heat 1 tablespoon of the olive oil over medium heat. Add cabbage wedges; cook for 8 to 10 minutes or until lightly browned and tender, turning occasionally to brown evenly.

2. Meanwhile, in a 4- to 5-quart Dutch oven, heat the remaining 1 tablespoon olive oil over medium-high heat. Add bratwurst and apples; cook for 2 minutes. In a small bowl, whisk together water and mustard. Add mustard mixture to bratwurst mixture. Bring to boiling; reduce heat. Simmer, covered, for 4 to 6 minutes or until apples are tender, stirring occasionally.

3. Transfer cabbage to a serving platter or bowl. Use a slotted spoon to remove bratwurst and apples to platter with cabbage. In a small bowl, combine sour cream and snipped sage. Gradually whisk in bratwurst cooking juices until well combined. Serve over bratwurst mixture. If desired, sprinkle fresh sage leaves.

Per serving: 456 cal., 38 g total fat (10 g sat. fat), 88 mg chol., 1,046 mg sodium, 13 g carbo., 2 g fiber, 15 g pro.

Pork and Pear Stir-Fry ♥

Sliced pears and plum preserves add a touch of sweetness to this spicy Asian-style dish.

Start to Finish: 30 minutes **Makes:** 4 servings

- 1 1/2 cups fresh pea pods or one 6-ounce package frozen pea pods
- 1 pound pork tenderloin
- 1/2 cup plum preserves or plum jam
- 3 tablespoons soy sauce
- 2 tablespoons lemon juice
- 1 tablespoon prepared horseradish
- 2 teaspoons cornstarch
- 1/2 teaspoon crushed red pepper
- 1 tablespoon vegetable oil
- 2 teaspoons grated fresh ginger

- 1 medium yellow or red sweet pepper, cut in thin strips
- 1 medium pear, cored and sliced
- 1/2 an 8-ounce can sliced water chestnuts, drained (about 1/2 cup)
- 1 to 2 tablespoons sliced almonds, toasted (optional)
- 2 cups hot cooked rice

1. Thaw pea pods, if frozen. Trim fat from pork. Cut pork in thin bite-size strips. Set aside.

2. For sauce, in a small bowl, stir together preserves, soy sauce, lemon juice, horseradish, cornstarch, and crushed red pepper. Set aside.

3. In a wok or large skillet, heat oil over medium-high heat. (Add more oil as necessary during cooking.) Add ginger; cook for 15 seconds. Add sweet pepper and pear; cook and stir for 1 1/2 minutes. Remove pepper strips and pear from wok. Add pork to wok; cook and stir for 2 to 3 minutes or until meat is no longer pink. Push pork from center of wok. Stir sauce; add to wok. Cook and stir until thickened and bubbly. Add water chestnuts. Return pepper strips and pear to wok; stir to coat. Cook and stir about 2 minutes more. Top with pea pods; cover and heat through. If desired, sprinkle with almonds. Serve with hot cooked rice.

Per serving: 482 cal., 7 g total fat (2 g sat. fat), 73 mg chol., 504 mg sodium, 72 g carbo., 4 g fiber, 29 g pro.

Pecan Pork Tenderloin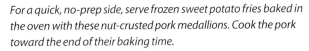

For a quick, no-prep side, serve frozen sweet potato fries baked in the oven with these nut-crusted pork medallions. Cook the pork toward the end of their baking time.

Start to Finish: 30 minutes **Makes:** 4 servings

- 12 ounces pork tenderloin
- 1 egg, lightly beaten
- 2 tablespoons Dijon-style mustard
- 1 tablespoon water
- 1/4 to 1/2 teaspoon cayenne pepper
- 1/2 cup fine dry bread crumbs
- 1/2 cup ground pecans, toasted
- 1/3 cup all-purpose flour
- 2 tablespoons olive oil or vegetable oil

1. Trim fat from pork. Cut pork crosswise in 1/4-inch slices. In a shallow bowl, combine egg, mustard, water, and cayenne pepper. In another shallow bowl, combine bread crumbs and pecans. Coat pork slices with flour. Dip slices into egg mixture; coat with crumb mixture.

2. In an extra-large skillet, heat oil over medium heat. (If necessary, add additional oil during cooking.) Cook pork in hot oil for 5 to 6 minutes or until slightly pink in center, turning once.

Per serving: 351 cal., 21 g total fat (3 g sat. fat), 108 mg chol., 488 mg sodium, 17 g carbo., 2 g fiber, 23 g pro.

Cornmeal-Crusted Pork ♥

Use either coarse-ground or fine-ground cornmeal to bread the pork. Coarse-ground provides more crunch than fine-ground provides.

Start to Finish: 20 minutes **Makes:** 4 servings

¹/₂	**cup yellow cornmeal**
¹/₂	**teaspoon salt**
¹/₂	**teaspoon ground black pepper**
1	**egg, lightly beaten**
1	**tablespoon water**
1	**pound pork tenderloin, cut in ¹/₂-inch slices**
2	**tablespoons olive oil or vegetable oil**
12	**ounces fresh green beans**
2	**medium zucchini and/or yellow summer squash, thinly bias-sliced**
2	**tablespoons fresh oregano leaves**

1. In a shallow bowl, combine cornmeal, salt, and pepper. In another shallow bowl, combine egg and water. Dip pork into egg mixture and then into cornmeal mixture to coat.

2. In an extra-large skillet, heat oil over medium-high heat. Add pork; cook about 2 minutes each side or until no pink remains. Transfer pork to a serving platter. Add beans and zucchini to skillet; cook and stir for 6 to 8 minutes or until crisp-tender. Season to taste with salt and pepper. Serve alongside pork. Sprinkle with oregano leaves.

Per serving: 310 cal., 13 g total fat (3 g sat. fat), 127 mg chol., 385 mg sodium, 21 g carbo., 5 g fiber, 29 g pro.

Classic Schnitzel

Classic Schnitzel ♥

This is the dish Julie Andrews sang praises to in The Sound of Music *hit "My Favorite Things." This take on the Austrian classic goes together in minutes and uses economical pork in place of traditional veal.*

Start to Finish: 35 minutes **Makes:** 6 servings

¹/₂	**cup all-purpose flour**
¹/₄	**teaspoon garlic salt**
¹/₄	**teaspoon celery salt**
¹/₄	**teaspoon seasoned salt**
¹/₄	**teaspoon paprika**
¹/₈	**teaspoon ground black pepper**
1	**egg, lightly beaten**
¹/₂	**cup milk**
6	**4-ounce pork sirloin cutlets, about ¹/₂ inch thick**
2	**to 3 tablespoons vegetable oil**
	Lemon wedges (optional)
	Sour Cream-Dill Sauce (optional)

1. In a shallow dish, combine flour, garlic salt, celery salt, seasoned salt, paprika, and pepper. In another shallow dish, stir together egg and milk. Coat each cutlet with flour mixture, then dip in egg mixture and again in flour mixture.

2. In a large skillet, heat oil over medium heat. Cook cutlets in hot oil for 12 to 15 minutes or until browned and meat is thoroughly cooked, turning once. (Remove meat from skillet and keep warm while preparing Sour Cream-Dill Sauce, if using.) If desired, serve with lemon wedges and/or sauce.

Per serving: 254 cal., 12 g total fat (3 g sat. fat), 108 mg chol., 242 mg sodium, 9 g carbo., 0 g fiber, 27 g pro.

Sour Cream-Dill Sauce: Pour 1¹/₄ cups chicken broth into the skillet used for cooking cutlets. Heat over medium heat, scraping up browned bits in skillet. Bring mixture to boiling. Meanwhile, in a small bowl, stir together ¹/₂ cup sour cream, 2 tablespoons all-purpose flour, and ¹/₂ teaspoon dried dill. Stir into hot broth in skillet. Cook and stir until thickened and bubbly. Cook and stir for 1 minute more. Makes about 2 cups.

Quick Tip The cornmeal breading in the Cornmeal-Crusted Pork recipe is incredibly versatile. Tailor it to your liking by adding dried herbs and spices, such as cayenne pepper, oregano, basil, marjoram, paprika, and cumin. Try it on fish fillets or skinless, boneless chicken breasts as well.

Cornmeal-Crusted Pork

Pork Lo Mein

Pork Lo Mein ♥

If you can't find dried lo mein noodles, substitute the same amount of dried thin spaghetti.

Start to Finish: 25 minutes **Makes:** 4 servings

12	ounces lean ground pork
2	cups sliced fresh mushrooms
1	cup shredded carrots (2 medium)
½	of a red or green sweet pepper, cut in bite-size strips
2	cloves garlic, minced
1	tablespoon cornstarch
1	cup reduced-sodium chicken broth
1	tablespoon reduced-sodium soy sauce
1	teaspoon grated fresh ginger
¼	teaspoon crushed red pepper
¼	teaspoon curry powder
4	ounces dried lo mein noodles, cooked and drained (2 cups cooked)
2	cups bean sprouts
½	cup sliced green onions (4)

1. In a large skillet, cook pork, mushrooms, carrots, sweet pepper, and garlic until meat is browned and vegetables are tender. Drain off fat.

2. Stir cornstarch into meat mixture. Stir in chicken broth, soy sauce, ginger, crushed red pepper, and curry powder.

Cook and stir until thickened and bubbly. Cook and stir for 2 minutes more.

3. Stir in cooked noodles, bean sprouts, and green onions; heat through. If desired, garnish with additional sliced green onions.

Per serving: 345 cal., 15 g total fat (5 g sat. fat), 49 mg chol., 367 mg sodium, 31 g carbo., 3 g fiber, 21 g pro.

Sausage with White Beans

This rich, hearty dish is infused with the flavor of fresh sage and topped with crispy fried leaves of the herb. Serve it with a robust red wine and rustic Italian bread.

Start to Finish: 30 minutes **Oven:** 425°F
Makes: 4 servings

1½	pounds fresh pork sausages (8)
3	tablespoons olive oil
15	fresh sage leaves
1½	tablespoons minced garlic
½	cup chopped onion (1 medium)
2	19-ounce cans white kidney (cannellini) beans, rinsed and drained
¾	cup chicken broth
½	cup chopped tomato (1 medium)
¼	teaspoon salt

1. Heat oven to 425°F. Arrange sausages on a 15×10×1-inch baking pan; drizzle with 1 tablespoon of the olive oil. Bake for 10 minutes. Turn sausage over; bake for 8 to 10 minutes more or until cooked through.

2. Meanwhile, in a large skillet, heat the remaining 1 tablespoon olive oil over medium heat. Add 5 of the sage leaves; cook for 3 to 4 minutes, until leaves begin to crisp. Transfer with tongs to paper towels.

3. Add garlic and onion to skillet; cook for 5 minutes. Chop the remaining 10 sage leaves. Add the chopped sage, beans, chicken broth, tomato, and salt. Simmer, uncovered, for 10 minutes. Slice sausages and add to beans; top with whole sage leaves.

Per serving: 510 cal., 27 g total fat (9 g sat. fat), 67 mg chol., 1,117 mg sodium, 36 g carbo., 12 g fiber, 31 g pro.

Pasta with Lamb and Feta Cheese ♥

Try another small pasta— such as ditalini or the pearl-shape pasta called Israeli couscous—in place of the rice-shape orzo in this dish.

Start to Finish: 30 minutes **Makes:** 4 servings

- 12 ounces lean boneless lamb or beef sirloin steak
- 1 tablespoon olive oil or vegetable oil
- 1 large onion, cut in wedges
- 2 cloves garlic, minced
- 1 6-ounce can tomato paste
- ½ cup tomato juice
- ½ cup water
- ¼ cup cider vinegar or red wine vinegar
- 1 teaspoon dried oregano, crushed
- ½ teaspoon ground cumin
- ¼ teaspoon ground cinnamon
- 1 medium zucchini, halved lengthwise and sliced (1¼ cups)
- 2 cups hot cooked orzo (rosamarina) or other pasta
- ¼ cup crumbled feta cheese (1 ounce)
  Chopped walnuts or snipped fresh parsley (optional)

1. Trim fat from meat. Thinly slice meat across the grain in bite-size pieces. In a large skillet, heat oil over medium heat. Add meat; cook and stir for 2 to 3 minutes or to desired doneness. Remove meat from skillet.

2. Add onion and garlic to skillet; cook and stir for 1 minute. Stir in tomato paste, tomato juice, water, vinegar, oregano, cumin, and cinnamon. Add zucchini. Bring to boiling; reduce heat. Simmer, covered, about 5 minutes or until zucchini is tender. Return meat to skillet; heat through. Serve over hot cooked orzo. Sprinkle with feta cheese and, if desired, walnuts or snipped parsley.

Per serving: 349 cal., 15 g total fat (5 g sat. fat), 51 mg chol., 323 mg sodium, 36 g carbo., 4 g fiber, 19 g pro.

Greek Lamb Stir-Fry ♥ [one]

Loaded with vegetables, this Mediterranean-style stir-fry is light on meat—just 8 ounces for three servings—which makes it economical and healthful.

Start to Finish: 20 minutes **Makes:** 3 servings

- 8 ounces lean boneless lamb
- 2 tablespoons vegetable oil
- 1 tablespoon lemon juice or balsamic vinegar
- ½ teaspoon dried rosemary, crushed
- ½ teaspoon dried oregano, crushed
- ¼ teaspoon ground black pepper
- 1 clove garlic, minced
- ½ cup thinly bias-sliced carrot (1 medium)
- ⅓ cup thinly sliced red onion (1 small)
- 4 cups torn fresh spinach (about 5 ounces)
- 2 small tomatoes, cut into thin wedges
- 2 cups hot cooked rice (optional)
- ¼ cup crumbled feta cheese (1 ounce)

1. Trim fat from lamb. Thinly slice across grain in bite-size strips. Set aside.

2. For sauce, in a small bowl, combine 1 tablespoon of the oil, lemon juice, rosemary, oregano, and pepper. Set aside.

3. In a wok or large skillet, heat the remaining 1 tablespoon oil over medium-high heat. (Add more oil as necessary during cooking.) Add garlic; cook and stir for 15 seconds. Add carrot and onion; cook and stir for 3 to 4 minutes or until crisp-tender. Remove vegetables from wok.

4. Add lamb to the hot wok. Cook and stir for 2 to 3 minutes or to desired doneness. Return cooked vegetables to the wok. Add the sauce, spinach, and tomato wedges. Stir all ingredients together to coat with sauce. Remove from heat. If desired, serve over hot cooked rice. Top with crumbled feta cheese.

Per serving: 244 cal., 15 g total fat (4 g sat. fat), 58 mg chol., 205 mg sodium, 8 g carbo., 3 g fiber, 19 g pro.

Greek Lamb Stir-Fry

Pan-Seared Lamb Chops with Mint Salad

Pan-Seared Lamb Chops with Mint Salad 🔲

Mint salad is a fresh, contemporary stand-in for traditional mint jelly to accompany these juicy pan-seared lamb chops.

Start to Finish: 30 minutes **Makes:** 4 servings

- ¼ **cup snipped fresh mint**
- ¼ **cup snipped fresh Italian (flat-leaf) parsley**
- ¼ **cup crumbled feta cheese (1 ounce)**
- ¼ **cup chopped pecans, toasted**
- 8 **lamb rib chops or loin chops, 1 inch thick (about 2 pounds)**
- 2 **teaspoons olive oil**
- ¼ **teaspoon salt**
- ⅛ **teaspoon ground black pepper**
  Olive oil (optional)
  Lemon juice (optional)
  Mixed salad greens (optional)

1. In a small bowl, combine mint, parsley, feta cheese, and pecans; set aside.

2. Trim fat from chops. Rub chops with the 2 teaspoons olive oil, salt, and pepper. Preheat a large heavy skillet over medium-high heat until hot. Add chops. Cook for 8 to 10 minutes or until medium-rare (145°F), turning once halfway through cooking.

3. To serve, sprinkle chops with mint mixture. If desired, drizzle additional olive oil and/or lemon juice over mint mixture and serve with salad greens.

Per serving: 252 cal., 17 g total fat (5 g sat. fat), 72 mg chol., 311 mg sodium, 2 g carbo., 1 g fiber, 22 g pro.

Quick Tip Two common types of lamb chops are rib chops and loin chops. Loin chops are thicker and meatier, while rib chops are generally more delicate. For nice presentation, buy Frenched rib chops. Frenching is the process of scraping the rib bones clean of fat and membrane for graceful-looking bones. Ask the butcher to do this for you.

Greek Lamb Salad with Yogurt Dressing ♥ 🔲

Dried tart cherries or golden raisins add a hint of sweetness to the otherwise savory (and classic) combination of lamb, yogurt, and cucumber.

Start to Finish: 30 minutes **Makes:** 4 servings

- 8 **ounces boneless lamb leg sirloin chops, ½ inch thick**
- 2 **teaspoons snipped fresh rosemary or ½ teaspoon dried rosemary, crushed**
- 2 **cloves garlic, minced**
- 8 **cups torn fresh spinach or torn mixed salad greens**
- 1 **15-ounce can garbanzo beans (chickpeas), rinsed and drained**
- ¼ **cup chopped, seeded cucumber**
- ½ **cup plain low-fat yogurt**
- ¼ **cup chopped green onions (2)**
- ⅛ **to ¼ teaspoon salt**
- ⅛ **teaspoon ground black pepper**
- ¼ **cup dried tart cherries or golden raisins**

1. Preheat broiler. Trim fat from lamb chops. Combine rosemary and half of the minced garlic; rub evenly onto chops. Place chops on the unheated rack of a broiler pan. Broil 4 to 5 inches from heat for 12 to 15 minutes for medium (160°F), turning once halfway through cooking. Cut lamb chops in thin bite-size slices.

2. Meanwhile, in a large bowl, toss together spinach, garbanzo beans, and cucumber. Divide spinach mixture among 4 plates. Arrange lamb slices on the spinach mixture.

3. For dressing, in a small bowl, combine yogurt, green onions, salt, pepper, and the remaining minced garlic clove. Drizzle dressing on salads. Sprinkle with cherries.

Per serving: 243 cal., 6 g total fat (2 g sat. fat), 36 mg chol., 569 mg sodium, 29 g carbo., 8 g fiber, 20 g pro.

Greek Lamb Salad with Yogurt Dressing

Greek-Style Pasta Skillet 🔲

This one-pan dish offers a quick fix of Greek-style flavors—lamb, tomato, pasta, and tangy feta cheese.

Start to Finish: 30 minutes **Makes:** 4 servings

12	ounces ground lamb or ground beef
½	cup chopped onion (1 medium)
1	14.5-ounce can diced tomatoes
1	5.5-ounce can tomato juice
½	cup water
½	teaspoon instant beef bouillon granules
½	teaspoon ground cinnamon
⅛	teaspoon garlic powder
1	cup packaged dried medium shell macaroni or elbow macaroni
1	cup frozen cut green beans
½	cup crumbled feta cheese (2 ounces)

1. In a large skillet, cook ground meat and onion until meat is no longer pink. Drain off fat. Stir in undrained tomatoes, tomato juice, water, bouillon granules, cinnamon, and garlic powder. Bring to boiling.

2. Stir uncooked macaroni and green beans into meat mixture. Return to boiling; reduce heat. Simmer, covered, about 15 minutes or until macaroni and green beans are tender. Sprinkle with feta cheese.

Per serving: 362 cal., 16 g total fat (7 g sat. fat), 70 mg chol., 647 mg sodium, 33 g carbo., 2 g fiber, 22 g pro.

Greek-Style Pasta Skillet

Herbed Lamb Steak Salad 🔲

Lamb arm steaks are a specialty cut and may not be wrapped, ready, and waiting in the meat case of your supermarket. Just ask the butcher to do it for you.

Start to Finish: 20 minutes **Makes:** 4 servings

1	pound lamb arm steaks, ½ inch thick
1	tablespoon olive oil
	Salt and ground black pepper
1	5-ounce package mixed salad greens with herbs
⅔	cup sliced fresh radishes
1	6-ounce container plain yogurt
1	to 2 tablespoons snipped fresh mint
	Herbed feta cheese

1. Heat a grill pan over medium-high heat. Trim fat from steaks. Brush steaks with oil; sprinkle lightly with salt and pepper. Place steaks on a grill pan. Cook steaks for 8 to 12 minutes for medium (160°F), turning once halfway through cooking. Transfer to a cutting board; cover and let stand for 2 minutes.

2. Meanwhile, divide salad greens and radishes among 4 plates. For dressing, in a small bowl, combine yogurt and mint; season to taste with salt and pepper.

3. Remove bones from lamb. Cut lamb in strips; place meat on salad greens. Sprinkle with feta cheese; pass dressing.

Per serving: 344 cal., 26 g total fat (10 g sat. fat), 82 mg chol., 258 mg sodium, 5 g carbo., 1 g fiber, 22 g pro.

Lamb Chops with Cranberry Relish ♥ 🔲

The supersimple glaze for the lamb is prepared cranberry-orange relish with additional orange flavor and chopped pecan crunch.

Start to Finish: 20 minutes **Makes:** 4 servings

¼	cup cranberry-orange relish
2	tablespoons chopped pecans
1	tablespoon orange juice
4	lamb loin chops or lamb shoulder chops, cut ¾ inch thick
	Salt and ground black pepper

1. In a small bowl, combine cranberry-orange relish, pecans, and orange juice. Set aside.

2. Preheat broiler. Trim fat from chops. Place chops on the unheated rack of a broiler pan. Lightly sprinkle chops with salt and pepper. Broil 3 to 4 inches from heat for 9 to 11 minutes for medium (160°F), turning once halfway through broiling. Spread relish mixture on chops. Broil for 1 minute more.

Per serving: 325 cal., 13 g total fat (3 g sat. fat), 100 mg chol., 245 mg sodium, 18 g carbo., 1 g fiber, 33 g pro.

Herbed Lamb Steak Salad

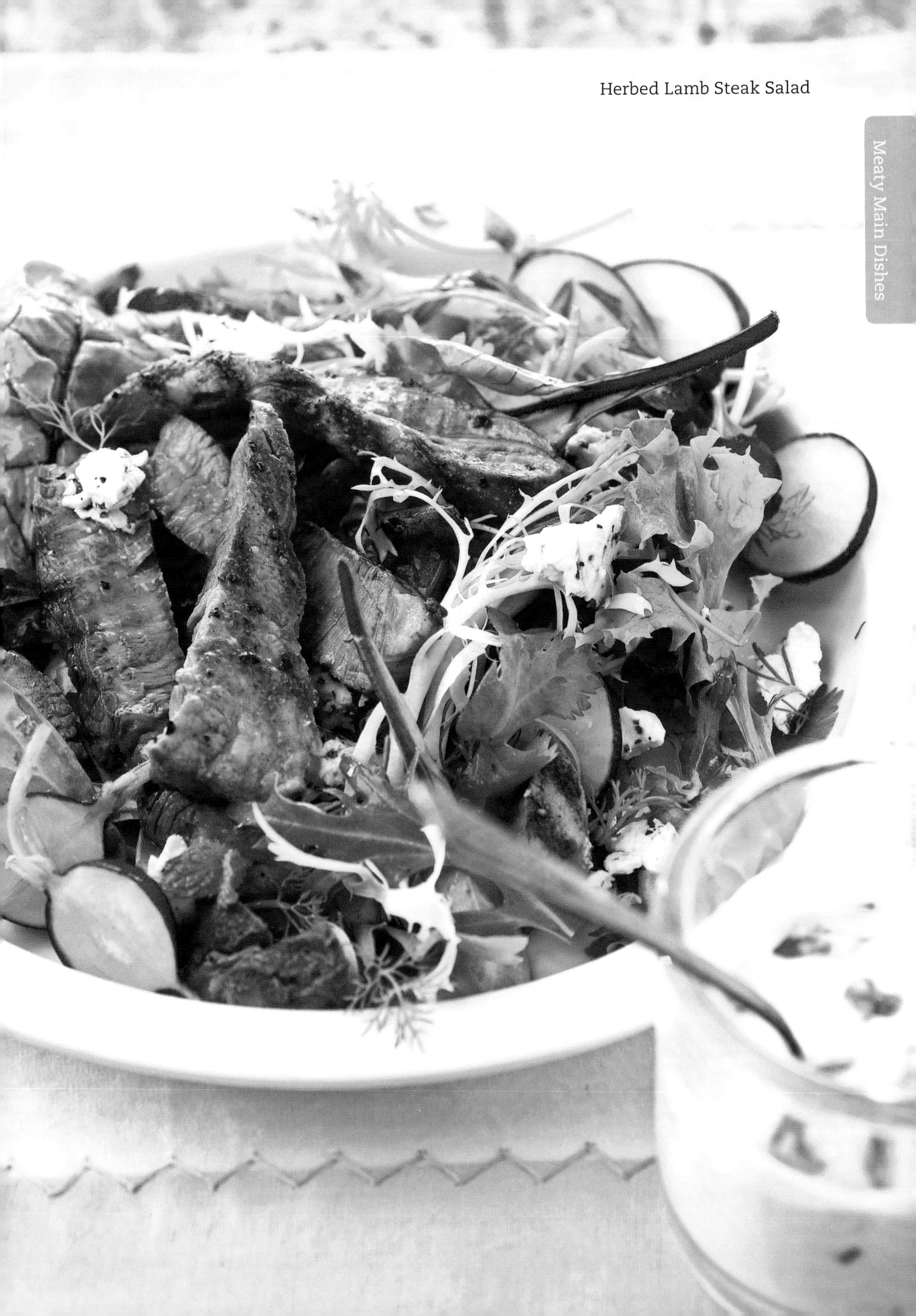

Chicken with Cherry-Ginger
Chutney, **page 65**

Chicken with Quick
Cornmeal Crust, **page 62**

Chicken with Parmesan
Noodles, **page 66**

Turkey Roulade,
page 103

Quick Poultry

Chicken is budget-friendly, quick to fix, and lends itself to all kinds of flavors and cooking methods. Broiled, baked, fried, roasted, or grilled, chicken (and turkey too) are sure to please.

Chicken Wellington

Apricots, Chicken, and Orzo

Combine the syrup from canned apricots with the savory pan juices, green onions, and curry to make a simple, delicious sauce.

Start to Finish: 20 minutes **Makes:** 4 servings

1¼   **cups dried orzo (about 8 ounces)**
1   **15-ounce can unpeeled apricot halves in light syrup**
4   **small skinless, boneless chicken breast halves (1 to 1¼ pounds)**
   Salt and ground black pepper
1½   **teaspoons curry powder**
2   **tablespoons olive oil or vegetable oil**
6   **green onions**

1. Cook orzo following package directions; drain. Drain apricot halves, reserving ½ cup syrup.

2. Meanwhile, sprinkle chicken with salt, pepper, and ½ teaspoon of the curry powder. In an extra-large skillet, heat oil over medium heat. Add chicken; cook for 8 to 10 minutes or until chicken is no longer pink (170°F), turning once, and adding apricots, cut sides down, to the skillet the last 2 minutes of cooking time.

3. Meanwhile, cut green tops of 2 of the green onions into thick diagonal slices; set aside. Chop remaining green onions. Add chopped green onions and remaining 1 teaspoon curry powder to skillet; cook for 1 minute. Stir in the reserved syrup and drained orzo. Serve chicken with apricots and orzo. Sprinkle with green onion tops.

Per serving: 458 cal., 9 g total fat (1 g sat. fat), 66 mg chol., 230 mg sodium, 59 g carbo., 4 g fiber, 34 g pro.

Chicken Wellington 🍳

To prepare ahead, cover unbaked pastries and refrigerate. Bake them the next day as directed. Or wrap unbaked pastries individually in waxed paper, then in foil. Freeze them up to 1 week. Thaw in the refrigerator overnight, then bake an additional 5 minutes.

Prep: 10 minutes **Roast:** 25 minutes **Oven:** 425°F
Makes: 6 servings

1   **10-ounce package frozen chopped broccoli, thawed and drained**
1   **5.2-ounce package semisoft cheese with garlic and fine herbs**
1   **17.25-ounce package frozen puff pastry sheets, thawed**
6   **skinless, boneless chicken breast halves (2 pounds)**
½   **teaspoon salt**
¼   **cup fine dry bread crumbs**
1   **egg, lightly beaten**
1   **tablespoon water**

1. Preheat oven to 425°F. In a medium bowl, stir together broccoli and cheese to combine. Set aside.

2. On lightly floured surface, roll out each pastry sheet to a 14×12-inch rectangle. Cut each sheet in four 7×6-inch rectangles.

3. Sprinkle both sides of chicken with salt. Spread ¼ cup of the broccoli mixture on one pastry rectangle. Place a chicken breast half on top. Sprinkle with 2 teaspoons bread crumbs. In a small bowl, combine egg and water. Brush some egg mixture onto edges of rectangle; fold pastry over chicken. Press edges to seal. Place, seam side down, in ungreased shallow baking pan. Repeat with remaining chicken, 5 of the remaining pastry rectangles, broccoli mixture, bread crumbs, and egg mixture.

Chicken and Pasta Stack

4. Using a small cookie cutter, cut decorative shapes from remaining pastry rectangles. Brush egg mixture on pastry packets. Place cutouts on packets; brush with additional egg mixture.

5. Bake about 25 minutes or until pastry is golden and an instant-read thermometer inserted in chicken breasts registers 170°F.

Per serving: 701 cal., 35 g total fat (11 g sat. fat), 163 mg chol., 751 mg sodium, 52 g carbo., 8 g fiber, 44 g pro.

Chicken and Pasta Stack

This is the ultimate summer pasta, made with fresh sweet corn and tomatoes and served warm or cool.

Start to Finish: 20 minutes **Makes:** 4 servings

- **6 ounces dried angel hair pasta**
- **3 ears fresh sweet corn**
- **4 small skinless, boneless chicken breast halves (1 to 1 1/4 pounds)**
- **1 1/2 teaspoons chili powder**
- **1/4 teaspoon salt**
- **1/4 teaspoon freshly ground black pepper**
- **4 tablespoons olive oil or vegetable oil**
- **3 tablespoons fresh lime or lemon juice**
- **2 medium tomatoes, sliced**
  Snipped fresh parsley (optional)
  Lime halves (optional)

1. Cook pasta and corn in lightly salted boiling water following pasta package directions. Drain in colander; rinse with cold water until cool.

2. Meanwhile, sprinkle chicken with 1 teaspoon of the chili powder, the salt, and pepper. In a large skillet, heat 1 tablespoon of the oil over medium heat. Add chicken; cook for 8 to 10 minutes or until no longer pink (170°F), turning once halfway through cooking.

3. In a screw top jar, combine the remaining 3 tablespoons oil, the remaining 1/2 teaspoon chili powder, and the lime juice; shake to combine.

4. Cut corn from cob. Arrange pasta, chicken, corn, and tomatoes on 4 dinner plates. Drizzle with dressing. Lightly sprinkle additional salt and pepper. If desired, sprinkle parsley and serve with lime halves.

Per serving: 515 cal., 17 g total fat (3 g sat. fat), 66 mg chol., 226 mg sodium, 58 g carbo., 5 g fiber, 36 g pro.

Chicken Tortellini Toss ⊡

This recipe employs a neat trick for any time you're making a quick pasta and veggies dish: Add fresh or frozen vegetables to the pasta pot the last few minutes of cooking time.

Start to Finish: 20 minutes **Makes:** 4 servings

- 2 9-ounce packages refrigerated cheese tortellini
- 4 cups fresh broccoli and/or cauliflower florets
- 1 14.5-ounce can diced tomatoes with Italian herbs, undrained
- 1 9-ounce package frozen roasted or grilled chicken breast strips, thawed
- ½ a 10-ounce jar dried-tomato pesto (½ cup) Shaved Parmesan cheese (optional) Fresh Italian (flat-leaf) parsley (optional)

1. In a 4-quart Dutch oven, cook tortellini following package directions, adding the broccoli the last 3 minutes of cooking. Drain. Return to pan.

2. Stir in undrained tomatoes, chicken, and pesto. Cook just until heated through, stirring occasionally. If desired, garnish with Parmesan cheese and parsley.

Per serving: 468 cal., 10 g total fat (4 g sat. fat), 81 mg chol., 1,372 mg sodium, 61 g carbo., 5 g fiber, 33 g pro.

Cucumber-Yogurt Chicken

Cayenne pepper gives the chicken fire; a cucumber-yogurt sauce cools the dish down.

Prep: 20 minutes **Bake:** 8 minutes **Oven:** 350°F
Makes: 4 servings

- 1 cup plain low-fat yogurt
- 1 cup chopped, peeled seedless cucumber
- ½ cup finely chopped radishes
- 2 tablespoons mayonnaise or salad dressing
- ¼ teaspoon finely shredded lemon peel
- 1 tablespoon fresh lemon juice
- 1 teaspoon salt
- ¼ teaspoon minced garlic
- ¼ teaspoon bottled red pepper sauce
- 1 tablespoon vegetable oil
- 4 skinless, boneless chicken breast halves (1½ to 1¾ pounds)
- ½ teaspoon cayenne pepper

1. Preheat oven to 350°F. For yogurt sauce, in a medium bowl, stir together yogurt, cucumber, radishes, mayonnaise, lemon peel, lemon juice, ½ teaspoon of the salt, the garlic, and red pepper sauce.

2. In an extra-large nonstick, ovenproof skillet, heat oil over medium heat. Sprinkle chicken with the remaining ½ teaspoon salt and the cayenne pepper. Cook chicken in hot oil about 6 minutes or until browned, turning once.

3. Bake chicken in skillet for 8 to 9 minutes or until no longer pink (170°F). Serve with yogurt sauce.

Per serving: 321 cal., 13 g total fat (3 g sat. fat), 105 mg chol., 760 mg sodium, 6 g carbo., 1 g fiber, 43 g pro.

Chicken with Quick Cornmeal Crust

Warm and homey, this 22-minute potpie-style dish cleverly makes use of refrigerated corn bread twists to form a pretty lattice crust.

Start to Finish: 22 minutes **Makes:** 4 servings

- 2 tablespoons vegetable oil
- ½ cup all-purpose flour
- ½ teaspoon ground sage
- ¼ teaspoon salt
- ¼ teaspoon ground black pepper
- 12 ounces skinless, boneless chicken breast halves
- 2 cups frozen mixed vegetables
- 1 14-ounce can reduced-sodium chicken broth
- ½ cup milk
- 1 11.5-ounce package (8) refrigerated corn bread twists
- ½ cup shredded Mexican-blend cheese (2 ounces)

1. Preheat oven to 450°F. In a large skillet, heat oil over medium-high heat. Meanwhile, in a large resealable plastic bag, combine flour, sage, salt, and pepper. Cut chicken in bite-size pieces. Add chicken to bag; seal bag and shake to coat.

2. Add chicken to hot oil; sprinkle any remaining flour mixture on chicken. Cook chicken over medium-high heat for 2 minutes (chicken will not be completely cooked), stirring to brown evenly. Place vegetables in a sieve or colander. Run cold water over vegetables to thaw. Add vegetables, broth, and milk to skillet. Bring to boiling, stirring once. Open package of corn bread twists and separate into 16 pieces.

3. Divide chicken mixture among 4 16-ounce gratin dishes or individual casserole dishes. Arrange corn bread pieces on top. Sprinkle with cheese. Bake for 9 to 10 minutes or until corn bread is golden brown.

Per serving: 612 cal., 25 g total fat (7 g sat. fat), 64 mg chol., 1,259 mg sodium, 60 g carbo., 3 g fiber, 34 g pro.

Quick Tip Dividing a large casserole that serves four or six into individual servings and baking it in gratin dishes or individual casseroles reduces baking time. Try it with some of your favorite casserole recipes. A large casserole that bakes at about 375°F for 25 to 30 minutes until golden brown and bubbly can be baked in individual dishes at 375°F for about half the time.

Chicken with Quick Cornmeal Crust

Chicken with Cherry-Ginger Chutney

Chicken with Cherry-Ginger Chutney ♥ one

This dish is equally good with dried cranberries in place of the dried cherries.

Start to Finish: 20 minutes **Makes:** 4 servings

- 4 **medium skinless, boneless chicken breast halves, each cut in 4 pieces**
  Salt and ground black pepper
- 1/2 **teaspoon ground ginger**
- 1 **tablespoon olive oil or vegetable oil**
- 1 **large apple, thinly sliced horizontally**
- 1/2 **cup dried tart red cherries**
- 1/3 **cup coarsely chopped walnuts**
- 4 **teaspoons packed brown sugar**
- 1/4 **cup water**
- 3 **tablespoons cider vinegar**

1. Sprinkle chicken with salt, pepper, and 1/4 teaspoon of the ginger.

2. In a large skillet, heat oil over medium heat. Add chicken; cook for 8 to 12 minutes or until no longer pink (170°F). Transfer chicken to a serving platter; cover and keep warm.

3. For cherry-ginger chutney, add apple, cherries, and walnuts to skillet; cook for 2 minutes, stirring frequently. In a small bowl, stir together brown sugar, water, vinegar, and the remaining 1/4 teaspoon ginger. Add to skillet. Cook and stir for 1 minute. Serve with chicken.

Per serving: 364 cal., 12 g total fat (2 g sat. fat), 82 mg chol., 249 mg sodium, 30 g carbo., 3 g fiber, 35 g pro.

Creamy Chicken and Penne

This dish is one great way to get kids to eat vegetables. When the chicken, pasta, and broccoli are coated in a rich, creamy Parmesan and dried-tomato sauce, who can resist?

Start to Finish: 25 minutes **Makes:** 6 servings

- 1 **pound dried penne pasta**
- 4 **cups broccoli florets**
- 1 **tablespoon olive oil**
- 1 **medium onion, sliced**
- 8 **ounces skinless, boneless chicken breast halves, cut in 3×1-inch strips**
- 3/4 **cup oil-packed dried tomato strips or pieces, drained and chopped**
- 1 **cup whipping cream**
- 1/2 **cup chicken broth**
- 2 **tablespoons balsamic vinegar**
- 1 **teaspoon salt**
- 1/4 **teaspoon ground black pepper**
- 3/4 **cup grated Parmesan cheese**

1. In a 4-quart Dutch oven, cook penne following package directions, adding broccoli the last 2 minutes.

2. Meanwhile, in a large skillet, heat olive oil over medium heat. Add onion; cook about 6 minutes or until softened. Add chicken; cook for 4 minutes. Stir in dried tomatoes, whipping cream, chicken broth, balsamic vinegar, salt, and pepper; simmer for 4 minutes.

3. Drain pasta and broccoli; return to Dutch oven. Add chicken mixture and Parmesan cheese; toss to mix.

Per serving: 554 cal., 25 g total fat (13 g sat. fat), 86 mg chol., 789 mg sodium, 59 g carbo., 5 g fiber, 24 g pro.

Quick Chicken Panzanella one

Panzanella is an Italian bread salad that was created to make good use of day-old bread. It always includes tomatoes and olive oil. The addition of chicken makes it a one-dish meal.

Start to Finish: 20 minutes **Makes:** 4 servings

- 1 **14.5-ounce can diced tomatoes with green pepper, celery, and onions, undrained**
- 3 **tablespoons olive oil**
  Dash salt
  Dash ground black pepper
- 1 **2- to 2¼-pound whole roasted chicken**
- 4 **cups cubed Italian bread**
- 2 **medium cucumbers, halved lengthwise and sliced**
- 1 **cup torn fresh basil or spinach**

1. Spoon off 2 tablespoons of the liquid from the diced tomatoes. Combine liquid with 1 tablespoon of the olive oil, the salt, and pepper; set aside. Remove meat from roasted chicken. Cut in pieces.

2. In a large skillet, heat the remaining 2 tablespoons olive oil over medium heat. Add bread cubes; cook and stir about 5 minutes or until golden. Remove skillet from heat. Add diced tomatoes; toss to mix. Divide bread mixture among 4 plates. Add chicken, cucumber, and basil. Pass tomato-oil mixture.

Per serving: 596 cal., 27 g total fat (6 g sat. fat), 92 mg chol., 824 mg sodium, 50 g carbo., 4 g fiber, 37 g pro.

Quick Tip Next time you're grocery shopping, pick up a rotisserie chicken—even if you don't plan to use it that night. When you get home, let it cool, then refrigerate it. The meat from a rotisserie chicken can be used in many healthful dishes. Keep a whole bird in the refrigerator for 3 to 4 days.

Chicken with
Parmesan Noodles

Chicken, Corn and Limas

With the addition of chicken, that classic American dish—succotash—becomes a main dish.

Start to Finish: 20 minutes **Makes:** 4 servings

- 2 **cups frozen whole kernel corn**
- 2 **cups frozen baby lima beans**
- ¼ **cup water**
- 1 **tablespoon vegetable oil**
- 1 **large onion, cut in thin wedges**
- 14 **to 16 ounces chicken breast tenderloins**
- 1 **14.5-ounce can stewed tomatoes, undrained**
- ¼ **teaspoon bottled hot pepper sauce**
- 1 **tablespoon snipped fresh oregano**

1. In a 1½-quart microwave-safe casserole, combine corn, lima beans, and the water; cover. Microwave on 100% power (high) for 5 to 7 minutes or until crisp-tender, stirring once. Drain.

2. Meanwhile, in an extra-large skillet, heat oil over medium heat. Add onion; cook for 2 minutes. Add chicken; cook about 8 minutes or until no longer pink (170°F), turning once halfway through cooking. Remove chicken and set aside. Add undrained tomatoes and bottled hot pepper sauce to the skillet. Bring to boiling. Stir in cooked vegetables. Cook and stir until heated through.

3. Transfer vegetable mixture to platter. Arrange chicken on top. Sprinkle with snipped oregano.

Per serving: 393 cal., 9 g total fat (2 g sat. fat), 70 mg chol., 859 mg sodium, 49 g carbo., 9 g fiber, 35 g pro.

Chicken with Parmesan Noodles

Serve this with a side of roasted baby carrots: Toss a 10- to 12-ounce ounce package of baby-cut carrots with olive oil, salt, and pepper, then roast in a single layer on a rimmed baking sheet at 400°F for 20 to 25 minutes or until lightly browned.

Start to Finish: 20 minutes **Makes:** 4 servings

- 1 **9-ounce package refrigerated angel hair pasta**
- 2 **tablespoons butter or margarine**
- 2 **cups thinly sliced carrots (4 large)**
- 1½ **pounds skinless, boneless chicken breast halves, cut in 1-inch cubes**
- ¼ **cup purchased basil pesto**
- ¼ **cup finely shredded Parmesan cheese (1 ounce)**
  Freshly ground black pepper
  Olive oil (optional)
  Fresh basil (optional)

1. Cook pasta following package directions.

2. Meanwhile, in an extra-large skillet, melt 1 tablespoon of the butter over medium heat. Add carrots; cook for 3 minutes. Add chicken; cook and stir for 4 to 5 minutes or until chicken is no longer pink. Add pesto; toss to coat.

3. Drain pasta; return to pan. Toss pasta with the remaining 1 tablespoon butter. Serve with chicken mixture. Sprinkle with Parmesan cheese and pepper. If desired, drizzle with olive oil and top with basil.

Per serving: 567 cal., 19 g total fat (8 g sat. fat), 164 mg chol., 452 mg sodium, 47 g carbo., 5 g fiber, 52 g pro.

Mediterranean Chicken Salad

Giardiniera, a mix of spicy, vinegary, pickled vegetables, gives this dish a major flavor boost. Also try it roughly chopped and layer it in homemade panini.

Start to Finish: 20 minutes **Makes:** 4 servings

- 12 **ounces chicken breast tenderloins**
  Ground black pepper
- ⅔ **cup bottled Greek salad dressing with feta cheese**
- 8 **cups packaged mixed baby greens**
- 1 **16-ounce jar pickled mixed vegetables (giardiniera), rinsed and drained**
- ½ **cup pitted kalamata olives, halved**
- ½ **cup onion and garlic croutons (optional)**

1. Sprinkle chicken lightly with pepper. Remove 2 tablespoons of the salad dressing. Brush on chicken.

2. Preheat a grill pan or large nonstick skillet over medium high heat; add chicken. Reduce heat to medium. Cook for 5 to 7 minutes or until chicken is no longer pink (170°F), turning once halfway through cooking.

3. In a salad bowl, toss together greens, chicken, drained vegetables, olives, and the remaining salad dressing. If desired, top with croutons.

Per serving: 305 cal., 21 g total fat (2 g sat. fat), 49 mg chol., 1,517 mg sodium, 9 g carbo., 2 g fiber, 21 g pro.

Chicken and Asparagus Skillet Supper 🗆

All you need to add to this dish to make a meal is purchased whole grain or regular rolls, hot from the oven.

Start to Finish: 20 minutes **Makes:** 4 servings

- 8   skinless, boneless chicken thighs
       Salt and ground black pepper
- 3   slices bacon, coarsely chopped
- ½   cup chicken broth
- 1   pound fresh asparagus spears, trimmed
- 1   small yellow summer squash, halved crosswise and cut in ½-inch strips
- 2   tablespoons water
- 4   green onions, cut in 2-inch pieces

1. Lightly sprinkle chicken with salt and pepper. In an extra-large skillet, cook chicken and bacon over medium-high heat for 12 minutes, turning to brown evenly. Carefully add chicken broth; cook, covered, for 3 to 5 minutes more or until chicken is no longer pink (180°F).

2. Meanwhile, in a microwave-safe 2-quart dish, combine asparagus, squash, and the water. Sprinkle with salt and pepper. Cover with vented plastic wrap. Microwave on 100% power (high) for 3 to 5 minutes or until vegetables are crisp-tender, stirring once. Transfer vegetables to 4 plates. Drizzle with cooking liquid from skillet; top with chicken, bacon, and green onions.

Per serving: 320 cal., 18 g total fat (6 g sat. fat), 134 mg chol., 626 mg sodium, 5 g carbo., 2 g fiber, 32 g pro.

Chicken and Asparagus Skillet Supper

Stroganoff-Style Chicken ♥

Chicken replaces beef and the sour cream is lower fat for a healthful—but still satisfying—version of this classic dish.

Start to Finish: 25 minutes **Makes:** 5 servings

- 12   ounces dried medium noodles or fettuccine
       Nonstick cooking spray
- 2   cups sliced fresh mushrooms
- ½   cup chopped onion (1 medium)
- 2   teaspoons vegetable oil (optional)
- 12   ounces skinless, boneless chicken breast halves, cut in 1-inch cubes
- 1   8-ounce container light sour cream
- 2   tablespoons all-purpose flour
- 1   teaspoon paprika
- ¼   teaspoon salt
- ½   cup reduced-sodium chicken broth

1. Cook noodles following package directions. Drain. Cover and keep warm.

2. Meanwhile, coat an unheated large skillet with nonstick cooking spray. Preheat over medium heat. Add mushrooms and onion; cook until onion is nearly tender.

3. Add oil to skillet, if necessary. Add chicken; cook for 3 to 4 minutes or until no longer pink.

4. In a small bowl, stir together sour cream, flour, paprika, and salt; stir in chicken broth. Add to skillet. Cook and stir until slightly thickened and bubbly. Cook and stir for 1 minute more. Serve over hot cooked noodles.

Per serving: 308 cal., 7 g total fat (2 g sat. fat), 79 mg chol., 257 mg sodium, 39 g carbo., 3 g fiber, 23 g pro.

Quick Tip Buying presliced mushrooms saves a prep step in making this creamy, comforting dish. Be sure to choose the freshest looking sliced mushrooms you can find (bright white and plump, not brown and starting to shrivel), then use them right away. Sliced mushrooms are a convenience, but they don't keep as long as whole mushrooms do. Cutting into any fruit or vegetable exposes more surface area to air, which hastens spoilage.

Chicken and Lemon-Broccoli Alfredo

Chicken and Lemon-Broccoli Alfredo 🔲

A touch of lemon brightens the flavor of this rich Alfredo sauce.

Start to Finish: 20 minutes **Makes:** 4 servings

- 4 **small skinless, boneless chicken breast halves (1 to 1¼ pounds)**
  Salt and ground black pepper
- 1 **tablespoon olive oil or vegetable oil**
- 8 **ounces fresh mushrooms, halved**
- 1 **lemon**
- 3 **cups fresh broccoli florets**
- 1 **10-ounce container refrigerated light Alfredo pasta sauce**

1. Lightly sprinkle chicken with salt and pepper. In a large skillet, heat oil over medium heat. Add chicken and mushrooms; cook 4 minutes or until chicken is browned, turning chicken once halfway through cooking.

2. Meanwhile, finely shred 2 teaspoons lemon peel; set aside. Slice lemon. Add broccoli and lemon slices to skillet. Cook, covered, about 8 minutes or until chicken is no longer pink (170°F).

3. Place chicken and vegetables on 4 plates. Add Alfredo sauce to skillet; heat through. Serve with chicken. Sprinkle with lemon peel and pepper.

Per serving: 295 cal., 12 g total fat (5 g sat. fat), 91 mg chol., 705 mg sodium, 16 g carbo., 4 g fiber, 35 g pro.

Ginger-Chicken and Garden-Vegetable Fried Rice 🔲

Fried rice is best made with cold, not just-cooked, rice. Use a precooked pouch of rice, as directed here, or cook extra rice one night and refrigerate the leftovers.

Start to Finish: 29 minutes **Makes:** 4 servings

- 1 **tablespoon vegetable oil**
- 4 **chicken drumsticks**
- 2 **tablespoons soy sauce**
- 1 **1-inch piece fresh ginger, peeled and finely chopped (2 tablespoons)**
- ½ **cup water**
- 1 **cup sliced or coarsely chopped carrots (2 large)**
- 2 **tablespoons water**
- 1 **14.8-ounce pouch cooked long grain rice**
- 8 **ounces fresh sugar snap peas**
- ½ **cup chopped red sweet pepper (optional)**
- 4 **eggs, lightly beaten**
  Sliced green onions (optional)
  Soy sauce and/or dark sesame oil (optional)

1. In a large nonstick skillet, heat vegetable oil over medium-high heat. Add chicken, the 2 tablespoons soy sauce, and half the ginger; stir to coat chicken. Cook chicken on all sides until browned; add the ½ cup water. Cook, covered, about 15 minutes or until chicken is no longer pink (180°F).

2. Meanwhile in a 2-quart microwave-safe casserole, combine carrots, the remaining ginger, and the 2 tablespoons water. Microwave, covered, on 100% power (high) for 4 minutes. Add rice from pouch, sugar snap peas, and, if desired, sweet pepper. Cook, covered, about 5 minutes or until heated through, stirring twice.

3. Remove chicken and pan juices from skillet; cover to keep warm. Using paper towels, wipe out skillet. Return skillet to heat; add eggs. Cook, stirring occasionally, for 30 seconds or just until scrambled. Stir in rice mixture. Divide among 4 shallow bowls or plates; top each with a chicken drumstick. Top with green onions. Pass any reserved pan juices and soy sauce.

Per serving: 421 cal., 17 g total fat (4 g sat. fat), 271 mg chol., 666 mg sodium, 42 g carbo., 4 g fiber, 25 g pro.

Cheesy Chicken and Noodles 🔲

A tiny splash of wine or sherry, if you choose to use it, adds flavor to the Alfredo sauce in this recipe.

Start to Finish: 25 minutes **Makes:** 6 servings

- 12 **ounces dried wide noodles**
- 2 **cups frozen vegetables (such as peas, carrots, sweet red pepper strips, and/or pea pods)**
- 1 **16-ounce jar light Parmesan-Alfredo pasta sauce**
- 1 **9-ounce package frozen cooked chicken breast strips, thawed**
- 1 **4-ounce can (drained weight) sliced mushrooms, drained**
- 2 **tablespoons dry white wine, dry sherry, chicken broth, or milk**
  Milk (optional)
  Grated Parmesan cheese (optional)

1. In a 4-quart Dutch oven, cook noodles following package directions, adding the frozen vegetables the last 3 minutes of cooking time. Drain; return noodle mixture to Dutch oven.

2. Stir in pasta sauce, chicken, mushrooms, and wine. Heat through. Stir in additional milk to reach desired consistency, if necessary. If desired, sprinkle servings with Parmesan cheese.

Per serving: 427 cal., 13 g total fat (7 g sat. fat), 109 mg chol., 966 mg sodium, 51 g carbo., 3 g fiber, 24 g pro.

Tuscan-Style Stuffed Chicken Breasts

For date night at home, serve these spiraled, stuffed chicken breasts with a side of sautéed fresh spinach and packaged risotto mix—and something chocolate for dessert.

Start to Finish: 30 minutes **Makes:** 2 servings

- **2 small skinless, boneless chicken breast halves (8 to 10 ounces)**
  Ground black pepper
- **2 ounces fontina cheese, crumbled or sliced**
- **½ cup bottled roasted red sweet pepper halves, drained**
- **6 fresh sage leaves or ½ teaspoon dried sage, crushed**
- **2 tablespoons all-purpose flour**
- **1 tablespoon olive oil**
- **½ cup dry white wine or chicken broth**

1. Place each chicken piece, bone side up, between 2 pieces of clear plastic wrap. Working from the center to the edges, lightly pound with the flat side of a meat mallet to ¼-inch thickness. Discard plastic wrap. Sprinkle chicken with pepper. Layer cheese, roasted pepper halves, and sage in center of each breast. Fold in edges; roll in a spiral, pressing edges to seal. Roll in flour.

2. In an 8-inch skillet, heat olive oil over medium heat. Add chicken; cook about 5 minutes, turning to brown evenly. Remove from skillet.

3. In the same skillet, heat wine to boiling; reduce heat. Simmer, uncovered, about 2 minutes or until ¼ cup liquid remains. Return chicken to skillet. Simmer, covered, for 7 to 8 minutes or until chicken is no longer pink. To serve, spoon juices over chicken.

Per serving: 364 cal., 19 g total fat (7 g sat. fat), 92 mg chol., 284 mg sodium, 8 g carbo., 1 g fiber, 30 g pro.

Chicken with Long Beans and Walnuts

Chinese long beans, which can grow to 18 inches, cook in much less time than other green beans. Look for them in Asian markets, farmers' markets, and supermarkets.

Prep: 30 minutes **Start to Finish:** 25 minutes **Makes:** 4 servings

- **12 ounces skinless, boneless chicken breast halves**
- **2 tablespoons hoisin sauce**
- **1 tablespoon soy sauce**
- **1 tablespoon water**
- **½ teaspoon sugar**
- **8 ounces fresh Chinese long beans, cut in 4-inch lengths, or fresh whole green beans**
- **1 tablespoon vegetable oil**
- **3 cloves garlic, minced**
- **1 medium onion, cut in thin wedges**
- **½ cup coarsely broken walnuts**
- **2 cups hot cooked rice**

1. Cut chicken in 1-inch pieces. Set aside. For sauce, in a small bowl, stir together hoisin sauce, soy sauce, water, and sugar. Set aside.

2. In a medium saucepan, cook long beans, covered, in a small amount of boiling water for 3 to 5 minutes (cook whole green beans about 10 minutes) or until crisp-tender. Drain; set aside.

3. In a wok or large skillet, heat oil over medium-high heat. (Add more oil as necessary during cooking.) Add garlic; cook and stir 15 seconds. Add onion; cook and stir 3 minutes or until crisp-tender. Remove onion mixture. Add walnuts to the wok; cook and stir for 2 to 3 minutes or until golden. Remove walnuts from the wok.

4. Add chicken to the wok; cook and stir for 3 to 4 minutes or until no longer pink. Return onion mixture and walnuts to the wok. Add beans.

5. Stir sauce. Add sauce to wok. Stir ingredients to coat with sauce. Cook and stir for 1 to 2 minutes or until heated through. Serve immediately over hot cooked rice.

Per serving: 368 cal., 15 g total fat (2 g sat. fat), 50 mg chol., 445 mg sodium, 34 g carbo., 4 g fiber, 26 g pro.

Crunchy Chicken and Fruit Salad

There are many ways to use deli-roasted rotisserie chickens. This fresh, fruity salad is just one of them—perfect for a summer dinner or light brunch.

Start to Finish: 20 minutes **Makes:** 4 servings

- **1 2½-pound roasted whole chicken**
- **3 oranges**
- **⅓ cup light mayonnaise**
  Ground black pepper
- **1 15-ounce package sweet baby lettuces**
- **2 small red and/or green apples, cored and coarsely chopped**
- **¼ cup pecan halves**

1. Remove chicken from bones. Tear chicken into bite-size chunks. Set aside.

2. For dressing, squeeze juice from 1 of the oranges. Stir enough juice into the mayonnaise to make dressing consistency. Season with pepper.

3. Peel and section the remaining 2 oranges. On 4 salad plates, arrange lettuce, chicken, apples, and orange sections. Sprinkle with pecan halves. Pass dressing.

Per serving: 455 cal., 30 g total fat (7 g sat. fat), 132 mg chol., 956 mg sodium, 23 g carbo., 5 g fiber, 29 g pro.

Crunchy Chicken and Fruit Salad

Pineapple Chicken

Pineapple Chicken

To reduce fat and calories, use light coconut milk. The sauce just won't have as much body as it does with regular coconut milk.

Start to Finish: 20 minutes **Makes:** 4 servings

1 1/2	**pounds skinless, boneless chicken thighs**
1/2	**teaspoon salt**
1/2	**teaspoon curry seasoning blend**
2	**tablespoons olive oil**
1	**red sweet pepper, cut in strips**
1	**pineapple, peeled, cored, and cut in large chunks**
1	**serrano pepper, thinly sliced**
3/4	**cup unsweetened coconut milk**
1	**tablespoon packed brown sugar**

1. Sprinkle chicken with salt and curry seasoning. In an extra-large skillet, heat 1 tablespoon of the olive oil over high heat. Add chicken; quickly brown chicken on all sides. Reduce heat to medium-high; cook about 12 minutes or until no longer pink (180°F). Transfer chicken to a plate; cover to keep warm.

2. For sauce, in a large skillet, heat the remaining 1 tablespoon olive oil over medium-high heat. Add sweet pepper; cook for 3 minutes. Remove sweet pepper from skillet; set aside. Add pineapple; cook about 5 minutes or until browned. Add serrano pepper; cook for 1 minute. Stir in coconut milk and brown sugar; heat through. Serve sauce with sweet pepper over chicken.

Per serving: 443 cal., 24 g total fat (12 g sat. fat), 141 mg chol., 448 mg sodium, 23 g carbo., 3 g fiber, 35 g pro.

Keys-Style Citrus Chicken

Cooking in the Florida Keys draws on fresh Florida citrus and Caribbean fiery peppers. Serve this flavorful dish with hot cooked rice.

Start to Finish: 20 minutes **Makes:** 4 servings

1	**tablespoon butter or margarine**
4	**small skinless, boneless chicken breast halves (1 to 1 1/4 pounds)**
2	**or 3 cloves garlic, peeled and thinly sliced**
1	**teaspoon finely shredded lime peel**
2	**tablespoons fresh lime juice**
1/4	**teaspoon ground ginger**
1/8	**teaspoon crushed red pepper**
1	**orange**

1. In a large skillet, melt butter over medium heat. Add chicken and garlic; cook for 8 to 10 minutes or until chicken is no longer pink (170°F), turning chicken once and stirring garlic occasionally.

2. Meanwhile, in a small bowl, combine lime peel, lime juice, ginger, and crushed red pepper; set aside. Peel orange. Reserving juice, cut orange in half lengthwise, then cut crosswise into slices. Add any reserved orange juice and the lime juice mixture to skillet. Place orange slices on top of chicken. Cook, covered, for 1 to 2 minutes or until heated through. To serve, spoon drippings over chicken.

Per serving: 167 cal., 6 g total fat (3 g sat. fat), 67 mg chol., 84 mg sodium, 5 g carbo., 1 g fiber, 22 g pro.

Basil-Stuffed Chicken `one`

Stuffed with tomato, basil, and melty mozzarella cheese, these crispy breaded chicken breasts are broiled, not fried.

Start to Finish: 25 minutes **Makes:** 6 servings

6	skinless, boneless chicken breast halves (1 1/2 to 2 pounds)
1/2	teaspoon salt
1/2	teaspoon ground black pepper
6	slices part-skim mozzarella cheese (4 ounces)
1	tomato, cut in 6 slices
6	fresh basil leaves
1/2	cup seasoned fine dry bread crumbs
2	tablespoons grated Parmesan cheese
2	tablespoons light mayonnaise or salad dressing Nonstick cooking spray

1. Preheat broiler. Cut each chicken piece horizontally in half, leaving one side intact. Sprinkle with salt and pepper.

2. Arrange a mozzarella slice, tomato slice, and basil leaf on bottom half of each chicken piece, keeping filling in center. Fold top of chicken over filling, pressing around edges to seal.

3. On waxed paper, combine bread crumbs and Parmesan cheese. Brush both sides of chicken with mayonnaise. Dip chicken in crumbs; press to adhere.

4. Place chicken on the greased rack of a broiling pan. Lightly coat both sides of chicken with cooking spray.

5. Broil chicken 8 inches from heat for about 10 minutes or until no longer pink (170°F), turning once halfway through broiling.

Per serving: 239 cal., 7 g total fat (3 g sat. fat), 81 mg chol., 627 mg sodium, 9 g carbo., 1 g fiber, 33 g pro.

Quick Tip Use finely grated—not shredded—Parmesan cheese in the breading for the chicken. The more fine the cheese, the more evenly it combines with the bread crumbs.

Maple-Glazed Chicken with Sweet Potatoes

Maple-Glazed Chicken with Sweet Potatoes `one`

A grilling seasoning blend makes spicing this supersimple dish a one-step proposition.

Start to Finish: 20 minutes **Makes:** 4 servings

1	24-ounce package refrigerated mashed sweet potatoes
1	pound chicken breast tenderloins
2	teaspoons steak grilling seasoning blend, such as Montreal
2	tablespoons butter or margarine
1/4	cup maple syrup
1/2	cup sliced green onions (4)

1. Prepare sweet potatoes following package directions for microwave cooking.

2. Meanwhile, sprinkle chicken with steak seasoning. In a large skillet, heat butter over medium-high heat. Add chicken; cook for 5 to 6 minutes or until no longer pink (170°F), turning once halfway through cooking. Remove chicken from skillet; cover to keep warm. Stir maple syrup into hot skillet; cook for 2 minutes. Stir in green onions.

3. Serve chicken with sweet potatoes. Drizzle with maple syrup mixture.

Per serving: 384 cal., 7 g total fat (4 g sat. fat), 81 mg chol., 505 mg sodium, 50 g carbo., 6 g fiber, 30 g pro.

Broccoli and Chicken Saltimbocca

Saltimbocca—"jumps in the mouth" in Italian—is a classic dish made with veal, sage, prosciutto, and white wine. This flavorful version calls for succulent chicken and rich Marsala.

Start to Finish: 30 minutes **Makes:** 4 servings

- 3 **tablespoons olive oil**
- 2 **cloves garlic, peeled and crushed**
- 1 **head broccoli, trimmed and cut into florets**
- ³/₄ **teaspoon salt**
- ¹/₄ **teaspoon crushed red pepper**
- 4 **thinly cut skinless, boneless chicken breast halves (about 1¹/₄ pounds)**
- ¹/₄ **teaspoon dried Italian herb seasoning**
- ¹/₈ **teaspoon ground black pepper**
- 8 **fresh sage leaves**
- 4 **ounces thinly sliced prosciutto**
- ¹/₂ **cup Marsala**
- ¹/₂ **cup beef broth**
- 1 **tablespoon cornstarch**
  Hot cooked orzo (optional)

1. In a large nonstick skillet, heat 1 tablespoon of the olive oil over medium-high heat. Add garlic; cook for 1 minute, stirring occasionally. Add broccoli, ¹/₂ teaspoon of the salt, and the crushed red pepper; cook for 7 to 8 minutes or until broccoli is crisp-tender, stirring occasionally. Remove from heat. Keep warm.

2. Meanwhile, sprinkle chicken with Italian seasoning, black pepper, and the remaining ¹/₄ teaspoon salt. Place 2 sage leaves on each piece; cover each with 1 ounce of prosciutto. Press prosciutto onto chicken.

3. In another large nonstick skillet, heat the remaining 2 tablespoons olive oil over medium-high heat. Place chicken, prosciutto sides down, in skillet; cook for 2 to 3 minutes or until prosciutto is seared. Turn chicken over; cook about 2 minutes more or until chicken is no longer pink. Remove chicken; cover to keep warm.

4. For sauce, remove skillet from heat; add Marsala to skillet. Return to heat, stirring to scrape up any browned bits from bottom of skillet. In small bowl, stir together beef broth and cornstarch. Add to skillet. Cook and stir until thickened and bubbly. Cook and stir for 2 minutes more. Remove from heat.

5. To serve, spread broccoli on a large serving platter. Place chicken on broccoli; spoon sauce over chicken. If desired, serve with orzo.

Per serving: 412 cal., 17 g total fat (3 g sat. fat), 101 mg chol., 1,370 mg sodium, 13 g carbo., 1 g fiber, 44 g pro.

Chicken and Peanut Noodles ♥ 📖

With peanut butter, noodles, and chicken, this dish has "kid-friendly" written all over it. For the kids, leave out the crushed red pepper. For adults who like spicy, stir it in last.

Prep: 15 minutes **Cook:** 12 minutes **Makes:** 6 servings

- 1 **tablespoon peanut oil**
- 1 **pound skinless, boneless chicken breast halves, cut in ¹/₄-inch slices**
- 3 **cloves garlic, minced**
- ³/₄ **cup reduced-fat creamy peanut butter**
- 2 **cups water**
- 2 **tablespoons balsamic vinegar**
- 1 **tablespoon reduced-sodium soy sauce**
- 1 **teaspoon crushed red pepper**
- 2 **3-ounce packages chicken-flavor ramen noodles**
- 1 **1-pound package frozen sliced green, red, and yellow peppers and white onion**
- ¹/₃ **cup thinly sliced green onions (3)**
  Unsalted peanuts (optional)

1. In a large skillet, heat peanut oil over medium-high heat. Add chicken and garlic; cook and stir about 3 minutes or until chicken is no longer pink. Remove skillet from heat; remove chicken from skillet.

2. Spoon peanut butter into skillet. Whisk in water, vinegar, soy sauce, crushed red pepper, and 1 seasoning packet from noodles. Reserve remaining seaosning packet for another use. Bring to boiling. Add noodles, breaking up slightly. Add chicken. Cook, covered, for 4 minutes, stirring occasionally to separate noodles. Place frozen pepper strips on top; simmer, covered, for 3 minutes. Stir to combine. Sprinkle with green onions and, if desired, peanuts.

Per serving: 384 cal., 15 g total fat (3 g sat. fat), 42 mg chol., 477 mg sodium, 35 g carbo., 4 g fiber, 30 g pro.

Chicken with Green Pumpkin Seed Mole

Traditional Mexican sauces known as moles (MOH-lays) generally take hours to make and require a long ingredient list. This version of chicken mole takes less than 30 minutes.

Start to Finish: 25 minutes **Makes:** 4 servings

- **Nonstick cooking spray**
- 4 **skinless, boneless chicken breast halves**
- 2 **teaspoons vegetable oil**
- ¹/₂ **cup chopped onion (1 medium)**
- 1 **clove garlic, minced**
- 1 **13-ounce can tomatillos, rinsed and drained**
- ¹/₃ **cup shelled raw pumpkin seeds (pepitas), toasted , (see Quick TIp, page 75)**

Chicken with
Green Pumpkin Seed Mole

<table>
<tr><td>1</td><td>4-ounce can diced green chiles, undrained</td></tr>
<tr><td>¼</td><td>cup chicken broth</td></tr>
<tr><td>3</td><td>tablespoons snipped fresh cilantro</td></tr>
<tr><td>¼</td><td>teaspoon salt</td></tr>
</table>

Shelled raw pumpkin seeds (pepitas), toasted
(optional), (see Quick Tip, right)
Cilantro (optional)

1. Coat an unheated large skillet with cooking spray. Heat skillet over medium heat. Cook chicken in hot skillet for 10 to 12 minutes or until no longer pink (170°F), turning once halfway through cooking. Remove chicken; cover to keep warm.

2. For the mole, in the same skillet, heat oil over medium heat. Add onion and garlic; cook about 5 minutes or until onion is tender. In a blender or food processor, combine onion mixture, tomatillos, the ⅓ cup toasted pumpkin seeds, the undrained chiles, chicken broth, cilantro, and salt. Cover and blend or process with several on-off turns to a coarse mixture. Transfer mole to the skillet; stir and cook until heated through.

3. To serve, spoon mole on chicken breasts. If desired, sprinkle with additional toasted pumpkin seeds.

Per serving: 202 cal., 7 g total fat (1 g sat. fat), 60 mg chol., 846 mg sodium, 11 g carbo., 3 g fiber, 24 g pro.

Quick Tip To toast pumpkin seeds, spread them in a shallow baking pan. Bake in a 350°F oven about 10 minutes or until toasted, stirring once or twice. Store toasted pumpkin seeds, tightly covered, in the refrigerator for 1 week. For longer storage, freeze them, raw or toasted, for up to 1 year.

Spanish Rice with Chicken and Shrimp

Rinse the fresh or thawed shrimp and pat dry with paper towels before cooking.

Start to Finish: 30 minutes **Makes:** 4 servings

- 8 **ounces fresh or frozen peeled and deveined large shrimp**
- 1 **6.75-ounce package Spanish rice pilaf mix or one 6.8-ounce package Spanish-flavor rice and vermicelli mix**
  Nonstick cooking spray
- 8 **ounces skinless, boneless chicken breast halves, cut in 1-inch pieces**
- ³/₄ **cup chopped green sweet pepper (1 medium)**
- ¹/₂ **cup chopped red onion (1 medium)**
- 1 **14.5-ounce can diced tomatoes, undrained**
- ¹/₄ **cup dry white wine or chicken broth**
- 1 **clove garlic, minced**
- ³/₄ **teaspoon dried thyme, crushed**
- 1 **cup frozen peas, thawed**
- 1 **4.5-ounce can diced green chiles, undrained**
  Salt and ground black pepper

1. Thaw shrimp, if frozen. Prepare the rice mix following package directions, omitting butter or vegetable oil.

2. Coat a large nonstick skillet with cooking spray. Heat skillet over medium heat. Cook the chicken, sweet pepper, and onion in the hot skillet until chicken is no longer pink and vegetables are tender.

3. Stir in the undrained tomatoes, wine, garlic, and thyme. Bring to boiling; reduce heat. Simmer, uncovered, for 10 minutes.

4. Add shrimp, peas, and undrained chiles. Cook and stir for 3 to 5 minutes or until shrimp turn opaque. Serve over rice. Season to taste with salt and pepper.

Per serving: 359 cal., 3 g total fat (0 g sat. fat), 119 mg chol., 1,322 mg sodium, 51 g carbo., 6 g fiber, 32 g pro.

Marsala Chicken Crepes

Make your crepes plain—or spice them up a bit by adding ¹/₂ teaspoon of ginger or curry powder to the batter.

Prep: 30 minutes **Cook:** 15 minutes **Makes:** 4 servings

- 2 **teaspoons vegetable oil**
- 2 **medium red sweet peppers, cut in thin strips**
- 12 **ounces skinless, boneless chicken breast halves, cut in thin strips**
- 1 **teaspoon dried coriander seeds, crushed**
- ¹/₄ **teaspoon freshly ground black pepper**
- ¹/₈ **teaspoon salt**
- ¹/₂ **cup Marsala**
- 1 **tablespoon water**
- 1 **teaspoon cornstarch**
- 1 **teaspoon grated fresh ginger**
- 8 **Basic Crepes or ready-to-use crepes**

1. In a large nonstick skillet, heat oil over medium-high heat. Add sweet peppers; cook, without stirring, about 3 minutes or until crisp-tender and charred slightly on one side. Add chicken, crushed coriander seeds, black pepper, and salt; cook and stir for 2 minutes more.

2. Carefully add Marsala; reduce heat. Cook, uncovered, 3 minutes more or until chicken is no longer pink.

3. In a small bowl, stir together water and cornstarch. Stir cornstarch mixture and ginger into chicken mixture. Cook and stir until thickened and bubbly. Cook and stir for 2 minutes more.

4. Using a slotted spoon, spoon chicken mixture on crepes. Roll or fold. Drizzle remaining sauce on crepes.

Per serving: 285 cal., 6 g total fat (2 g sat. fat), 84 mg chol., 167 mg sodium, 24 g carbo., 2 g fiber, 24 g pro.

Basic Crepes: In a medium mixing bowl, combine 2 eggs, 1¹/₂ cups milk, 1 cup all-purpose flour, 1 tablespoon vegetable oil, and ¹/₄ teaspoon salt; beat with an electric mixer on medium speed until combined. Heat a lightly greased 6-inch skillet; remove from heat. Spoon in 2 tablespoons of the batter; lift and tilt skillet to spread batter. Return to heat; brown on one side only. Invert crepe onto a paper towel. Repeat with remaining batter, greasing skillet occasionally. Use 8 crepes to make Marsala Chicken Crepes. Layer remaining cooled crepes with sheets of waxed paper in an airtight container; freeze up to 4 months. Thaw crepes at room temperature 1 hour before using.

Spanish Rice with Chicken and Shrimp

Chicken and Dried-Tomato Cream

Chicken and Dried-Tomato Cream [one]

Look for chicken breasts labeled "cutlets" for this dish. They've been cut extra thin to cook quickly.

Prep: 10 minutes **Cook:** 20 minutes **Makes:** 6 servings

1½	**pounds thin-sliced skinless, boneless chicken breast halves**
¼	**teaspoon salt**
⅛	**teaspoon ground black pepper**
2	**tablespoons olive oil**
⅓	**cup chopped onion (1 small)**
¼	**teaspoon crushed red pepper**
¼	**cup dry white wine or chicken broth**
1	**cup chicken broth**
½	**cup whipping cream**
½	**cup dried-tomato pesto**
¼	**cup niçoise olives, pitted and quartered**

1. Sprinkle both sides of chicken with salt and pepper. In a large skillet, heat 1 tablespoon of the olive oil over medium-high heat. Add half the chicken; cook about 6 minutes or until no longer pink, turning once halfway through cooking. Remove chicken to platter; cover to keep warm. Repeat with remaining olive oil and chicken.

2. For dried-tomato cream, add onion and crushed red pepper to skillet; cook for 3 minutes. Carefully add wine; cook for 1 minute, stirring to scrape up browned bits. Add chicken broth, whipping cream, pesto, and olives. Bring to boiling; cook, uncovered, about 4 minutes or until slightly thickened. Pour dried-tomato cream over chicken. Serve immediately.

Per serving: 304 cal., 19 g total fat (7 g sat. fat), 91 mg chol., 746 mg sodium, 7 g carbo., 1 g fiber, 25 g pro.

Sesame and Ginger Chicken

Chicken with Tomato-Caper Sauce ⬛

Capers are the pickled flower buds of the Mediterranean caper bush.

Prep: 10 minutes **Cook:** 20 minutes **Makes:** 4 servings

- 4 **skinless, boneless chicken breast halves (about 1½ pounds)**
- 2 **tablespoons all-purpose flour**
- ½ **teaspoon salt**
- ¼ **teaspoon ground white pepper**
- 1 **tablespoon olive oil**
- ½ **cup dry white wine**
- 2 **cloves garlic, minced**
- 6 **medium plum tomatoes, coarsely chopped**
- ¾ **cup reduced-sodium chicken broth**
- 2 **tablespoons capers, drained and crushed**
- 6 **large basil leaves, thinly shredded**

1. Place each chicken piece between 2 pieces of plastic wrap. Working from center to edges, pound lightly with flat side of meat mallet until pieces are ½ inch thick.

2. In a small bowl, combine flour, salt, and pepper. Coat chicken with flour mixture.

3. In an extra-large nonstick skillet, heat oil over high heat. Add chicken; cook 8 to 10 minutes or until and no longer pink inside (170°F), turning once halfway through cooking. Remove chicken from skillet; keep warm.

4. For sauce, carefully add wine and garlic to skillet; cook until bubbly, stirring to scrape up any browned bits from bottom of skillet. Add tomatoes and chicken broth. Bring to boiling; cook about 5 minutes or until liquid is reduced by half. Stir in capers and basil. Season to taste with salt and white pepper. Pour the sauce on chicken.

Per serving: 258 cal., 8 g total fat (2 g sat. fat), 94 mg chol., 582 mg sodium, 8 g carbo., 1 g fiber, 36 g pro.

Sesame and Ginger Chicken ♥ ⬛

This take on Asian chicken salad is delicious with the addition of mandarin oranges and crispy chow mein noodles.

Start to Finish: 20 minutes **Makes:** 4 servings

- 1 **pound skinless, boneless chicken breast, cut in bite-size strips**
  Salt and ground black pepper
  Nonstick cooking spray
- 2 **cups packaged julienned carrots**
- ¼ **cup bottled light Asian-style dressing with sesame and ginger**
- ⅛ **teaspoon crushed red pepper**
- 1 **head butterhead lettuce, leaves separated**
- ¼ **cup honey-roasted peanuts, chopped**

1. Sprinkle chicken with salt and pepper. Lightly coat a large skillet with cooking spray. Heat skillet over medium-high heat. Add chicken; cook and stir about 3 minutes or until browned. Add carrots and 1 tablespoon of the dressing to the skillet; cook and stir for 2 minutes more or until carrots are crisp-tender and chicken is no longer pink. Stir in crushed red pepper.

2. On a large platter, arrange 4 stacks of lettuce leaves. Top with chicken mixture. Sprinkle with peanuts. Serve with remaining dressing.

Per serving: 231 cal., 7 g total fat (1 g sat. fat), 66 mg chol., 436 mg sodium, 12 g carbo., 3 g fiber, 29 g pro.

Savoy Cabbage Salad with Grilled Chicken

If you have a food processor, attach the slicing blade and use it to make quick work of slicing the vegetables.

Start to Finish: 30 minutes **Makes:** 4 servings

- 4 **cups thinly sliced savoy cabbage**
- 4 **cups thinly sliced celery**
- 2 **cups thinly sliced red sweet peppers**
- 2 **cups thinly sliced green onions**
- ½ **cup snipped fresh cilantro**
- ¼ **cup rice wine vinegar**
- 2 **tablespoons honey**
- 2 **tablespoons molasses**
- 2 **tablespoons peanut oil**
- 1 **teaspoon grated fresh ginger**
- 2 **cloves garlic, peeled**
- ½ **teaspoon red chile sauce**
- ½ **teaspoon kosher salt**
- ½ **teaspoon freshly ground black pepper**
- 2 **skinless, boneless chicken breast halves**
- ¼ **cup coarsely chopped peanuts**

1. For salad, in a large bowl, toss together cabbage, celery, sweet peppers, green onions, and cilantro. Set aside.

2. For dressing, in a blender, combine vinegar, honey, molasses, 1 tablespoon of the peanut oil, ginger, garlic, chile sauce, ¼ teaspoon of the salt, and ¼ teaspoon of the black pepper. Cover and blend until smooth. Set aside.

3. Sprinkle chicken with remaining ¼ teaspoon salt and ¼ teaspoon black pepper. Brush a grill pan or large skillet with remaining 1 tablespoon peanut oil. Heat over medium-high heat. Add chicken; cook 8 to 12 minutes or until no longer pink (170°F), turning once. Cool slightly.

4. Shred chicken into a small bowl. Add 2 tablespoons of the dressing; toss to coat. Toss remaining dressing with salad; divide among 4 plates. Arrange chicken on salad. Sprinkle with peanuts.

Per serving: 320 cal., 13 g total fat (2 g sat. fat), 33 mg chol., 400 mg sodium, 35 g carbo., 8 g fiber, 19 g pro.

Fast Chicken and Rice

Fast Chicken and Rice ♥

Faster than takeout, this dish is on the table in 10 minutes.

Start to Finish: 10 minutes **Makes:** 4 servings

- ½ **cup frozen peas**
- 1 **8.8-ounce package cooked brown or white rice**
- 1 **tablespoon vegetable oil**
- 1 **pound chicken breast tenderloins, halved crosswise**
- ¼ **cup bottled stir-fry sauce**
  Packaged oven-roasted sliced almonds (optional)

1. Stir peas into rice package. Heat in microwave following package directions for rice.

2. Meanwhile, in a large skillet, heat oil over medium-high heat. Add chicken; cook and stir for 2 to 3 minutes or until no longer pink. Stir rice mixture into skillet. Stir in stir-fry sauce; heat through. If desired, sprinkle with almonds.

Per serving: 311 cal., 9 g total fat (1 g sat. fat), 66 mg chol., 453 mg sodium, 25 g carbo., 2 g fiber, 31 g pro.

Lebanese Chicken

Middle Eastern cooks often use sweet spices such as cinnamon and allspice, as well as citrus and fresh mint, to flavor poultry and meat.

Prep: 10 minutes **Cook:** 16 minutes **Makes:** 4 servings

- 1 **tablespoon butter or margarine**
- 8 **skinless, boneless chicken thighs (about 1½ pounds)**
- ⅓ **cup chopped onion (1 small)**
- 1 **clove garlic, minced**
- 2 **teaspoons finely shredded orange peel**
- ½ **cup fresh orange juice**
- ¼ **teaspoon salt**
- ¼ **teaspoon ground cinnamon**
- ⅛ **teaspoon ground allspice**
- 2 **tablespoons honey**
  Orange wedges (optional)
  Fresh mint leaves (optional)

1. In a large skillet, melt butter over medium heat. Add chicken, onion, and garlic. Cook about 6 minutes or until chicken is browned, turning once.

2. Add orange peel, orange juice, and salt to skillet. Bring to boiling; reduce heat. Simmer, covered, for 5 minutes. Sprinkle chicken with cinnamon and allspice; drizzle with honey. Simmer, uncovered, for 5 to 7 minutes more or until chicken is no longer pink (180°F). If desired, serve with orange wedges and fresh mint.

Per serving: 408 cal., 11 g total fat (3 g sat. fat), 69 mg chol., 238 mg sodium, 49 g carbo., 8 g fiber, 26 g pro.

Bow Tie Pasta with Chicken and Broccoli ♥

Adobo seasoning is a blend of dried ground chiles, garlic, onion, black pepper, Mexican oregano, and cumin. Find it in Hispanic markets and many supermarkets.

Start to Finish: 30 minutes **Makes:** 6 servings

- 8 **ounces dried multigrain or regular bow tie or penne pasta (about 2½ cups)**
- 3 **cups fresh broccoli florets**
- 4 **skinless, boneless chicken breast halves (1 to 1¼ pounds), cut in bite-size pieces**
- 1 **teaspoon adobo seasoning**
- 2 **tablespoons olive oil, butter, or margarine**
- 1 **clove garlic, minced**
- ¼ **cup light mayonnaise or salad dressing**
- ⅛ **teaspoon ground black pepper**
- 2 **tablespoons finely shredded Parmesan cheese**

1. In a Dutch oven, cook pasta following package directions, adding broccoli the last 5 minutes of cooking. Drain well. Return to the Dutch oven.

2. Meanwhile, in a medium bowl, sprinkle chicken with adobo seasoning; toss to coat. In a large skillet, heat olive oil over medium-high heat. Add garlic; cook for 30 seconds. Add chicken; cook for 3 to 4 minutes or until chicken is no longer pink, stirring occasionally.

3. Add chicken to drained pasta and broccoli in Dutch oven. Stir in mayonnaise and pepper. Cook over low heat for 1 minute or until heated through, stirring occasionally. Top servings with Parmesan cheese.

Per serving: 309 cal., 9 g total fat (1 g sat. fat), 48 mg chol., 399 mg sodium, 30 g carbo., 4 g fiber, 26 g pro.

Bow Tie Pasta with Chicken and Broccoli

Chicken Cutlet Parmigiana

Chicken Parmesan is a family favorite. Add a green salad and crusty bread and you're set.

Prep: 10 minutes **Bake:** 4 minutes **Cook:** 8 minutes **Oven:** 375°F **Makes:** 4 servings

4   **skinless, boneless chicken breast halves (1 1/2 pounds)**
2   **eggs, lightly beaten**
1/2   **teaspoon salt**
1/8   **teaspoon ground black pepper**
2   **tablespoons all-purpose flour**
3/4   **cup seasoned fine dry bread crumbs**
3   **tablespoons vegetable oil**
2   **tablespoons butter or margarine**
1   **8-ounce can tomato sauce**
1 1/2   **cups shredded mozzarella cheese (6 ounces)**
2   **tablespoons chopped fresh parsley**
12   **ounces spaghetti, cooked and tossed with tomato sauce**

1. Place each chicken breast between 2 pieces of plastic wrap. Using the flat side of a meat mallet, lightly pound chicken to about 1/4-inch thickness. Discard plastic wrap.

2. In a shallow dish, combine eggs, salt, and pepper. Place flour in a second dish. Place bread crumbs in a third dish. Dip each chicken piece in flour to coat both sides; shake off excess. Dip in egg mixture. Coat both sides with crumbs. Place on waxed paper.

3. Preheat oven to 375°F. In a large nonstick skillet, heat oil and butter over medium heat. Add chicken; cook for 6 to 8 minutes or until golden and no longer pink, turning once halfway through cooking. Transfer chicken to a rimmed baking sheet. Spoon tomato sauce on each piece. Top with cheese.

4. Bake chicken for 4 to 5 minutes or until cheese is melted. Sprinkle with parsley. Serve with spaghetti tossed with tomato sauce.

Per serving: 959 cal., 35 g total fat (13 g sat. fat), 254 mg chol., 1,493 mg sodium, 95 g carbo., 7 g fiber, 63 g pro.

Quick Tip Chicken cutlets—thin pieces of chicken breast—cook quicker and crispier than thick pieces. You can flatten the chicken breasts one of two ways: Place the breast on a flat surface and press down on it with the heel of your hand, or place it between two pieces of plastic wrap and pound it lightly with a meat mallet.

Chicken Pad Thai [one]

Make Thailand's most famous noodle dish at home. Be sure not to oversoak the rice noodles—they'll break when cooked.

Prep: 15 minutes **Cook:** 15 minutes **Makes:** 4 servings

8   **ounces rice noodles (Vietnamese banh pho)**
1/4   **cup salted peanuts, finely chopped**
1   **tablespoon granulated sugar**
1/2   **teaspoon finely shredded lime peel**
2   **tablespoons fresh lime juice**
2   **tablespoons fish sauce**
1 1/2   **teaspoons dried shrimp paste or mashed anchovy**
1   **tablespoon Asian chili sauce**
2   **tablespoons packed brown sugar**
4 1/2   **teaspoons rice vinegar**
3   **tablespoons vegetable oil**
1/4   **cup chopped shallots**
1   **pound skinless, boneless chicken breast halves, cut in 3-inch strips**
1   **tablespoon minced garlic**
1   **egg, lightly beaten**
1   **cup fresh bean sprouts**
1/3   **cup sliced green onions (6)**
2   **tablespoons snipped fresh cilantro**

1. Place noodles in a large bowl. Add enough hot water to cover; let stand for 10 to 15 minutes or until pliable but not soft. Drain well in a colander.

2. Meanwhile, for peanut topping, in a small bowl, combine peanuts, sugar, and lime peel. Set aside.

3. For fish sauce, in another small bowl, combine lime juice, fish sauce, shrimp paste, chili sauce, brown sugar, and rice vinegar. Stir until smooth. Set aside.

4. In an extra-large nonstick skillet, heat 1 tablespoon of the oil over medium-high heat. Add shallots; cook about 2 minutes or until softened and lightly browned. Add chicken and garlic; cook and stir 6 minutes or until chicken is no longer pink. Transfer chicken mixture to a bowl.

5. Add egg to skillet; cook for 30 seconds. Turn egg with spatula and cook for 30 to 60 seconds more or just until set. Remove egg from skillet. Chop egg and set aside.

6. Heat the remaining 2 tablespoons oil in the skillet over high heat for 30 seconds. Add drained noodles and sprouts; cook and stir for 2 minutes. Add fish sauce mixture and chicken; cook for 1 to 2 minutes or until heated through. Divide among 4 plates. Sprinkle with chopped egg and peanut topping. Garnish with green onions and cilantro.

Per serving: 565 cal., 19 g total fat (3 g sat. fat), 120 mg chol., 838 mg sodium, 68 g carbo., 1 g fiber, 33 g pro.

Chicken Pad Thai

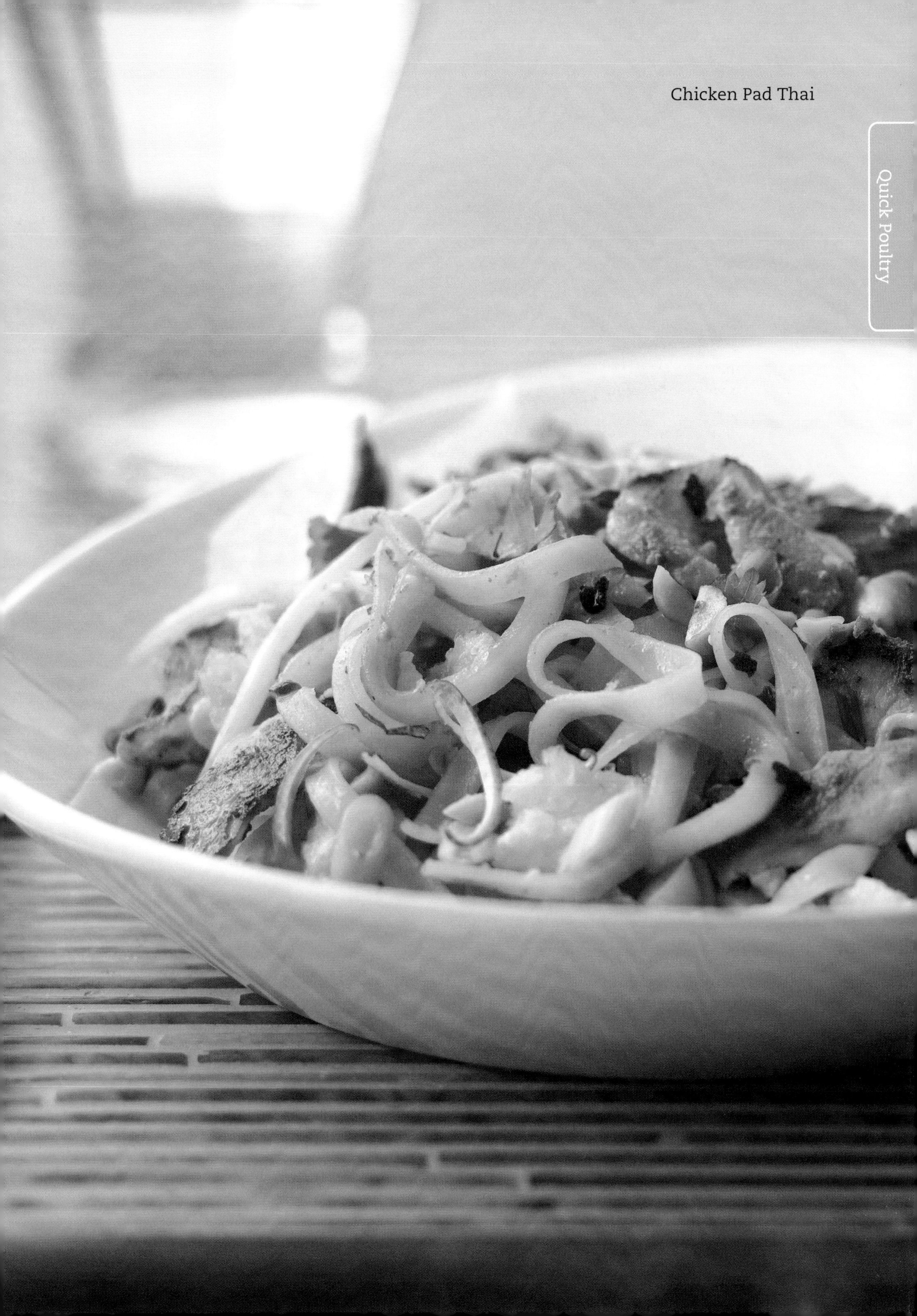

Kung Pao Chicken

Kung Pao Chicken

This dish originates from the Chinese province of Szechwan, known for its fiery foods. Make it hotter with more pepper sauce, if you like, or by stirring crushed red pepper into the sauce mixture before cooking it.

Prep: 15 minutes **Marinate:** 15 minutes
Cook: 8 minutes **Makes:** 4 servings

- 12   **ounces skinless, boneless chicken breast halves**
- 1   **tablespoon dry sherry**
- 5   **teaspoons cornstarch**
- 1/4   **cup water**
- 1/4   **cup soy sauce**
- 1   **tablespoon sugar**
- 1   **teaspoon vinegar**
  Few dashes bottled hot pepper sauce
- 1   **tablespoon vegetable oil**
- 2   **teaspoons grated fresh ginger**
- 2   **cloves garlic, minced**
- 6   **green onions, cut in 1/2-inch pieces (1 cup)**
- 1/2   **cup dry-roasted peanuts**
- 2   **cups hot cooked rice**
  Green onion fans (optional)

1. Cut chicken in 3/4-inch pieces. In a medium bowl, stir together chicken, sherry, and 1 teaspoon of the cornstarch. Let stand to marinate for 15 minutes.

2. For sauce, in a small bowl, stir together water, soy sauce, sugar, vinegar, hot pepper sauce, and the remaining 4 teaspoons cornstarch. Set aside.

3. Pour oil into a wok or large skillet. (Add more oil as necessary during cooking.) Heat over medium-high heat. Add ginger and garlic; cook and stir for 15 seconds. Add marinated chicken mixture; cook and stir for 3 to 4 minutes or until chicken is no longer pink. Push chicken from the center of the wok.

4. Stir sauce. Add sauce to the center of the wok. Cook and stir until thickened and bubbly. Add green onion pieces and peanuts. Stir all ingredients to coat with sauce. Cook and stir for 1 to 2 minutes more or until heated through. Serve immediately with hot cooked rice. If desired, garnish with green onion fans.

Per serving: 378 cal., 14 g total fat (2 g sat. fat), 49 mg chol., 1,078 mg sodium, 35 g carbo., 3 g fiber, 28 g pro.

Quick Tip Adding vinegar to recipes boosts flavor and tenderizes meats. The acid in vinegar breaks down meat fibers. For this recipe, use either rice vinegar or rice wine vinegar—seasoned or plain.

Thai Curried Noodle Bowl

Prepared Thai curry pastes—yellow, red, and green—are versatile convenience condiments. They save hours of prep time and lend an authentic taste to dishes.

Start to Finish: 30 minutes **Makes:** 4 servings

1	**12- to 14-ounce package wide rice stick noodles**
1	**tablespoon vegetable oil**
³/₄	**cup coarsely chopped carrots**
1	**cup sliced fresh shiitake mushrooms, stems removed, or sliced fresh white mushrooms**
³/₄	**cup coarsely chopped red sweet pepper**
2	**green onions, bias-sliced in ¹/₄-inch pieces**
1	**14-ounce can unsweetened lite coconut milk**
3	**to 4 teaspoons red curry paste**
1¹/₂	**teaspoons sugar**
2	**cups cooked chicken cut or pulled in bite-size pieces (10 ounces)**
1	**tablespoon fresh lime juice**
¹/₄	**cup chopped dry-roasted peanuts**
2	**tablespoons snipped fresh cilantro**

1. In a Dutch oven, cook noodles in lightly salted boiling water for 5 minutes. Drain and return noodles to Dutch oven; keep warm.

2. Meanwhile, in a large skillet, heat oil over medium-high heat. Add carrots; cook and stir for 3 minutes. Add mushrooms, sweet pepper, and green onions; cook and stir for 2 minutes more. Add coconut milk, curry paste, and sugar. Reduce heat to medium; stir until combined. Add chicken, lime juice, and cooked noodles; heat through. Remove from heat. Add peanuts and cilantro. Toss gently to mix. (Mixture will thicken as it stands.)

3. Transfer noodle mixture to a warm serving bowl. Serve immediately.

Per serving: 642 cal., 19 g total fat (6 g sat. fat), 62 mg chol., 425 mg sodium, 89 g carbo., 5 g fiber, 27 g pro.

Quick Tip When you make any pasta or noodle dish, set aside ¹/₂ cup or so of the cooking water before draining. When you toss the pasta or noodles with the sauce, if it seems a little dry, thin the sauce with some of the hot cooking water.

Thai Curried Noodle Bowl

Chicken and Polenta

Boneless chicken thighs are a bargain—and if they're skinless, a healthful option too. A 4-ounce portion is generally about 150 calories, with about 7 grams of fat.

Start to Finish: 35 minutes **Makes:** 4 servings

- 1½ **pounds skinless, boneless chicken thighs**
- ¾ **teaspoon salt**
  Nonstick cooking spray
- 1½ **cups coarsely chopped green sweet peppers (2 medium)**
- ½ **cup coarsely chopped onion (1 medium)**
- 2 **teaspoons ground cumin**
- 1 **10-ounce can diced tomatoes with green chiles, undrained**
- 1 **tablespoon olive oil**
- 1 **1-pound tube refrigerated cooked polenta, cut crosswise in 8 slices**
- 2 **tablespoons snipped fresh cilantro**

1. Sprinkle chicken with ½ teaspoon of the salt. Lightly coat an extra-large nonstick skillet with cooking spray. Heat skillet over medium-high heat. Add chicken; cook about 3 minutes or until browned, turning once. Add sweet peppers and onion; cook for 3 minutes. Add cumin; cook and stir for 30 seconds. Add undrained tomatoes and the remaining ¼ teaspoon salt. Bring to boiling; reduce heat. Simmer, covered, for 6 to 7 minutes or until chicken is no longer pink and cooked through (180°F).

2. Meanwhile, in a large nonstick skillet, heat olive oil over medium-high heat; add the polenta slices. Cook for 10 to 12 minutes or until polenta is golden, turning once halfway through cooking.

3. Divide polenta and chicken among 4 shallow bowls. Sprinkle with cilantro.

Per serving: 355 cal., 11 g total fat (2 g sat. fat), 141 mg chol., 1,071 mg sodium, 25 g carbo., 5 g fiber, 37 g pro.

Pomegranate Chicken ♥

Antioxidant-rich pomegranate juice lends sweet-tart flavor and ruby red color to the chicken marinade.

Prep: 10 minutes **Marinate:** 10 minutes
Cook: 8 minutes **Makes:** 2 servings

- ½ **cup snipped fresh parsley**
- ¼ **cup unsweetened pomegranate juice**
- 2 **tablespoons fresh lemon or lime juice**
- 1 **teaspoon olive oil**
- 2 **cloves garlic, minced**
  Salt and freshly ground pepper
- 2 **skinless, boneless chicken breast halves, cut in thin bite-size strips**
  Olive oil nonstick cooking spray
- 3 **cups chopped romaine**

1. For marinade, in a large bowl, combine parsley, pomegranate juice, lemon juice, olive oil, and garlic. Season with salt and pepper. Add chicken and coat with the marinade. Marinate in the refrigerator for 10 minutes.

2. Lightly coat a large skillet with cooking spray. Heat over medium heat. Drain chicken; discard marinade. Cook chicken in hot skillet for 8 to 12 minutes or until no longer pink, turning occasionally to cook evenly. Line 2 plates with romaine. Serve chicken on romaine.

Per serving: 192 cal., 4 g total fat (1 g sat. fat), 66 mg chol., 381 mg sodium, 11 g carbo., 2 g fiber, 28 g pro.

Szechwan-Style Chicken 🔲

If you can find baby bok choy, use it rather than mature bok choy. Instead of chopping, quarter it to keep its shape.

Start to Finish: 30 minutes **Makes:** 6 servings

- ⅓ **cup teriyaki sauce**
- 3 **tablespoons Szechwan spicy stir-fry sauce**
- 2 **teaspoons cornstarch**
- 1 **tablespoon vegetable oil**
- 1 **cup chopped onion (1 large)**
- 3 **cups chopped bok choy**
- 1 **cup fresh broccoli florets**
- 1 **medium red sweet pepper, cut into strips**
- 2 **cups fresh pea pods, stings removed, or one 6-ounce package frozen pea pods, thawed**
- 1 **pound skinless, boneless chicken breast halves, cut in thin bite-size strips**
- 1 **14-ounce can whole baby sweet corn, drained and halved crosswise**
- 1 **7-ounce jar whole straw mushrooms, drained**
- 3 **cups hot cooked rice noodles or rice**

1. For sauce, in a small bowl, stir together teriyaki sauce, stir-fry sauce, and cornstarch. Set aside.

2. Pour oil into a wok or large skillet. (Add more oil as necessary during cooking.) Heat over medium-high heat. Add onion; cook and stir for 2 minutes. Add bok choy, broccoli, and sweet pepper; cook and stir for 1 minute. Add fresh pea pods (if using); cook and stir for 1 to 2 minutes more or until vegetables are crisp-tender. Remove vegetables from the wok.

3. Add half the chicken to the hot wok. Cook and stir for 2 to 3 minutes or until no longer pink. Remove chicken from wok. Repeat with remaining chicken. Return all the chicken to the wok. Push chicken from center of the wok.

4. Stir sauce. Add sauce to the center of wok. Cook and stir until thickened and bubbly. Return cooked vegetables to the wok. Add corn, mushrooms, and thawed frozen pea pods (if using). Stir all ingredients to coat with sauce. Cook and stir about 1 minute more or until heated through. Serve over hot cooked rice noodles.

Per serving: 205 cal., 4 g total fat (1 g sat. fat), 44 mg chol., 1,153 mg sodium, 17 g carbo., 4 g fiber, 23 g pro.

Chicken Breasts with Jalapeño Jelly

Chicken Breasts with Jalapeño Jelly ♥ ▣

This recipe calls for red jalapeño jelly, but green works equally well. Either one adds a touch of sweet heat.

Start to Finish: 25 minutes **Makes:** 4 servings

- **4** skinless, boneless chicken breast halves (about 1¼ pounds)
  Salt and freshly ground black pepper
- **2** tablespoons butter or margarine
- **1** tablespoon water
- **2** cups bias-sliced celery (4 stalks)
- **¼** cup red jalapeño chile pepper jelly
- **2** tablespoons lemon juice
- **1** tablespoon Dijon-style mustard

1. Place each chicken breast half between 2 pieces of plastic wrap. Pound lightly with the flat side of a meat mallet to about ½-inch thickness. Discard plastic wrap. Sprinkle chicken with salt and pepper.

2. In an extra-large skillet, melt butter over medium-high heat. Add chicken; cook for 8 to 10 minutes or until chicken is no longer pink, turning once halfway through cooking. Remove chicken from skillet.

3. For sauce, carefully add the water to the skillet, stirring to scrape up browned bits. Add celery; cook and stir for 1 minute. Add jelly, lemon juice, and mustard; cook and stir about 3 minutes more or until slightly thickened. Return chicken to skillet; heat through.

Per serving: 281 cal., 9 g total fat (4 g sat. fat), 99 mg chol., 236 mg sodium, 16 g carbo., 1 g fiber, 34 g pro.

Crispy Chicken Scaloppine
♥ ▣

Scaloppine, which refers to a thin slice or cutlet of meat, is usually pan-fried. For this light broiled version, a little olive oil is sprinkled on both sides of the chicken during cooking to make the breading crisp.

Start to Finish: 26 minutes **Makes:** 4 servings

- **1** egg white, lightly beaten
- **2** tablespoons water
- **1** cup fresh bread crumbs
- **2** tablespoons snipped fresh parsley
- **2** cloves garlic, minced
- **¼** teaspoon freshly ground black pepper
- **4** skinless, boneless chicken breast halves
  Salt
- **4** thin slices prosciutto
- **2** tablespoons olive oil
  Lemon wedges (optional)

1. Preheat broiler. In a shallow dish, whisk together egg white and water. In another shallow dish, combine bread crumbs, parsley, garlic, and pepper.

2. Place each chicken breast half between 2 pieces of plastic wrap. Using the flat side of a meat mallet, pound chicken lightly to ½-inch thickness. Discard plastic wrap. Sprinkle chicken lightly with salt. Press 1 slice of prosciutto onto each piece of chicken. Dip in egg white mixture, then in crumbs. Place on the rack of a broiler pan; sprinkle with 1 tablespoon of the olive oil.

3. Broil 4 to 5 inches from heat for 3 minutes; turn and sprinkle with the remaining 1 tablespoon olive oil. Broil about 3 minutes more or until chicken is no longer pink. If desired, serve with lemon wedges.

Per serving: 343 cal., 16 g total fat (1 g sat. fat), 82 mg chol., 832 mg sodium, 6 g carbo., 0 g fiber, 42 g pro.

Spicy Coconut Chicken ▣

Tiny Scotch bonnet chiles are among the hottest peppers and range in color from yellow and orange to red.

Prep: 15 minutes **Cook:** 10 minutes **Makes:** 4 servings

- **8** skinless, boneless chicken thighs (2 pounds)
- **¾** teaspoon salt
- **1** cup chopped onion (1 large)
- **1** tablespoon minced garlic
- **3** plum tomatoes, diced
- **¾** teaspoon ground turmeric
- **½** teaspoon minced Scotch bonnet or habanero chile, or 1 teaspoon minced jalapeño chile with seeds (see tip, page 22)
- **1** cup unsweetened lite coconut milk
- **1** tablespoon fresh lime juice
  Hot cooked rice (optional)

1. Sprinkle chicken with ½ teaspoon of the salt. Heat an extra-large nonstick skillet over medium-high heat. Add chicken; cook about 6 minutes or until crisp and browned, turning once halfway through cooking. Remove chicken from skillet.

2. Add onion and garlic to drippings in skillet; cook about 2 minutes or until tender. Add tomatoes, turmeric, chile, and the remaining ¼ teaspoon salt. Cook for 2 minutes. Return chicken to skillet; add coconut milk. Bring to boiling; reduce heat. Simmer, uncovered, for 10 to 12 minutes or until chicken is cooked through (180°F) and sauce is thickened. Remove from heat; stir in lime juice. If desired, serve with hot cooked rice.

Per serving: 225 cal., 9 g total fat (3 g sat. fat), 114 mg chol., 574 mg sodium, 9 g carbo., 1 g fiber, 29 g pro.

Chicken and Pasta in Peanut Sauce

The safest way to cut a chicken breast in half horizontally is to lay it flat on a work surface. Place one hand firmly on top of the chicken, pressing down lightly to hold it steady. Use the other hand to cut horizontally through the meat.

Start to Finish: 20 minutes **Makes:** 4 servings

8	ounces dried thin spaghetti
1	bunch Broccolini, cut in 2-inch lengths
1	medium red sweet pepper, cut in bite-size strips
1	pound skinless, boneless chicken breast halves
	Salt and ground black pepper
1	tablespoon olive oil
½	cup bottled peanut sauce
	Crushed red pepper (optional)

1. In a Dutch oven, cook spaghetti following package directions, adding Broccolini and sweet pepper during the last 2 minutes of cooking. Drain. Return pasta and vegetables to Dutch oven; set aside.

2. Meanwhile, halve chicken breasts horizontally. Sprinkle chicken with salt and pepper. In an extra-large skillet, heat olive oil over medium-high heat. Add chicken; cook about 4 minutes or until chicken is no longer pink, turning once halfway through cooking. Transfer chicken to a cutting board. Slice chicken; add to pasta and vegetables. Heat through. Add peanut sauce. If desired, pass crushed red pepper.

Per serving: 467 cal., 10 g total fat (2 g sat. fat), 66 mg chol., 634 mg sodium, 55 g carbo., 5 g fiber, 37 g pro.

Chicken and Pasta in Peanut Sauce

Chicken Marsala ♥

Marsala is a fortified wine—one that has had spirits such as brandy added to it—that comes from the island of Sicily.

Prep: 11 minutes **Cook:** 8 minutes **Makes:** 4 servings

- **4   small boneless, skinless chicken breast halves (12 ounces total)**
     Nonstick cooking spray
- 1½ **cups sliced fresh mushrooms**
- **2   tablespoons sliced green onion (1)**
- **2   tablespoons water**
- ¼ **teaspoon salt**
- ¼ **cup dry Marsala or dry sherry**

1. Place each chicken breast half between 2 pieces of plastic wrap. Using the flat side of a meat mallet, pound lightly to about ¼-inch thickness. Discard plastic wrap.

2. Lightly coat a large skillet with cooking spray. Heat skillet over medium heat. Add 2 chicken pieces. Cook for 2 to 3 minutes or until no longer pink, turning once halfway through cooking. Transfer chicken to a platter; cover to keep warm. Repeat with remaining chicken.

3. Carefully add mushrooms, green onions, water, and salt to skillet. Cook over medium heat until mushrooms are tender and most of the liquid has evaporated (about 3 minutes). Add Marsala to skillet. Heat through. Spoon vegetable mixture over chicken.

Per serving: 190 cal., 6 g total fat (1 g sat. fat), 66 mg chol., 210 mg sodium, 2 g carbo., 0 g fiber, 28 g pro.

Chicken Marsala

Chicken and Tabbouleh Salad

If your supermarket deli doesn't have prepared tabbouleh, substitute a savory rice salad instead.

Start to Finish: 10 minutes **Makes:** 3 servings

- **4   cups purchased torn mixed salad greens**
- **2   cups purchased tabbouleh salad**
- **1   tablespoon snipped fresh mint or 1 teaspoon dried mint, crushed**
- **2   purchased broiled or roasted chicken breast halves**
- ½ **cup bottled oil-and-vinegar salad dressing**

1. Arrange salad greens on a large platter. Toss together tabbouleh salad and mint. Spoon over greens. Remove bones from chicken breasts; cut meat into ¼-inch slices. Arrange chicken on tabbouleh mixture. Drizzle salad dressing over all.

Per serving: 426 cal., 31 g total fat (4 g sat. fat), 51 mg chol., 797 mg sodium, 23 g carbo., 1 g fiber, 20 g pro.

Chicken Fried Rice

Using cold rice to make fried rice ensures that the grains will separate when stir-fried and not stick to each other as warm, freshly cooked rice does.

Start to Finish: 30 minutes **Makes:** 4 servings

- **12   ounces skinless, boneless chicken breast halves**
- **2   tablespoons soy sauce**
- ⅛ **teaspoon ground black pepper**
- **2   tablespoons vegetable oil**
- **3   eggs, lightly beaten**
- **2   cloves garlic, minced**
- **8   green onions, bias-sliced in 1-inch pieces (1½ cups)**
- **1   cup sliced fresh button mushrooms or enoki mushrooms**
- **3   cups cooked rice, chilled**
- ½ **cup frozen peas, thawed**

1. Finely chop the chicken. In a small bowl, stir together soy sauce and pepper. Set aside.

2. Pour 1 tablespoon of the oil into a wok or large skillet. Heat over medium heat. Add eggs. Lift and tilt the wok to form a thin sheet of egg. Cook, without stirring, about 2 minutes or just until set. Slide the egg sheet onto a cutting board. Use a knife to finely shred the cooked egg. Set aside.

3. Pour the remaining 1 tablespoon oil into the wok. (Add more oil as necessary during cooking.) Heat over medium-high heat. Add garlic; cook and stir for 15 seconds. Add green onion and, if using, the button mushrooms; cook and stir about 1 to 2 minutes or until

crisp-tender. Remove vegetables from the wok. Add the chicken to the wok. Cook and stir for 2 to 3 minutes or until no longer pink. Remove chicken from the wok.

4. Add the cooked rice to the wok. Cook and stir for 2 to 3 minutes or until lightly browned. Drizzle the soy sauce mixture over the rice. Return the cooked vegetables and chicken to the wok. Add the shredded egg and thawed peas. Cook and stir until well mixed and heated through. Carefully stir in enoki mushrooms, if using.

Per serving: 389 cal., 12 g total fat (2 g sat. fat), 208 mg chol., 423 mg sodium, 38 g carbo., 3 g fiber, 31 g pro.

Chicken Adobo

This sweet-and-sour dish is so easy. Toss the ingredients together in a saucepan and cook for fewer than 20 minutes. The flavor is terrific.

Start to Finish: 30 minutes **Makes:** 4 servings

8	**skinless, boneless chicken thighs (1¼ pounds)**
¼	**cup white wine vinegar**
¼	**cup soy sauce**
2	**tablespoons sugar**
1	**tablespoon vegetable oil**
1	**tablespoon minced garlic**
1	**bay leaf, broken in half**
¼	**teaspoon freshly ground black pepper**

1	**cup snow peas, trimmed**
1	**tablespoon water**
	Hot cooked rice noodles or rice (optional)
1	**cup diced fresh or canned pineapple**

1. Cook rice following package directions.

2. Meanwhile, in a 3-quart saucepan, combine chicken, vinegar, soy sauce, sugar, oil, garlic, bay leaf, and pepper. Bring to boiling, stirring occasionally; reduce heat. Simmer, covered, for 12 minutes, stirring occasionally. Using a slotted spoon, transfer chicken to a platter; cover to keep warm.

3. Discard bay leaf. Return vinegar mixture in saucepan to boiling. Cook about 5 minutes or until syrupy.

4. Place snow peas and water in a microwave-safe bowl; cover with vented plastic wrap. Microwave on 100% power (high) for 1 minute. Drain snow peas; add to platter with chicken.

5. Serve chicken on rice noodles. Top with sauce and sprinkle with pineapple.

Per serving: 274 cal., 9 g total fat (2 g sat. fat), 113 mg chol., 1,020 mg sodium, 13 g carbo., 1 g fiber, 31 g pro.

Chicken Adobo

Chicken Cordon Bleu

These breaded ham- and Swiss cheese-stuffed chicken breasts will be a hit with kids. Top them with a little tomato sauce, if you like.

Prep: 25 minutes **Bake:** 45 minutes **Oven:** 375°F
Makes: 6 servings

- 6 small chicken breast halves with bone (3½ to 4 pounds)
- ½ cup finely chopped reduced-sodium ham (about 2 ounces)
- ½ cup shredded Swiss cheese (2 ounces)
- ¼ cup refrigerated or frozen egg product, thawed, or 1 egg, lightly beaten
- 1 tablespoon water
- ½ cup fine dry bread crumbs
- 2 tablespoons olive oil

1. Preheat oven to 375°F. Line a 15×10×1-inch baking pan with foil; set aside. Remove skin from chicken breast halves and discard. Using a small sharp knife, cut a horizontal pocket about 2 inches long and 1 inch deep in the meaty side of each chicken breast half.

2. In a small bowl, combine ham and cheese. Divide ham mixture among pockets in chicken breast halves.

3. In a shallow dish, whisk together egg and the water. Place bread crumbs in another shallow dish. Dip stuffed chicken breast halves into egg mixture, then into bread crumbs to coat. Arrange chicken, meaty sides up, in prepared baking pan. Drizzle with olive oil.

4. Bake for 45 to 55 minutes or until no longer pink (170°F).

Per serving: 322 cal., 10 g total fat (3 g sat. fat), 114 mg chol., 278 mg sodium, 7 g carbo., 0 g fiber, 47 g pro.

Moo Goo Gai Pan

This light and fresh Chinese dish has lots of color and crunch—from carrots, snow peas, and water chestnuts.

Start to Finish: 30 minutes **Makes:** 4 servings

- ½ cup chicken broth
- 2 tablespoons soy sauce
- 2 tablespoons rice wine or dry white wine
- 4 teaspoons cornstarch
- ½ teaspoon sugar
- 1 tablespoon vegetable oil
- 3 cloves garlic, minced
- 1 cup thinly bias-sliced carrots (2 medium)
- 8 ounces whole small fresh mushrooms (3 cups) or large fresh mushrooms, halved (3 cups)
- 2 cups fresh snow peas or one 6-ounce package frozen snow peas, thawed
- 12 ounces skinless, boneless chicken breast halves, cut in thin bite-size strips
- ½ an 8-ounce can sliced water chestnuts, drained
- 3 cups hot cooked rice

1. For sauce, in a small bowl, stir together chicken broth, soy sauce, rice wine, cornstarch, and sugar. Set aside.

2. Pour oil into a wok or large skillet. (Add more oil as necessary during cooking.) Heat over medium-high heat. Add garlic; cook and stir for 15 seconds. Add carrots; cook and stir for 3 minutes. Add mushrooms and, if using, fresh pea pods; cook and stir about 1 minute more or until carrots and pea pods are crisp-tender. Remove the vegetables from the wok.

3. Add the chicken to the hot wok. Cook and stir for 2 to 3 minutes or until chicken is no longer pink. Push the chicken from the center of the wok. Stir sauce. Add the sauce to the center of the wok. Cook and stir until thickened and bubbly.

4. Return the cooked vegetables to the wok. Add water chestnuts and, if using, thawed pea pods. Stir all ingredients together to coat with sauce. Cook and stir about 1 minute more or until heated through. Serve immediately over hot cooked rice.

Per serving: 377 cal., 6 g total fat (1 g sat. fat), 50 mg chol., 720 mg sodium, 51 g carbo., 4 g fiber, 28 g pro.

Quick Tip Remove the tough strings from fresh snow peas and sugar snap peas to make them more palatable. To remove, grab one end of the string from the top of the pod and pull it across the pod.

Chicken Cordon Bleu

Spicy Shrimp with Lime in Lettuce Cups

CHRIS TRACY

1 pound medium raw shrimp, shelled and deveined, cut in half

1 large (2- to 2½-inch) jalepeño, trimmed, seeded and cut into small dice

½ medium green pepper, cut into ¼-inch strips and then into 1-inch lengths

½ medium red pepper, cut into ¼-inch strips and then into 1-inch lengths

½ cup spanish onion, cut into ¼-inch dice

zest and juice of 1 large lime

1 tablespoon rice wine vinegar

4 tablespoons soy sauce

1 tablespoon honey

2 to 3 hearts of romaine lettuce

Wash and dry the hearts of romaine lettuce and separate the leaves or ribs. Place the romaine cups around the edge of a platter and set aside.

Combine all the remaining ingredients in a large plastic storage bag or glass bowl and refrigerate. Allow to marinate for 1 hour. To ensure proper cooking, remove prepared ingredients from the refrigerator approximately 10 minutes prior to cooking to take the chill off.

Preheat a Calphalon 2 qt. chef's skillet. When the rim of the pan is hot-to-the-touch, add ½ of the shrimp mixture and cook. When the shrimp has turned pink, place the cooked shrimp mixture in the middle of the platter with the romaine cups. Cook the remaining shrimp and add to the platter.

To serve, place some of the shrimp into a lettuce cup and enjoy.

Serves 4 as a hearty appetizer or 2 as a light but filling meal.

Serve with a light, dry white wine.

Chris Tracy

Chris Tracy brings more than twenty years broad-based culinary experience to his position as **Calphalon Executive Chef and Culinary Events Manager**–from restaurant management to recipe writing to retail merchandising of gourmet foods. Over the years, he has been fortunate to study, teach and dine alongside some of the culinary community's most prominent citizens, including Guiliano Bugialli, Hugh Carpenter, Madeleine Kamman, Nina Simmonds and Zona Spray.

Here at Calphalon, we count on Chris to always be at the center of "what's happening" in the culinary world. He helps us keep current with trends in restaurant cuisine and to design cookware to satisfy the most exacting professional standards. And it's through the many classes and special events Chris hosts and the recipes he writes that we are able to share our enthusiasm for cooking with home chefs like you.

We're pleased to be able to share some of Chris' uniquely delicious recipes with you.

Bon appetit!

Chicken and Gnocchi with Squash

Chicken and Gnocchi with Squash

This quick-to-fix dish features the flavors of fall—earthy sage and sweet acorn squash—cooked in a flash in a microwave.

Start to Finish: 18 minutes **Makes:** 4 servings

1	**1-pound package shelf-stable potato gnocchi**
1	**small acorn squash, halved and seeded**
2	**tablespoons water**
14	**to 16 ounces chicken breast tenderloins**
	Salt and ground black pepper
1	**tablespoon oil**
¾	**cup chicken broth**
1	**tablespoon chopped fresh sage**
2	**tablespoons milk**
	Tiny whole sage leaves (optional)
	Grated nutmeg (optional)

1. Prepare gnocchi following package directions. Drain. Cover to keep warm.

2. Meanwhile, place squash, cut sides down, in a microwave-safe baking dish. Add the water. Cover with vented plastic wrap. Microwave on 100% power (high) for 7 to 10 minutes, rearranging once halfway through cooking. Let stand, covered, for 5 minutes.

3. Meanwhile, sprinkle chicken with salt and pepper. In a large skillet, heat oil over medium heat. Add chicken; cook for 6 to 8 minutes or until no longer pink (170°F). Remove chicken from skillet; cover to keep warm.

4. Scrape the flesh from the squash into a large bowl; mash. Transfer squash to hot skillet; stir in chicken broth and snipped sage. Bring to boiling; reduce heat. Simmer for 1 minute. Stir in milk. Spoon into bowls. Top with the chicken and gnocchi. If desired, garnish with sage leaves and nutmeg.

Per serving: 366 cal., 6 g total fat (1 g sat. fat), 59 mg chol., 796 mg sodium, 50 g carbo., 4 g fiber, 29 g pro.

Chicken-Vegetable Ratatouille ♥

Chicken and pasta added to the familiar Provençal vegetable dish featuring eggplant and tomatoes makes a one-dish meal.

Start to Finish: 30 minutes **Makes:** 4 or 5 servings

2²/₃   **cups dried penne (mostaccioli), cut ziti, or wagon wheel macaroni (ruote) (8 ounces)**
  1   **tablespoon olive oil**
  1   **cup chopped onion (1 large)**
  2   **cloves garlic, minced**
  1   **medium eggplant, cut in 1-inch pieces**
  2   **cups frozen zucchini, carrots, cauliflower, lima beans, and Italian beans**
  1   **14.5-ounce can diced tomatoes, undrained**
  1   **teaspoon dried Italian seasoning, crushed**
  ³/₄ **teaspoon seasoned salt**
  ¹/₄ **teaspoon ground black pepper**
1¹/₂   **cups chopped cooked chicken (about 8 ounces)**

1. In a large saucepan, cook pasta following package directions. Drain. Cover and keep warm.

2. Meanwhile, in another large saucepan, heat olive oil over medium-high heat. Add onion and garlic; cook for 2 minutes. Stir in eggplant, frozen vegetables, undrained tomatoes, Italian seasoning, seasoned salt, and pepper. Bring to boiling; reduce heat. Simmer, covered, for 12 to 15 minutes or until eggplant is tender.

3. Add chicken to vegetable mixture; cook about 1 minute more or until heated through. Serve chicken and vegetable mixture over pasta.

Per serving: 442 cal., 9 g total fat (2 g sat. fat), 50 mg chol., 578 mg sodium, 64 g carbo., 11 g fiber, 28 g pro.

Chicken with Creamy Mushrooms

Pick up marinated chicken breasts in the meat department of your supermarket. Plain chicken breasts work well too—just salt them lightly before cooking.

Start to Finish: 30 minutes **Makes:** 6 servings

- 3 tablespoons butter or margarine
- 1 pound sliced fresh mushrooms, such as button or shiitake
- 6 Italian-marinated skinless, boneless chicken breast halves (about 2 pounds)
- 3 tablespoons rice vinegar or white wine vinegar
- 1½ cups whipping cream
- 3 tablespoons capers, drained
- ¼ teaspoon freshly ground black pepper
  Steamed fresh vegetables (optional)

1. In an extra-large skillet, melt 1 tablespoon of the butter over medium-high heat. Add mushrooms; cook, uncovered, about 5 minutes or until tender. Remove mushrooms from skillet.

2. Reduce heat to medium. Add the remaining 2 tablespoons of the butter and the chicken to skillet. Cook, uncovered, for 8 to 12 minutes or until chicken is no longer pink (170°F), turning once halfway through cooking. Remove chicken from skillet; keep warm.

3. Remove skillet from heat; add vinegar, stirring to scrape up browned bits in bottom of skillet. Return skillet to heat. Stir in whipping cream, capers, and pepper. Bring to boiling; boil gently, uncovered, for 2 to 3 minutes or until sauce is slightly thickened. Return mushrooms to skillet; heat through. Cut each chicken piece in half horizontally to make 2 thin pieces. Top with mushroom mixture. If desired, serve with steamed vegetables.

Per serving: 456 cal., 34 g total fat (19 g sat. fat), 183 mg chol., 967 mg sodium, 7 g carbo., 1 g fiber, 33 g pro.

Chicken with Creamy Mushrooms

Chicken Cacciatore

Porcini mushrooms impart a rich, woodsy taste to this Italian "hunter's-style" dish. You need only a small amount of the fairly expensive mushrooms for big flavor.

Start to Finish: 30 minutes **Makes:** 4 servings

- 1½ pounds skinless, boneless chicken thighs
- ¾ teaspoon salt
- ¼ teaspoon freshly ground black pepper
  Nonstick cooking spray
- 1 0.35-ounce package dried porcini mushrooms
- ¼ cup boiling water
- 1 tablespoon olive oil
- 1 8- to 10-ounce package button mushrooms, sliced
- ½ cup chopped onion (1 medium)
- 1 28-ounce can whole tomatoes in puree, chopped (reserve puree)
- 2 teaspoons snipped fresh oregano or ½ teaspoon dried oregano, crushed
- 1 tablespoon snipped fresh Italian (flat-leaf) parsley

1. Sprinkle chicken with ½ teaspoon of the salt and the pepper. Coat an extra-large nonstick skillet with cooking spray. Heat skillet over medium-high heat. Add chicken and cook 5 minutes or until well browned, turning once. Remove chicken from skillet.

2. Meanwhile, place porcini in a sieve and rinse well. Transfer to a 1-cup glass measuring cup; add boiling water and let stand for 10 minutes. Transfer porcini to a cutting board; reserve 2 tablespoons of the mushroom liquid. Chop porcini. Set aside.

3. Heat olive oil in same skillet over medium-high heat for 30 seconds. Add sliced mushrooms and onion. Cook about 3 minutes or until vegetables soften. Sprinkle with the remaining ¼ teaspoon salt; cook for 1 to 2 minutes or until lightly browned. Return chicken to skillet; add chopped porcini mushrooms and the reserved 2 tablespoons mushroom liquid, tomatoes and puree, and oregano. Bring to boiling; reduce heat. Simmer, covered, for 15 to 17 minutes or until chicken is no longer pink (180°F). Transfer to a serving platter; sprinkle with parsley.

Per serving: 330 cal., 11 g total fat (2 g sat. fat), 141 mg chol., 902 mg sodium, 20 g carbo., 3 g fiber, 38 g pro.

Quick Tip In general, fresh herbs and dried herbs are interchangeable—just use different amounts. Substitute one for the other in the following proportions: 1 tablespoon snipped fresh herb is equal to ½ to 1 teaspoon crushed dried herb or ½ teaspoon ground herb.

Pappardelle with Chicken and Peas

Pappardelle with Chicken and Peas

Pappardelle is an especially hearty and toothsome ribbonlike pasta. Cooked, it measures about 3/4 to 1 inch wide.

Prep: 10 minutes **Cook:** 10 minutes **Makes:** 4 servings

6	ounces dried pappardelle or other wide egg noodles
1½	cups shelled sweet peas
½	a 14.5-ounce can Italian-style stewed tomatoes, undrained
2	teaspoons olive oil
8	ounces skinless, boneless chicken breast halves, cut in large bite-size pieces
1	small onion, cut in thin wedges
¼	teaspoon coarsely ground black pepper
¼	cup chicken broth
¼	cup whipping cream
2	tablespoons finely shredded Parmigiano-Reggiano cheese (optional)

1. Cook pasta following package directions, adding peas the last 3 minutes of cooking time. Meanwhile, place undrained tomatoes in a blender or food processor. Cover and blend or process until smooth; set aside.

2. In a large skillet, heat olive oil over medium-high heat. Add chicken, onion, and pepper; cook for 2 to 4 minutes or until chicken is no longer pink.

3. Carefully stir in chicken broth and the pureed tomatoes. Return to boiling; reduce heat. Boil gently, uncovered, for 2 minutes. Stir in cream; boil gently about 3 minutes more or until sauce thickens slightly.

4. Drain pasta and peas; transfer to a warm serving dish. Spoon chicken mixture over noodles and peas; toss gently. If desired, top with Parmigiano-Reggiano cheese.

Per serving: 378 cal., 11 g total fat (4 g sat. fat), 94 mg chol., 214 mg sodium, 46 g carbo., 5 g fiber, 23 g pro.

Smoked Chicken Salad with Raspberry Vinaigrette

This simple and so-pretty smoked chicken and fruit salad is perfect for a bridal luncheon or baby shower. Serve it with fresh croissants or dinner rolls.

Start to Finish: 20 minutes **Makes:** 4 servings

⅓	cup balsamic vinegar
⅓	cup seedless raspberry jam
¼	cup olive oil
12	ounces boneless smoked chicken breast* or turkey, cut in thin strips
8	cups mixed salad greens
2	cups fresh raspberries
¼	cup sliced almonds, toasted

1. For the vinaigrette, in a screw-top jar, combine balsamic vinegar, jam, and olive oil; shake well.

2. In a large bowl, toss chicken with about half the vinaigrette. Line a large platter with greens. Top with chicken mixture, raspberries, and almonds. Pass remaining dressing.

Per serving: 382 cal., 18 g total fat (2 g sat. fat), 37 mg chol., 924 mg sodium, 36 g carbo., 6 g fiber, 20 g pro.

*Note: To smoke chicken on a barbecue grill, soak 3 cups of wood chips in enough water to cover for at least 1 hour. Brush 4 skinless, boneless chicken breast halves lightly with olive oil and sprinkle with salt and pepper. Arrange medium-hot coals around a drip pan. Test for medium heat above drip pan. Add 1 inch of water to dip pan. Drain wood chips. Sprinkle wood chips on hot coals. Place rack on grill. Place chicken breast halves on grill rack above the drip pan. Close grill hood. Grill for 15 to 18 minutes or until chicken is tender and no longer pink (170°F).

Smoked Chicken Salad with Raspberry Vinaigrette

Chicken, Bean, and Tomato Stir-Fry

Chicken, Bean, and Tomato Stir-Fry ♥

Add tomatoes at the end of cooking time so they warm through and don't become mushy.

Start to Finish: 25 minutes **Makes:** 4 servings

- **6 ounces dried wide rice noodles or egg noodles**
- **12 ounces skinless, boneless chicken breast halves, cut in thin bite-size strips**
- **1 teaspoon Cajun seasoning or other spicy seasoning blend**
- **4 teaspoons vegetable oil**
- **2 cloves garlic, minced**
- **1 pound Chinese long beans or whole green beans, cut in 3-inch pieces**
- **¼ cup water**
- **2 medium tomatoes, cut in thin wedges**
- **2 tablespoons raspberry vinegar**

1. In a Dutch oven, cook rice noodles in boiling lightly salted water for 3 to 5 minutes or until tender. (Or cook egg noodles following package directions.) Drain; cover and keep warm. Meanwhile, combine chicken and Cajun seasoning; toss to coat. Set aside.

2. In a large skillet, heat 2 teaspoons of the oil over medium-high heat. Add garlic; cook and stir for 15 seconds. Add beans; cook and stir for 2 minutes. Add water; reduce heat to low. Simmer, covered, for 6 to 8 minutes or until beans are crisp-tender. Remove beans from skillet.

3. Add the remaining 2 teaspoons oil to the skillet. Add chicken. Cook and stir for 2 to 3 minutes or until no longer pink. Return cooked beans to skillet. Add tomato wedges and vinegar. Stir all ingredients together to coat. Cook and stir for 1 to 2 minutes more or until heated through. Serve immediately over hot cooked noodles.

Per serving: 336 cal., 6 g total fat (1 g sat. fat), 49 mg chol., 188 mg sodium, 46 g carbo., 5 g fiber, 24 g pro.

Chicken Saltimbocca 🔲

Vermouth is a fortified wine (spirits are added), infused with herbs and spices for complex flavor, and is available in both sweet and dry varieties. The dry version is usually white; the sweet one, red.

Start to Finish: 11 minutes **Makes:** 4 servings

- **4** **skinless, boneless chicken breast halves (about 1 ¼ pounds)**
- **½** **teaspoon dried sage, crushed**
- **⅛** **teaspoon ground black pepper**
- **4** **slices prosciutto or ham (about 4 ounces)**
- **2** **tablespoons butter**
- **½** **cup sweet vermouth**
- **¼** **cup beef broth**

1. Place each chicken breast half between 2 pieces of plastic wrap. Using the flat side of a meat mallet, pound chicken lightly to ½-inch thickness. Discard plastic wrap. Sprinkle chicken with sage and pepper. Place 1 slice of prosciutto on each chicken piece.

2. In a large heavy nonstick skillet, melt 1 tablespoon of the butter over high heat. When butter begins to brown, add chicken, prosciutto sides down; cook about 4 minutes or until no longer pink in center, turning once. Transfer chicken to a platter. Cover to keep warm.

3. Add vermouth and beef broth to skillet; cook for 2 minutes, stirring to scrape up browned bits from bottom of skillet. Add the remaining 1 tablespoon butter; swirl just until incorporated into a creamy sauce. Pour over chicken.

Per serving: 348 cal., 15 g total fat (4 g sat. fat), 97 mg chol., 693 mg sodium, 4 g carbo., 0 g fiber, 40 g pro.

Asian Chicken and Cabbage Slaw

Serve this fresh and light Thai-inspired salad with sesame-topped rice crackers.

Start to Finish: 25 minutes **Makes:** 4 servings

- **½** **teaspoon finely shredded lime peel**
- **3** **tablespoons fresh lime juice**
- **3** **tablespoons Thai fish sauce (nam pla)**
- **3** **tablespoons vegetable oil**
- **2** **tablespoons finely chopped jalapeño chile (see tip, page 22)**
- **4** **teaspoons minced garlic**
- **1** **tablespoon rice wine vinegar**
- **¼** **teaspoon freshly ground black pepper**
- **1** **2- to 2¼-pound whole roasted chicken, boned, skinned, and shredded**
- **1** **16-ounce package shredded cabbage with carrots (coleslaw mix)**
- **½** **cup thinly sliced green onions (4)**
- **½** **cup thinly sliced fresh mint leaves**

1. For the dressing, in small bowl, stir together lime peel, lime juice, fish sauce, oil, chile, garlic, vinegar, and black pepper.

2. In a large bowl, toss chicken with ¼ cup of the dressing; let stand for 5 minutes.

3. In another large bowl, toss together the coleslaw mix, green onions, mint, and the remaining dressing. Add the chicken; toss to mix.

Per serving: 574 cal., 40 g total fat (10 g sat. fat), 200 mg chol., 2,389 mg sodium, 14 g carbo., 4 g fiber, 46 g pro.

Chicken-Broccoli Salad

This crunchy main-dish salad is perfect for a summer potluck.

Start to Finish: 20 minutes **Makes:** 4 servings

- **½** **cup mayonnaise or salad dressing**
- **2** **tablespoons cider vinegar**
- **4** **cups broccoli florets or packaged shredded broccoli (broccoli slaw mix)**
- **2** **cups cubed cooked chicken (10 ounces)**
- **1** **cup chopped apples (2 small)**
- **2** **slices bacon, crisp-cooked, drained, and crumbled, or 2 tablespoons cooked bacon pieces**

1. For dressing, in a small bowl, stir together mayonnaise and vinegar; set aside.

2. In a large bowl, toss together broccoli, chicken, and apples. Pour dressing over chicken mixture; toss lightly to coat. Sprinkle with bacon. Serve immediately or, if desired, cover and chill up to 8 hours.

Per serving: 417 cal., 29 g total fat (5 g sat. fat), 75 mg chol., 284 mg sodium, 16 g carbo., 5 g fiber, 24 g pro.

Chicken-Broccoli Salad

Chicken Francese 🔲

Although "Francese" means "in the French manner," these lightly battered chicken breasts are served in a lemon-butter sauce and are standard fare at Italian-American restaurants.

Start to Finish: 27 minutes **Makes:** 4 servings

- **2 eggs**
- **¼ cup all-purpose flour**
- **2 tablespoons vegetable oil**
- **4 skinless, boneless chicken breast halves (1 to 1¼ pounds)**
- **½ teaspoon salt**
- **½ cup chicken broth**
- **½ cup dry white wine**
- **¼ cup fresh lemon juice**
- **¼ cup butter, cut up**
- **1 tablespoon snipped fresh parsley**
   Freshly ground black pepper

1. In a shallow dish, lightly beat eggs. Spread flour in another shallow dish.

2. In an extra-large skillet, heat oil over medium-high heat. Sprinkle chicken with salt. Dip each chicken piece in flour, shaking off excess, then dip in egg. Cook chicken in hot oil about 12 minutes or until no longer pink (170°F), turning once halfway through cooking. Transfer chicken to a plate; cover to keep warm.

3. For sauce, discard oil from skillet. Add chicken broth, wine, and lemon juice; bring to boiling. Boil for 6 minutes or until mixture is reduced to ⅓ cup. Remove pan from heat; whisk butter into sauce. Stir in parsley. Season to taste with pepper; pour sauce over chicken.

Per serving: 370 cal., 23 g total fat (10 g sat. fat), 211 mg chol., 651 mg sodium, 7 g carbo., 0 g fiber, 34 g pro.

Rigatoni with Chicken and Gorgonzola Cheese

Serve this dish made with shiitake mushrooms, whipping cream, and Gorgonzola when entertaining. It's elegant and easy.

Start to Finish: 26 minutes **Makes:** 4 servings

- **8 ounces dried rigatoni or penne pasta**
- **8 ounces skinless, boneless chicken breast halves, cut in ½-inch slices**
- **½ teaspoon salt**
- **½ teaspoon ground black pepper**
- **1 tablespoon olive oil**
- **4 ounces shiitake mushrooms (stems removed), sliced**
- **1 cup whipping cream**
- **½ cup crumbled Gorgonzola cheese (2 ounces)**
- **⅓ cup finely shredded Parmesan cheese**
- **2 tablespoons snipped fresh Italian (flat-leaf) parsley**

1. In a Dutch oven, cook pasta following package directions. Drain; keep warm.

2. Meanwhile, sprinkle chicken with ¼ teaspoon of the salt and ¼ teaspoon of the pepper. In an extra-large nonstick skillet, heat olive oil over medium-high heat. Add chicken; cook about 1½ minutes or until edges are lightly browned. Add mushrooms; cook and stir for 2 to 4 minutes or until softened. Stir in whipping cream. Cook about 3 minutes or until mixture is reduced by half. Stir in ¼ cup of the Gorgonzola cheese and the Parmesan cheese. Cook and stir about 1 minute more or until cheese is melted. Stir in the remaining ¼ teaspoon salt and the remaining ¼ teaspoon pepper.

3. Toss hot pasta with chicken mixture. Divide among 4 plates. Sprinkle with the remaining ¼ cup Gorgonzola cheese and the parsley.

Per serving: 605 cal., 34 g total fat (19 g sat. fat), 133 mg chol., 699 mg sodium, 46 g carbo., 2 g fiber, 29 g pro.

Basil, Chicken, and Tomatoes

Make this composed main-dish salad during the summer, when tomatoes are juicy and ripe.

Start to Finish: 20 minutes **Makes:** 4 servings

- **3 to 4 medium tomatoes**
- **1 2- to 2½-pound whole roasted chicken**
- **1 avocado, peeled, seeded, and sliced**
- **¼ cup olive oil**
- **1 medium lime, quartered**
- **½ cup small fresh basil leaves**
   Salt and cracked black pepper

1. Cut tomatoes in wedges and divide among 4 plates. Use two forks to pull chicken meat off the bones and shred into large pieces. Discard bones and skin. Layer chicken and avocado on tomatoes.

2. Drizzle with olive oil. Squeeze juice from lime quarters on tomato, chicken, and avocado. Sprinkle with basil leaves, salt, and cracked black pepper.

Per serving: 470 cal., 31 g total fat (6 g sat. fat), 120 mg chol., 170 mg sodium, 9 g carbo., 5 g fiber, 41 g pro.

Quick Tip To prepare an avocado, first make a horizontal cut around the fruit to the seed. Twist the halves slightly to separate. Use a small spoon to scoop the seed out of the avocado. Cut each half in half again, then gently peel away the skin from each quarter using your fingers or a small paring knife.

Basil, Chicken, and Tomatoes

Creamy Turkey Fettuccine

Creamy Turkey Fettuccine ♥

Another time substitute pork tenderloin for the turkey.

Start to Finish: 35 minutes **Makes:** 8 servings

- **1** **pound dried spinach fettuccine and/or plain fettuccine**
- **2** **8-ounce containers fat-free sour cream**
- **¼** **cup all-purpose flour**
- **1** **cup reduced-sodium chicken broth**
- **1** **teaspoon dried sage, crushed**
- **¼** **teaspoon ground black pepper**
- **1½** **pounds turkey breast tenderloin**
- **¼** **teaspoon salt**
  Nonstick cooking spray
- **3** **cups sliced fresh mushrooms**
- **1** **cup sliced green onions (8)**
- **4** **cloves garlic, minced**

1. Cook pasta following package directions; drain. Meanwhile, in a large bowl, stir together sour cream and flour. Gradually stir in chicken broth, sage, and pepper. Cut turkey in bite-size strips; sprinkle with salt. Set aside.

2. Coat a large skillet with cooking spray. Heat over medium-high heat. Add half the turkey; cook and stir for 3 to 5 minutes or until no longer pink (170°F). Remove turkey from skillet. Add remaining turkey, mushrooms, green onions, and garlic to skillet. Cook and stir for 3 to 5 minutes or until turkey is no longer pink (170°F). Return all of the turkey to the skillet.

3. Stir the sour cream mixture into turkey mixture in skillet. Cook and stir until thickened and bubbly. Cook and stir for 1 minute more. Serve over hot cooked pasta.

Per serving: 400 cal., 3 g total fat (1 g sat. fat), 51 mg chol., 327 mg sodium, 58 g carbo., 1 g fiber, 34 g pro.

Turkey with Creamy Morel Sauce 🔲

Fresh morels are available briefly—usually in May—and the price makes them a special treat. Rehydrate dried morels by covering with warm water for 30 to 45 minutes—then drain and use.

Start to Finish: 30 minutes **Makes:** 4 servings

- 4 tablespoons all-purpose flour
- ¼ teaspoon salt
- ¼ teaspoon lemon-pepper seasoning
- 4 turkey breast steaks or skinless, boneless chicken breast halves (1 to 1¼ pounds)
- 3 tablespoons butter or margarine
- 2 ounces fresh morels or ½ ounce dried morels, rehydrated
- 2 tablespoons sliced green onion (1)
- 1 clove garlic, minced
- 1¼ cups half-and-half, light cream, or milk
- 1 tablespoon dry sherry
  Salt and ground black pepper
  Fresh herbs (optional)

1. In a shallow dish, combine 3 tablespoons of the flour, the ¼ teaspoon salt, and the lemon-pepper seasoning; coat turkey with flour mixture.

2. In a large skillet, heat 2 tablespoons of the butter over medium heat. Add turkey; cook for 8 to 10 minutes or until no longer pink (170°F), turning once halfway through cooking. Transfer turkey to 4 plates; cover to keep warm.

3. Cut any large morels in bite-size strips. For sauce, in the same skillet, melt the remaining 1 tablespoon butter. Add morels, green onion, and garlic; cook for 3 minutes or until tender.

4. In a small bowl, stir together half-and-half and the remaining 1 tablespoon flour; add to vegetables in skillet. Cook and stir until thickened and bubbly; stir in sherry. Cook and stir for 1 minute more. Season to taste with additional salt and ground black pepper.

5. Spoon some of the sauce over turkey; pass remaining sauce. If desired, garnish with fresh herbs.

Per serving: 340 cal., 18 g total fat (11 g sat. fat), 121 mg chol., 421 mg sodium, 10 g carbo., 0 g fiber, 32 g pro.

> **Quick Tip** Any time you rehydrate dried mushrooms—such as morels or porcini—save the soaking liquid. It is intensely flavored and can be used in soups, stews, and sauces. Be sure to strain it well through cheesecloth to remove any grit, then refrigerate to use within 2 days or freeze it.

Turkey Roulade 🔲

The rolled turkey bundles—filled with crisp snow peas—have colorful, crunchy centers.

Start to Finish: 25 minutes **Makes:** 4 servings

- 1 4.1- to 6-ounce package long grain and wild rice mix
- 2 turkey breast tenderloins (about 1 pound)
- ½ a 6-ounce package frozen pea pods
- 2 tablespoons vegetable oil
- ⅓ cup bottled barbecue sauce
- ⅓ cup orange juice
  Orange slices, quartered (optional)

1. Prepare rice mix following package directions.

2. Meanwhile, cut each turkey tenderloin in half horizontally to make 2 steaks each. Place each turkey steak between 2 pieces of plastic wrap. Using the flat side of a meat mallet, pound turkey lightly to ¼-inch thickness. Discard plastic wrap. Arrange the pea pods across the turkey steaks. Roll up and secure with wooden toothpicks.

3. In a large skillet, heat oil over medium-high heat. Add turkey rolls; cook until browned, turning to brown evenly.

4. Meanwhile, in a small bowl, stir together the barbecue sauce and orange juice. Add orange juice mixture to skillet with turkey rolls. Bring to boiling; reduce heat. Simmer, covered, for 10 to 15 minutes or until turkey is no longer pink (170°F). Serve with rice. If desired garnish with orange slices.

Per serving: 332 cal., 8 g total fat (1 g sat. fat), 70 mg chol., 701 mg sodium, 34 g carbo., 2 g fiber, 31 g pro.

Turkey Roulade

Mango Salad with Smoked Turkey

Turkey Breasts with Raspberry Sauce ♥ 🔲

The traditional poultry herbs of thyme and sage add savory flavor to the sweet and fruity sauce.

Start to Finish: 20 minutes **Makes:** 4 servings

½	teaspoon dried thyme, crushed
½	teaspoon dried sage, crushed
¼	teaspoon salt
¼	teaspoon ground black pepper
1	tablespoon olive oil or vegetable oil
4	turkey breast slices, cut ½ inch thick
¼	cup seedless raspberry jam
2	tablespoons orange juice
2	tablespoons wine vinegar

1. In a small bowl, combine thyme, sage, salt, and pepper; rub evenly over turkey slices.

2. In a large skillet, heat oil over medium heat. Add turkey; cook for 8 to 10 minutes or until no longer pink (170°F), turning once halfway through cooking. Remove turkey from skillet; keep warm.

3. For sauce, in a small bowl, stir together raspberry jam, orange juice, and vinegar; carefully add to skillet. Bring to boiling; reduce heat. Boil gently, uncovered, about 2 minutes or until sauce is desired consistency. Serve sauce over turkey.

Per serving: 184 cal., 4 g total fat (1 g sat. fat), 56 mg chol., 185 mg sodium, 15 g carbo., 0 g fiber, 21 g pro.

Mango Salad with Smoked Turkey ♥

Leave out the turkey and lettuce for a fruit salsa to serve with grilled meat and fish.

Start to Finish: 30 minutes **Makes:** 4 servings

6	cups torn mixed salad greens
4	mangoes, cut from seed, peeled, and cut in thin slices
8	ounces cooked smoked turkey or chicken, cut in thin bite-size strips; or smoked trout, catfish, or other white fish, crumbled
2	tablespoons thinly sliced green onion (1)
¼	cup snipped fresh cilantro
¼	cup salad oil
¼	teaspoon finely shredded lime peel
2	tablespoons fresh lime juice
¼	teaspoon grated fresh ginger or ¼ teaspoon ground ginger
	Edible flowers, such as nasturtiums, chive flowers, pansies, or snapdragons (optional)
	Lime wedges (optional)

1. Divide greens among 4 salad plates. Arrange mangoes, smoked turkey, and green onion on greens. Sprinkle with cilantro.

2. For dressing, in a screw-top jar, combine salad oil, lime peel, lime juice, and ginger. Cover and shake well.

3. Drizzle dressing over salad. If desired, garnish with edible flowers and lime wedges.

Per serving: 333 cal., 16 g total fat (3 g sat. fat), 29 mg chol., 582 mg sodium, 39 g carbo., 6 g fiber, 13 g pro.

Parmesan Turkey with Pasta Sauce ♥

Nutty cereal creates a crunchy crust on the turkey and gives this family favorite a nutritional boost.

Prep: 15 minutes **Bake:** 12 minutes **Oven:** 400°F
Makes: 6 servings

- 12   **ounces dried spinach or plain fettuccine**
- 4   **medium zucchini and/or yellow summer squash, halved lengthwise and thinly sliced (about 3¹⁄₂ cups)**
- 12   **ounces turkey tenderloin**
- 3   **tablespoons wheat and barley nugget cereal**
- 3   **tablespoons grated Parmesan or Romano cheese**
- ³⁄₄   **teaspoon dried Italian seasoning, crushed**
- ¹⁄₈   **to ¹⁄₄ teaspoon cayenne pepper**
- 1   **egg white**
- 1   **tablespoon water**
- 2   **cups low-fat, chunky tomato pasta sauce**

1. Preheat oven to 400°F. Cook pasta following package directions, adding zucchini the last 2 minutes of cooking. Drain pasta and zucchini; keep warm.

2. Meanwhile, cut turkey tenderloin in 6 pieces. In a shallow bowl, combine cereal, Parmesan cheese, Italian seasoning, and cayenne pepper. In another shallow bowl, lightly beat together egg white and water. Dip turkey pieces in egg white mixture, then coat with cereal mixture. Place turkey in a lightly greased shallow baking pan. Bake for 12 to 15 minutes or until turkey is no longer pink (170°F), turning once halfway through cooking.

3. In a small saucepan, heat pasta sauce. Serve turkey with pasta, zucchini, and pasta sauce.

Per serving: 340 cal., 4 g total fat (1 g sat. fat), 27 mg chol., 126 mg sodium, 55 g carbo., 3 g fiber, 23 g pro.

Turkey Steaks with Apple and Maple Sauce ♥ 🔲

Serve these turkey tenderloins for two with prepared mashed sweet potatoes and steamed green beans.

Start to Finish: 20 minutes **Makes:** 2 servings

- 1   **turkey tenderloin steak or 2 skinless, boneless chicken breast halves (8 ounces)**
- 1   **tablespoon butter or margarine**
- 2   **tablespoons pure maple or maple-flavor syrup**
- 1   **tablespoon cider or wine vinegar**
- 1   **teaspoon Dijon-style mustard**
- ¹⁄₂   **teaspoon instant chicken bouillon granules**
- 1   **medium tart red apple, cored and thinly sliced Fresh sage (optional)**

1. If using turkey, cut tenderloin horizontally in half to make 2 steaks. In a medium skillet, melt butter over medium heat. Add turkey or chicken; cook for 8 to 10 minutes or until no longer pink (170°F), turning once halfway through cooking. Transfer to 2 plates, reserving drippings in the skillet. Cover to keep warm.

2. Stir maple syrup, vinegar, mustard, and bouillon granules into drippings in the skillet. Add the apple slices. Cook and stir over medium heat for 2 to 3 minutes or until the apple is tender. To serve, spoon the apple mixture over the turkey. If desired, garnish with sage.

Per serving: 264 cal., 7 g total fat (4 g sat. fat), 65 mg chol., 376 mg sodium, 23 g carbo., 2 g fiber, 26 g pro.

Layered Turkey Enchiladas

Whole-berry cranberry sauce adds a sweet-tart flavor to these 20-minute turkey enchiladas.

Start to Finish: 20 minutes **Oven:** 450°F
Makes: 4 servings

- 1   **tablespoon vegetable oil**
- 1   **pound turkey breast tenderloin, cut into bite-size strips**
- 1   **16-ounce package frozen (yellow, green, and red) peppers and onion stir-fry vegetables**
- 1   **10-ounce can enchilada sauce**
- ¹⁄₂   **cup canned whole-berry cranberry sauce Salt and ground black pepper**
- 9   **6-inch corn tortillas, halved**
- 1   **8-ounce package shredded Mexican-blend cheese (2 cups)**
     Lime wedges (optional)
     Cilantro sprigs (optional)

1. Position oven rack in the top third of the oven. Preheat oven to 450°F. In an extra-large skillet, heat oil over medium heat. Add turkey; cook about 4 minutes or until no longer pink. Add frozen vegetables, enchilada sauce, and cranberry sauce. Bring to boiling. Remove from heat. Sprinkle with salt and pepper.

2. In a 2-quart baking dish, layer one-third of the tortillas, then one-third of the cheese. Using a slotted spoon, layer half the turkey and vegetables. Layer one-third of the tortillas, one-third of the cheese, the remaining turkey and vegetables (with slotted spoon), and the remaining tortillas. Spoon on remaining sauce from skillet; sprinkle with remaining cheese.

3. Bake about 5 minutes or until cheese is melted. Cut in squares. If desired, serve with lime and cilantro.

Per serving: 615 cal., 25 g total fat (11 g sat. fat), 120 mg chol., 1,171 mg sodium, 52 g carbo., 6 g fiber, 45 g pro.

Layered Turkey Enchiladas

Sautéed Apple and Smoked Turkey Salad

The vinaigrette in this recipe is infused with nut flavor. Because nut oils are highly perishable, store them in the refrigerator.

Start to Finish: 30 minutes **Makes:** 4 servings

- 1   red or green crisp-tart apple
- 1   tablespoon butter or margarine
- 1   tablespoon pure maple or maple-flavor syrup
- ¼   cup fresh or dried cranberries
- 1   6- to 8-ounce package torn mixed salad greens
- 2   cups bite-size cubes smoked turkey (10 ounces)
- 2   ounces goat cheese, crumbled
       Apple Cider Vinaigrette
- 1   to 2 tablespoon coarsely chopped pecans or almonds, toasted, and/or snipped fresh chives

1. Core and thinly slice apple. In a large skillet, melt butter over medium heat. Stir in maple syrup. Add apple slices; cook for 6 to 8 minutes or until apple slices are golden on both sides and still slightly crispy, turning as needed. Stir in cranberries; set aside.

2. Arrange greens on a large platter. Top with turkey and apple mixture. Sprinkle with goat cheese. Drizzle with Apple Cider Vinaigrette. Sprinkle with toasted nuts.

Apple Cider Vinaigrette: In a small bowl, whisk together ½ cup cider vinegar, 2 tablespoons pure maple or maple-flavor syrup, 1 teaspoon grainy mustard, ¼ teaspoon salt, and ¼ teaspoon ground black pepper. Gradually whisk in ⅓ cup nut oil (such as pecan or almond). Use at once. Makes about 1 cup.

Per serving: 424 cal., 28 g total fat (7 g sat. fat), 53 mg chol., 1,107 mg sodium, 25 g carbo., 2 g fiber, 19 g pro.

Sautéed Apple and Smoked Turkey Salad

Creamy Turkey Dijon

Spicy Dijon mustard, garlic, and onions give new zing to an old favorite—turkey à la king.

Start to Finish: 35 minutes **Makes:** 4 servings

- 2   tablespoons all-purpose flour
- 2   tablespoons Dijon-style mustard
- 2   tablespoons dry white wine
- ½   teaspoon salt
- ⅛   teaspoon ground black pepper
- 1   cup half-and-half or light cream
- 1   tablespoon vegetable oil
- 1   clove garlic, minced
- 1   medium red or green sweet pepper, cut in thin bite-size strips
- ½   cup chopped onion (1 medium)
- 1½   cups sliced fresh mushrooms
- 12   ounces turkey breast tenderloin, cut in bite-size strips
- ¾   cup frozen peas, thawed
- 2   cups hot cooked noodles or fettuccine
       Fresh whole mushrooms (optional)
       Fresh basil sprigs (optional)

1. For sauce, in a small bowl, stir together flour, mustard, wine, salt, and black pepper. Slowly stir in half-and-half until well mixed; set aside.

2. In a wok or large skillet, heat oil over medium-high heat. (Add more oil as necessary during cooking.) Add garlic; cook and stir for 15 seconds. Add sweet pepper and onion; cook and stir for 2 minutes. Add sliced mushrooms; cook and stir about 2 minutes more or until tender yet firm. Remove vegetables from wok.

3. Add turkey to hot wok; cook and stir for 2 to 3 minutes or until no longer pink. Push turkey from center of wok.

4. Stir sauce. Add sauce to center of wok; cook and stir until thickened and bubbly. Return cooked vegetables to the wok. Add thawed peas. Stir all ingredients together to coat with sauce. Cook and stir for 1 to 2 minutes more or until heated through. Serve over hot cooked noodles. If desired, garnish with whole mushrooms and fresh basil.

Per serving: 388 cal., 13 g total fat (5 g sat. fat), 98 mg chol., 575 mg sodium, 35 g carbo., 4 g fiber, 30 g pro.

Quick Tip When a recipe calls for dry white wine, choose a Chardonnay, Chablis, Sauvignon Blanc, Pinot Grigio, or another white table wine. Riesling and Gewürztraminer contain a fair amount of sugar, which will give the dish a sweet, rather than savory, flavor.

Spiced Jerk Turkey
with Mango Salsa

Spiced Jerk Turkey
with Mango Salsa [one]

*The spicy-sweet salsa is also delicious served on grilled chicken,
steak, or fish.*

Start to Finish: 30 minutes **Makes:** 4 servings

- 4 **teaspoons Jamaican jerk seasoning**
- 1 **teaspoon ground cumin**
- ½ **teaspoon salt**
- ½ **teaspoon ground ginger**
- ⅛ **teaspoon cayenne pepper**
- 2 **tablespoons olive oil**
- 2 **cloves garlic, minced**
- 8 **turkey breast slices, cut ¼ to ⅜ inch thick**
  (about 1 pound)
- 1 **cup chopped, peeled mango, peeled peach,**
  or nectarine
- ¼ **cup finely chopped red sweet pepper**
- ¼ **cup finely chopped red onion**
- 2 **tablespoons snipped fresh cilantro**
- 1 **tablespoon fresh lime juice**
- 1 **teaspoon finely chopped, seeded fresh**
  serrano chile (see tip, page 22)
  Torn mixed salad greens

1. In a small bowl, combine Jamaican jerk seasoning, cumin,
   salt, ginger, and cayenne pepper; remove and set aside
   1 teaspoon of the cumin mixture. Add 1 tablespoon of
   the olive oil and the garlic to the remaining cumin
   mixture. Using your fingers, rub the cumin mixture
   evenly onto both sides of turkey slices. Set turkey aside.

2. For salsa, in a small bowl, combine mango, sweet pepper,
   onion, cilantro, lime juice, serrano chile, and the reserved
   1 teaspoon cumin mixture. Set salsa aside.

3. In a large skillet, heat the remaining 1 tablespoon olive
   oil over medium heat. Add half the turkey slices; cook for
   4 to 6 minutes or until turkey is no longer pink, turning
   once halfway through cooking. Repeat with remaining
   turkey slices. (Add more olive oil if necessary during
   cooking.) If desired, cut turkey in bite-size strips. Serve on
   salad greens; top with salsa.

Per serving: 243 cal., 8 g total fat (1 g sat. fat), 70 mg chol., 648 mg sodium,
13 g carbo., 3 g fiber, 30 g pro.

Parmesan-Crusted Fish, **page 131**

Salmon with Fresh Citrus Salsa, **page 119**

Chile-Lime Snapper, **page 125**

Cajun Snapper with Red Beans and Rice, **page 126**

Seafood Favorites

Fish and seafood are smart choices for meals in a flash. Fresh, light, healthful, and versatile, they cook quickly for a tasty, anytime dinner. Dressed up a bit, they can be an effortless special-occasion meal.

Dill-Baked Salmon

Serve this fresh dill-flavored salmon on a bed of basil-infused creamed spinach—yum!

Prep: 15 minutes **Bake:** 15 minutes **Oven:** 350°F
Makes: 4 servings

- 4 **5- to 6-ounce fresh or frozen salmon fillets**
- ¾ **teaspoon salt**
- ¼ **teaspoon ground black pepper**
- 2 **tablespoons fresh lemon juice**
- 1 **tablespoon snipped fresh dill**
- 4 **lemon slices**
- 2 **tablespoons butter or margarine**
- 3 **shallots, chopped**
- 1 **clove garlic, chopped**
- 2 **10-ounce packages fresh spinach**
- 2 **cups lightly packed basil**
- ¼ **cup whipping cream**

1. Thaw fish, if frozen. Preheat oven to 350°F. Place fish in baking pan. Mix salt and pepper; sprinkle half over fish. Sprinkle fish with lemon juice and dill; top with lemon slices. Bake about 15 minutes or until fish begins to flake when tested with a fork.

2. Meanwhile, in a large nonstick skillet, melt butter over medium heat. Add shallots and garlic; cook for 6 minutes. Add spinach and basil; cook for 8 minutes. Add whipping cream and the remaining salt mixture. Bring to boiling; boil for 4 minutes. Arrange spinach mixture on 4 plates. Top with salmon.

Per serving: 429 cal., 25 g total fat (9 g sat. fat), 138 mg chol., 601 mg sodium, 15 g carbo., 5 g fiber, 38 g pro.

Herb-Crusted Salmon with Roasted Pepper Cream

If you didn't know that this elegant dish called for only five ingredients and three simple steps, you'd guess by the flavor that it called for more.

Prep: 10 minutes **Bake:** 20 minutes **Cook:** 15 minutes
Oven: 400°F **Makes:** 4 servings

- 4 **5- to 6-ounce fresh or frozen skinless, boneless salmon fillets**
- 3 **tablespoons honey-Dijon mustard**
- 3 **tablespoons seasoned fine dry bread crumbs**
- ½ **cup chopped bottled roasted red sweet peppers, drained**
- 1 **cup whipping cream**

1. Thaw fish, if frozen. Preheat oven to 400°F. Brush 1 side of each fillet with 2 tablespoons of the mustard. Sprinkle with bread crumbs. Place fish, crumb sides up, in a 3-quart rectangular baking dish.

2. Bake, uncovered, for 20 to 25 minutes or until crumbs are golden and fish begins to flake when tested with a fork.

3. Meanwhile, for sauce, in a medium saucepan, combine the remaining 1 tablespoon mustard, roasted peppers, and cream. Bring to boiling; reduce heat. Boil gently, uncovered, about 15 minutes or until reduced to 1 cup. Serve sauce over fish.

Per serving: 576 cal., 32 g total fat (15 g sat. fat), 227 mg chol., 359 mg sodium, 11 g carbo., 0 g fiber, 57 g pro.

Maple Salmon with Greens, Edamame, and Walnuts

The main ingredients of this dish—salmon, edamame, and walnuts—are loaded with heart-healthy omega-3 fatty acids.

Start to Finish: 29 minutes **Makes:** 4 servings

- 4 **5- to 6-ounce fresh or frozen skinless salmon fillets, about 1 inch thick**
- 3 **tablespoons pure maple syrup**
- 2 **tablespoons balsamic vinegar**
- 1 **tablespoon fresh lemon juice**
- 1 **tablespoon Dijon-style mustard**
- 1 **tablespoon finely chopped shallot**
- ¼ **teaspoon kosher salt or salt**
- ¼ **teaspoon freshly ground black pepper**
- 2 **tablespoons olive oil**
- 2 **teaspoons snipped fresh rosemary**
- 1 **6-ounce package fresh baby spinach**
- ½ **cup cooked sweet soybeans (edamame)**
- ½ **cup red sweet pepper strips**
- ¼ **cup chopped walnuts, toasted**

1. Thaw fish, if frozen. In a small saucepan, combine maple syrup, vinegar, lemon juice, mustard, shallot, salt, and black pepper. Remove 2 tablespoons of maple syrup mixture. For dressing, in a small bowl, stir together the 2 tablespoons maple syrup mixture and the olive oil; set dressing aside.

2. For glaze, heat remaining maple syrup mixture to boiling; reduce heat. Simmer, uncovered, about 5 minutes or until syrupy. Remove from heat; stir in rosemary.

3. Preheat broiler. Place fish on the greased unheated rack of a broiler pan, tucking under thin edges. Brush fish with half of the glaze. Broil 6 to 7 inches from heat for 5 minutes. Turn fish over; brush with remaining glaze. Broil for 3 to 5 minutes more or until fish begins to flake when tested with a fork.

4. Meanwhile, in a large bowl, combine spinach, edamame, sweet pepper strips, and nuts. Drizzle spinach mixture with dressing; toss to coat. Arrange on 4 serving plates. Add a fillet to each plate.

Per serving: 460 cal., 28 g total fat (5 g sat. fat), 84 mg chol., 313 mg sodium, 18 g carbo., 3 g fiber, 33 g pro.

Seared Sesame Salmon 🔲

There's something so perfect about the combination of salmon and asparagus. Here they're served with a rich and creamy hollandaise sauce.

Start to Finish: 20 minutes **Makes:** 4 servings

- **4** **4- to 5-ounce fresh or frozen skinless salmon fillets, ³/₄ inch thick**
- **¹/₄** **cup seasoned fine dry bread crumbs**
- **2** **tablespoons sesame seeds**
- **1** **tablespoon soy sauce**
  Salt and ground black pepper
- **2** **to 3 tablespoons vegetable oil**
- **12** **ounces fresh asparagus spears, trimmed**
- **¹/₄** **cup bottled hollandaise or tartar sauce**

1. Thaw fish, if frozen. In a shallow dish, combine bread crumbs and sesame seeds; set aside.

2. Brush both sides of fish with soy sauce. Sprinkle lightly with salt and pepper. Coat fish with crumb mixture.

3. In an extra-large skillet, heat 2 tablespoons of the oil over medium heat. Add fish to hot oil in skillet. Cook for 4 minutes; turn fish over. Cook for 3 to 4 minutes more or until fish begins to flake when tested with a fork. Transfer fish to a serving platter; cover to keep warm.

4. Add remaining oil to skillet, if needed. Add asparagus; cook about 3 minutes or until crisp-tender, turning occasionally. Add asparagus to serving platter. Serve with hollandaise sauce.

Per serving: 347 cal., 23 g total fat (4 g sat. fat), 70 mg chol., 615 mg sodium, 9 g carbo., 2 g fiber, 26 g pro.

Salmon Steaks with Pistachios

Gingery Asian-style barbecue sauce flavors the vegetable accompaniment of stir-fried mushrooms, asparagus, and crunchy green onions.

Start to Finish: 25 minutes **Oven:** 450°F
Makes: 4 servings

- **4** **5- to 6-ounce fresh or frozen salmon steaks, cut ³/₄ inch thick, or 1 pound salmon, cut in serving-size pieces**
- **¹/₄** **cup finely chopped natural pistachios, toasted**
- **1** **tablespoon vegetable oil**
- **1** **pound asparagus, bias-sliced into 1-inch pieces**
- **4** **ounces shiitake mushrooms or button mushrooms, sliced (about 1¹/₂ cups)**
- **6** **green onions, cut in bite-size pieces (1 cup)**
  Barbecue Sauce

1. Thaw fish, if frozen. Preheat oven to 450°F. Place salmon in a greased shallow baking pan. Sprinkle with pistachios.

2. Bake for 8 to 12 minutes or until fish begins to flake when tested with a fork.

3. Meanwhile, in a skillet or wok, heat oil over medium-high heat. Add asparagus; cook and stir for 3 minutes. Add mushrooms and green onions. Cook and stir for 1 to 2 minutes or until the vegetables are crisp-tender. Stir in ¹/₂ cup of the Barbecue Sauce; heat through.

4. Spoon vegetable mixture on 4 plates; place salmon on top.

Per serving: 445 cal., 27 g total fat (5 g sat. fat), 78 mg chol., 304 mg sodium, 19 g carbo., 4 g fiber, 33 g pro.

Barbecue Sauce: In a covered container, combine ¹/₂ cup hoisin sauce; ¹/₂ cup honey; 3 tablespoons soy sauce; 2 to 3 tablespoons sesame seeds, toasted; 1 jalapeño, Asian, or other hot chile, diced (see tip, page 22); 4 teaspoons finely shredded orange peel, 2 teaspoons finely shredded lemon peel or 1¹/₂ teaspoons finely shredded lime peel; 1 tablespoon dry sherry; 1 tablespoon triple sec or Grand Marnier (optional); 1 teaspoon grated fresh ginger; 1 teaspoon dark sesame oil; and 1 clove garlic, minced. Mix well. Cover and refrigerate for up to 2 weeks. Use with fish, chicken, pork, or beef. Makes 3 cups.

Salmon with Matzo Crust 🔲

Look for matzo—unleavened flatbread—in the kosher section of supermarkets.

Start to Finish: 20 minutes **Oven:** 450°F
Makes: 4 servings

- **4** **4- to 5-ounce fresh or frozen skinless salmon fillets, 1 inch thick**
- **1¹/₂** **6-inch squares matzo (1¹/₂ ounces), broken up**
- **2** **tablespoons fresh dill or 1¹/₂ teaspoon dried dill**
- **¹/₂** **teaspoon salt**
- **¹/₄** **teaspoon ground black pepper**
- **3** **tablespoons olive or vegetable oil**
  Lemon wedges (optional)
  Fresh dill sprigs (optional)
  Steamed green beans (optional)

1. Thaw fish, if frozen. Preheat oven to 450°F. In a blender or food processor, combine matzo, the 2 tablespoons dill, the salt, and pepper. Cover; blend or process until coarse crumbs form. Transfer crumb mixture to a sheet of waxed paper or shallow dish.

2. Brush shallow baking pan with oil. Brush fish with oil. Roll in crumb mixture; place in prepared pan. Drizzle with remaining oil.

3. Bake, uncovered, for 10 to 12 minutes or until fish begins to flake when tested with a fork. If desired, serve with lemon wedges, fresh dill sprigs, and steamed green beans.

Per serving: 340 cal., 23 g total fat (4 g sat. fat), 67 mg chol., 358 mg sodium, 9 g carbo., 0 g fiber, 24 g pro.

Salmon with Matzo Crust

Salmon-Buckwheat
Noodle Bowl

Salmon-Buckwheat Noodle Bowl

Crushing the anise seeds releases oils, flavor, and aroma. Crush them with a mortar and pestle or by putting the seeds in a small plastic bag and crushing with a rolling pin.

Start to Finish: 30 minutes **Makes:** 4 servings

- 1 1/4 **pounds fresh or frozen skinless salmon fillets, about 1 inch thick**
- 1/4 **cup olive oil**
- 1/4 **cup balsamic vinegar**
- 1 1/2 **teaspoons cracked black pepper**
- 8 **ounces dried buckwheat (soba) noodles or whole wheat noodles**
- 2 **oranges, peeled, sectioned, and chopped**
- 1/3 **cup fresh orange juice**
- 1/2 **a red onion or 2 green onions, thinly sliced**
- 2 **teaspoons anise seeds, crushed**
- 1 **clove garlic, minced**

1. Thaw fish, if frozen. Cut fish in four portions. Preheat broiler. In a small bowl, combine 1 tablespoon of the olive oil, 1 tablespoon of the balsamic vinegar, and the cracked pepper. Place salmon on the unheated rack of a broiler pan. Brush both sides of fish with olive oil mixture. Broil 4 inches from the heat for 8 to 12 minutes or until fish begins to flake when tested with a fork.

2. Meanwhile, in a large saucepan, cook buckwheat noodles in boiling water about 4 minutes or until slightly chewy. (Cook whole wheat noodles for 8 to 10 minutes.) Drain; place in a large bowl. Add the remaining 3 tablespoons oil, the remaining 3 tablespoons vinegar, the chopped oranges, orange juice, onion, anise seeds, and garlic; toss to coat.

3. To serve, divide the noodle mixture among 4 bowls. Top each with a piece of salmon.

Per serving: 548 cal., 19 g total fat (3 g sat. fat), 74 mg chol., 549 mg sodium, 59 g carbo., 5 g fiber, 38 g pro.

Ancho-Glazed Salmon with Broiled Sweet Potato Fries

If you can't find ground ancho chile pepper at your supermarket, look for it at a Hispanic market. Try sprinkling it on hot chocolate—it's surprisingly good!

Start to Finish: 20 minutes **Makes:** 4 servings

- 4 **5- to 6-ounce fresh or frozen skinless salmon fillets**
- 2 **medium sweet potatoes**
- 1 **tablespoon sugar**

1   **teaspoon salt**

1   **teaspoon ground cumin**

1   **teaspoon ground ancho chile pepper or chili powder**
     Olive oil nonstick cooking spray

1   **tablespoon olive oil**

2   **tablespoons fresh cilantro sprigs (optional)**

1. Thaw fish, if frozen. Preheat broiler. If desired, halve sweet potatoes lengthwise. Cut lengthwise again into 1/4-inch slices. In a small bowl, combine sugar, salt, cumin, and chili powder. Place sweet potatoes on the greased rack of an unheated broiler pan; coat both sides of potato slices with cooking spray; sprinkle both sides with about half of the sugar mixture. Broil 4 inches from the heat about 10 minutes or until tender, turning once halfway through cooking.

2. Meanwhile, sprinkle fish with the remaining sugar mixture. In a large skillet, heat oil over medium heat. Add salmon; cook for 8 to 12 minutes or until fish begins to flake when tested with a fork, turning once halfway through cooking.

3. Serve salmon with sweet potato fries. If desired, garnish with cilantro.

Per serving: 363 cal., 19 g total fat (4 g sat. fat), 84 mg chol., 710 mg sodium, 17 g carbo., 2 g fiber, 29 g pro.

Easy Citrus Salmon Steaks ♥

Whichever citrus you choose—lemon or orange—zest it first, then juice it and use fresh juice for the best flavor.

Start to Finish: 18 minutes **Makes:** 2 servings

1   **8-ounce fresh or frozen salmon steak, cut 1 inch thick**

1   **teaspoon finely shredded lemon or orange peel**

1   **tablespoon fresh lemon or orange juice**

1   **clove garlic, minced**

1/8 **teaspoon ground black pepper**
     Nonstick cooking spray

1   **tablespoon sliced green onion (1)**

1   **medium orange, peeled and sliced crosswise**

1. Thaw fish, if frozen. In a small bowl, stir together lemon peel, lemon juice, garlic, and pepper.

2. Coat the unheated rack of a broiler pan with cooking spray. Place fish on rack. Brush with half the lemon juice mixture. Broil 4 inches from the heat for 5 minutes. Using a wide spatula, carefully turn fish. Brush with the remaining lemon juice mixture. Broil for 3 to 7 minutes more or until fish begins to flake when tested with a fork.

3. To serve, cut the fish in 2 portions and sprinkle with green onion. Serve with orange slices.

Per serving: 226 cal., 10 g total fat (2 g sat. fat), 70 mg chol., 54 mg sodium, 9 g carbo., 2 g fiber, 25 g pro.

Cold Roasted Salmon

This is a fabulous make-ahead dish for brunch or for dinner on a warm summer evening on the patio. Serve it with chilled white wine or Champagne.

Prep: 30 minutes **Bake:** 15 minutes **Chill:** 4 to 24 hours **Oven:** 475°F **Makes:** 6 servings

     Olive oil

6   **5- to 6-ounce fresh or frozen center-cut salmon fillets, skinned**

2   **tablespoons peppercorn or tarragon mustard**

6   **slices bacon, crisp-cooked, drained, and coarsely crumbled**

3   **ounces goat cheese (chèvre), crumbled**
     Snipped fresh chives (optional)

1. Thaw fish, if frozen. Preheat oven to 475°F. Lightly brush a 15×10×1-inch baking pan with olive oil. Arrange fish in prepared pan, tucking under any thin edges to make uniform thickness. Spread mustard on fillets.

2. Bake for 15 to 18 minutes or until fish begins to flake when tested with a fork. Transfer to plate; cover and refrigerate for at least 4 hours or up to 24 hours.

3. To serve, arrange fish on a serving plate. Sprinkle with bacon, goat cheese, and, if desired, chives.

Per serving: 407 cal., 26 g total fat (8 g sat. fat), 118 mg chol., 387 mg sodium, 1 g carbo., 0 g fiber, 40 g pro.

Roasted Salmon Sandwiches: Roast and chill fish as above. Spread 6 split French rolls with mayonnaise and mustard. Top with fish, bacon, goat cheese, and, if desired, chives. Makes 6 sandwiches.

Cold Roasted Salmon

Poached Salmon with Green Sauce

Mayonnaise serves as the base for a creamy herbed sauce to accompany the salmon. Use light mayo, if you like.

Start to Finish: 25 minutes **Makes:** 4 servings

- 5   5- to 6-ounce fresh or frozen salmon steaks, cut 1 inch thick
- 1   lemon, thinly sliced
- 2¼   teaspoons salt
- ¾   cup mayonnaise or salad dressing
- 3   tablespoons snipped fresh chives
- 3   tablespoons fresh parsley leaves
- 2   tablespoons fresh lemon juice
- ¼   teaspoon freshly ground black pepper
- 1   cucumber, peeled, seeded, and diced

1. Thaw fish, if frozen. Fill a large skillet with water to the depth of 1 inch. Add lemon and 2 teaspoons of the salt. Bring to boiling. Carefully add salmon to liquid; reduce heat to low. Simmer, covered, for 8 to 12 minutes or until fish begins to flake when tested with a fork.

2. Meanwhile, for green sauce, in a blender, combine mayonnaise, chives, parsley, lemon juice, the remaining ¼ teaspoon salt, and the pepper. Cover; blend until smooth. Transfer to a medium bowl; stir in cucumber.

3. Using a slotted spatula, transfer salmon to 4 plates. Serve with green sauce.

Per serving : 365 cal., 24 g total fat (3.5 g sat. fat), 103 mg chol., 497 mg sodium, 1 g carbo., 34 g pro.

Coriander-Crusted Salmon with Tropical Rice

Coriander-Crusted Salmon with Tropical Rice ♥

The taste of coriander is a bit like a cross between caraway and sage, with a lemon bite. In seed form, it makes a crisp crust for the fish. Crush the seeds with a mortar and pestle or by placing them in a small plastic bag and crushing with a rolling pin.

Prep: 15 minutes **Bake:** 4 minutes per ½-inch thickness **Oven:** 450°F **Makes:** 4 servings

- 1   1½-pound fresh or frozen salmon fillet
- 2   tablespoons coriander seeds, coarsely crushed
- 1   tablespoon packed brown sugar
- 1   teaspoon lemon-pepper seasoning
- 1   tablespoon butter or margarine, melted
- 2   cups cooked rice
- 1   medium mango, peeled, seeded, and chopped
- 1   tablespoon snipped fresh cilantro
- 1   teaspoon finely shredded lemon peel
    Finely shredded lemon peel (optional)
    Fresh cilantro sprigs (optional)

1. Thaw salmon, if frozen. Preheat oven to 450°F. Measure thickness of fish. Place fish, skin side down, in a greased shallow baking pan. In a small bowl, stir together coriander seeds, brown sugar, and lemon-pepper seasoning. Brush top and sides of fish with melted butter. Sprinkle fish with coriander mixture, pressing in slightly.

2. In a medium bowl, stir together rice, mango, the 1 tablespoon snipped cilantro, and the 1 teaspoon lemon peel. Spoon rice mixture around fish.

3. Bake, uncovered, until fish begins to flake when tested with a fork. (Allow 4 to 6 minutes per ½-inch thickness.) To serve, cut fish in 4 pieces. Serve fish on rice mixture. If desired, garnish with additional lemon peel and cilantro sprigs.

Per serving: 336 cal., 9 g total fat (2 g sat. fat), 31 mg chol., 406 mg sodium, 36 g carbo., 1 g fiber, 27 g pro.

Quick Tip If you crush or grind many spices from whole seeds, consider purchasing an electric spice grinder or coffee mill designated for grinding spices. After you use the grinder, clean it by grinding torn bits of soft white bread, which will pick up the remaining ground spices. If there are residual ground spices, use a clean, damp cloth to wipe out the grinder.

Salmon with Fresh Citrus Salsa ♥

Sweet and spicy jalapeño jelly does double duty here—to glaze the broiled salmon and to flavor the salsa.

Start to Finish: 20 minutes **Makes:** 4 servings

4   4- to 5-ounce fresh or frozen skinless salmon fillets,
      ³/₄ to 1 inch thick
      Salt and ground black pepper
¹/₃ cup red jalapeño jelly
3   medium oranges, peeled, seeded, and coarsely
      chopped
1   medium grapefruit, peeled and sectioned
1   cup grape or cherry tomatoes, halved

1. Thaw fish, if frozen. Preheat broiler. Sprinkle fish lightly
    with salt and pepper. Melt jelly in a small saucepan. Brush
    2 tablespoons of the melted jelly on fish. Place fish on the
    unheated rack of a broiler pan. Broil 4 inches from heat
    for 8 to 10 minutes or until fish begins to flake when
    tested with a fork.

2. Meanwhile, for fresh citrus salsa, in a medium bowl,
    combine orange, grapefruit, tomatoes, and the
    remaining jelly. Season to taste with salt and pepper.
    Serve fish with citrus salsa.

Per serving: 362 cal., 13 g total fat (3 g sat. fat), 67 mg chol., 223 mg sodium,
40 g carbo., 4 g fiber, 24 g pro.

Chipotle Salmon Tacos

Chipotle Salmon Tacos

Leftover chipotle peppers and sauce can be frozen in small containers in portions of 1 or 2 peppers. Thaw what you need next time you cook with them.

Prep: 10 minutes **Bake:** 18 minutes **Oven:** 450°F
Makes: 4 servings (2 tacos per serving)

- 1   **1¼-pound fresh or frozen salmon fillet, with skin**
- ¼   **teaspoon salt**
- 1   **canned chipotle pepper in adobo sauce, seeded, chopped, and mixed with 1 tablespoon adobo sauce**
- 8   **taco shells**
- 1   **11-ounce can whole kernel corn with sweet peppers**
- 1   **cup hot salsa**

1. Thaw fish, if frozen. Preheat oven to 450°F. Place fish, skin side down, in a 2-quart rectangular baking dish. Sprinkle with salt. Spread chipotle pepper and sauce over fish.

2. Bake about 18 minutes or until fish begins to flake when tested with a fork. Place taco shells in the oven the last 3 minutes of baking.

3. Meanwhile, in a small saucepan, heat corn over medium heat. Remove fish from oven; flake fish. Divide corn and fish among warm taco shells. Serve with salsa.

Per serving: 349 cal., 10 g total fat (2 g sat. fat), 66 mg chol., 1,079 mg sodium, 31 g carbo., 5 g fiber, 32 g pro.

Salmon with Wilted Greens ♥

The greens in this recipe—spinach, Swiss chard, radicchio, mustard, and collards—are partially cooked in this recipe. The hot dressing wilts the greens, increasing flavor.

Start to Finish: 21 minutes **Makes:** 4 servings

- 1   **pound fresh or frozen salmon steaks, cut ¾ inch thick**
- 3   **tablespoons orange juice concentrate**
- 3   **tablespoons water**
- 2   **tablespoons reduced-sodium soy sauce**
- 1   **tablespoon honey**
- 2   **teaspoons vegetable oil**
- 1   **teaspoon dark sesame oil**
- ½   **teaspoon grated fresh ginger or ¼ teaspoon ground ginger**
- 6   **cups torn mixed salad greens (such as spinach, Swiss chard, radicchio, mustard, and collard)**
- 1   **medium orange, peeled and sectioned**
- 1   **small red sweet pepper, cut in thin strips**

1. Thaw fish, if frozen. Preheat broiler. Cut fish in 4 pieces. Set aside.

2. For dressing, in a small bowl, combine orange juice concentrate, water, soy sauce, honey, vegetable oil, sesame oil, and ginger.

3. Place fish on the greased unheated rack of a broiler pan. Broil 4 inches from the heat for 6 to 9 minutes or until fish begins to flake when tested with a fork, brushing with 1 tablespoon of the dressing halfway through broiling. (Or grill fish on the greased rack of an uncovered grill directly over medium coals for 6 to 9 minutes, gently turning and brushing with 1 tablespoon of the dressing halfway through grilling.) Cover to keep warm while preparing the greens.

4. In a large bowl, combine greens and orange sections. In a large skillet, bring the remaining dressing to boiling. Boil gently, uncovered, for 1 minute. Add red pepper strips. Remove from heat. Pour over greens mixture; toss to coat.

5. To serve, divide the greens mixture among 4 plates. Top with the fish. Serve immediately.

Per serving: 281 cal., 14 g total fat (2 g sat. fat), 70 mg chol., 383 mg sodium, 14 g carbo., 5 g fiber, 27 g pro.

Quick Tip To section an orange, cut a slice off the top and bottom of the fruit to expose the flesh. Stand the orange on one end and cut down to the bottom of the fruit, removing pieces of peel as you cut. When the fruit is peeled, take a very thin knife and cut toward the center of the fruit on either side of the membranes, slipping the sections out. Work over a bowl to catch both the fruit and juice.

Salmon with
Wilted Greens

Seared Tuna with Citrus Relish ♥

Tuna has so little fat, it's easy to overcook and make dry—so watch it carefully. When tuna is perfectly cooked, it's still pink in the center.

Start to Finish: 30 minutes **Makes:** 4 servings

- 4 **4-ounce fresh or frozen tuna steaks, cut ¾ inch thick**
  Salt and ground black pepper
- 2 **teaspoons white wine vinegar**
- 2 **teaspoons soy sauce**
- ½ **teaspoon grated fresh ginger**
- 1 **tablespoon canola oil**
- 1 **medium grapefruit, peeled and coarsely chopped**
- 1 **medium orange, peeled and coarsely chopped**
- 2 **tablespoons finely chopped red onion**
- 2 **tablespoons snipped fresh cilantro**
- 2 **teaspoons canola oil**

1. Thaw fish, if frozen. Sprinkle fish with salt and pepper; set aside.

2. For citrus relish, in a medium bowl, combine vinegar, soy sauce, and ginger. Whisk in the 1 tablespoon canola oil. Gently stir grapefruit, orange, red onion, and cilantro into the vinegar mixture. Set relish aside.

3. In a large skillet, heat the 2 teaspoons canola oil over medium heat. Add fish; cook for 6 to 9 minutes or until fish begins to flake when tested with a fork, carefully turning once halfway through cooking. Serve with citrus relish.

Per serving: 210 cal., 7 g total fat (1 g sat. fat), 51 mg chol., 342 mg sodium, 9 g carbo., 2 g fiber, 28 g pro.

Tuna-Potato Cakes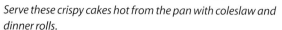

Serve these crispy cakes hot from the pan with coleslaw and dinner rolls.

Start to Finish: 18 minutes **Makes:** 4 servings

- 1 **cup packaged refrigerated mashed potatoes with garlic**
- 1 **12-ounce can tuna (water pack), drained and broken in chunks**
- ⅓ **cup seasoned fine dry bread crumbs**
- ½ **cup finely chopped celery (1 stalk)**
- ¼ **teaspoon ground black pepper**
- 2 **tablespoons vegetable oil**
- ¼ **cup bottled tartar sauce**

1. In a medium bowl, combine mashed potatoes, tuna, bread crumbs, celery, and pepper.

2. In a large skillet, heat oil over medium heat. Drop about ⅓ cup of the tuna-potato mixture into the hot oil; flatten to ½-inch-thick cake. Cook about 4 minutes or until browned. Carefully turn; cook about 4 minutes more. Serve with tartar sauce.

Per serving: 267 cal., 14 g total fat (2 g sat. fat), 22 mg chol., 621 mg sodium, 16 g carbo., 1 g fiber, 19 g pro.

Seared Tuna with Citrus Relish

California Tuna
Parmesan

California Tuna Parmesan

A simple lemon vinaigrette brightens the flavor of this fresh, light, and superhealthy main-dish salad.

Start to Finish: 20 minutes **Oven:** 450°F
Makes: 4 servings

4	**4-ounce fresh or frozen tuna steaks**
2	**lemons**
1/3	**cup olive oil**
1/2	**teaspoon freshly ground black pepper**
1/4	**teaspoon salt**
12	**ounces fresh asparagus spears, trimmed**
1	**5-ounce package mixed baby greens**
1/3	**cup finely shaved Parmesan cheese**

1. Thaw fish, if frozen. Preheat oven to 450°F. Finely shred 2 teaspoons peel from 1 lemon. Squeeze juice from lemon. For dressing, in a small bowl, whisk together olive oil, lemon peel and juice, pepper, and salt; set aside. Cut remaining lemon in wedges; set aside.

2. Place asparagus in a single layer in a shallow baking pan. Drizzle with 2 tablespoons of the dressing. Bake, uncovered, for 8 minutes.

3. Meanwhile, in a large skillet, heat 1 tablespoon of the dressing. Add fish; cook for 8 to 12 minutes or until browned and center is slightly pink, turning once halfway through cooking.

4. Divide greens among 4 plates; top with tuna and asparagus. Drizzle with remaining dressing. Sprinkle with Parmesan cheese; pass lemon wedges.

Per serving: 377 cal., 26 g total fat (5 g sat. fat), 48 mg chol., 312 mg sodium, 9 g carbo., 4 g fiber, 31 g pro.

Skillet Tuna and Noodles [one]

In the mood for tuna and noodles but don't have time to wait for a casserole to bake? Here's the ticket.

Prep: 20 minutes **Cook:** 10 minutes **Makes:** 4 servings

- 2 **cups dried rotini pasta**
- 2 **tablespoons butter or margarine**
- ½ **cup soft bread crumbs**
- 1 **tablespoon olive oil**
- ½ **cup chopped onion (1 medium)**
- ½ **cup chopped green sweet pepper**
- ⅓ **cup chopped celery**
- 1 **teaspoon dried herbes de Provence**
- ½ **teaspoon salt**
- 1¼ **cups half-and-half or light cream**
- 1 **12-ounce can chunk white tuna (water pack), drained and broken in chunks**
- 2 **tablespoons dry white wine (optional)**

1. Cook pasta following package directions; drain.

2. Meanwhile, in a large skillet, melt 1 tablespoon of the butter over medium heat; stir in bread crumbs to coat. Cook over medium heat about 3 minutes or until lightly browned, stirring occasionally. Remove from skillet and set aside.

3. In the same skillet, heat olive oil and the remaining 1 tablespoon butter over medium heat. Add onion, sweet green pepper, celery, dried herbs, and salt. Cook for 4 to 5 minutes or until vegetables are tender, stirring occasionally. Add half-and-half; heat just until bubbly. Reduce heat. Simmer, uncovered, about 5 minutes or until slightly thickened, stirring occasionally. Add cooked pasta, tuna, and, if desired, wine. Heat through. Just before serving, sprinkle with toasted bread crumbs.

Per serving: 453 cal., 21 g total fat (10 g sat. fat), 79 mg chol., 731 mg sodium, 37 g carbo., 2 g fiber, 28 g pro.

Roasted Red Snapper with Tomatoes and Feta Cheese ♥

The most familiar way to prepare snapper is Veracruz style—always with tomatoes and olives. The addition of feta cheese and oregano gives this version a Greek twist.

Start to Finish: 30 minutes **Oven:** 450°F
Makes: 4 servings

- 1 **pound fresh or frozen red or black snapper fillets, about 1 inch thick, or other firm white fish fillets**
- 1 **14.5-ounce can no-salt-added diced tomatoes, undrained**
- ½ **cup sliced green onions (4)**
- ¼ **cup thinly sliced celery**
- 2 **tablespoons fresh lemon juice**
- 1 **teaspoon dried oregano, crushed**
  Nonstick cooking spray
- ¼ **teaspoon ground black pepper**
- ¼ **teaspoon ground coriander**
- ¼ **cup crumbled feta cheese (1 ounce)**
- 2 **tablespoons sliced ripe olives**
  Fresh parsley sprigs (optional)

1. Thaw fish, if frozen. Preheat oven to 450°F. Cut fish in 4 pieces.

2. For sauce, in a large skillet, combine undrained tomatoes, green onions, celery, lemon juice, and oregano. Bring to boiling; reduce heat. Simmer, uncovered, about 15 minutes or until most of the liquid has evaporated.

3. Meanwhile, lightly coat a 2-quart rectangular baking dish with cooking spray. Place the fish in the dish, tucking under any thin edges to make uniform thickness. Sprinkle with pepper and coriander.

4. Bake, uncovered, for 8 to 10 minutes or until fish begins to flake when tested with a fork.

5. Transfer fish to 4 plates. Spoon sauce over fish. Sprinkle with feta cheese and olives. If desired, garnish with parsley.

Per serving: 169 cal., 4 g total fat (2 g sat. fat), 48 mg chol., 189 mg sodium, 7 g carbo., 1 g fiber, 26 g pro.

Broiled Red Snapper with Tomatoes, Olives, and Garlic ♥ [one]

Black snapper and farm-raised sea bass have firm flesh and are good choices for the grill. When the weather is calling you outdoors, cook this fish on the grill instead of the broiler, placing the fillets in a fish basket.

Start to Finish: 20 minutes **Makes:** 4 servings

- 4 **6-ounce fresh or frozen red or black snapper fillets with skin or other firm white fish fillets with skin**
- 1 **large tomato, cored, seeded, and chopped**
- ¼ **cup pitted kalamata olives, coarsely chopped**
- 1 **clove garlic, minced**
- 2 **teaspoons olive oil**
- ¼ **teaspoon salt**
- ¼ **teaspoon ground black pepper**
  Nonstick cooking spray
- ¼ **cup snipped Italian (flat-leaf) parsley**

1. Thaw fish, if frozen. Preheat broiler. In a small bowl, combine tomato, olives, garlic, olive oil, ⅛ teaspoon of the salt, and ⅛ teaspoon of the pepper. Set aside.

2. Coat the unheated rack of a broiler pan with cooking spray. Place fish, skin sides down, on the broiler pan. Sprinkle fish with the remaining salt and pepper.

Chile-Lime Snapper

3. Broil fish 4 inches from the heat for 5 minutes. Spoon the tomato mixture on the fillets. Broil for 3 to 4 minutes or until fish begins to flake when tested with a fork and tomatoes begin to brown slightly. Place lemon slice on each fillet; broil 1 minute more. Transfer fish to plates. Sprinkle with parsley.

Per serving: 224 cal., 7 g total fat (1 g sat. fat), 63 mg chol., 426 mg sodium, 5 g carbo., 1 g fiber, 34 g pro.

Chile-Lime Snapper 🔲one

Asian chili paste is a blend of ground chiles, garlic, oil, and salt. If your supermarket doesn't carry it, look for it at an Asian market.

Prep: 15 minutes **Cook:** 12 minutes **Makes:** 4 servings

- 4   **5- to 6-ounce fresh or frozen red snapper fillets, or other firm white fish fillets**
- 1/2 **teaspoon salt**
- 1/4 **teaspoon ground black pepper**
- 3   **tablespoons all-purpose flour**
- 1/2 **cup water**
- 2   **tablespoons fresh lime juice**
- 1   **tablespoon sugar**
- 1   **tablespoon Asian fish sauce**
- 1   **teaspoon Asian chili paste**
- 3   **tablespoons vegetable oil**
- 3   **green onions, sliced**
- 3   **cloves garlic, minced**
- 2   **cups hot cooked rice**

1. Thaw fish, if frozen. Sprinkle fish with salt and pepper. Place flour in a shallow dish. Coat both sides of fish with flour.

2. For sauce, in a small bowl, stir together water, lime juice, sugar, fish sauce, and chili paste.

3. In a large nonstick skillet, heat oil over medium heat. Add fish; cook about 10 minutes or until fish begins to flake when tested with a fork, turning once halfway through cooking. Transfer fish to a platter. Cover to keep warm.

4. Add green onions, garlic, and sauce to skillet. Bring to boiling; boil for 1 minute. Pour over fish. Serve fish with hot cooked rice.

Per serving: 455 cal., 12 g total fat (1 g sat. fat), 42 mg chol., 700 mg sodium, 55 g carbo., 1 g fiber, 29 g pro.

Cajun Snapper with Red Beans and Rice one

Red beans and rice was traditionally a long-simmered dish reserved for laundry day in New Orleans. This quick version—with pan-fried fish—is on the table in 20 minutes.

Start to Finish: 20 minutes **Makes:** 4 servings

- **2 10-ounce fresh or frozen red snapper fillets with skin or other firm white fish fillets with skin**
- **2 teaspoons Creole or Cajun seasoning**
- **1 14.8-ounce pouch cooked long grain rice**
- **1 15-ounce can red beans, rinsed and drained**
- **2 lemons**
- **2 tablespoons butter or margarine, melted**
  Snipped fresh Italian (flat-leaf) parsley (optional)

1. Thaw fish, if frozen. Cut fillets in half crosswise. Sprinkle fish with 1 teaspoon of the Creole seasoning. Heat an extra-large heavy nonstick skillet over medium-high heat. Add fish, skin sides up; cook for 4 minutes; turn. Cook for 2 to 4 minutes more or until fish begins to flake when tested with fork.

2. Meanwhile, in large microwave-safe bowl, combine rice, beans, and the remaining 1 teaspoon seasoning. Cover with vented plastic wrap. Microwave on 100% power (high) for 3 to 3½ minutes or until heated through, stirring twice.

3. Finely shred 2 teaspoons peel from one lemon; cut the remaining lemon into wedges.

4. Drizzle melted butter over fish; sprinkle with lemon peel and, if desired, parsley. Serve fish with rice and beans. Pass lemon wedges.

Per serving: 447 cal., 11 g total fat (4 g sat. fat), 68 mg chol., 1,055 mg sodium, 51 g carbo., 6 g fiber, 38 g pro.

Crispy Potato-Crusted Fish 🔲

Kids will love the crunchy fried potato-flake coating. Cut the fillets in tot-friendly strips to make fish sticks, if you like. Serve with green beans and mashed potatoes on the side.

Prep: 5 minutes **Cook:** 6 minutes **Makes:** 4 servings

4	**5- to 6-ounce fresh or frozen black snapper, tilapia, rockfish, or other firm white fish fillets**
½	**cup buttermilk**
2	**cloves garlic, minced**
¼	**teaspoon salt**
¼	**teaspoon ground black pepper**
¾	**cup instant potato flakes (not granules)**
1	**tablespoon butter or margarine**
4	**lemon wedges**

1. Thaw fish, if frozen. In a shallow dish, combine buttermilk, garlic, salt, and pepper. Place the potato flakes in another shallow dish. Dip the fish fillets into the buttermilk mixture, shaking off any excess liquid, then dip in potato flakes to coat.

2. In a large nonstick skillet, melt butter over medium-high heat. Add fish; cook for 6 to 10 minute or until fish is golden and begins to flake when tested with a fork. Serve with lemon wedges.

Per serving: 217 cal., 5 g total fat (2 g sat. fat), 61 mg chol., 299 mg sodium, 11 g carbo., 1 g fiber, 31 g pro.

Halibut with Creamy Dijon Sauce

Use coarse-ground or country-style Dijon mustard in the creamy mustard sauce for a pleasant crunch.

Start to Finish: 28 minutes **Makes:** 4 servings

1½	**pounds fresh or frozen halibut or sea bass steaks, about 1 inch thick**
1	**tablespoon butter or margarine, melted**
¼	**teaspoon onion salt**
¼	**teaspoon dried marjoram, crushed**
¼	**teaspoon dried thyme, crushed**
½	**cup sour cream**
1	**tablespoon all-purpose flour**
1	**tablespoon Dijon-style mustard**
⅛	**teaspoon salt**
⅛	**teaspoon ground black pepper**
⅛	**teaspoon dried thyme, crushed**
½	**cup chicken broth**
4	**cups shredded fresh spinach (5 ounces)**
½	**cup shredded carrot (1 medium)**
	Lemon wedges (optional)

1. Thaw fish, if frozen. Preheat broiler. Cut fish in 4 pieces, if necessary. Set aside.

2. For brushing sauce, in a small bowl, combine melted butter, onion salt, marjoram, and the ¼ teaspoon thyme.

3. Place fish steaks on the rack of an unheated broiler pan. Brush fish steaks with brushing sauce. Broil 4 inches from the heat for 5 minutes. Turn fish. Brush with remaining brushing sauce. Broil for 3 to 7 minutes more or until fish begins to flake when tested with a fork.

4. Meanwhile, for Dijon sauce, in a small saucepan, stir together sour cream, flour, mustard, salt, pepper, and the ⅛ teaspoon thyme. Add chicken broth, stirring until well mixed. Cook and stir over medium heat until mixture is thickened and bubbly. Cook and stir for 1 minute more. Keep warm.

5. In a large bowl, toss together spinach and carrot. Line 4 plates with the spinach mixture. Serve fish on spinach mixture. Top with Dijon sauce. If desired, garnish with lemon wedges.

Per serving: 281 cal., 12 g total fat (5 g sat. fat), 74 mg chol., 563 mg sodium, 4 g carbo., 3 g fiber, 37 g pro.

Quick Tip You can thaw frozen fish in the refrigerator—overnight or during the day. If you forget to take the fish out of the freezer, place it in a sealed plastic bag, then submerge in cool water until thawed, about 10 to 15 minutes. Cook the thawed fish immediately.

Halibut with Creamy Dijon Sauce

Halibut with Tomato-Basil Relish ♥

This summery, fresh relish is delicious on just about anything that comes off the grill—fish, chicken, or steak.

Start to Finish: 20 minutes **Makes:** 4 servings

- **4** **5- to 6-ounce fresh or frozen halibut, tuna, or salmon steaks, cut 1 inch thick**
- **1/2** **cup chopped tomato (1 medium)**
- **1** **tablespoon finely chopped red onion**
- **1** **tablespoon snipped fresh basil or 1/2 teaspoon dried basil, crushed**
- **2** **teaspoons olive oil**
- **2** **teaspoons red wine vinegar or cider vinegar**
- **1** **clove garlic, minced**
- **1/4** **teaspoon salt**
- **1/8** **teaspoon ground black pepper**
- **1** **tablespoon olive oil or vegetable oil**

1. Thaw fish, if frozen. For tomato-basil relish, in a small bowl, combine tomato, onion, basil, the 2 teaspoons olive oil, the vinegar, garlic, salt, and pepper. Set aside.

2. Brush fish with the 1 tablespoon olive oil. Place fish on the rack of an uncovered grill directly over medium heat. Grill for 8 to 12 minutes or until fish begins to flake with a fork, turning once halfway through grilling. Serve fish with tomato-basil relish.

Per serving: 245 cal., 10 g total fat (1 g sat. fat), 54 mg chol., 239 mg sodium, 2 g carbo., 0 g fiber, 36 g pro.

Halibut with Tomato-Basil Relish

Flounder with Zucchini Relish 🗓

The fish is flash-fried in a pan to create a nice crust, then finished in the oven. If you don't have two skillets, fry the fish in stages— transferring the first batch to a baking sheet in the oven while frying the second batch.

Prep: 10 minutes **Cook:** 5 minutes **Bake:** 4 minutes
Oven: 350°F **Makes:** 4 servings

- **4** **6- to 8-ounce fresh or frozen skinless flounder fillets**
- **1/4** **cup finely chopped onion (1 large)**
- **1** **medium zucchini, cut in 1/2-inch pieces**
- **1** **medium carrot, cut in 1/2-inch pieces**
- **1** **small jalapeño chile, finely chopped (see tip, page 22)**
- **1** **tablespoon white wine vinegar**
- **2** **tablespoons olive oil**
- **1/2** **teaspoon sugar**
- **3/4** **teaspoon salt**
- **1/4** **teaspoon freshly ground black pepper**
- **1/4** **teaspoon ground cumin**
- **4** **teaspoons olive oil**
  Tomato wedges (optional)

1. Thaw fish, if frozen. Preheat oven to 350°F.

2. For zucchini relish, place onion in a small strainer and rinse under cold running water. Drain well. Transfer to a medium bowl. Stir in zucchini, carrot, chile, vinegar, olive oil, sugar, and 1/4 teaspoon of the salt. Mix well; set aside.

3. Cut each fillet crosswise in half. In a small bowl, combine the remaining 1/2 teaspoon salt, the black pepper, and cumin. Sprinkle on both sides of fish. Heat 2 large nonstick ovenproof skillets over medium-high heat for 2 minutes. Add 2 teaspoons oil to each skillet and swirl to coat. Place 4 pieces of flounder, skinned sides down, in each skillet. Cook for 3 minutes; transfer skillets to oven. Bake, uncovered, for 4 to 5 minutes or until fish begins to flake when tested with a fork.

4. Using a flexible metal spatula, carefully transfer fish to 4 plates. Serve with zucchini relish. If desired, garnish with tomato wedges.

Per serving: 300 cal., 14 g total fat (2 g sat. fat), 95 mg chol., 602 mg sodium, 5 g carbo., 1 g fiber, 38 g pro.

Quick Tip When you use raw onion in salsas and relishes, first rinse the chopped onion in a small strainer under cold running water. Rinsing raw onion removes some of the pungency that can bring tears to the eyes as well as overwhelm the flavors of other ingredients it's mixed with. It's especially important to rinse white onions, which have a stronger flavor than yellow onions.

Baked Fish in White Wine

Baked Fish in White Wine ♥

This dish is equally good with hot cooked rice. Add the salt and butter to the cooking water—and use ground white pepper if you have it.

Prep: 10 minutes **Bake:** 17 to 18 minutes
Oven: 450°F **Makes:** 4 servings

4	4- to 5-ounce fresh or frozen flounder or sole fillets
	Nonstick spray coating
2	large tomatoes, seeded and chopped
1/3	cup dry white wine
3	tablespoons capers packed in oil, drained and chopped
3	tablespoons snipped fresh mint
1/2	teaspoon salt
1/4	teaspoon ground black pepper
4	slices lemon
1 1/2	cups couscous
1 1/2	cups water
4	tablespoons butter or margarine

1. Thaw fish, if frozen. Heat oven to 450°F. Coat a shallow baking pan just large enough to hold the fish with cooking spray.

2. In a medium bowl, gently stir together tomatoes, wine, capers, and mint. Set tomato mixture aside.

3. Sprinkle fish with 1/4 teaspoon of the salt and 1/8 teaspoon of the pepper. Place fish in the prepared pan. Spoon tomato mixture on fish. Place a lemon slice on each fillet.

4. Bake, uncovered, for 17 to 18 minutes or until fish begins to flake when tested with a fork.

5. Meanwhile, prepare couscous following package directions, using the water, 2 tablespoons of the butter, the remaining 1/4 teaspoon salt, and the remaining 1/8 teaspoon pepper.

6. Transfer fish to 4 plates. Divide couscous among the plates. Whisk the remaining 2 tablespoons butter into pan juices; spoon pan juices over couscous.

Per serving: 492 cal., 14 g total fat (8 g sat. fat), 98 mg chol., 599 mg sodium, 55 g carbo., 4 g fiber, 33 g pro.

Parmesan-Crusted Fish

Spinach-Stuffed Flounder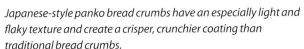

Assemble this dish the night before, then cover and refrigerate. If you make it ahead, complete it up to arranging the fish rolls in the baking dish. Add the tomatoes and season the fish right before baking and broiling.

Prep: 20 minutes **Bake:** 10 minutes **Broil:** 1 minute
Oven: 350°F **Makes:** 4 servings

- **4 6-ounce fresh or frozen flounder fillets**
- **1 10-ounce package frozen chopped spinach, thawed and drained**
- **3 tablespoons seasoned fine dry bread crumbs**
- **3 tablespoons grated Parmesan cheese**
- **1 14.5-ounce can diced tomatoes, undrained**
   Salt and ground black pepper

1. Thaw fish, if frozen. Preheat oven to 350°F. In a medium bowl, combine spinach, 2 tablespoons of the bread crumbs, and 2 tablespoons of the Parmesan cheese. Spread mixture evenly among the fish fillets; roll up. Place fish rolls, seam sides down, in a baking dish. Spoon undrained tomatoes around fish on bottom of dish. Lightly sprinkle fish rolls with salt and pepper.

2. Bake, uncovered, about 10 minutes or until fish begins to flake when tested with a fork. Change oven to broiler setting. In a small bowl, combine the remaining 1 tablespoon bread crumbs and the remaining 1 tablespoon Parmesan cheese. Sprinkle on fish rolls. Broil for 1 to 2 minutes or until topping is golden.

Per serving: 230 cal., 4 g total fat (1 g sat. fat), 85 mg chol., 742 mg sodium, 11 g carbo., 3 g fiber, 37 g pro.

Parmesan-Crusted Fish ♥

Japanese-style panko bread crumbs have an especially light and flaky texture and create a crisper, crunchier coating than traditional bread crumbs.

Start to Finish: 20 minutes **Oven:** 450°F
Makes: 4 servings

- **4 fresh or frozen skinless cod fillets**
   Nonstick cooking spray
   Salt and ground black pepper
- **¹⁄₃ cup panko (Japanese-style) bread crumbs**
- **¹⁄₄ cup finely shredded Parmesan cheese (1 ounce)**
- **¹⁄₂ cup water**
- **1 10-ounce package shredded fresh carrots (3 cups)**
- **1 tablespoon butter or margarine**
- **³⁄₄ teaspoon ground ginger**
   Mixed salad greens (optional)

1. Thaw fish, if frozen. Preheat oven to 450°F. Lightly coat a baking sheet with cooking spray. Measure thickness of fish. Arrange fish on baking sheet. Sprinkle lightly with salt and pepper. In a small bowl, stir together bread crumbs and Parmesan cheese. Sprinkle on fish.

2. Bake, uncovered, until crumbs are golden and fish begins to flake when tested with a fork. Allow 4 to 6 minutes per ¹⁄₂-inch thickness of fish.

3. Meanwhile, in a large skillet, bring water to boiling. Add carrots; reduce heat to medium. Cook, covered, 5 minutes. Uncover and cook about 2 minutes or until water is evaporated. Add butter and ginger; toss until butter is melted and carrots are coated. Season with salt and pepper. Serve fish with carrot mixture and, if desired, greens.

Per serving: 233 cal., 6 g total fat (3 g sat. fat), 84 mg chol., 407 mg sodium, 11 g carbo., 2 g fiber, 34 g pro.

Roasted Cod with Peppers and Potatoes

Roasting turns the garlic into a soft and creamy—and much mellowed—flavoring for the sweet peppers.

Prep: 10 minutes **Roast:** 15 minutes **Oven:** 450°F
Makes: 4 servings

- **1³⁄₄ pounds fresh or frozen center-cut cod fillets with skin**
- **1 pound fingerling or small red potatoes, halved**
- **1 yellow sweet pepper, cut in 1-inch-wide strips**
- **1 red sweet pepper, cut in 1-inch-wide strips**
- **4 garlic cloves, skins on**
- **4 tablespoons olive oil**
- **1 teaspoon salt**
- **¹⁄₂ teaspoon freshly ground pepper**
- **3 sprigs fresh rosemary**
   Lemon wedges

1. Thaw fish, if frozen. Cut fish in 4 pieces. Adjust rack in lower third of oven. Preheat oven to 450°F.

2. In a 15×10×1-inch baking pan, arrange potatoes, sweet peppers, and garlic. Toss with 2 tablespoons of the olive oil, ¹⁄₄ teaspoon of the salt, and ¹⁄₄ teaspoon of the pepper. Roast for 15 to 20 minutes or until potatoes are tender and sweet peppers are browned. Transfer sweet peppers and garlic to a cutting board. Squeeze garlic out of skin; finely chop garlic and sweet peppers. Toss potatoes with 1 tablespoon of the oil. Cover with foil to keep warm.

3. Meanwhile, sprinkle both sides of fish with the remaining ³⁄₄ teaspoon salt and ¹⁄₄ teaspoon pepper. In a large ovenproof skillet, heat the remaining 1 tablespoon oil over medium-high heat. Add fish, skin sides down, and cook for 2 to 3 minutes or until skin is crisp and golden brown. Arrange rosemary on fish. Transfer skillet to oven; roast for 3 minutes. Turn fish; roast about 3 minutes more or until fish begins to flake when tested with a fork.

4. Spoon sweet pepper mixture on each fillet. Serve with potatoes and lemon wedges.

Per serving: 375 cal., 15 g total fat (2 g sat. fat), 78 mg chol., 691 mg sodium, 24 g carbo., 3 g fiber, 35 g pro.

Cod Fillets Adobo ♥

Give these supersimple fillets a smoky touch by using smoked paprika in place of regular paprika. Smoked paprika comes in sweet and hot varieties.

Prep: 5 minutes **Broil:** 5 minutes **Chill:** 20 minutes
Makes: 4 servings

- **4** **5-ounce fresh or frozen cod fillets**
- **2** **tablespoons vegetable oil**
- **2** **tablespoons lemon juice**
- **³/₄** **teaspoon paprika**
- **³/₄** **teaspoon dried oregano**
- **¹/₄** **teaspoon ground cumin**
- **¹/₄** **teaspoon salt**
- **¹/₈** **teaspoon ground black pepper**

1. Thaw fish, if frozen. In a small bowl, combine oil, lemon juice, paprika, oregano, cumin, salt, and pepper. Brush mixture on both sides of fish. Place fish in pie plate. Cover and chill for 20 minutes.

2. Preheat broiler. Place fish on the unheated rack of a broiler pan. Broil 4 inches from heat for 5 to 7 minutes or until fish begins to flake when tested with a fork.

Per serving: 178 cal., 8 g total fat (1 sat fat) 60 mg chol., 222 mg sodium, 1 g carbo., 0 g fiber, 25 g pro.

Quick Tip Marinate the fish no longer than 20 minutes. Longer than that and the acid in the lemon juice will begin to cook the fish and make it mushy.

Citrus-Baked Sea Bass ♥

To keep the other half of the avocado fresh, sprinkle the cut surface with lime juice. Wrap and store in the refrigerator.

Prep: 10 minutes **Bake:** 12 minutes **Oven:** 400°F
Makes: 4 servings

- **4** **4- to 5-ounce fresh or frozen sea bass fillets**
- **¹/₄** **teaspoon salt**
- **¹/₈** **teaspoon freshly ground black pepper**
- **1** **red onion, cut in half**
- **1** **lime, cut in half**
- **2** **oranges**
- **¹/₂** **ripe avocado, peeled and cubed**
- **¹/₂** **cup finely chopped jicama**
- **1** **tablespoon snipped fresh cilantro**
- **1** **teaspoon finely chopped fresh jalapeño chile (see tip, page 22)**

1. Thaw fish, if frozen. Preheat oven to 400°F. Sprinkle fish with ¹/₈ teaspoon of the salt and the pepper. Place fish in a glass baking dish. Cut one onion half into thin slices. Cut one lime half into thin slices. Arrange onion and lime slices on each fillet. Bake, uncovered, for 12 to 15 minutes or until fish begins to flake when tested with a fork.

2. Meanwhile, peel oranges and remove white membranes. Cut into segments, then cut each segment in half. Transfer orange pieces to a medium bowl. Finely chop 1 tablespoon onion from the remaining onion half and squeeze 1 tablespoon lime juice from the remaining lime half; add to orange pieces. Gently stir in avocado, jicama, cilantro, jalapeño chile, and the remaining ¹/₈ teaspoon salt. Serve with baked fish.

Per serving: 225 cal., 7 g total fat (2 g sat. fat), 52 mg chol., 238 mg sodium, 18 g carbo., 4 g fiber, 25 g pro.

Citrus-Baked Sea Bass

Sea Bass with Hot Chili Oil

Sea Bass with Hot Chili Oil ♥ 🔲

An everyday kitchen tool—a vegetable peeler—cuts elegant carrot ribbons for this Asian-style fish dish. Serve jasmine rice as a side dish.

Start to Finish: 25 minutes **Makes:** 4 servings

1¼	**pounds fresh or frozen sea bass fillets**
2	**medium carrots**
5	**cups shredded cabbage**
2	**tablespoons water**
1	**tablespoon fresh lemon juice**
½	**teaspoon salt**
¼	**teaspoon ground black pepper**
2	**to 3 teaspoons chili oil**
2	**teaspoons grated fresh ginger**
2	**cloves garlic, minced**

1. Thaw fish, if frozen. Cut in 4 pieces; set aside. Using a vegetable peeler, cut the carrots in long thin ribbons (about 1 cup). In an extra-large skillet, combine the carrot ribbons, cabbage, water, lemon juice, ¼ teaspoon of the salt, and the pepper.

2. Sprinkle fish with the remaining ¼ teaspoon salt. In a small bowl, stir together the chili oil, ginger, and garlic; spread on fish. Place fish on vegetable mixture in skillet.

3. Bring mixture in skillet to boiling; reduce heat. Simmer, covered, for 9 to 12 minutes or until fish begins to flake when tested with a fork. Transfer fish and vegetable mixture to plates. Serve immediately.

Per serving: 196 cal., 5 g total fat (1 g sat. fat), 58 mg chol., 415 mg sodium, 9 g carbo., 3 g fiber, 28 g pro.

Mahi Mahi with Black Bean
and Avocado Relish

Mahi Mahi with Black Bean and Avocado Relish ♥

Serve this Mexican-style fish dish with warmed flour tortillas or wedges of crusty flatbread.

Prep: 20 minutes **Grill:** 4 to 6 minutes per ¹/₂-inch thickness **Makes:** 4 servings

- 1 **pound fresh or frozen skinless mahi mahi fillets**
- 2 **tablespoons snipped fresh cilantro**
- 2 **tablespoons snipped fresh oregano**
- ¹/₂ **teaspoon finely shredded lime peel**
- 2 **tablespoons lime juice**
- 1 **tablespoon olive oil**
- 1 **to 2 cloves garlic, minced**
- ¹/₄ **to ¹/₂ teaspoon bottled hot pepper sauce**
- 1 **15-ounce can black beans, rinsed and drained**
- 1 **medium avocado, halved, seeded, peeled, and chopped**
  Salt and ground black pepper

1. Thaw fish, if frozen. In a small bowl, combine cilantro, oregano, lime peel, lime juice, olive oil, garlic, and hot pepper sauce. For relish, in a medium bowl, combine drained beans and avocado; stir in half the cilantro mixture. Cover and refrigerate until ready to serve.

2. Measure thickness of fish; sprinkle with salt and pepper. Brush remaining cilantro mixture on both sides of fish. Place fish on the greased rack of an uncovered grill. Grill fish directly over medium heat until fish begins to flake when tested with a fork, turning once halfway through grilling. Allow for 4 to 6 minutes per ¹/₂-inch thickness.

3. To serve, cut fish in serving-size pieces. Divide three-fourths of the relish among 4 plates. Arrange fish on relish; spoon the remaining relish over fish.

Per serving: 255 cal., 10 g total fat (1 g sat. fat), 83 mg chol., 369 mg sodium, 18 g carbo., 6 g fiber, 29 g pro.

Fish Fillets with Baby Spinach, Red Pepper, and Onion Wedges ♥ 🔲

Baby spinach is an ideal ingredient for quick cooking—it doesn't have to be stemmed.

Prep: 20 minutes **Cook:** 15 minutes **Makes:** 4 servings

- 1 **pound fresh or frozen mahi mahi or cod fillets, ³/₄ to 1 inch thick**
- 4 **cups chopped fresh baby spinach**
- 3 **tablespoons olive oil or vegetable oil**
- 1 **medium onion, cut in thin wedges**
- 4 **tablespoons red jalapeño jelly**
- 1 **small red or yellow sweet pepper, cut in thin strips**
- ¹/₄ **teaspoon salt**
- ¹/₄ **teaspoon ground black pepper**
- 1 **tablespoon balsamic vinegar**

1. Thaw fish, if frozen. Place spinach in a large bowl; set aside. In a large skillet, heat 1 tablespoon of the oil over medium heat. Add onion; cook until tender and slightly golden, stirring occasionally. Stir in 1 tablespoon of the jalapeño jelly. Add sweet pepper; cook and stir for 1 minute more. Remove from heat. Stir onion mixture into spinach; cover and set aside. Wipe skillet clean.

2. Meanwhile, cut fish in 4 pieces. Sprinkle fish with salt and black pepper. In the same large skillet, heat remaining 2 tablespoons oil over medium-high heat. Add fish; cook 2 minutes on each side. Reduce heat to medium; cook about 5 minutes more or until fish begins to flake when tested. Transfer fish to serving platter; cover to keep warm.

3. Add remaining 3 tablespoons jalapeño jelly to skillet. Cook and stir until melted; spoon on fish. Toss spinach mixture with vinegar. Serve with fish.

Per serving: 241 cal., 9 g total fat (1 g sat. fat), 83 mg chol., 275 mg sodium, 18 g carbo., 2 g fiber, 22 g pro.

Baked Haddock with Mushroom Sauce ♥

If you have the time, substitute a little bit of freshly grated lemon peel and black pepper for the lemon-pepper seasoning.

Prep: 10 minutes **Bake:** 4 to 6 minutes per ¹/₂-inch thickness **Oven:** 450°F **Makes:** 4 servings

- 1 **pound fresh or frozen haddock or cod fillets**
  Lemon-pepper seasoning
- 1 **tablespoon butter or margarine**
- 2 **cups sliced fresh mushrooms**
- ¹/₃ **cup sliced green onions (2 to 3)**
- ¹/₃ **cup chicken broth**
- ¹/₄ **cup dry white wine or chicken broth**
- 2 **teaspoons cornstarch**

1. Thaw fish, if frozen. Preheat oven to 450°F. Cut fish in 4 pieces. Measure thickness of fish. Place fish in a 2-quart rectangular baking dish, tucking under thin edges to make uniform thickness. Sprinkle with lemon-pepper.

2. Bake, uncovered, until fish begins to flake when tested with a fork. (Allow 4 to 6 minutes per ¹/₂-inch thickness.)

3. Meanwhile, for mushroom sauce, in a small saucepan, melt butter over medium heat. Add mushrooms and green onions; cook until tender. In a small bowl, stir together chicken broth, wine, and cornstarch; add to mushroom mixture. Cook and stir until mixture is thickened and bubbly; cook and stir for 2 minutes more.

4. Transfer fish to 4 plates; spoon mushroom sauce on fish.

Per serving: 200 cal., 8 g total fat (2 g sat. fat), 44 mg chol., 323 mg sodium, 9 g carbo., 1 g fiber, 19 g pro.

Swordfish with Cucumber Sauce 🖤

The cucumber-yogurt sauce is a simplified version of tzatziki (dzah-DZEE-kee), a Greek dipping sauce served with pita bread or on gyros. Add a clove of minced garlic, salt, and a squeeze of fresh lemon juice, if you like.

Prep: 10 minutes **Grill:** 6 minutes **Makes:** 4 servings

- 2 **8-ounce fresh or frozen swordfish or halibut steaks, cut ³/₄ inch thick**
- ¹/₃ **cup plain low-fat yogurt**
- ¹/₄ **cup finely chopped cucumber**
- 1 **teaspoon snipped fresh mint or dill or ¹/₄ teaspoon dried mint, crushed, or dried dill**
  Nonstick cooking spray

1. Thaw fish, if frozen. Cut each fish steak in half. For cucumber sauce, in a small bowl, stir together yogurt, cucumber, and mint. Cover and chill until serving time.

2. Coat an unheated grill rack with cooking spray. Place fish on grill rack over medium-high heat. Grill for 6 to 9 minutes or until fish is lightly browned. Turn and grill for 2 to 3 minutes more or until fish flakes easily when tested with a fork. Serve fish with cucumber sauce.

Per serving: 149 cal., 5 g total fat (1 g sat. fat), 44 mg chol., 116 mg sodium, 2 g carbo., 0 g fiber, 24 g pro.

Sesame-Coated Tilapia Salad

Brush the fillets with honey-Dijon salad dressing for flavor and to help the sesame seeds stick to the fish.

Start to Finish: 20 minutes **Makes:** 4 servings

- 1 **pound fresh or frozen tilapia fillets**
- ¹/₄ **cup all-purpose flour**
- ¹/₄ **cup sesame seeds**
- ¹/₂ **teaspoon ground black pepper**
- ²/₃ **cup bottled honey-Dijon salad dressing**
- 2 **tablespoons vegetable oil**
- 1 **5-ounce package baby spinach and red leaf lettuce or baby spinach with radicchio**

1. Thaw fish, if frozen. Cut fish in 4 pieces. In a shallow bowl, combine flour, sesame seeds, and pepper. Transfer 2 tablespoons of the salad dressing to a small bowl. Brush all sides of the fish pieces with the 2 tablespoons dressing. Firmly press both sides of each fish piece into sesame mixture.

2. In an extra-large skillet, heat oil over medium heat. Add fish; cook about 6 minutes or until fish begins to flake when tested with a fork, turning once halfway through cooking.

3. Divide spinach mixture among 4 plates; top each with fish. Drizzle with the remaining salad dressing.

Per serving: 418 cal., 30 g total fat (3 g sat. fat), 0 mg chol., 247 mg sodium, 16 g carbo., 4 g fiber, 22 g pro.

Tilapia with Ginger-Marinated Cucumbers 🖤

A brief soak in vinegar, sugar, ginger, and salt quickly turns the cucumbers into Asian-style pickles to serve with the broiled fish.

Start to Finish: 20 minutes **Makes:** 4 servings

- 4 **4-ounce fresh or frozen tilapia fillets, ¹/₂ to ³/₄ inch thick**
- ¹/₂ **cup cider vinegar**
- ¹/₄ **cup packed brown sugar**
- 2 **teaspoons grated fresh ginger**
- ¹/₂ **teaspoon salt**
- 3¹/₂ **cups sliced cucumbers (2 medium)**
- 2 **tablespoons coarsely chopped fresh mint**
  Nonstick cooking spray
- 1 **6-ounce container plain yogurt**
- 1 **teaspoon packed brown sugar**
  Strips of lemon peel and lemon wedges (optional)
  Cracked peppercorns (optional)

1. Thaw fish, if frozen. Preheat broiler. In a medium bowl, combine vinegar, the ¹/₄ cup brown sugar, the ginger, and salt; stir until sugar is dissolved. Remove ¹/₄ cup of the mixture. Add cucumbers and 1 tablespoon of the mint to the remaining mixture in bowl; toss to coat and set aside.

2. Lightly coat the rack of an unheated broiler pan with cooking spray. Place fish on rack. Brush the ¹/₄ cup vinegar mixture on the fish. Broil 4 inches from the heat for 4 to 6 minutes or until fish begins to flake when tested with a fork.

3. Meanwhile, in another small bowl, combine yogurt, the remaining 1 tablespoon mint, and the 1 teaspoon brown sugar.

4. Using a slotted spoon, place cucumbers on 4 plates. Top with fish and yogurt mixture. If desired, garnish with lemon peel, lemon wedges, and cracked peppercorns.

Per serving: 210 cal., 3 g total fat (1 g sat. fat), 59 mg chol., 388 mg sodium, 23 g carbo., 0 g fiber, 26 g pro.

Tilapia with Ginger-Marinated Cucumbers

Pecan-Cornmeal Fried Catfish

Like your catfish nice and spicy? Add a little more cayenne to the breading—then serve the fish with a creamy bottled rémoulade to cool the fire.

Prep: 20 minutes **Cook:** 4 minutes per batch
Oven: 300°F **Makes:** 6 servings

- 1½ **pounds fresh or frozen catfish fillets**
- ¾ **cup ground pecans or peanuts**
- ⅔ **cup yellow cornmeal**
- ¾ **teaspoon salt**
- ¼ **teaspoon ground black pepper**
- ¼ **teaspoon cayenne pepper**
- ¼ **cup milk**
- 1 **egg, lightly beaten**
  Vegetable oil for deep-fat frying

1. Thaw fish, if frozen. Preheat oven to 300°F. Cut fish in 6 pieces, if necessary.

2. In a shallow dish, combine pecans, cornmeal, salt, black pepper, and cayenne pepper. In another shallow dish, combine milk and egg.

3. Dip each fish piece into milk mixture; then dip into nut mixture to coat.

4. Meanwhile, in a large heavy saucepan or deep fryer, heat 2 inches of oil to 375°F. Fry fish in hot oil, 1 or 2 pieces at a time, about 2 minutes on each side or until golden brown. Carefully remove with a slotted spoon; drain on paper towels. Keep warm in oven while frying the remaining fish.

Per serving: 397 cal., 28 g total fat (4 g sat. fat), 89 mg chol., 367 mg sodium, 15 g carbo., 2 g fiber, 21 g pro.

Pecan-Cornmeal Fried Catfish

Trout Amandine

"Amandine" is a French term that refers to a garnish of sliced almonds. This buttery combination of trout and almonds has been a favorite for generations.

Prep: 10 minutes **Cook:** 4 minutes per batch
Oven: 250°F **Makes:** 6 servings

- 6 **4- to 6-ounce fresh or frozen trout fillets with skin**
- 1½ **cups all-purpose flour**
- 12 **tablespoons butter**
- 1 **tablespoon fresh lemon juice**
- 1½ **cups sliced almonds, toasted**
- 6 **lemon wedges**

1. Thaw fish, if frozen. Heat oven to 250°F. Dip each fillet in flour, shaking off excess. In an extra-large skillet, heat 3 tablespoons of the butter over medium-high heat until bubbly. Add 3 fillets, skin sides down; cook for 2 to 3 minutes or until golden brown and skin is crisp. Turn and cook for 2 to 3 minutes more or until fish begins to flake when tested with a fork. Transfer fish to a platter; keep warm in oven.

2. Wipe out skillet. Melt 3 tablespoons butter in skillet and repeat cooking with remaining fish.

3. In a small saucepan, melt the remaining 6 tablespoons butter on medium heat. Stir in lemon juice. Sprinkle almonds over fish on platter. Drizzle with butter mixture. Serve with lemon wedges.

Per serving: 600 cal., 41 g total fat (14.5 g sat. fat), 134 mg chol., 272 mg sodium, 22 g carbo., 2 g fiber, 37 g pro.

Prosciutto-Wrapped Trout

Smoked sea salt gives this dish an outdoorsy, cooked-over-an-open-flame flavor—even when it's grilled inside. Look for smoked sea salt at gourmet shops and specialty food stores. If you can't find it, regular sea salt works well.

Prep: 20 minutes **Cook:** 10 minutes **Makes:** 4 servings

- 4 **fresh or frozen skinless trout, flounder, or catfish fillets, about ¼ inch thick, or 2 fresh or frozen orange roughy or cod fillets, ½ inch thick**
- 4 **2-inch sprigs fresh rosemary or 2 teaspoons dried rosemary, crushed**
- 4 **slices thinly sliced prosciutto or thinly sliced cooked ham**
- 3 **tablespoons fresh lemon juice**
  Freshly ground black pepper
- 2 **medium plum tomatoes**
  Olive oil
- 1 **19-ounce can cannellini (white kidney) beans, rinsed and drained**
- 1 **tablespoon olive oil**

Prosciutto-Wrapped Trout

1 **clove garlic, minced**
2 **teaspoons snipped fresh rosemary or ½ teaspoon dried rosemary, crushed**
¼ **teaspoon smoked sea salt, crushed, or ⅛ teaspoon salt**

1. Thaw fish, if frozen. Cut each fillet in half crosswise. If using trout, flounder, or catfish, place rosemary sprigs on half the pieces (or sprinkle with dried rosemary) and top with remaining pieces to make 4 stacks. (If using roughy or cod, place a rosemary sprig on each fillet half or sprinkle with the 2 teaspoons dried rosemary.) Wrap 1 slice of prosciutto around fish and rosemary. Sprinkle with 1 tablespoon of the lemon juice and the pepper; set aside.

2. Heat a nonstick or well-seasoned grill pan on stovetop over medium heat until hot. Meanwhile, cut tomatoes in half lengthwise. Brush tomatoes lightly with olive oil.

Add tomato halves to grill pan, cut sides down. Cook for 6 to 8 minutes or until very tender, turning once. Remove tomatoes from grill; set aside to cool slightly.

3. Place the fish fillets on grill pan, rosemary sprig sides up. Cook for 4 to 6 minutes or until fish begins to flake when tested with a fork, turning once halfway through cooking.

4. Coarsely chop grilled tomatoes. In a medium bowl, gently toss together tomato, the remaining 2 tablespoons lemon juice, the beans, the 1 tablespoon olive oil, garlic, the 2 teaspoons snipped rosemary, and salt. Serve fish with bean mixture.

Per serving: 332 cal., 15 g total fat (3 g sat. fat), 77 mg chol., 731 mg sodium, 21 g carbo., 7 g fiber, 36 g pro.

Spicy Jalapeño Shrimp Pasta ♥

Tail-on shrimp looks pretty, but the shrimp may be easier to eat in this dish if you cut the tails off when you're peeling and deveining the shrimp.

Start to Finish: 30 minutes **Makes:** 4 servings

- 12 **ounces fresh or frozen large shrimp in shells**
- 8 **ounces dried linguini**
- 2 **tablespoons olive oil**
- 1 **or 2 fresh jalapeño chiles, finely chopped (see tip, page 22)**
- 2 **cloves garlic, minced**
- 1/2 **teaspoon salt**
- 1/8 **teaspoon ground black pepper**
- 2 **cups chopped tomatoes and/or cherry tomatoes, halved or quartered**
  Finely shredded Parmesan cheese (optional)

1. Thaw shrimp, if frozen. Peel and devein shrimp. Rinse shrimp; pat dry with paper towels. Cook linguini following package directions; drain well. Return to pan. Cover and keep warm.

2. In a large skillet, heat olive oil over medium-high heat. Add jalapeño chile, garlic, salt, and black pepper; cook and stir for 1 minute. Add shrimp; cook about 3 minutes more or until shrimp are opaque. Stir in tomatoes; heat through.

3. Toss cooked linguini with shrimp mixture. If desired, sprinkle with Parmesan cheese.

Per serving: 363 cal., 9 g total fat (1 g sat. fat), 97 mg chol., 396 mg sodium, 48 g carbo., 3 g fiber, 21 g pro.

Quick Coconut Shrimp

This quick-to-fix coconut shrimp is yummy—and more healthful—than the fried version on restaurant menus.

Prep: 10 minutes **Bake:** 8 minutes **Oven:** 450°F
Makes: 4 servings

- 1 **pound fresh or frozen peeled and deveined large shrimp**
  Nonstick cooking spray
  Salt and ground black pepper
- 1/3 **cup bottled sweet-and-sour sauce**
- 1 1/2 **cups shredded coconut**
- 2 **medium yellow summer squash**

1. Thaw shrimp, if frozen. Rinse and pat dry with paper towels. Preheat oven to 450°F. Lightly coat a baking sheet and a 15×10×1-inch baking pan with cooking spray; set aside. Sprinkle shrimp lightly with salt and pepper. Place sweet-and-sour sauce in a medium bowl; place coconut in a small bowl. Add shrimp to bowl with sauce and stir to

coat. Add shrimp, a few at a time, to dish with coconut; turn shrimp to coat. Arrange shrimp in a single layer on the prepared baking sheet.

2. Trim ends from squash; cut squash in 1/2-inch slices. Arrange squash in a single layer in the prepared pan. Sprinkle squash with salt and pepper; lightly coat with cooking spray.

3. Bake for 8 to 10 minutes or until shrimp are opaque and squash is tender. Serve shrimp with squash slices.

Per serving: 380 cal., 17 g total fat (14 g sat. fat), 172 mg chol., 659 mg sodium, 31 g carbo., 4 g fiber, 27 g pro.

Shrimp Celeste

This creamy, elegant curried shrimp dish for two is perfect for a romantic dinner.

Start to Finish: 25 minutes **Makes:** 2 servings

- 1 **pound fresh or frozen prawns or jumbo shrimp in shells (6 to 8)**
- 3 **tablespoons butter or margarine**
- 1/2 **cup sliced fresh mushrooms**
- 1/2 **cup chopped tomato (1 medium)**
- 1/4 **cup sliced green onions (2)**
- 1 **tablespoon minced garlic (6 cloves)**
- 1 **teaspoon curry powder**
- 1/4 **teaspoon salt**
- 1/4 **teaspoon ground black pepper**
- 1/2 **cup half-and-half or light cream**
- 1 **tablespoon all-purpose flour**
- 1/4 **cup brandy**
- 1 1/2 **cups hot cooked rice or couscous**
  Snipped fresh parsley (optional)

1. Thaw prawns, if frozen. Peel and devein prawns. Rinse prawns; pat dry with paper towels. In a large skillet, melt butter over medium heat. Add prawns; cook for 5 minutes, turning once. Add mushrooms, tomato, green onions, garlic, curry powder, salt, and pepper. Cook and stir for 2 to 3 minutes more or until prawns turn opaque.

2. Meanwhile, in a small bowl, whisk together half-and-half and flour until smooth. Add flour mixture and brandy to shrimp mixture in skillet. Cook and stir until thickened and bubbly; cook and stir for 1 minute more. Serve in shallow bowls with rice. If desired, sprinkle with parsley.

Per serving: 767 cal., 29 g total fat (16 g sat. fat), 413 mg chol., 781 mg sodium, 53 g carbo., 2 g fiber, 54 g pro.

Quick Tip To peel and devein shrimp, first remove the legs from the underside of the shrimp, then slip the tip of your fingers under the shell and gently peel it off. Use the tip of a paring knife to make a shallow cut down the back of the shrimp, from the top to the bottom. Use the tip of the knife to scrape and pull out the vein—discard it—then thoroughly rinse the shrimp under cold running water.

Shrimp on Grits with Fresh Cilantro Sauce

If you like, spice up the creamy, cheesy, sweet-pepper grits with a bit of finely chopped fresh jalapeño chile.

Start to Finish: 25 minutes **Makes:** 4 servings

1 1/2	pounds fresh or frozen medium shrimp
1 3/4	cups water
1/2	cup quick cooking (hominy) grits
2	small red and/or yellow sweet peppers, coarsely chopped
1/2	cup shredded Mexican-blend cheese (2 ounces)
	Salt and ground black pepper
1/4	cup olive oil
1/2	teaspoon chili powder
1	cup cilantro sprigs
1	tablespoon cider vinegar
2	tablespoons water
	Lemon wedges (optional)
	Cilantro sprigs (optional)

1. Thaw shrimp, if frozen. Peel and devein shrimp, leaving tails intact. Rinse shrimp; pat dry with paper towels. Set aside.

2. For grits, in a medium saucepan, bring the 1 3/4 cup water to boiling; stir in grits and sweet peppers. Return to boiling; reduce heat. Simmer, covered, about 5 minutes or until most of the water is absorbed and grits are tender. Stir in cheese. Season to taste with salt and pepper. Cover and keep warm.

3. In a large skillet, heat 1 tablespoon of the olive oil over medium heat. Toss shrimp with chili powder. Add shrimp to skillet. Cook and stir for 3 to 4 minutes or until shrimp are opaque.

4. For fresh cilantro sauce, in a food processor, combine the remaining 3 tablespoons olive oil, the 1 cup cilantro sprigs, cider vinegar, and 2 tablespoons water. Cover and process until almost smooth. Season to taste with salt and black pepper.

5. Serve shrimp on grits; drizzle with fresh cilantro sauce. If desired, garnish with lemon wedges and additional cilantro sprigs.

Per serving: 385 cal., 21 g total fat (5 g sat. fat), 185 mg chol., 423 mg sodium, 21 g carbo., 3 g fiber, 29 g pro.

Quick Tip To make quick work of removing the stems and seeds from sweet peppers, hold the pepper upright on a cutting surface. Slice down each of the sides using a sharp knife. You should have 4 large flat pieces of pepper that are free of seeds and stem—ready to be sliced or chopped. The stem, seeds, and ribs should all be in one tidy unit you can discard.

Thai Shrimp and Fresh Vegetable Rice ♥ 🔲

The marinade does double duty here as a flavorful bath for the shrimp and as a stir-fry sauce for the whole dish. It's safe to use after having raw shrimp in it because it is boiled.

Start to Finish: 30 minutes **Makes:** 4 servings

3/4	pound fresh or frozen peeled and deveined medium shrimp
2	tablespoons fresh lime juice
4	teaspoons soy sauce
1	fresh jalapeño chile, seeded and finely chopped
1	teaspoon grated fresh ginger
1	clove garlic, minced
1	tablespoon vegetable oil
1	pound fresh asparagus spears, bias-sliced in 1-inch pieces
1	small red sweet pepper, cut in thin bite-size strips
3	cups hot cooked rice
1/4	cup chopped peanuts

1. Thaw shrimp, if frozen. Rinse shrimp; pat dry. Place shrimp in a medium bowl. For marinade, combine lime juice, soy sauce, jalapeño chile, ginger, and garlic. Pour over shrimp; toss to coat. Marinate at room temperature for 15 minutes, stirring occasionally. Drain shrimp well, reserving marinade.

2. In a wok or large skillet, heat oil over medium-high heat. (Add more oil if necessary during cooking.) Add shrimp; cook and stir for 2 to 3 minutes or until shrimp turn opaque. Remove from wok; cover and keep warm. Add asparagus and pepper strips to wok; cook and stir for 2 to 3 minutes or until crisp-tender. Add reserved marinade to wok and bring to boiling. Stir in cooked rice and peanuts.

3. To serve, transfer rice mixture to 4 bowls or plates. Spoon shrimp on top.

Per serving: 331 cal., 9 g total fat (1 g sat. fat), 131 mg chol., 571 mg sodium, 41 g carbo., 2 g fiber, 11 g pro.

Thai Shrimp and Fresh Vegetable Rice

Speedy Paella

Speedy Paella ♥

This shortcut version of the classic Spanish dish takes advantage of precooked shrimp and rice with vegetables already stirred in.

Start to Finish: 14 minutes **Makes:** 4 servings

- **8 ounces fresh or frozen sea scallops**
- **8 ounces fresh or frozen cooked peeled, deveined shrimp**
- **1 10-ounce package frozen long grain white rice with vegetables (peas, corn, and carrots)**
- **1 tablespoon vegetable oil**
- **4 plum tomatoes, coarsely chopped**
- **1/2 to 1 teaspoon ground turmeric**
  Salt and ground black pepper
  Chopped fresh parsley (optional)

1. Thaw the scallops and shrimp, if frozen. Rinse scallops and shrimp; pat dry. Cut any large scallops in half. Prepare the rice following the microwave package directions.

2. Meanwhile, in a large skillet, heat oil over medium heat. Add scallops; cook about 3 minutes or until scallops are opaque. Add shrimp and tomatoes; heat through.

3. Transfer the rice to a bowl; stir in turmeric. Spoon seafood-tomato mixture over rice; lightly toss. Season to taste with salt and pepper. If desired, sprinkle dish with fresh parsley.

Per serving: 229 cal., 5 g total fat (1 g sat. fat), 129 mg chol., 374 mg sodium, 22 g carbo., 2 g fiber, 24 g pro.

Crab Mornay

Mornay sauce is a white sauce with cheese. This one uses two Swiss cheeses—one process cheese for creaminess and a traditional aged cheese—for flavor and convenience.

Start to Finish: 30 minutes **Makes:** 6 servings

- **1 1/2 cups fresh or frozen cooked crab meat**
- **1 10-ounce package (6) frozen patty shells**
- **2 tablespoons butter or margarine**
- **1 cup sliced fresh mushrooms**
- **1 small leek, sliced, or 1/2 cup sliced green onions**
- **1 clove garlic, minced**
- **2 tablespoons all-purpose flour**
  Dash ground white pepper
- **2 cups half-and-half, light cream, or milk**
- **1/2 cup shredded Swiss cheese (2 ounces)**
- **1/2 cup shredded process Swiss cheese (2 ounces)**
- **2 tablespoons dry sherry**
  Fresh chives (optional)
  Fresh thyme (optional)

1. Thaw crab meat, if frozen. Bake patty shells following package directions.

2. In a medium saucepan, melt butter over medium heat. Add mushrooms, leek, and garlic; cook until tender. Stir in flour and white pepper. Add half-and-half all at once. Cook and stir until mixture is thickened and bubbly; cook and stir for 1 minute more. Reduce heat.

3. Add Swiss cheese and process Swiss cheese to cream mixture; stir gently until cheese is melted. Stir in the crabmeat and sherry. Heat through; do not boil. Serve immediately in patty shells. If desired, garnish with fresh chives and thyme.

Per serving: 484 cal., 34 g total fat (11 g sat. fat), 99 mg chol., 526 mg sodium, 26 g carbo., 0 g fiber, 19 g pro.

White Clam Sauce with Spaghetti ♥

This dish is made mostly from pantry staples and ingredients you're likely to have on hand.

Start to Finish: 22 minutes **Makes:** 4 servings

- 8   **ounces dried spaghetti, linguini, or twisted spaghetti**
- 2   **6.5-ounce cans minced clams, undrained**
- 2   **teaspoons olive oil**
- 1/2 **cup chopped onion (1 medium)**
- 2   **cloves garlic, minced**
- 3/4 **cup milk**
- 1/3 **cup all-purpose flour**
- 1/4 **teaspoon salt**
- 1/4 **teaspoon lemon-pepper seasoning**
- 1/2 **cup frozen peas**
- 1/4 **cup snipped fresh parsley**
- 1/4 **cup dry white wine or chicken broth**
- 1   **tablespoon snipped fresh basil or 1/2 teaspoon dried basil, crushed**
     Grated Parmesan cheese (optional)

1. Cook pasta following package directions; drain pasta and keep warm.

2. Meanwhile, drain clams, reserving the liquid. Set clams aside. Add water, if necessary, to the reserved liquid to equal 1 cup. Set aside.

3. For sauce, in a medium saucepan, heat olive oil over medium heat. Add onion and garlic; cook until onion is tender. In a screw-top jar, combine milk and flour; cover and shake until smooth. Add milk mixture to saucepan. Stir in salt, lemon-pepper seasoning, and the clam liquid. Cook and stir over medium heat until thickened and bubbly. Cook and stir for 1 minute more. Stir in the clams, peas, parsley, wine, and basil. Heat through. Serve sauce over hot pasta. If desired, sprinkle with Parmesan cheese.

Per serving: 384 cal., 6 g total fat (1 g sat. fat), 24 mg chol., 364 mg sodium, 59 g carbo., 3 g fiber, 19 g pro.

Pan-Seared Scallops ♥

This is a flash in the pan! Scallops are given a spicy Cajun-flavored crust, then tossed with balsamic vinegar-dressed spinach and crisp-cooked bacon. Serve this with corn bread and a cold beer or iced tea.

Start to Finish: 20 minutes **Makes:** 4 servings

- 1   **pound fresh or frozen sea scallops**
- 2   **tablespoons all-purpose flour**
- 1   **to 2 teaspoons blackened steak seasoning or Cajun seasoning**
- 1   **tablespoon vegetable oil**
- 1   **10-ounce package prewashed spinach**
- 1   **tablespoon water**
- 2   **tablespoons balsamic vinegar**
- 1/4 **cup cooked bacon pieces**

1. Thaw scallops, if frozen. Rinse scallops; pat dry. In a resealable plastic bag, combine flour and steak seasoning. Add scallops; toss gently to coat. In a large skillet, heat oil over medium heat. Add scallops; cook for 3 to 5 minutes or until browned and opaque, turning once halfway through cooking. Remove scallops.

2. Add spinach to skillet; sprinkle with water. Cook, covered, over medium-high heat about 2 minutes or until spinach starts to wilt. Add vinegar; toss to coat evenly. Return scallops to skillet; heat through. Sprinkle with bacon.

Per serving: 158 cal., 6 g total fat (1 g sat. fat), 37 mg chol., 323 mg sodium, 9 g carbo., 2 g fiber, 18 g pro.

Pan-Seared Scallops

Quick Tip There are two types of scallops—sea scallops and bay scallops. Sea scallops are generally larger than bay scallops. Choose scallops that are plump and moist with a translucent color and a fresh, sweet smell. The best scallops are dry-packed. Scallops that are packed in liquid tend to steam in the pan rather than sear. Quick searing gives them a crust on the outside and creamy, tender centers.

Pasta with Zucchini and Walnuts, **page 161**

Bean and Potato Chowder,
page 151

Skillet Vegetables on
Cheese Toast, **page 155**

Portobello Burgers,
page 164

Meatless Main Dishes

These delicious dishes
based on grains, pasta,
cheese, and vegetables
prove that you don't
have to eat meat to feel
totally satisfied. Even
the most dedicated meat
eaters will enjoy the
variety of great flavors
and hearty textures.

Black Bean Cakes with Salsa

Corn muffin mix is the base for these Mexican-style black bean cakes topped with chili-spiked sour cream.

Start to Finish: 25 minutes
Makes: 4 servings (2 cakes per serving)

1½	**cups prepared salsa**
1	**jalapeño chile (see tip, page 22)**
2	**15-ounces cans black beans, rinsed and drained**
1	**8.5-ounce package corn muffin mix**
3	**teaspoons chili powder**
2	**tablespoons olive oil**
½	**cup sour cream**
½	**teaspoon chili powder**

1. In a colander, drain ½ cup of the salsa. Seed and finely chop half the jalapeño; thinly slice remaining half. In a large bowl, mash beans with vegetable masher or fork. Stir in muffin mix, drained salsa, 2½ teaspoons of the chili powder, and the chopped jalapeño.

2. In an extra-large skillet, heat 1 tablespoon of the olive oil over medium-high heat. Add four ½-cup mounds bean mixture to skillet. Flatten mounds with spatula to 3½-inch-round cakes. Cook about 3 minutes on each side or until browned. Remove from skillet. Repeat with remaining olive oil and bean mixture.

3. In a small bowl, combine sour cream and ½ teaspoon chili powder. Top cakes with remaining salsa, sliced jalapeño, and seasoned sour cream.

Per serving: 519 cal., 19 g total fat (4 g sat. fat), 11 mg chol., 1,553 mg sodium, 79 g carbo., 12 g fiber, 20 g pro.

Lentil and Veggie Tostadas ♥

Red lentils cook much more quickly than brown lentils. In just 12 to 15 minutes, they're done, compared to 35 to 45 minutes for brown lentils.

Start to Finish: 25 minutes **Makes:** 4 servings

1¾	**cups water**
¾	**cup dry red lentils, rinsed and drained**
¼	**cup chopped onion**
1	**to 2 tablespoons snipped fresh cilantro**
1	**clove garlic, minced**
½	**teaspoon salt**
½	**teaspoon ground cumin**
4	**tostada shells**

Black Bean Cakes
with Salsa

Lentil and Veggie Tostadas

2 cups chopped assorted fresh vegetables (such as broccoli, tomato, zucchini, and/or yellow summer squash)
¾ cup shredded Monterey Jack cheese (3 ounces)

1. In a medium saucepan, stir together water, lentils, onion, cilantro, garlic, salt, and cumin. Bring to boiling; reduce heat. Simmer, covered, for 12 to 15 minutes or until lentils are tender and most of the liquid is absorbed. Use a fork to mash the cooked lentils.

2. Preheat broiler. Place tostada shells on a large baking sheet. Spread the lentil mixture on tostada shells; top with vegetables and cheese. Broil 3 to 4 inches from the heat about 2 minutes or until cheese is melted. Serve the tostadas immediately.

Per serving: 288 cal., 11 g total fat (5 g sat. fat), 20 mg chol., 497 mg sodium, 34 g carbo., 7 g fiber, 16 g pro.

Black-Eyed Pea Cakes with Spicy Dressing

Spritz the cakes with nonstick cooking spray before they go in the oven to crisp them up as they bake.

Prep: 25 minutes Bake: 20 minutes Oven: 425°F
Makes: 4 servings

1 egg, lightly beaten
⅔ cup soft bread crumbs
¼ cup mayonnaise or salad dressing

1 teaspoon ground cumin
1 teaspoon dried minced onion
1 teaspoon coarse-grain brown mustard
1 15- to 16-ounce can black-eyed peas, rinsed, drained, and mashed
 Nonstick cooking spray
⅓ cup mayonnaise or salad dressing
¼ cup sour cream
2 tablespoons bottled salsa
1 teaspoon prepared horseradish
½ teaspoon Cajun seasoning

1. Preheat oven to 425°F. In a medium bowl, combine egg, bread crumbs, the ¼ cup mayonnaise, cumin, dried onion, and mustard; mix well. Add black-eyed peas; mix well (mixture will be soft).

2. Lightly coat a baking sheet with cooking spray. Using a scant ¼ cup for each, drop pea mixture in 8 mounds on the baking sheet. Spread each mound in a 3-inch patty. Coat patties with additional cooking spray. Bake, uncovered, for 20 minutes, turning once halfway through cooking.

3. Meanwhile, in a small bowl, stir together the ⅓ cup mayonnaise, the sour cream, salsa, horseradish, and Cajun seasoning. Serve with black-eyed pea cakes.

Per serving: 456 cal., 31 g total fat (6 g sat. fat), 70 mg chol., 742 mg sodium, 34 g carbo., 6 g fiber, 11 g pro.

Rice and Bean Frittata one

Eggs are the go-to ingredient to make this a fast and light supper. Serve this veggie-packed frittata with a green salad and rolls or bread.

Start to Finish: 20 minutes **Makes:** 4 servings

- 2 **tablespoons vegetable oil**
- 1 **large yellow summer squash, halved lengthwise and sliced**
- 1 **8.8-ounce pouch cooked long grain and wild rice**
- 1 **15-ounce can navy beans, red beans, or garbanzo beans (chickpeas), rinsed and drained**
- 6 **eggs, lightly beaten**
- ¼ **cup milk**
- ¼ **teaspoon salt**
- ¼ **teaspoon ground black pepper**
- 1 **cup shredded Colby and Monterey Jack cheese, cheddar cheese, or Swiss cheese (4 ounces)**

1. In a large skillet, heat oil over medium heat. Add summer squash; cook until crisp-tender. Meanwhile, microwave rice following the package directions; stir into skillet. Stir in beans.

2. In a large bowl, combine eggs, milk, salt, and pepper; pour into skillet. Continue to cook over medium heat. As mixture sets, run a spatula around the edge of the eggs, lifting egg mixture so uncooked portion flows underneath. Cook just until egg mixture is set. Sprinkle with cheese.

Per serving: 510 cal., 26 g total fat (9 g sat. fat), 343 mg chol., 1,127 mg sodium, 43 g carbo., 7 g fiber, 26 g pro.

Bean and Potato Chowder one

This creamy, warming chowder is ideal for a cold night. If you don't have Italian seasoning, use ½ teaspoon each of dried oregano and dried basil.

Start to Finish: 20 minutes **Makes:** 4 servings

- 1 **20-ounce package refrigerated diced potatoes with onions**
- 1 **14-ounce can vegetable broth**
- ⅓ **cup all-purpose flour**
- 1 **cup shredded Swiss cheese (4 ounces)**
- 3 **cups milk**
- 1 **teaspoon dried Italian seasoning, crushed**
- 1 **15-ounce can navy beans, rinsed and drained**
  Salt and ground black pepper
  Bottled roasted red sweet peppers (optional)
  Snipped fresh Italian (flat-leaf) parsley (optional)
- 8 **slices toasted Italian bread with shredded Swiss cheese (optional)**

1. In a 4-quart Dutch oven, combine potatoes and vegetable broth. Cover and bring to boiling; reduce heat. Simmer, covered, for 4 minutes.

2. In a large bowl, toss together flour and cheese until cheese is coated. Gradually stir in milk until combined. Add cheese mixture and Italian seasoning to potato mixture in Dutch oven. Cook and stir over medium heat until thickened and bubbly. Stir in beans; cook and stir for 1 minute more. Season to taste with salt and pepper. If desired, top servings with roasted pepper and parsley and serve with toasted cheese-topped bread.

Per serving: 494 cal., 12 g total fat (7 g sat. fat), 41 mg chol., 1,344 mg sodium, 70 g carbo., 9 g fiber, 25 g pro.

Pumpkin-Bean Soup one

Stir together pumpkin, coconut milk, beans, and broth for a fresh, healthful soup in just 15 minutes.

Start to Finish: 15 minutes **Makes:** 4 servings

- 1 **15-ounce can pumpkin**
- 1 **14-ounce can unsweetened coconut milk**
- 1 **15-ounce can white kidney (cannellini) beans, rinsed and drained**
- 1 **14-ounce can vegetable broth**
- 1 **teaspoon dried leaf sage, crushed**
  Salt and ground black pepper
  Cracked black peppercorns (optional)
  Fresh lime slices (optional)

1. In a medium saucepan, combine pumpkin, coconut milk, beans, vegetable broth, and sage. Heat through.

2. Season to taste with salt and pepper. If desired, sprinkle with cracked peppercorns and serve with lime.

Per serving: 285 cal., 19 g total fat (17 g sat. fat), 0 mg chol., 729 mg sodium, 28 g carbo., 8 g fiber, 9 g pro.

Pumpkin-Bean Soup

Vegetable Curry 🔲

A drizzle of olive oil right before serving adds flavor and aroma to this extremely simple dish. Use a fruity extra virgin olive oil for the best results.

Prep: 10 minutes **Cook:** 8 minutes **Makes:** 4 servings

- 1 **16-ounce package frozen baby lima beans**
- ½ **cup water**
- 1 **15-ounce can tomato sauce with garlic and onion**
- 1½ **teaspoons curry powder**
- 2 **8.8-ounce pouches cooked Spanish-style rice**
- ¼ **cup sliced green onion (2) or snipped fresh cilantro**
  Olive oil (optional)

1. In a medium saucepan, combine lima beans and water. Bring to boiling; reduce heat. Simmer, covered, for 5 minutes. Stir in tomato sauce and curry powder; return to boiling. Reduce heat. Simmer, covered, for 3 minutes.

2. Meanwhile, microwave rice following package directions. Spoon rice on one side of 4 plates; spoon bean mixture and green onions alongside rice. If desired, drizzle with olive oil.

Per serving: 385 cal., 3 g total fat (0 g sat. fat), 0 mg chol., 939 mg sodium, 72 g carbo., 9 g fiber, 14 g pro.

Saucy Beans and Eggplant

This version of no-bake eggplant Parmesan uses crumbled salty, tangy feta cheese instead of mozzarella.

Start to Finish: 20 minutes **Makes:** 4 servings

- 1 **small eggplant (about 10 to 12 ounces), cut in 8 slices**
- 3 **tablespoons olive oil**
  Salt and freshly ground black pepper
- ¼ **cup seasoned fine dry bread crumbs**
- 1 **cup instant brown rice**
  Sliced green onions (optional)
- 1 **15-ounce can navy or Great Northern beans, rinsed and drained**
- 1 **26-ounce jar roasted garlic pasta sauce**
  Crumbled feta cheese (optional)

1. Lightly brush eggplant slices with olive oil; sprinkle with salt and pepper. Place bread crumbs in a shallow dish. Dip eggplant slices in bread crumbs to coat both sides. In an extra-large skillet, heat the remaining olive oil over medium-high heat. Add eggplant in a single layer. Cook about 5 minutes each side or until browned and tender, turning often for even browning.

Vegetable Curry

Spinach Tortellini with Beans and Feta

2. Meanwhile, in a medium saucepan, cook the rice following package directions; if desired, stir in green onions. In another saucepan, combine beans and pasta sauce; heat through.

3. Arrange eggplant slices on 4 plates; serve with rice and beans. If desired, top with feta cheese and additional ground black pepper.

Per serving: 511 cal., 14 g total fat (2 g sat. fat), 0 mg chol., 1,099 mg sodium, 82 g carbo., 13 g fiber, 17 g pro.

Spinach Tortellini with Beans and Feta 📋

For a meat version of this recipe, add chicken-filled tortellini.

Start to Finish: 18 minutes **Makes:** 4 servings

- 1 **9-ounce package refrigerated cheese-filled spinach tortellini**
- 1 **15-ounce can white kidney (cannellini) beans, rinsed and drained**
- ¾ **cup crumbled garlic-and-herb-flavored feta cheese (3 ounces)**
- 2 **tablespoons olive oil**
- 1 **cup chopped tomato (1 large)**
  Ground black pepper
- 4 **cups baby spinach**

1. Cook tortellini following package directions. Drain and return to pan.

2. Add drained beans, feta cheese, and olive oil to tortellini in saucepan. Cook over medium heat until beans are hot and cheese begins to melt; gently stir occasionally. Add tomato; cook for 1 minute more. Sprinkle with pepper.

3. Divide spinach among 4 plates or shallow salad bowls. Top with tortellini mixture.

Per serving: 448 cal., 18 g total fat (7 g sat. fat), 61 mg chol., 858 mg sodium, 55 g carbo., 9 g fiber, 24 g pro.

Quick Tip Although cannellini beans are nice for this recipe because of their big, buttery bite, most canned white beans are interchangeable in many recipes. Canned Great Northern beans or tiny navy beans are good options.

Skillet Vegetables on Cheese Toast

Skillet Vegetables on Cheese Toast

Made with hearty bread, goat cheese, and loaded with vegetables, this open-face sandwich does grilled cheese one better.

Start to Finish: 20 minutes **Makes:** 4 servings

8	slices rustic wheat bread
2	tablespoons olive oil
½	an 8-ounce package peeled fresh whole baby carrots, halved lengthwise
1	8-ounce package button mushrooms, halved
1	small red onion, cut in thin wedges
4	cloves garlic, peeled and coarsely chopped
2	tablespoons water
	Salt and ground black pepper
4	ounces soft goat cheese (chèvre)
	Fresh basil (optional)

1. Preheat broiler. Place bread on baking sheet; set aside.

2. In a large skillet, heat olive oil over medium-high heat. Add carrots, mushrooms, onion, and garlic; cook for 2 to 3 minutes or until vegetables just begin to brown. Add water. Cook, covered, over medium heat about 5 minutes or until vegetables are crisp-tender, stirring once. Sprinkle with salt and pepper.

3. Meanwhile, for cheese toast, lightly toast bread 3 inches from boiler heat for 1 to 2 minutes. Spread goat cheese on one side of each slice. Broil 3 inches from heat for 1 to 2 minutes or until cheese is softened. Place cheese toasts on 4 plates; top with vegetables. If desired, drizzle additional olive oil and sprinkle basil.

Per serving: 461 cal., 21 g total fat (6 g sat. fat), 13 mg chol., 596 mg sodium, 56 g carbo., 8 g fiber, 15 g pro.

Red Beans and Couscous

Walnuts—a central ingredient in this dish—are rich in protein and heart-healthy omega-3 fatty acids.

Start to Finish: 20 minutes **Oven:** 350°F
Makes: 4 servings

¾	cup walnuts, coarsely chopped
2	cups packaged shredded fresh carrots
2	cups water
1	15- to 16-ounce can red beans, rinsed and drained
1½	cups couscous
1½	cups refrigerated salsa
	Salt

1. Preheat oven to 350°F. Place walnuts in a shallow baking pan. Bake about 8 minutes or until toasted.

2. Meanwhile, in a large saucepan, combine carrots, water, and drained beans; bring to boiling. Stir in couscous.

Remove from heat and let stand for 5 minutes. Stir in salsa and walnuts. Season to taste with salt.

Per serving: 796 cal., 16 g total fat (2 g sat. fat), 0 mg chol., 955 mg sodium, 139 g carbo., 17 g fiber, 30 g pro.

Vegetarian Chili with Rice

If you like chili with a fair amount of fire, increase the amount of cayenne pepper.

Prep: 15 minutes **Cook:** 15 minutes **Makes:** 4 servings

1	15.5-ounce can red kidney beans, rinsed and drained
1	15-ounce can Great Northern beans, rinsed and drained
1	14.5-ounce can diced tomatoes, undrained
1	8-ounce can tomato sauce
1	cup water
¾	cup chopped green sweet pepper (1 medium)
½	cup chopped onion (1 medium)
1	tablespoon chili powder
1	teaspoon sugar
2	cloves garlic, minced
½	teaspoon dried basil, crushed
½	teaspoon ground cumin
¼	teaspoon salt
	Dash cayenne pepper
2	cups hot cooked rice

1. In large saucepan, combine kidney beans, Great Northern beans, undrained tomatoes, tomato sauce, water, green pepper, onion, chili powder, sugar, garlic, basil, cumin, salt, and cayenne pepper. Bring to boiling; reduce heat. Simmer, covered, for 15 minutes, stirring occasionally.

2. Serve chili in bowls. Top with hot cooked rice.

Per serving: 386 cal., 1 g total fat (0 g sat. fat), 0 mg chol., 777 mg sodium, 78 g carbo., 14 g fiber, 20 g pro.

Vegetarian Chili with Rice

Tex-Mex Beans with Dumplings

Two kinds of legumes give this dish texture and flavor. Swap the red kidney beans for black beans or pinto beans.

Start to Finish: 35 minutes **Makes:** 5 servings

- ⅓ **cup all-purpose flour**
- ⅓ **cup yellow cornmeal**
- 1 **teaspoon baking powder**
- ¼ **teaspoon salt**
- 1 **egg white, lightly beaten**
- ¼ **cup fat-free milk**
- 2 **tablespoons vegetable oil**
- 1 **cup chopped onion (1 large)**
- ¾ **cup water**
- 1 **clove garlic, minced**
- 1 **15-ounce can garbanzo beans (chickpeas), rinsed and drained**
- 1 **15-ounce can red kidney beans, rinsed and drained**
- 2 **8-ounce cans no-salt-added tomato sauce**
- 1 **4.5-ounce can diced green chiles, drained**
- 2 **teaspoons chili powder**
- 1 **tablespoon water**
- 1½ **teaspoons cornstarch**
  Shredded cheddar cheese (optional)

1. In a bowl, mix flour, cornmeal, baking powder, and salt. In a bowl, combine egg white, milk, and oil; set aside.

2. In a large skillet, combine onion, the ¾ cup water, and garlic. Bring to boiling; reduce heat. Simmer, covered, about 5 minutes or until tender. Stir in garbanzo beans, kidney beans, tomato sauce, green chiles, chili powder, and salt.

3. In a small bowl, stir together the 1 tablespoon water and cornstarch. Stir into bean mixture. Cook and stir until slightly thickened and bubbly. Reduce heat.

4. Add milk mixture to cornmeal mixture; stir just until combined. Drop from a tablespoon to make 5 mounds on the hot bean mixture.

5. Simmer, covered, for 10 to 12 minutes or until a toothpick inserted into the center of a dumpling comes out clean. If desired, sprinkle with cheese.

Per serving: 351 cal., 7 g total fat (1 g sat. fat), 0 mg chol., 695 mg sodium, 61 g carbo., 12 g fiber, 15 g pro.

Spaghetti Squash with Balsamic Beans ♥

When cooked, the golden flesh of spaghetti squash separates into strands that look like pasta and have a wonderful, nutty flavor and toothsome texture.

Start to Finish: 30 minutes **Makes:** 4 servings

- ¼ **cup balsamic vinegar**
- 3 **tablespoons olive oil**
- 1 **tablespoon honey mustard**
- 2 **cloves garlic, minced**
- 1 **medium spaghetti squash (2½ to 3 pounds), halved and seeded**
- 1 **10-ounce package frozen baby lima beans**
- 1 **15-ounce can red kidney beans, rinsed and drained**
- ½ **a 7-ounce jar (½ cup) roasted red sweet peppers, rinsed, drained, and cut in short strips**
- ½ **teaspoon salt**
  Freshly ground black pepper (optional)

Tex-Mex Beans with Dumplings

1. For vinaigrette, in a screw-top jar, combine vinegar, olive oil, honey mustard, and garlic. Cover and shake well. Set vinaigrette aside.

2. Place squash halves in a large Dutch oven with about 1 inch of water. Bring to boiling. Cook, covered, for 15 to 20 minutes or until tender.

3. Meanwhile, in a medium saucepan, cook lima beans following package directions, adding kidney beans during the last 3 minutes of cooking; drain and return to pan. Stir in roasted peppers and salt; heat through. Pour vinaigrette over warm bean mixture; toss to coat.

4. Using a fork, scrape the squash pulp from the shells into strands. Spoon warm bean mixture over squash strands; drizzle any remaining vinaigrette. If desired, sprinkle with pepper.

Per serving: 387 cal., 12 g total fat (2 g sat. fat), 0 mg chol., 563 mg sodium, 61 g carbo., 14 g fiber, 15 g pro.

Spicy Black Beans and Rice

Indian Lentils and Rice

Like curry powder, garam masala is a ground spice blend that varies by the region of India from which it originates. Common are cloves, black and white peppers, cumin, cinnamon, nutmeg, cardamom, and coriander.

Start to Finish: 20 minutes **Makes:** 4 to 6 servings

- 1 **tablespoon vegetable oil**
- ½ **cup chopped onion (1 medium)**
- 2 **teaspoons garam masala**
- 2 **cups bite-size cauliflower florets**
- ½ **cup bias-sliced carrot (1 medium)**
- 1 **cup water**
- 1 **17.3-ounce package refrigerated steamed lentils or one 15-ounce can lentils, rinsed and drained***
- 1 **8.8-ounce pouch cooked long grain rice**
- 1 **cup frozen peas**
- ⅓ **cup golden raisins**
  Salt and ground black pepper

1. In an extra-large skillet, heat oil over medium heat. Add onion and garam masala; cook about 5 minutes or until onion is tender. Add cauliflower, carrot, and water. Bring to boiling; reduce heat. Simmer, covered, about 5 minutes or until tender.

2. Stir in lentils, rice, peas, and raisins. Cook and stir until heated through and water is absorbed. Season to taste with salt and pepper.

Per serving: 373 cal., 6 g total fat (0 g sat. fat), 0 mg chol., 510 mg sodium, 65 g carbo., 14 g fiber, 17 g pro.

*Note: If refrigerated steamed lentils are not available, in a large saucepan, combine 8 ounces dry lentils and 2½ cups water. Bring to boiling; reduce heat. Simmer, covered, about 30 minutes or until tender.

Spicy Black Beans and Rice

This dish is made easy with Mexican-style stewed tomatoes or a same-size can of fire-roasted tomatoes, which give it a nice, smoky flavor.

Start to Finish: 30 minutes **Makes:** 4 servings

- 2 **tablespoons olive oil or vegetable oil**
- ½ **cup chopped onion (1 medium)**
- 4 **cloves garlic, minced**
- 1 **15-ounce can black beans, rinsed and drained**
- 1 **14.5-ounce can Mexican-style stewed tomatoes**
- ⅛ **to ¼ teaspoon cayenne pepper**
- 2 **cups hot cooked brown or long grain rice**
  Chopped onion (optional)

1. In a medium saucepan, heat oil over medium heat. Add the ½ cup onion and garlic; cook until until onion is tender. Carefully stir in beans, undrained tomatoes, and cayenne pepper. Bring to boiling; reduce heat. Simmer, uncovered, for 15 minutes.

2. To serve, mound rice on 4 dinner plates; make a well in the center of each. Spoon bean mixture into centers. If desired, sprinkle with additional chopped onion.

Per serving: 279 cal., 8 g total fat (1 g sat. fat), 0 mg chol., 631 mg sodium, 47 g carbo., 7 g fiber, 11 g pro.

Quick Tip Brown rice differs from white rice in that it is less processed. The outer husk and bran—which contain fiber and nutrients—are removed on white rice. Only the husk is removed on brown rice, while the bran is left intact. For most recipes, you can substitute one for the other. Brown rice adds distinct, nutty flavor to dishes.

Polenta with Portobello Sauce

Polenta with Portobello Sauce

Meaty portobello mushrooms in chunky sauce contrasts deliciously with creamy, cheesy polenta.

Start to Finish: 25 minutes **Makes:** 2 servings

- **1 tablespoon olive oil**
- **1 8-ounce fresh portobello mushroom, stem removed, quartered, and sliced (2½ cups)**
- **½ cup finely chopped onion (1 medium)**
- **3 cloves garlic, minced**
- **2 tablespoons dry red wine**
- **2 teaspoons snipped fresh oregano or ½ teaspoon dried oregano, crushed**
- **3 plum tomatoes, chopped**
   Salt and freshly ground black pepper
- **1 cup water**
- **⅓ cup cornmeal**
- **1 tablespoon butter or margarine**
- **⅛ teaspoon salt**
- **⅓ cup shredded Havarti or brick cheese**
   Fresh oregano (optional)

1. In a large skillet, heat oil over medium-high heat. Add mushroom, onion, and garlic. Cook and stir for 4 to 5 minutes or until mushroom is tender. Add the wine and the ½ teaspoon dried oregano (if using). Bring to boiling; reduce heat. Simmer, covered, for 5 minutes to blend flavors. Stir in tomatoes and the 2 teaspoons fresh oregano (if using); heat through. Remove from heat. Season to taste with salt and freshly ground black pepper. Cover and keep warm.

2. Meanwhile, for polenta, in a small bowl, stir together ½ cup of the water and the cornmeal; set aside. In a small saucepan, bring the remaining ½ cup water, the butter, and the ⅛ teaspoon salt just to boiling. Slowly add the cornmeal mixture, stirring constantly. Reduce heat to low. Cook and stir about 10 minutes or until polenta is thick. Remove from heat. Stir in cheese.

3. To serve, divide the polenta between 2 shallow pasta bowls or soup bowls. Top with mushroom mixture. If desired, garnish with additional fresh oregano.

Per serving: 373 cal., 22 g total fat (5 g sat. fat), 42 mg chol., 455 mg sodium, 35 g carbo., 6 g fiber, 11 g pro.

Saffron Pilaf with Grilled Vegetables ♥

Like Spanish paella, this sunny-color saffron rice dish bursts with flavor from a rainbow of grilled vegetables.

Prep: 20 minutes **Grill:** 10 minutes **Makes:** 4 servings

- 1 **14-ounce can vegetable broth**
- 1 **cup jasmine, basmati, or wild-pecan long grain rice**
- ¼ **cup water**
- ⅛ **teaspoon saffron threads or dash ground saffron***
- 2 **tablespoons olive oil**
- 1 **clove garlic, minced**
- 1 **red sweet pepper, seeded and quartered**
- 1 **large zucchini, halved lengthwise**
- 1 **eggplant, sliced ½ inch thick**
  Salt and ground black pepper
- 1 **ounce herbed semisoft goat cheese (chèvre), crumbled**
- 2 **tablespoons coarsely chopped hazelnuts or pecans, toasted**

1. In a large saucepan, combine vegetable broth, rice, water, and saffron. Heat to boiling; reduce heat. Simmer, covered, about 15 minutes or until rice is tender and liquid is absorbed; keep warm.

2. Meanwhile, in a small bowl, combine olive oil and garlic; brush over sweet pepper, zucchini, and eggplant. Place vegetables on the lightly greased rack of an uncovered grill directly over medium heat. Grill about 10 minutes or until tender, turning once halfway through grilling. Sprinkle with salt and pepper.

3. Transfer vegetables to a cutting board; cool slightly. Cut vegetables in bite-size pieces; stir into cooked rice. Top with goat cheese and nuts.

Per serving: 333 cal., 12 g total fat (2 g sat. fat), 7 mg chol., 443 mg sodium, 48 g carbo., 5 g fiber, 9 g pro.

***Note:** You may substitute ¼ teaspoon turmeric for the saffron.

Corn and Bean Quesadillas

Look for good-quality prepared guacamole—it adds so much flavor to these quesadillas.

Start to Finish: 20 minutes **Makes:** 3 or 4 servings

- ½ **cup drained canned corn**
- ¼ **teaspoon chili powder**
- 1 **cup fat-free refried beans**
- 4 **7- to 8-inch fat-free flour tortillas**
- 1 **cup chopped, peeled papaya, mango, or peaches**
- 1 **4-ounce can green chiles, drained and cut in strips (see tip, page 22)**
- ¾ **to 1 cup shredded Chihuahua or Monterey Jack cheese (3 to 4 ounces)**
  Nonstick cooking spray
  Fat-free sour cream (optional)
  Guacamole (optional)
  Fresh cilantro leaves (optional)

1. In a small bowl, combine corn and chili powder; set aside. Spread about ¼ cup of the refried beans on half of each tortilla. Layer papaya, the corn mixture, and green chiles. Sprinkle with cheese. Fold tortillas in half, pressing gently.

2. Lightly coat a large nonstick skillet with cooking spray. Cook quesadillas over medium heat for 2 to 3 minutes or until lightly browned, turning once. Cut each quesadilla in wedges. If desired, serve with sour cream, guacamole, and/or cilantro leaves.

Per serving: 382 cal., 10 g total fat (6 g sat. fat), 34 mg chol., 1,260 mg sodium, 58 g carbo., 6 g fiber, 18 g pro.

Quick Tip Mexican cheeses are categorized as fresh, soft, semisoft, semifirm, and firm. Chihuahua—also called asadero—is a semifirm cheese that is a terrific melting cheese. Monterey Jack is a good replacement if you can't find it. The most familiar firm cheese—perfect for crumbling over refried beans—is called Cotija (co-TEE-ah). Dry feta is a good stand-in—though Cotija is widely available.

Saffron Pilaf with Grilled Vegetables

Pasta with Zucchini and Walnuts

Pasta with Zucchini and Walnuts

Pasta is best served in warm bowls—one big serving bowl or individual bowls. To warm, place bowls in a 200°F oven for 2 to 3 minutes.

Start to Finish: 18 minutes **Makes:** 4 servings

- 1 **9-ounce package refrigerated whole wheat or plain cheese ravioli**
- 2 **tablespoons olive oil**
- ½ **cup walnuts, coarsely chopped**
- 2 **medium zucchini, halved lengthwise and sliced**
- 6 **green onions, diagonally sliced in ¼-inch pieces**
- ⅓ **cup milk**
- 1 **cup finely shredded Parmesan cheese (4 ounces) or grated Parmesan cheese**
  Salt and ground black pepper

1. In a large saucepan, cook ravioli in 4 cups boiling lightly salted water for 6 to 8 minutes or until tender; drain.

2. Meanwhile, in a large skillet, heat oil over medium heat. Add walnuts; cook for 2 to 3 minutes or until toasted. Using a slotted spoon, remove walnuts from skillet. Add zucchini and green onions; cook and stir for 2 to 3 minutes or until crisp-tender.

3. Add drained ravioli, walnuts, milk, and ¾ cup of the cheese to skillet; cook and toss for 1 minute. Season to taste with salt and pepper. Transfer to a serving bowl; sprinkle with the remaining ¼ cup cheese.

Per serving: 466 cal., 29 g total fat (9 g sat. fat), 59 mg chol., 859 mg sodium, 33 g carbo., 6 g fiber, 21 g pro.

Linguini with Fresh Tomato Sauce and Basil Garlic Toast ♥

Just a little sugar heightens the natural sweetness of tomatoes in this dish—a contrast to the salty, briny flavor of the olives.

Start to Finish: 20 minutes **Makes:** 4 servings

- 10 **ounces dried linguini**
- 3 **tablespoons olive oil**
- 6 **cloves garlic, minced**
- 2 **English muffins, split**
- ⅔ **cup fresh basil, chopped**
- 2 **cups grape tomatoes, halved, or 4 plum tomatoes, chopped**
- ½ **cup chicken broth or pasta water**
- 1 **teaspoon sugar**
  Salt and ground black pepper
- ½ **cup halved, pitted kalamata olives (optional)**
  Grated Parmesan cheese (optional)
  Fresh basil (optional)

1. Preheat broiler. Cook pasta following package directions.

2. Meanwhile, in a small bowl, combine 1 tablespoon of the olive oil and 2 cloves of the garlic; brush on cut sides of English muffins. Place on baking sheet. Broil 3 to 4 inches from heat for 2 to 3 minutes or until edges begin to brown and tops are golden. Sprinkle with 1 tablespoon of the basil; set aside.

3. Meanwhile, in a large saucepan, heat remaining 2 tablespoons oil over medium-high heat; add remaining 4 cloves garlic, the remaining basil, and the tomatoes. Cook about 2 minutes or until garlic is tender. Add chicken broth and sugar. Cook for 3 to 4 minutes or until tomatoes have softened. Season with salt and pepper. Add drained pasta and, if desired, olives; heat through.

4. Serve pasta with toasted muffins. If desired, sprinkle Parmesan cheese and additional basil.

Per serving: 450 cal., 12 g total fat (2 g sat. fat), 0 mg chol., 403 mg sodium, 72 g carbo., 3 g fiber, 12 g pro.

Ravioli in Browned Butter Sauce

When browned, butter has a deliciously nutty flavor. In French, browned butter is "beurre noisette," or "hazelnut butter," a reference to its color and flavor.

Start to Finish: 18 minutes **Makes:** 4 servings

- 2 **9-ounce packages refrigerated four-cheese ravioli**
- 8 **ounces fresh green beans, trimmed and cut in 2-inch pieces**
- ¼ **cup butter**
- 1 **tablespoon snipped fresh sage**
- ½ **cup whipping cream**
- 2 **ounces Gorgonzola cheese, crumbled**
- ½ **cup milk**
  Salt and ground black pepper
  Fresh sage leaves (optional)

1. In a 4-quart Dutch oven, bring 2 quarts lightly salted water to boiling. Add ravioli and green beans. Return to boiling. Simmer, uncovered, for 6 to 8 minutes or until ravioli is tender. Drain; set aside.

2. Meanwhile, in a large skillet, melt butter. Add the 1 tablespoon snipped sage. Continue cooking sage and butter until the butter is lightly browned. Stir in whipping cream and Gorgonzola cheese. Bring to boiling; reduce heat. Simmer about 2 minutes or until thickened and cheese is melted, stirring frequently. Whisk in milk. Cook and stir about 2 minutes or until mixture is slightly thickened. Stir in ravioli; toss to coat.

3. Season with salt and pepper. If desired, garnish with fresh sage leaves.

Per serving: 623 cal., 33 g total fat (21 g sat. fat), 137 mg chol., 1,014 mg sodium, 60 g carbo., 5 g fiber, 23 g pro.

Pasta with Three Cheeses

Pasta with Three Cheeses 🔲

For a delicious twist on this rich, creamy dish, use smoked Gouda.

Start to Finish: 30 minutes **Makes:** 4 servings

- 10 **ounces dried medium shell macaroni or rotini**
- 2 **cups frozen cauliflower, broccoli, and carrots or other vegetable combination**
- 1 **cup milk**
- 1 **3-ounce package cream cheese, cut up**
- ¼ **teaspoon ground black pepper**
- ¾ **cup shredded Gouda, Edam, Havarti, fontina, cheddar, or Swiss cheese (3 ounces)**
- ¼ **cup grated Parmesan cheese**
  Grated Parmesan cheese (optional)

1. In a large saucepan, cook pasta following package directions, adding the frozen vegetables the last 5 minutes of cooking. Drain.

2. In the hot saucepan, combine milk, cream cheese, and pepper. Cook and stir over low heat until cheese is melted.

3. Return pasta mixture to saucepan. Toss to coat with cream cheese mixture. Gently stir in the shredded cheese and the ¼ cup Parmesan cheese. If desired, sprinkle with additional Parmesan cheese.

Per serving: 598 cal., 25 g total fat (14 g sat. fat), 86 mg chol., 596 mg sodium, 66 g carbo., 3 g fiber, 28 g pro.

Mixed Vegetables and Tofu Chow Mein 🔲

Serve this stir-fry with hot jasmine or oolong tea and purchased fortune cookies—just for fun.

Start to Finish: 35 minutes **Makes:** 2 servings

- 1 **cup fresh pea pods or half a 6-ounce package frozen pea pods, thawed**
- ½ **cup water**
- 2 **tablespoons dry sherry or dry white wine**
- 1 **tablespoon soy sauce**
- 2 **teaspoons cornstarch**
- ½ **teaspoon instant chicken bouillon granules**
- 1 **tablespoon vegetable oil**
- 2 **cloves garlic, minced**
- ½ **cup thinly sliced carrot (1 medium)**
- 1 **cup shredded Chinese cabbage or cabbage**
- 1 **small yellow summer squash or zucchini, thinly sliced (about 1 cup)**
- 2 **green onions, bias-sliced in 1-inch lengths**
- 4 **ounces firm tofu, cut in ½-inch cubes**
- 1 **7-ounce jar whole straw mushrooms or one 4.5-ounce jar sliced mushrooms, drained**
- ½ **cup cashews or peanuts**
  Chow mein noodles (optional)

1. Slice the pea pods in half crosswise; set aside. For sauce, in a small bowl, stir together water, sherry, soy sauce, cornstarch, and chicken bouillon granules. Set aside.

2. In a wok or large skillet, heat oil over medium-high heat. (Add more oil as necessary during cooking.) Add garlic; cook and stir for 15 seconds. Add carrot; cook and stir for 1 minute. Add the fresh pea pods (if using), regular cabbage (if using), summer squash, and green onions; cook and stir for 3 to 4 minutes more or until vegetables are crisp-tender. Remove the vegetables from the wok.

3. Add the tofu to the hot wok. Cook and gently stir for 2 to 3 minutes or until tofu is lightly browned. Remove tofu from wok.

4. Stir the sauce. Add the sauce to the wok. Cook and stir until thickened and bubbly. Return cooked vegetables and tofu to the wok. Add the thawed pea pods (if using), Chinese cabbage (if using), and mushrooms. Stir all ingredients to coat with sauce. Cook and stir about 1 minute more or until heated through. Stir in cashews. If desired, spoon over chow mein noodles. Serve immediately.

Per serving: 443 cal., 27 g total fat (4 g sat. fat), 0 mg chol., 1,149 mg sodium, 33 g carbo., 8 g fiber, 18 g pro.

Penne with Fennel ♥

The slightly sweet licorice flavor of the fennel complements the spiciness of crushed red pepper in this light pasta dish.

Start to Finish: 30 minutes **Makes:** 4 servings

- 6 ounces dried penne or mostaccioli
- 2 medium fennel bulbs
- 1 tablespoon olive oil or vegetable oil
- 1 tablespoon butter or margarine
- 3 cloves garlic, minced
- 1/4 teaspoon crushed red pepper
- 1 cup red and/or green sweet pepper cut in thin bite-size strips

Penne with Fennel

- 1 15-ounce can Great Northern beans, rinsed and drained
- 1/4 teaspoon dried thyme, crushed
  Ground black pepper
- 1/4 cup shaved or shredded Parmesan cheese

1. Cook penne following package directions. Drain penne. Return to pan. Cover; keep warm.

2. Cut off and discard upper stalks from fennel bulbs. If desired, reserve some of the feathery leaves for garnish. Cut fennel bulbs lengthwise in quarters. Remove and discard cores. Cut fennel in thin strips.

3. In a large skillet, heat oil and butter over medium-high heat. Add garlic; cook for 30 seconds. Add fennel and crushed red pepper; cook and stir for 5 minutes. Add sweet pepper strips; cook for 3 minutes. Add beans and thyme; cook about 2 minutes or until heated through.

4. To serve, add fennel mixture to hot cooked pasta; toss gently. Season with black pepper. Sprinkle with Parmesan cheese. If desired, garnish with reserved fennel leaves.

Per serving: 349 cal., 9 g total fat (2 g sat. fat), 5 mg chol., 309 mg sodium, 53 g carbo., 4 g fiber, 15 g pro.

Spicy Thai Peanut Noodles

With a few fresh ingredients and a bottle of peanut sauce, your favorite Thai takeout can be on the table in 20 minutes—less time than it takes to drive to a restaurant.

Start to Finish: 20 minutes **Makes:** 4 servings

- 1 9-ounce package refrigerated linguini
- 1 cup packaged fresh shredded carrots
- 1 medium red or yellow sweet pepper, seeded and cut into thin strips
- 1/2 a medium cucumber, seeded and cut in thin strips
- 1/3 cup bias-sliced green onions
- 1/3 cup torn fresh basil
- 1 11.5-ounce bottle peanut sauce
- 1/3 cup dry-roasted peanuts

1. Cook linguini following package directions; drain. Rinse under cold running water until cooled; drain again. If desired, with clean kitchen scissors, snip linguini in short lengths.

2. In a large bowl, toss together drained linguini, carrots, sweet pepper, cucumber, green onions, and basil. Add peanut sauce and toss to coat. Sprinkle with peanuts.

Per serving: 496 cal., 20 g total fat (4 g sat. fat), 68 mg chol., 1,288 mg sodium, 62 g carbo., 4 g fiber, 16 g pro.

Caramelized Onions and Garlic with Cavatelli ♥

Caramelizing onions is the simple process of heating them until the natural sugars brown and caramelize for a sweet, mellow flavor.

Start to Finish: 30 minutes **Makes:** 4 servings

10	ounces dried cavatelli or other medium size pasta (3½ cups)
1	tablespoon olive oil
2	medium onions, sliced (about 2 cups)
1	teaspoon sugar
1	medium zucchini, halved lengthwise and sliced
4	cloves garlic, minced
2	tablespoons water
1	to 2 tablespoons balsamic vinegar
¼	cup pine nuts or chopped walnuts, toasted
1	tablespoon snipped fresh thyme
	Salt and ground black pepper

1. Cook pasta following package directions; drain and keep warm.

2. Meanwhile, in a large heavy skillet, heat olive oil over medium-low heat. Add onions; cook, covered, for 13 to 15 minutes or until onions are tender. Uncover; add sugar. Cook and stir over medium-high heat for 4 to 5 minutes more or until onions are golden.

3. Add zucchini and garlic. Cook and stir for 2 minutes. Stir in water and vinegar; cook for 2 to 3 minutes more or until zucchini is crisp-tender.

4. To serve, in a large bowl, toss together warm pasta, onion mixture, nuts, and thyme. Season with salt and pepper.

Per serving: 386 cal., 10 g total fat (1 g sat. fat), 0 mg chol., 97 mg sodium, 64 g carbo., 3 g fiber, 12 g pro.

Apple-Brie Grilled Sandwiches

Use a sweet variety of yellow onion, such as Vidalia, Walla Walla, or Maui, to make these fruit-and-vegetable sandwiches.

Start to Finish: 20 minutes **Makes:** 4 sandwiches

1	tablespoon vegetable oil
1	medium sweet onion, cut in thin wedges
2	tablespoons apple jelly
1	5-ounce package soft-style spreadable Brie cheese*
8	slices whole grain bread
1	medium Granny Smith apple, cored and thinly sliced
¼	cup butter, softened

1. In a large skillet, heat oil over medium heat. Add onion; cook until tender and beginning to brown. Transfer onion to a small bowl; stir in apple jelly. If desired, snip onion in small pieces.

2. Spread Brie on half the bread slices. Top with apple slices and onion mixture. Top with remaining bread slices.

3. Spread top slices of bread with half the butter. Place sandwiches, butter sides down, in an extra-large skillet over medium heat. Carefully spread unbuttered bread with remaining butter. Cook for 4 to 6 minutes or until cheese is melted and bread is browned, turning once.

Per sandwich: 484 cal., 28 g total fat (14 g sat. fat), 66 mg chol., 529 mg sodium, 44 g carbo., 9 g fiber, 19 g pro.

*Note: If you can't find soft-style spreadable Brie, thinly slice regular Brie and place on the bread slice; carefully spread cheese together.

Portobello Burgers

Even the most dedicated hamburger fans will enjoy these hearty grilled mushroom burgers.

Start to Finish: 20 minutes **Makes:** 4 burgers

4	portobello mushrooms
2	tablespoons olive oil
	Salt and ground black pepper
1	teaspoon dried Italian seasoning, crushed
4	slices provolone cheese
4	ciabatta rolls, split
¼	cup mayonnaise or salad dressing
4	to 8 pieces bottled, roasted red sweet pepper
¾	cup fresh basil leaves

1. If desired, scrape gills from mushroom caps. Drizzle mushrooms with olive oil. Sprinkle with salt, pepper, and Italian seasoning.

2. Place mushrooms on the rack of an uncovered grill directly over medium heat. Grill for 6 to 8 minutes or until almost tender, turning once halfway through grilling. Top each mushroom with a cheese slice. Place rolls, split sides down, on grill rack. Grill 2 minutes more or until cheese is melted, mushrooms are tender, and rolls are toasted.

3. Serve mushrooms on rolls. Pass mayonnaise, roasted pepper pieces, and basil leaves.

Per burger: 520 cal., 29 g total fat (9 g sat. fat), 25 mg chol., 972 mg sodium, 49 g carbo., 4 g fiber, 17 g pro.

Quick Tip Because of their size and meaty texture, portobello mushrooms—the mature version of golden-brown cremini mushrooms—are perfect for making grilled sandwiches. Look for portobellos that are plump, fresh, and spotless. The gills—accordianlike folds under the cap—should be tightly closed. The tighter the gills, the fresher the mushroom.

Portobello Burgers

Zucchini Cakes with Mushroom Ragout

For the sauce, use several different mushrooms, such as button, cremini, chanterelle, and shiitake. Remove the stems from the shiitake—they're woody and inedible.

Prep: 10 minutes **Bake:** 11 minutes **Oven:** 400°F
Makes: 4 servings

　　Nonstick cooking spray
1　**cup shredded zucchini (1/2 a medium)**
1　**8.5-ounce package corn muffin mix**
1　**cup shredded cheddar cheese (4 ounces)**
1/4　**cup milk**
1　**egg, lightly beaten**
1/4　**teaspoon cayenne pepper**
1　**tablespoon olive oil**
12　**ounces assorted mushrooms, quartered (4 1/2 cups)**
　　Salt and ground black pepper
1　**cup drained bottled roasted red sweet peppers**

1. Preheat oven to 400°F. Lightly coat twelve 2 1/2-inch muffin cups with cooking spray; set aside.

2. In a large bowl, combine zucchini, muffin mix, cheese, milk, egg, and cayenne pepper; mix well. Spoon evenly into prepared muffin cups. Bake for 11 to 14 minutes or until golden.

3. Meanwhile, in a large skillet, heat olive oil over medium-high heat. Add mushrooms; cook for 3 to 4 minutes or until tender, stirring occasionally. Season with salt and black pepper. Place roasted peppers in blender. Cover; blend until nearly smooth.

4. For each serving, arrange 3 cakes on a plate with some of the mushrooms and puréed peppers.

Per serving: 443 cal., 21 g total fat (7 g sat. fat), 84 mg chol., 701 mg sodium, 49 g carbo., 2 g fiber, 16 g pro.

Three-Grain Risotto

Caciotta (kah-COH-tah) is a semifirm Italian cheese that's often flavored with sage. If it's not available, use provolone or mozzarella—and add 1/2 teaspoon of crushed dried sage leaves along with the cheese.

Prep: 30 minutes **Cook:** 28 minutes **Makes:** 6 servings

2　**medium fennel bulbs with tops**
1　**tablespoon olive oil**
1/3　**cup finely chopped onion (1 small)**
3　**cloves garlic, minced**
1/2　**teaspoon ground white pepper**
1/2　**cup Arborio or short grain rice**
1/2　**cup quick-cooking barley**
1/4　**cup quinoa or quick-cooking brown rice**
1　**14-ounce can reduced-sodium vegetable broth**
1　**cup water**
1/4　**cup dry white wine or water**
1　**tablespoon snipped fresh rosemary**
　　or 1 teaspoon dried rosemary, crushed
1　**teaspoon snipped fresh marjoram**
　　or 1/2 teaspoon dried marjoram, crushed
1　**cup shredded Caciotta with sage, provolone, or mozzarella cheese (4 ounces)**
1/2　**cup half-and-half or light cream**
　　Fresh rosemary sprigs (optional)

1. Remove any tough or brown outer layers of fennel bulbs. Rinse whole fennel with cold water; gently shake dry. Remove and discard the top 2 inches of fennel stalks, reserving green fronds. Snip fronds; set aside. Remove and finely chop remaining fennel stalks.

2. Cut one fennel bulb in six 1/4-inch slices; set aside. Pull apart leaf and stalk sections of remaining bulb. Chop and set aside (about 1 cup).

3. In a small saucepan, cook fennel bulb slices, covered, in a small amount of lightly salted water about 5 minutes or just until tender. Drain; set aside. In a large saucepan, heat olive oil over medium heat. Add chopped fennel, onion, garlic, and pepper; cook for 4 to 5 minutes or until tender, stirring often. Add rice, barley, and quinoa; cook and stir for 3 minutes more.

4. Stir in broth, water, white wine, snipped or dried rosemary, and marjoram. Return to boiling; reduce heat. Simmer, covered, about 20 minutes or until grains are tender, stirring often.

5. Remove saucepan from heat. Add cheese and half-and-half, stirring until cheese is melted. To serve, sprinkle with fennel leaves. Garnish with reserved cooked fennel slices and, if desired, fresh rosemary sprigs.

Per serving: 283 cal., 11 g total fat (5 g sat. fat), 21 mg chol., 386 mg sodium, 35 g carbo., 9 g fiber, 10 g pro.

Quick Tip Fennel is an anise-flavor bulb commonly used in Italian cooking. The bulb itself, the stalks, and feathery fronds, or leaves, all can be used. The bulb and stalks are eaten raw or cooked—the fronds are most often used as a fresh garnish. Choose fennel that is bright white, with no bruises or scuff marks, and that feels heavy for its size. Fronds should be bright green and fresh—not wilted or wet.

Italian Mozzarella Salad

This take on "insalata caprese," the Italian mozzarella salad, gets a protein and fiber boost from two kinds of beans.

Start to Finish: 30 minutes **Makes:** 4 servings

- ¼ **cup red wine vinegar**
- ¼ **cup olive oil**
- 1½ **teaspoons snipped fresh basil or ½ teaspoon dried basil, crushed**
- 1 **teaspoon Dijon-style mustard**
- ¼ **teaspoon crushed red pepper**
- 1 **clove garlic, minced**
- 1 **15-ounce can black beans or garbanzo beans (chickpeas), rinsed and drained**
- 1 **15-ounce can butter beans or Great Northern beans, rinsed and drained**
- 1 **small cucumber, quartered lengthwise and sliced (1 cup)**
- 1 **8-ounce round or log fresh mozzarella cheese or part-skim Scamorza, thinly sliced**
- 2 **red and/or yellow tomatoes, thinly sliced**
- ½ **cup thinly sliced green onions (4)**
   Fresh basil sprigs (optional)

1. For dressing, in a screw-top jar, combine vinegar, olive oil, snipped basil, mustard, crushed red pepper, and garlic. Cover and shake well.

2. In a large bowl, combine beans, cucumber, and the dressing; toss to mix. Divide among 4 plates. Arrange cheese and tomato slices alternately on bean mixture. Sprinkle with green onions. If desired, garnish with basil sprigs.

Per serving: 433 cal., 23 g total fat (8 g sat. fat), 32 mg chol., 834 mg sodium, 36 g carbo., 11 g fiber, 26 g pro.

The New Chef's Salad

Traditional 1970s-era chef's salad is composed of iceberg lettuce and strips of meat and cheese. This meatless version gets a makeover that features spinach, cabbage, kidney beans, fresh vegetables, and a low-fat dressing.

Start to Finish: 25 minutes **Makes:** 4 servings

- ⅓ **cup fat-free mayonnaise dressing or salad dressing**
- ⅓ **cup light sour cream**
- 2 **teaspoons white wine vinegar**
- 2 **cloves garlic, minced**
- 1½ **teaspoons snipped fresh marjoram or ½ teaspoon dried marjoram, crushed**
- ¼ **teaspoon dry mustard**
- ⅛ **teaspoon salt**
- 3 **tablespoons fat-free milk**
- 2 **cups Boston or Bibb lettuce**
- 2 **cups torn fresh spinach**
- 1 **15-ounce can reduced-sodium kidney beans or garbanzo beans (chickpeas), rinsed and drained**
- 1 **cup shredded red cabbage**
- 1 **cup thinly sliced zucchini (1 small)**
- 1 **cup shredded reduced-fat cheddar cheese (4 ounces)**
- 1 **small green or red sweet pepper, cut in thin bite-size strips**
- ½ **cup thinly sliced radishes**
- ½ **cup halved cherry tomatoes**
- 1 **hard-cooked egg, sliced**

1. For dressing, in a small bowl, combine mayonnaise dressing, sour cream, vinegar, garlic, marjoram, mustard, and salt. Stir in the milk.

2. In a large salad bowl, toss together lettuce, spinach, kidney beans, cabbage, zucchini, cheddar cheese, sweet pepper, radishes, and tomatoes. Pour the dressing over all; toss to coat. Divide mixture among 4 plates. Arrange egg slices on salad.

Per serving: 275 cal., 8 g total fat (4 g sat. fat), 76 mg chol., 740 mg sodium, 34 g carbo., 7 g fiber, 20 g pro.

Poached Eggs with Polenta and Black Beans

Great for brunch or supper, this dish calls for tubes of prepared polenta—just slice and fry.

Start to Finish: 35 minutes **Makes:** 4 servings

- 3 **medium plum tomatoes, seeded and chopped**
- ½ **cup canned black beans, rinsed and drained**
- 2 **tablespoons chopped red onion**
- 1 **fresh jalapeño chile, seeded and finely chopped (see tip, page 22)**
- 1 **tablespoon snipped fresh cilantro**
- 2 **teaspoons balsamic vinegar**
- 1 **teaspoon olive oil**
- ⅛ **teaspoon salt**
- ⅛ **teaspoon ground black pepper**
- 1 **16-ounce tube refrigerated plain cooked polenta**
- 1 **tablespoon olive oil**
- 4 **eggs**
- 2 **teaspoons snipped fresh cilantro**
   Lime wedges

1. For salsa, in a small bowl, combine tomatoes, black beans, red onion, jalapeño chile, the 1 tablespoon cilantro, the balsamic vinegar, the 1 teaspoon oil, the salt, and black pepper. Set aside until ready to serve.

2. Unwrap the polenta and cut into 12 slices. In an extra-large nonstick skillet, heat the 1 tablespoon olive oil over medium heat. Add polenta; cook for 14 to 16 minutes or until polenta is browned and crisp, turning once halfway through cooking.

Poached Eggs with
Polenta and Black Beans

3. Meanwhile, to poach eggs, fill a large skillet half full with water. Bring to boiling; reduce heat to simmering (bubbles begin to break the surface of the water). Break 1 of the eggs into a measuring cup. Carefully slide egg into simmering water, holding the lip of the cup as close to the water as possible. Repeat with remaining eggs, allowing each egg an equal amount of space. Simmer, uncovered, for 3 to 5 minutes or until the egg whites are completely set and yolks begin to thicken but are not hard. Using a slotted spoon, remove eggs.

4. To serve, divide polenta slices among 4 plates. Top with salsa and poached eggs. Sprinkle eggs with additional salt and black pepper. Sprinkle with the 2 teaspoons cilantro. Serve with lime wedges.

Per serving: 254 cal., 10 g total fat (2 g sat. fat), 213 mg chol., 768 mg sodium, 29 g carbo., 6 g fiber, 11 g pro.

Quick Tip If you have trouble keeping poached eggs intact, add a teaspoon or so of vinegar to the boiling water, then slip in the eggs. Vinegar helps the eggs keep their shape by quickly firming up and congealing the edges.

Summer Stew, **page 175**

Teriyaki Beef Soup, **page 177**

Chunky Bean and Chicken Chili, **page 182**

Creamy Tomato and Shrimp Chowder, **page 189**

Soups and Stews

Soups and stews are always comfort foods for any season. From whisper-light broth-based soups to stick-to-your ribs stews, these recipes offer variety and good taste in little time.

Easy Beef Borscht ⬚

Borscht is a classic Eastern European and Russian soup of beets and cabbage. The addition of beef makes it a main dish. Serve it with dark rye or pumpernickel bread.

Start to Finish: 18 minutes **Makes:** 4 servings

- 1 **17-ounce package refrigerated cooked beef roast au jus**
- 1 **15-ounce can julienne beets, undrained**
- 3 **cups reduced-sodium beef broth**
- 2 **cups coarsely chopped cabbage (about ⅓ a small head)**
- ½ **cup chopped tomato (1 medium)**
   Ground black pepper
   Sour cream (optional)

1. Place beef roast and juices in a large saucepan. Add undrained beets and beef broth. Bring to boiling, breaking up meat with a spoon. Add cabbage and tomato. Simmer, covered, for 5 minutes. Season to taste with pepper. If desired, serve with sour cream.

Per serving: 222 cal., 9 g total fat (4 g sat. fat), 64 mg chol., 1,014 mg sodium, 13 g carbo., 3 g fiber, 26 g pro.

French Onion and Beef Soup

This quick soup is a great way to use up leftover steak or beef roast. Serve the soup with a salad of vinaigrette-dressed baby greens.

Start to Finish: 25 minutes **Makes:** 4 servings

- 3 **tablespoons butter or margarine**
- 1 **medium onion, thinly sliced and separated in rings**
- 2 **10.5-ounce cans condensed French onion soup**
- 2½ **cups water**
- 2 **cups cubed cooked beef (10 ounces)**
- 4 **1-inch slices French bread**
- ½ **cup shredded Gruyère or Swiss cheese (2 ounces)**

1. Preheat broiler. In a large skillet, melt butter over medium heat. Add onion; cook about 5 minutes or until tender. Stir in soup, water, and beef. Bring to boiling, stirring occasionally.

2. Meanwhile, place the bread slices on a baking sheet. Broil 4 inches from the heat about 1 minute or until toasted on one side. Top the toasted sides of bread slices with shredded cheese; broil about 1 minute more or until cheese is melted.

3. To serve, ladle soup into soup bowls. Top with bread slices, cheese sides up.

Per serving: 465 cal., 21 g total fat (10 g sat. fat), 82 mg chol., 1,701 mg sodium, 40 g carbo., 3 g fiber, 28 g pro.

Quick Meatball Minestrone ⬚

Using small ½-ounce meatballs in this soup makes it easy to eat with a spoon. (Larger ones might end up on your lap.)

Start to Finish: 25 minutes **Makes:** 6 to 8 servings

- 1 **12- to 16-ounce package frozen cooked Italian-style meatballs**
- 3 **14-ounce cans lower-sodium beef broth**
- 1 **15- to 16-ounce can Great Northern beans or white kidney (cannellini) beans, rinsed and drained**
- 1 **14.5-ounce can diced tomatoes with basil, garlic, and oregano, undrained**
- 1 **10-ounce package frozen mixed vegetables**
- 1 **cup dried small pasta (such as macaroni, small shell, mini penne, or rotini)**
- 1 **teaspoon sugar**
   Finely shredded Parmesan cheese (optional)

1. In a 4-quart Dutch oven, stir together meatballs, beef broth, beans, undrained tomatoes, and frozen vegetables. Bring to boiling. Stir in pasta. Return to boiling; reduce heat. Simmer, uncovered, about 10 minutes or until pasta is tender and meatballs are heated through. Stir in sugar. If desired, sprinkle servings with Parmesan.

Per serving: 413 cal., 15 g total fat (7 g sat. fat), 40 mg chol., 1,242 mg sodium, 47 g carbo., 8 g fiber, 24 g pro.

Sweet Chili with Beef and Beans ⬚

The sweet in this bowl of red comes from peach salsa and a ripe fresh mango.

Start to Finish: 20 minutes **Makes:** 4 servings

- 1 **pound lean ground beef**
- 2 **15-ounce cans chili beans in chili sauce, undrained**
- 1 **16-ounce jar peach salsa**
- 1 **8-ounce can tomato sauce**
- 1 **mango, seeded, peeled, and chopped**

1. In a very large skillet, cook ground beef over medium-high heat until browned. Drain off fat. Stir in undrained chili beans, salsa, and tomato sauce. Bring to boiling; reduce heat. Simmer, covered, for 10 minutes. Stir in mango just before serving.

Per serving: 576 cal., 19 g total fat (7 g sat. fat), 77 mg chol., 954 mg sodium, 67 g carbo., 15 g fiber, 34 g pro.

Quick Meatball Minestrone

Summer Stew

Summer Stew

This vegetable-packed stew is cooked just long enough for the vegetables to stay crisp-tender and fresh-tasting.

Start to Finish: 20 minutes **Makes:** 4 servings

- 1 **17-ounce package refrigerated cooked beef roast au jus**
- 1 **8-ounce package peeled fresh baby carrots, sliced**
- 3½ **cups water**
- ½ **a 16-ounce package refrigerated rosemary- and-roasted garlic-seasoned diced red-skinned potatoes (about 2 cups)**
- 1 **14.5-ounce can diced fire-roasted tomatoes with garlic, undrained**
- 2 **tablespoons snipped fresh oregano**
  Salt
  Freshly ground black pepper

1. Pour juices from beef roast into a large saucepan; set meat aside. Add carrots and 1 cup water to saucepan. Bring to boiling; reduce heat. Simmer, covered, for 3 minutes. Add remaining 2½ cups water, the potatoes, undrained tomatoes, and 1 tablespoon of the oregano. Return to boiling. Simmer, covered, about 3 minutes or until vegetables are tender. Break beef into bite-size pieces and add to stew; heat through. Season with salt.

2. Spoon into shallow bowls; top with freshly ground pepper and the remaining 1 tablespoon oregano.

Per serving: 253 cal., 9 g total fat (4 g sat. fat), 64 mg chol., 948 mg sodium, 20 g carbo., 3 g fiber, 25 g pro.

Hamburger-Vegetable Soup

If frozen succotash isn't in the freezer section of your supermarket, use 1 cup each frozen corn and frozen lima beans.

Prep: 20 minutes **Cook:** 10 minutes **Makes:** 6 servings

- 1 **pound lean ground beef or ground pork**
- ½ **cup chopped onion (1 medium)**
- ½ **cup chopped green sweet pepper**
- 4 **cups beef broth**
- 1 **14.5-ounce can diced tomatoes, undrained**
- 1 **10-ounce package frozen succotash**
- ½ **cup chopped, peeled potato or ½ cup frozen diced hash brown potatoes**
- ½ **cup purchased shredded carrot or 1 medium carrot, cut in short thin strips**
- 1 **teaspoon dried basil, crushed**
- 1 **teaspoon Worcestershire sauce**
- ⅛ **teaspoon ground black pepper**

1. In a large saucepan, cook ground meat, onion, and sweet pepper over medium heat until meat is browned and onion is tender; drain off fat.

2. Stir beef broth, undrained tomatoes, succotash, potato, carrot, basil, Worcestershire sauce, and black pepper into meat mixture in saucepan. Bring to boiling; reduce heat. Simmer, covered, for 10 to 15 minutes or until vegetables are tender.

Per serving: 227 cal., 8 g total fat (3 g sat. fat), 48 mg chol., 613 mg sodium, 19 g carbo., 3 g fiber, 20 g pro.

Taco Soup

Make this family-friendly soup vegetarian-friendly with the Taco Bean Soup variation.

Prep: 10 minutes **Cook:** 10 minutes
Makes: 4 to 6 servings

- 1 **pound lean ground beef**
- 2 **cups water**
- 1 **15-ounce can black beans, rinsed and drained**
- 1 **14.5-ounce can Mexican-style stewed tomatoes, undrained and cut up**
- 1 **10.75-ounce can condensed fiesta nacho cheese soup**
  Broken tortilla chips (optional)

1. In a large saucepan, cook ground beef over medium heat until browned. Drain off fat.

2. Stir water, black beans, undrained tomatoes, and cheese soup into meat mixture in saucepan. If necessary, use a wire whisk to stir mixture until smooth. Bring to boiling; reduce heat. Simmer, covered, for 10 minutes. If desired, top servings with tortilla chips.

Per serving: 355 cal., 16 g total fat (7 g sat. fat), 78 mg chol., 1,148 mg sodium, 27 g carbo., 5 g fiber, 30 g pro.

Taco Bean Soup: Prepare as above, except omit ground beef. Stir in one 16-ounce can refried beans before cooking.

Per serving: 266 cal., 6 g total fat (2 g sat. fat), 6 mg chol., 1,646 mg sodium, 43 g carbo., 11 g fiber, 15 g pro.

Taco Soup

Italian Wedding Soup

This classic Italian soup always features the trio of meatballs, greens—usually spinach or escarole—and pasta.

Prep: 20 minutes **Cook:** 12 minutes **Makes:** 6 servings

- 1 **tablespoon cooking oil**
- 2 **medium red and/or yellow sweet peppers, chopped (1 1/2 cups)**
- 1 **medium red onion or fennel bulb, chopped (1/2 cup)**
- 3 **14-ounce cans chicken broth with roasted garlic**
- 1 **cup bottled marinara pasta sauce**
- 1 **16-ounce package frozen cooked Italian-style meatballs (32 bite-size meatballs)**
- 1 **cup dried mini penne pasta**
- 3 **cups packaged prewashed fresh baby spinach, chopped**
   Shredded Italian-blend cheese

1. In a Dutch oven, heat oil over medium heat. Add sweet peppers and onion; cook and stir about 5 minutes or until tender.

2. Add chicken broth and marinara sauce to sweet pepper mixture; bring to boiling. Carefully stir in meatballs and pasta. Return to boiling; reduce heat. Simmer, uncovered, for 12 to 15 minutes or until pasta is tender. Stir in spinach. Sprinkle servings with shredded cheese.

Per serving: 387 cal., 23 g total fat (10 g sat. fat), 58 mg chol., 1,605 mg sodium, 25 g carbo., 5 g fiber, 19 g pro.

Quick Tip If you can't find mini penne for this soup, substitute any small pasta, such as elbow macaroni, mini shells, or ditalini—a short, fat tubular pasta.

Teriyaki Beef Soup ♥

Add crunch to this Asian-style soup by adding a couple handfuls of bean sprouts to the soup right before serving.

Start to Finish: 30 minutes **Makes:** 5 servings

- 8 **ounces boneless beef top sirloin steak**
- 2 **teaspoons olive oil**
- 1 **large shallot, cut in thin rings**
- 2 **14-ounce cans lower-sodium beef broth**
- 1 **cup water**
- 1/2 **cup apple juice or apple cider**
- 2 **medium carrots, cut in thin bite-size strips (1 cup)**
- 1/3 **cup instant brown rice or quick-cooking barley**
- 2 **tablespoons light teriyaki sauce**
- 1 **tablespoon grated fresh ginger**
- 3 **cloves garlic, minced**
- 1/4 **teaspoon crushed red pepper**
- 2 **cups coarsely chopped broccoli**

1. Trim fat from steak. Cut steak in thin bite-size strips. In a large saucepan, heat olive oil over medium-high heat. Add steak and shallot; cook and stir for 2 to 3 minutes or until beef is browned. Using a slotted spoon, remove beef mixture from saucepan; set aside.

2. In the same saucepan, combine beef broth, water, apple juice, carrots, rice, teriyaki sauce, ginger, garlic, and crushed red pepper. Bring to boiling; reduce heat. Simmer, covered, for 10 minutes.

3. Stir in broccoli and the beef mixture. Bring to boiling; reduce heat. Simmer, covered, for 3 to 5 minutes or until rice and vegetables are tender.

Per serving: 162 cal., 4 g total fat (1 g sat. fat), 28 mg chol., 481 mg sodium, 18 g carbo., 2 g fiber, 13 g pro.

Teriyaki Beef Soup

Italian Beef Soup 🔲

Although pesto from a jar is a great convenience product, refrigerated pesto stays fresher longer and has better color and flavor.

Start to Finish: 25 minutes **Makes:** 6 servings

- 1 **pound lean ground beef**
- 2 **14-ounce cans beef broth**
- 1 **16-ounce package frozen broccoli and/or cauliflower florets**
- 1 **14.5-ounce can diced tomatoes, undrained**
- 1 **5.5-ounce can tomato juice (³⁄₄ cup)**
- 1 **cup dried rotini, wagon wheel, or other small pasta**
- ¹⁄₂ **cup basil pesto**

1. In a 4-quart Dutch oven, cook ground beef over medium heat until browned. Drain off fat.

2. Stir beef broth, broccoli, undrained tomatoes, and tomato juice into meat mixture in saucepan. Bring to boiling; stir in pasta. Reduce heat. Simmer, covered, about 10 minutes or until vegetables and pasta are tender. Stir in pesto.

Per serving: 317 cal., 16 g total fat (5 g sat. fat), 54 mg chol., 905 mg sodium, 20 g carbo., 4 g fiber, 21 g pro.

Spicy BBQ Stew 🔲

Spark this soup with color by using a combination of green, red, yellow, and orange sweet peppers.

Start to Finish: 20 minutes **Makes:** 4 servings

- 1 **18-ounce container prepared barbecue shredded pork**
- 2 **cups coarsely chopped green sweet peppers (2 large)**
- 1¹⁄₂ **cups frozen corn, thawed**
- 1 **cup water**
- 1 **15-ounce can sweet potatoes in syrup**
- ¹⁄₄ **cup shredded cheddar cheese (1 ounce)**

1. In a large saucepan, combine pork, sweet peppers, corn, and water. Cook, covered, over medium-high heat about 7 minutes or until peppers are crisp-tender, stirring occasionally.

2. Meanwhile, drain sweet potatoes. If whole, cut in cubes. Stir sweet potatoes into pork mixture; cook for 2 to 3 minutes or until heated through. Sprinkle servings with cheese.

Per serving: 358 cal., 8 g total fat (3 g sat. fat), 42 mg chol., 1,022 mg sodium, 53 g carbo., 5 g fiber, 21 g pro.

Italian Beef Soup

Corn and Sausage Chowder

Corn and Sausage Chowder

This creamy, hearty chowder starts with a package of quick-cooking shredded hash browns rather than whole potatoes.

Start to Finish: 20 minutes **Makes:** 5 servings

1	**20-ounce package refrigerated shredded hash brown potatoes**
1	**14-ounce can reduced-sodium chicken broth**
1	**10-ounce package frozen whole kernel corn**
2	**cups milk**
12	**ounces cooked link sausage, halved lengthwise and sliced**
1/3	**cup sliced green onions (3)**
1/4	**teaspoon ground black pepper**
	Salt
	Green or red bottled hot pepper sauce (optional)
2	**tablespoons snipped fresh cilantro**

1. In a 4-quart Dutch oven, combine hash brown potatoes, chicken broth, and corn. Bring to boiling; reduce heat. Simmer, covered, about 10 minutes or until potatoes are tender, stirring occasionally.

2. Using a potato masher, slightly mash potatoes. Stir in milk, sausage, green onions, and black pepper. Heat through. Season to taste with salt and, if desired, bottled hot pepper sauce. Sprinkle with cilantro.

Per serving: 439 cal., 22 g total fat (8 g sat. fat), 65 mg chol., 873 mg sodium, 41 g carbo., 3 g fiber, 22 g pro.

Quick Tip Most chowder recipes call for whole or 2% milk so the chowder has body and creaminess. If you're trying to trim calories and fat, however, substitute an equal amount of condensed fat-free milk in most chowders without sacrificing flavor and richness.

Pizza Soup

Italian Pumpkin Soup 🔲

Pumpkin adds sweetness—and good amounts of vitamins A and C—to this savory soup.

Start to Finish: 25 minutes **Makes:** 6 servings

- 1 **pound bulk mild Italian sausage**
- 2 **14-ounces cans reduced-sodium chicken broth**
- 2 **medium potatoes, peeled and chopped (10 ounces)**
- 1 **cup canned pumpkin**
- 1 **cup milk**
- 1 **teaspoon dried thyme, crushed**
- 2 **cups shredded fresh spinach**

1. In a Dutch oven, cook sausage over medium-high heat until browned. Drain off fat. Add chicken broth and potatoes. Bring to boiling; reduce heat. Simmer, covered, for 10 minutes.

2. Stir in pumpkin, milk, and thyme. Return to boiling; remove from heat. Stir in spinach.

Per serving: 354 cal., 25 g total fat (9 g sat. fat), 60 mg chol., 896 mg sodium, 18 g carbo., 2 g fiber, 15 g pro.

Pizza Soup 🔲

Here's a fun soup to please everyone—especially kids. Serve it with focaccia or Italian bread, if you like.

Start to Finish: 20 minutes **Makes:** 6 servings

- 1 **cup chopped onion (1 large)**
- 1 **cup chopped green sweet pepper (1 large)**
- 1 **cup sliced fresh mushrooms**
- 1 **cup halved, sliced zucchini**
- 1 **14-ounce can beef broth**
- 1 **14.5-ounce can Italian-style tomatoes, undrained and cut up**
- 1 **8-ounce can pizza sauce**
- 4 **ounces cooked smoked sausage links, thinly sliced**
- ½ **teaspoon pizza seasoning**
- ½ **cup shredded reduced-fat mozzarella cheese (2 ounces)**

1. In a medium saucepan, combine onion, sweet pepper, mushrooms, zucchini, and ¼ cup of the beef broth. Bring to boiling; reduce heat. Simmer, covered, for 5 minutes.

2. Stir in the remaining beef broth, the undrained tomatoes, pizza sauce, sausage, and pizza seasoning. Simmer, covered, for 5 to 10 minutes more or until vegetables are tender. Top servings with cheese.

Per serving: 163 cal., 9 g total fat (3 g sat. fat), 18 mg chol., 919 mg sodium, 12 g carbo., 2 g fiber, 10 g pro.

Country Captain Soup 🔲

The roots of this Southern dish reach back to India. It's thought to have been brought to North America by an English sea captain who was stationed in Bengal and who introduced it to friends when he visited the port city of Savannah.

Prep: 10 minutes **Cook:** 20 minutes **Makes:** 6 servings

- 2 **teaspoons olive oil**
- ¾ **cup chopped green sweet pepper (1 medium)**
- ⅔ **cup chopped, peeled Granny Smith apple (1 medium)**
- ½ **cup chopped onion (1 medium)**
- 2 **cloves garlic, minced**
- 1 **tablespoon curry powder**
- 1 **teaspoon grated fresh ginger**
- 1¼ **pounds skinless, boneless chicken thighs, cut in 1-inch pieces**
- 2 **14-ounce cans chicken broth**
- 1 **14.5-ounce can petite diced tomatoes with jalapeños, undrained**

1. In a large saucepan, heat olive oil over medium heat. Add sweet pepper, apple, onion, and garlic. Cook about 4 minutes or until tender. Add curry powder and ginger; cook for 1 minute.

2. Add chicken, chicken broth, and undrained tomatoes. Bring to boiling; reduce heat. Simmer, covered, about 15 minutes or until chicken is no longer pink.

Per serving: 225 cal., 11 g total fat (3 g sat. fat), 67 mg chol., 909 mg sodium, 11 g carbo., 2 g fiber, 20 g pro.

Country Captain Soup

Chunky Bean and Chicken Chili

Crushed tortilla chips thicken the chili, while whole chips sprinkled with cheese add crunch.

Start to Finish: 20 minutes **Makes:** 4 servings

- 3 **cups tortilla chips**
- 2 **teaspoons vegetable oil**
- 1 **pound skinless, boneless chicken breasts or thighs, cut in bite-size pieces**
- 2 **19-ounces cans white kidney (cannelini) beans, rinsed and drained**
- 1½ **cups shredded Monterey Jack cheese with jalapeño peppers (6 ounces)**
- 1 **4.5-ounce can diced green chiles, undrained**
- 1 **14-ounce can reduced-sodium chicken broth**
- ½ **cup water**
  Fresh cilantro (optional)

1. Preheat broiler. Coarsely crush 2 cups of the chips.

2. In 4- to 5- quart Dutch oven, heat vegetable oil over medium-high heat. Add chicken; cook until browned. Add beans, 1 cup of the cheese, the undrained chiles, chicken broth, water, and the 2 cups crushed chips. Bring to boiling; reduce heat. Simmer, uncovered, for 5 minutes, stirring occasionally.

3. Meanwhile, for tortilla crisps, place the remaining 1 cup chips on a baking sheet lined with nonstick foil. Sprinkle with the remaining ½ cup cheese. Broil 6 inches from heat for 1 to 2 minutes or until cheese is melted and begins to brown. Serve chili with tortilla crisps. If desired, sprinkle with cilantro.

Per serving: 575 cal., 23 g total fat (10 g sat. fat), 111 mg chol., 1,172 mg sodium, 52 g carbo., 14 g fiber, 55 g pro.

Coconut Lime Chicken Soup [one]

There are several Thai seasoning blends on the market. Most have some combination of ground chile, ginger, coriander, red pepper, cumin, cinnamon, star anise, garlic, lemon peel, and onion.

Start to Finish: 25 minutes **Makes:** 4 servings

- 1 **2- to 2½-pound whole roasted chicken**
- 1 **15-ounce can unsweetened coconut milk**
- 2 **cups water**
- ¼ **cup fresh lime juice (2 medium limes)**
- 1½ **cups bias-sliced carrots (3 medium)**
- 1 **tablespoon soy sauce**
- 2 **teaspoons Thai seasoning blend**
- ¼ **teaspoon salt**
  Thai seasoning blend (optional)
  Fresh cilantro (optional)
  Lime wedges (optional)

1. Remove and discard skin and bones from chicken. Shred chicken. In a large saucepan, combine shredded chicken, coconut milk, water, lime juice, carrots, soy sauce, the 2 teaspoons Thai seasoning, and salt. Bring to boiling; reduce heat. Simmer, covered, about 8 minutes or until carrot are crisp-tender.

2. If desired, sprinkle bowls of soup with additional Thai seasoning and cilantro and serve with lime wedges.

Per serving: 487 cal., 38 g total fat (24 g sat. fat), 125 mg chol., 1,437 mg sodium, 11 g carbo., 1 g fiber, 29 g pro.

Chicken and Dumpling Soup [one]

Serve this quintessential soup in 30 minutes by using leftover chicken and biscuit mix.

Start to Finish: 30 minutes **Makes:** 6 servings

- 5 **cups reduced-sodium chicken broth**
- 1 **cup sliced carrots (2 medium)**
- 1 **cup chopped celery (2 stalks)**
- ⅛ **teaspoon ground black pepper**
- 1½ **cups chopped cooked chicken (8 ounces)**
- 1½ **cups packaged biscuit mix**
- ½ **cup milk**

1. In a medium saucepan, combine chicken broth, carrots, celery, and pepper. Bring to boiling; reduce heat. Simmer, covered, for 10 minutes. Stir in chicken.

2. Meanwhile, for dumplings, in a medium bowl, combine biscuit mix and milk. Stir just until combined.

3. Spoon dough in 12 mounds on top of hot chicken mixture. Cook, covered, about 10 minutes or until a toothpick inserted into dumplings comes out clean.

Per serving: 222 cal., 8 g total fat (2 g sat. fat), 33 mg chol., 916 mg sodium, 23 g carbo., 1 g fiber, 15 g pro.

Chicken and Dumpling Soup

Wild Rice-Chicken Soup

Wild Rice-Chicken Soup ♥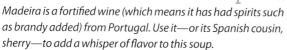

Madeira is a fortified wine (which means it has had spirits such as brandy added) from Portugal. Use it—or its Spanish cousin, sherry—to add a whisper of flavor to this soup.

Start to Finish: 25 minutes **Makes:** 8 servings

- 1 **6.2-ounce package quick-cooking long grain and wild rice mix**
- 2 **14-ounce cans reduced-sodium chicken broth**
- 4 **cloves garlic, minced**
- 1 **tablespoon snipped fresh thyme or 1 teaspoon dried thyme, crushed**
- 4 **cups chopped tomatoes (4 large)**
- 2 **cups chopped cooked chicken (10 ounces)**
- 1 **cup finely chopped zucchini (1 small)**
- ¼ **teaspoon freshly ground black pepper**
- 1 **tablespoon Madeira or dry sherry (optional)**

1. Prepare rice mix following package directions, except omit the seasoning packet and the butter.

2. Meanwhile, in a Dutch oven, combine chicken broth, garlic, and dried thyme (if using); bring to boiling. Stir in tomato, chicken, zucchini, fresh thyme (if using), and pepper. Return to boiling; reduce heat. Simmer, covered, for 5 minutes. Stir in cooked rice and, if desired, Madeira. Heat through.

Per serving: 174 cal., 3 g total fat (1 g sat. fat), 31 mg chol., 311 mg sodium, 22 g carbo., 2 g fiber, 15 g pro.

Chicken and Lentil Soup with Garlic-Cheese Toasts

Canned soups can be the starting point for quick, tasty meals. The base for this recipe is lentil soup and cooked chicken.

Start to Finish: 20 minutes **Makes:** 4 servings

- 1 **18.5-ounce can ready-to-serve lentil soup**
- 1 **cup frozen crinkle-cut carrots**
- ¼ **teaspoon dried thyme, crushed**
- 8 **slices French bread**
- 2 **tablespoons butter or margarine**
- ¼ **teaspoon garlic powder**
- ¾ **cup shredded mozzarella or cheddar cheese (3 ounces)**
- 1 **cup cubed cooked chicken (5 ounces)**
- 1 **5.5-ounce can tomato juice (²/₃ cup)**

1. Preheat broiler. In a medium saucepan, stir together soup, carrots, and thyme. Bring to boiling; reduce heat. Simmer, covered, for 8 to 9 minutes or until carrots are tender.

2. Meanwhile, for garlic-cheese toasts, place bread slices on the unheated rack of a broiler pan. Spread with butter; sprinkle with garlic powder. Broil 5 inches from heat about 1 minute or until golden. Top with cheese. Return to broiler; broil for 30 to 60 seconds or until cheese is slightly melted and edges are golden brown.

3. Stir the chicken and tomato juice into soup; heat through. Serve garlic-cheese toasts with soup.

Per serving: 459 cal., 14 g total fat (8 g sat. fat), 60 mg chol., 1,225 mg sodium, 56 g carbo., 6 g fiber, 28 g pro.

Tex-Mex Cream of Chicken Soup

Add a little more zing to this soup by using Monterey Jack with hot peppers in place of the plain cheese.

Start to Finish: 30 minutes **Makes:** 4 servings

8	ounces uncooked ground chicken or turkey
¼	cup chopped onion
2	cloves garlic, minced
2	cups milk
1	10.75-ounce can condensed cream of chicken soup
¾	cup chopped tomato (1 medium)
1	7-ounce can whole kernel corn with sweet peppers, drained
1	4-ounce can diced green chiles, drained
2	tablespoons snipped fresh cilantro or parsley
¼	teaspoon cayenne pepper
1	cup shredded Monterey Jack cheese (4 ounces)
	Fresh cilantro or parsley (optional)

1. In a large saucepan or Dutch oven, cook ground chicken, onion, and garlic over medium-high heat until chicken is browned and onion is tender. Drain off fat.

2. Stir in milk, soup, tomato, corn, chiles, the 2 tablespoons cilantro, and the cayenne pepper. Bring to boiling; reduce heat. Simmer, uncovered, for 5 minutes, stirring occasionally. Add cheese; cook and stir until cheese is melted. If desired, garnish servings with additional cilantro.

Per serving: 375 cal., 19 g total fat (9 g sat. fat), 68 mg chol., 1,481 mg sodium, 29 g carbo., 3 g fiber, 24 g pro.

Quick Tip If you're watching calories and fat grams, choose ground chicken or turkey made from breast meat only. If you can't find ground chicken or turkey breast in the meat department of your supermarket, ask a butcher to grind some for you. Most ground chicken or turkey is made from white and dark meat, as well as some skin. Ground turkey breast is about 3 percent fat, while regular ground turkey is about 10 percent fat.

Tex-Mex Cream of Chicken Soup

Chicken Paprikash Soup

Chicken Paprikash Soup

Try ladling this Hungarian-style soup over hot cooked spaetzle or egg noodles.

Prep: 10 minutes **Cook:** 15 minutes **Makes:** 6 servings

- ¼ **cup all-purpose flour**
- 2 **tablespoons paprika**
- ½ **teaspoon salt**
- ¼ **teaspoon ground black pepper**
- 1½ **pounds chicken breast tenderloins, cut in half**
- 2 **14-ounce cans chicken broth**
- 1 **tablespoon vegetable oil**
- 1 **cup frozen chopped onion, thawed and drained**
- 2 **teaspoons bottled minced garlic**
- ½ **of a 2-ounce package refrigerated sliced potatoes**
- 6 **tablespoons dairy sour cream**

1. In a resealable plastic bag, combine flour, paprika, salt, and pepper. Add half of the chicken; shake to coat. Place coated chicken on a plate and set aside. Repeat with remaining chicken.

2. In a small bowl, stir together flour mixture remaining in the plastic bag and 3 tablespoons of the chicken broth.

3. In a large saucepan, heat oil over medium-high heat. Add chicken; cook about 4 minutes or until browned. Add onion and garlic; cook for 1 minute. Stir in the remaining chicken broth and potatoes. Bring to boiling; reduce heat. Simmer, covered, for 5 minutes.

4. Stir in flour mixture. Cook and stir until thickened and bubbly. Cook and stir for 1 minutes more.

5. Ladle soup into 6 bowls; top with sour cream.

Per serving: 262 cal., 11 g total fat (4 g sat. fat), 72 mg chol., 821 mg sodium, 16 g carbo., 2 g fiber, 26 g pro.

Confetti Chicken Big Bowl

Prepared curry paste is available in red, green, and yellow varieties. This terrific product is complex and intense, so a little packs a big punch.

Prep: 30 minutes **Cook:** 6 minutes **Makes:** 6 servings

- 2 **tablespoons vegetable oil**
- 1 **pound skinless, boneless chicken breast halves, cut in 1-inch cubes**
- 4 **teaspoons minced garlic (8 cloves)**
- 4 **teaspoons minced fresh ginger**
- 1 **tablespoon red curry paste or ¼ teaspoon cayenne pepper**
- 1 **teaspoon ground cumin**
- 4 **cups water**
- 1 **14-ounce can unsweetened coconut milk**

2 cups shredded carrots (4 medium)
2 cups small broccoli florets
1 medium red sweet pepper, cut into bite-size strips
2 3-ounce packages chicken-flavor ramen noodles, coarsely broken
2 cups snow pea pods, halved crosswise
2 tablespoons soy sauce
4 teaspoons fresh lime juice
1 cup slivered fresh basil
1/3 cup snipped fresh cilantro

1. In a 4-quart Dutch oven, heat 1 tablespoon of the oil over medium-high heat. Add chicken; cook for 3 to 4 minutes or until lightly browned and no longer pink. Remove chicken from pan; set aside.

2. Add the remaining 1 tablespoon oil to pan. Add garlic, ginger, curry paste, and cumin; cook and stir for 30 seconds. Stir in water, coconut milk, carrots, broccoli, sweet pepper, and noodles (set seasoning packets aside). Bring to boiling; reduce heat. Simmer, covered, for 3 minutes. Stir in cooked chicken, pea pods, soy sauce, lime juice, and contents of seasoning packets. Stir in the basil and cilantro.

Per serving: 454 cal., 25 g total fat (12 g sat. fat), 44 mg chol., 1,087 mg sodium, 33 g carbo., 4 g fiber, 26 g pro.

Lemongrass Chicken Soup ♥ one

Add fire to this Asian-style soup by bundling up a hot chile pepper along with the lemongrass.

Start to Finish: 20 minutes **Makes:** 4 servings

2 large stalks lemongrass, peeled, trimmed, and cut in 4-inch pieces
3 cups chicken broth
1/4 cup sliced shiitake or button mushrooms
1/8 teaspoon cracked black pepper
1/2 cup cooked chicken breast, cut in pieces
6 thin fresh asparagus spears, cut up
1/4 cup thinly bias-sliced green onions (2)
Fresh basil leaves (optional)

1. Cut lemongrass pieces in half lengthwise. Tie lemongrass into a bundle with 100-percent-cotton string. In a medium saucepan, combine chicken broth, mushrooms, pepper, and lemongrass bundle. Bring to boiling; reduce heat. Simmer, uncovered, for 10 minutes.

2. Discard lemongrass. Add chicken and asparagus. Simmer, uncovered, about 3 minutes or until asparagus is crisp-tender. Remove from heat. Stir in green onions. Ladle into warm soup bowls. If desired, top with fresh basil leaves.

Per serving: 67 cal., 2 g total fat (1 g sat. fat), 15 mg chol., 597 mg sodium, 2 g carbo., 1 g fiber, 10 g pro.

Confetti Chicken Big Bowl

Creamy Tomato
and Shrimp Chowder

Creamy Tomato and Shrimp Chowder 🔲

This beautifully hued soup is incredibly elegant but so simple to make.

Start to Finish: 18 minutes **Makes:** 4 servings

- 1 tablespoon olive oil
- 1 cup chopped celery (2 stalks)
- 1/2 cup chopped onion (1 medium)
- 2 14.5-ounce cans diced tomatoes with basil, garlic, and oregano, undrained
- 8 ounces peeled and deveined cooked medium shrimp
- 1/2 cup whipping cream
- 1/2 cup water
   Ground black pepper
   Slivered fresh basil (optional)
   Focaccia, cut in wedges (optional)

1. In a large saucepan, heat olive oil over medium heat. Add celery and onion; cook just until tender.

2. Stir in undrained tomatoes; heat through. Add shrimp, whipping cream, and water. Cook over medium heat just until heated through. Season to taste with pepper. If desired, top with basil and serve with focaccia wedges.

Per serving: 245 cal., 15 g total fat (8 g sat. fat), 152 mg chol., 1,056 mg sodium, 14 g carbo., 2 g fiber, 15 g pro.

Thai Coconut-Shrimp Soup 🔲

Fish sauce provides the distinctive sweet-salty flavor that distinguishes Thai and Southeast Asian cooking. The sauce is widely available in the Asian section of supermarkets.

Start to Finish: 25 minutes **Makes:** 5 servings

- 12 ounces fresh or frozen medium shrimp, peeled and deveined
- 3 cups reduced-sodium chicken broth
- 1 14-ounce can unsweetened lite coconut milk
- 1 tablespoon fish sauce (nam pla)
- 2 teaspoons grated fresh ginger
- 1 teaspoon red curry paste
- 1 clove garlic, minced
- 1/2 teaspoon kosher salt
- 1 cup green beans, cut in 1-inch pieces (4 ounces)
- 1/4 cup thinly sliced green onions (2)
   Lime wedges (optional)

1. Thaw shrimp, if frozen. In a large saucepan, combine chicken broth, coconut milk, fish sauce, ginger, curry paste, garlic, and salt. Bring to boiling; reduce heat.

2. Add green beans; cook for 2 minutes. Add shrimp; cook

about 5 minutes or until shrimp turn opaque. Sprinkle servings with green onions. If desired, serve with lime.

Per serving: 160 cal., 7 g total fat (3.5 g sat. fat), 103 mg chol., 656 mg sodium, 9 g carbo., 1 g fiber, 18 g pro.

Soba Noodles in Broth 🔲

Look for soba noodles, mirin, and dashi in the Asian section of supermarkets or at Asian grocery stores.

Start to Finish: 20 minutes **Makes:** 2 servings

- 8 ounces fresh or frozen shrimp in shells
- 6 ounces soba (buckwheat noodles) or dried vermicelli
- 2 cups reduced-sodium chicken broth
- 1/4 cup mirin (Japanese sweet rice wine)
- 1/4 cup reduced-sodium soy sauce
- 2 teaspoons sugar
- 1/2 teaspoon instant dashi granules (dried tuna-and-seaweed-flavor soup stock)
- 1/4 cup thinly bias-sliced green onions (2)

1. Thaw shrimp, if frozen. Peel and devein shrimp, leaving tails intact. Rinse shrimp; pat dry with paper towels; set shrimp aside. In a large saucepan, cook soba noodles in boiling water about 4 minutes or until tender.

2. Meanwhile, in a medium saucepan, combine chicken broth, mirin, soy sauce, sugar, and dashi granules. Bring to boiling; reduce heat. Add shrimp; simmer, uncovered, about 2 minutes or until shrimp are opaque.

3. Drain noodles; divide noodles between 2 soup bowls. Pour the shrimp mixture over the noodles. Sprinkle with green onions.

Per serving: 515 cal., 2 g total fat (0 g sat. fat), 129 mg chol., 2,698 mg sodium, 93 g carbo., 4 g fiber, 35 g pro.

Soba Noodles in Broth

Tuscan Bean Soup

Tuscan Bean Soup

Rather than being stirred into the soup, the spinach is given a quick sauté in a hot skillet, then scooped on top of each serving. Add a little minced garlic to the pan, if you like.

Start to Finish: 20 minutes **Makes:** 4 servings

- 3 **tablespoons olive oil**
- 1 **cup packaged peeled baby carrots, coarsely chopped**
- ⅓ **cup chopped onion (1 small)**
- 2 **15-ounces cans white kidney (cannellini) beans, rinsed and drained**
- 1 **32-ounce carton reduced-sodium chicken broth**
- 2 **to 3 teaspoons dried Italian seasoning, crushed**
- 1 **5-ounce package fresh baby spinach**
  Freshly cracked black pepper
  Cracker bread (optional)

1. In a 4-quart Dutch oven, heat 1 tablespoon of the olive oil over medium-high heat. Add carrots and onion; cook and stir for 3 minutes. Add beans, chicken broth, and Italian seasoning. Bring to boiling; slightly mash beans. Reduce heat. Simmer, uncovered, for 8 minutes, stirring occasionally.

2. Meanwhile, in a large skillet, heat the remaining 2 tablespoons olive oil over medium-high heat. Add spinach; toss with tongs for 1 to 2 minutes or just until wilted. Remove from heat. Ladle soup into bowls; top with spinach and sprinkle with pepper. If desired, serve with cracker bread.

Per serving: 254 cal., 11 g total fat (2 g sat. fat), 0 mg chol., 919 mg sodium, 36 g carbo., 12 g fiber, 16 g pro.

Peanut Butter-Vegetable Soup one

This recipe is inspired by groundnut soup or stew—an African dish based on peanuts or peanut butter.

Start to Finish: 30 minutes **Makes:** 4 servings

- 2 **tablespoons butter or margarine**
- 1½ **cups sliced celery (3 stalks)**
- 1 **cup chopped carrots (2 medium)**
- 1 **cup chopped onion (1 large)**
- 3 **cloves garlic, minced**
- 3 **cups water**
- 1 **cup diced potato (1 medium)**
- 1 **cup sliced zucchini (1 medium)**
- 4 **teaspoons instant vegetable or chicken bouillon granules**
- ½ **teaspoon ground black pepper**
- 1 **14.5-ounce can diced tomatoes, undrained**
- 2 **tablespoons snipped fresh parsley**
- ½ **cup peanut butter**

1. In a large saucepan or Dutch oven, melt butter over medium heat. Add celery, carrots, onion, and garlic. Cook, covered, about 5 minutes or until onion is tender. Stir in water, potato, zucchini, bouillon granules, and pepper. Bring to boiling; reduce heat. Simmer, covered, for 10 minutes. Stir in undrained tomatoes and parsley.

2. In a small bowl, gradually stir about 1 cup of the broth into the peanut butter until smooth. Add peanut butter mixture to vegetable mixture in saucepan. Cook and stir until heated through.

Per serving: 337 cal., 22 g total fat (7 g sat. fat), 15 mg chol., 1,247 mg sodium, 28 g carbo., 7 g fiber, 11 g pro.

White Bean and Cabbage Soup one

Serve this veggie-rich soup with garlicky focaccia bread or olive-studded ciabatta.

Prep: 20 minutes **Cook:** 10 minutes **Makes:** 6 servings

- 1 **tablespoon olive oil**
- 3 **cups thinly sliced cabbage**
- 1 **cup sliced carrots (2 medium)**
- 1 **teaspoon dried thyme, crushed**
- ¼ **teaspoon ground black pepper**
- 6 **cloves garlic, minced**
- 2 **14-ounce cans chicken broth**
- 1 **14.5-ounce can diced tomatoes, undrained**
- 1 **cup water**
- ¼ **cup tomato paste**
- 2 **15-ounce cans white kidney (cannellini) beans, rinsed and drained**

1. In a 4-quart Dutch oven, heat olive oil over medium heat. Add cabbage, carrots, thyme, pepper, and garlic; cook and stir for 2 to 3 minutes or until cabbage begins to wilt. Stir in chicken broth, undrained tomatoes, water, and tomato paste. Bring to boiling; reduce heat. Simmer, covered, for 7 to 9 minutes or until vegetables are tender, stirring occasionally.

2. Meanwhile, slightly mash half the drained beans with a potato masher or fork. Add all the beans to the mixture in Dutch oven; heat through.

Per serving: 164 cal., 4 g total fat (1 g sat. fat), 0 mg chol., 1,006 mg sodium, 30 g carbo., 9 g fiber, 11 g pro.

Quick Tip Mash a portion of the beans for almost any broth-based bean soup to give the soup creaminess and body without adding cream.

Black Bean and Corn Soup

Black Bean and Corn Soup [one]

Make this Tex-Mex soup as spicy or mild as you like depending on the salsa you choose. You can also use either tomato-based salsa or a green salsa based on lemony-flavor tomatillos.

Start to Finish: 20 minutes **Makes:** 6 servings

- 2 **tablespoons vegetable oil**
- 1/2 **cup chopped red onion (1 medium)**
- 2 **15-ounce cans black beans, rinsed and drained**
- 1 **14-ounce can chicken broth**
- 1 **11-ounce can whole kernel corn, drained**
- 1 **cup bottled chunky salsa**
- 1 **tablespoon fresh lime juice**
- 1/2 **teaspoon salt**
- 1/8 **teaspoon ground black pepper**
  Sour cream (optional)
  Lime wedges (optional)

1. In a large saucepan, heat oil over medium heat. Add onion; cook until tender. Mash 1 cup of the beans with a potato masher or fork.

2. Add mashed beans, whole beans, chicken broth, corn, salsa, lime juice, salt, and pepper to saucepan. Bring to boiling; reduce heat. Simmer, uncovered, about 10 minutes or until heated through. If desired, serve with sour cream and lime wedges.

Per serving: 191 cal., 7 g total fat (1 g sat. fat), 2 mg chol., 1,171 mg sodium, 25 g carbo., 7 g fiber, 8 g pro.

Broccoli-Beer-Cheese Soup [one]

If you prefer not to use beer with alcohol in this soup, use a nonalcoholic beer. You'll get the flavor without the alcohol.

Start to Finish: 30 minutes **Makes:** 4 servings

- 3 **slices bacon, chopped**
- 1/2 **cup chopped onion (1 medium)**
- 2 **tablespoons all-purpose flour**
- 1/4 **teaspoon ground black pepper**
- 2 3/4 **cups chicken broth**
- 2 **cups bite-size broccoli florets**
- 2/3 **cup beer**

12 ounces smoked turkey breast, chopped
6 ounces process Swiss cheese, torn
⅓ cup half-and-half or light cream

1. In a large saucepan, cook bacon and onion until bacon is crisp and onion is tender, stirring occasionally. Stir in flour and pepper until well combined. Add chicken broth, broccoli, and beer. Bring to boiling; reduce heat. Simmer, uncovered, for 3 to 5 minutes or until broccoli is nearly tender. Add turkey, cheese, and half-and-half. Cook and stir until cheese is melted

Per serving: 386 cal., 22 g total fat (11 g sat. fat), 97 mg chol., 2,048 mg sodium, 13 g carbo., 2 g fiber, 31 g pro.

Golden Onion Soup

Cooking the onions slowly and adding just a pinch of sugar brings out the natural sweetness in the onions.

Start to Finish: 30 minutes **Makes:** 4 servings

4 large sweet onions (2 pounds), such as Oso, Maui, Walla Walla, or Vidalia
3 tablespoons butter
1 teaspoon sugar
¼ cup dry wine
3 cups chicken broth
2 cups water
Freshly ground black pepper or bottled hot sauce
4 1-inch slices French bread, lightly toasted
½ cup shredded Gruyère cheese

1. Cut onions in half, then thinly slice. In a large deep pot, heat butter over medium-high heat. Add sliced onions and stir to coat with butter. Cook, covered, for 10 minutes, stirring often. Add sugar; cook over high heat, uncovered, about 6 more minutes or until onions are golden. Add wine; cook for 1 minute. Add chicken broth and water. Bring to boiling; reduce heat. Simmer, covered, for 5 minutes. Stir in pepper to taste.

2. Meanwhile, preheat broiler. Arrange toasted bread slices on a baking sheet. Divide cheese among bread slices. Broil 3 to 4 inches from heat for 2 to 3 minutes or until cheese is light brown and bubbly. Divide soup among 4 bowls; top each with a bread slice.

Per serving: 336 cal., 17 g total fat (9 g sat. fat), 42 mg chol., 956 mg sodium, 35 g carbo., 5 g fiber, 10 g pro.

Quick Tip Simple dishes with few ingredients rely on those ingredients to be as good as they can be. To effortlessly improve the quality of cooking, use freshly ground black pepper. Grinding peppercorns when you need them releases natural oils—and that's where the flavor is. Buy a refillable grinder or whole peppercorns packaged in a disposable grinder.

Smoky Cheese and Corn Chowder ♥ 🄴

Brightened with red pimiento and green chives, this rich, creamy soup makes a warming and delicious supper for a casual holiday party.

Start to Finish: 25 minutes **Makes:** 4 servings

1 10-ounce package frozen whole kernel corn (2 cups)
½ cup chopped onion (1 medium)
½ cup water
1 teaspoon instant chicken bouillon granules
¼ teaspoon ground black pepper
2½ cups milk
3 tablespoons all-purpose flour
1 cup shredded smoked process cheddar cheese (4 ounces)
1 tablespoon chopped pimiento, drained
Fresh chives (optional)
Chopped pimiento (optional)

1. In a large saucepan, combine corn, onion, water, bouillon granules, and pepper. Bring to boiling; reduce heat. Simmer, covered, about 4 minutes or until corn is tender.

2. Stir together ½ cup of the milk and the flour; add to corn mixture along with the remaining milk. Cook and stir until slightly thickened and bubbly. Add cheese and the 1 tablespoon pimiento; heat and stir until cheese is melted.

3. If desired, garnish with chives and additional pimiento.

Per serving: 283 cal., 13 g total fat (8 g sat. fat), 42 mg chol., 462 mg sodium, 28 g carbo., 2 g fiber, 15 g pro.

Smoky Cheese and Corn Chowder

Lamb Chops with Tomatoes, **page 210**

Pizza Burgers,
page 202

Stuffed Veal Chops with
Gorgonzola, **page 204**

Mediterranean Lamb
Burgers, **page 212**

From the Grill

There's something special about food cooked over hot coals. Smoke and fire bring out flavors and textures in foods that make them succulent and absolutely delicious—with no (or very little) fuss required.

Chipotle Steak and Tomatoes

Chipotle Steak and Tomatoes

For a creamy dressing instead of vinaigrette, leave out the oil and vinegar and stir the chopped chipotle into $1/2$ cup bottled ranch dressing.

Prep: 10 minutes **Grill:** 10 minutes **Makes:** 4 servings

- 2 6- to 8-ounces beef shoulder petite tenders or beef ribeye steaks
  Salt and ground black pepper
- 1 canned chipotle pepper in adobo sauce, finely chopped, plus 2 teaspoons adobo sauce
- $1/4$ cup olive oil
- $1/4$ cup vinegar
- 3 medium tomatoes, thickly sliced (1 pound)
- 2 medium avocados, halved, seeded, peeled, and sliced
- $1/2$ a small red onion, thinly sliced

1. Trim fat from steaks. Sprinkle steaks lightly with salt and black pepper. Spread each with 1 teaspoon adobo sauce.

2. Place steaks on the rack of an uncovered grill directly over medium heat. Grill until desired doneness, turning once halfway through grilling. Allow 10 to 12 minutes for medium rare (145°F) or 12 to 15 minutes for medium (160°F).

3. Meanwhile, for dressing, in a screw-top jar, combine the chopped chipotle pepper, olive oil, and vinegar. Shake to combine.

4. Slice steaks. Arrange steak, tomato, and avocado on 4 plates. Top with onion slices; drizzle with dressing.

Per serving: 421 cal., 33 g total fat (6 g sat. fat), 50 mg chol., 221 mg sodium, 13 g carbo., 7 g fiber, 20 g pro.

Herbed Tenderloin Steaks and Vegetables ♥

For a simple side, stir bottled roasted garlic into refrigerated mashed potatoes.

Prep: 15 minutes **Grill:** 8 minutes **Makes:** 4 servings

- 2 cloves garlic
- $1/4$ cup loosely packed fresh basil leaves
- 2 tablespoons fresh thyme leaves
- 1 tablespoon fresh rosemary
- 1 tablespoon fresh mint leaves
- 2 tablespoons olive oil
- $1/2$ teaspoon salt
- $1/2$ teaspoon ground black pepper
- 4 4- to 5-ounce beef tenderloin steaks, cut 1 inch thick
- 2 large yellow tomatoes, halved crosswise
- 1 pound fresh asparagus spears, trimmed

1. For herb mixture, in a food processor or blender, process or blend garlic until finely chopped. Add basil, thyme, rosemary, and mint. Cover and process or blend until herbs are chopped. With food processor or blender running, add oil in a thin, steady stream through feed tube or opening in lid. (When necessary, stop food processor or blender and use a rubber scraper to scrape the sides of bowl or container.) Stir in salt and pepper.

2. Trim fat from steaks. Spread some of the herb mixture evenly on both sides of the steaks and cut sides of tomatoes; set aside. Fold an 18×12-inch piece of heavy foil in half to make a 9×12-inch double thickness of foil. Place asparagus in the center of the foil. Add remaining herb mixture, turning asparagus to coat evenly.

3. Place steaks and asparagus (on foil) on rack of an uncovered grill directly over medium heat. Grill for 5 minutes. Turn steaks and asparagus spears; add tomatoes to grill. Grill until steaks are desired doneness. Allow 3 to 7 minutes more for medium rare (145°F) or 7 to 10 minutes more for medium (160°F). Grill vegetables until asparagus is crisp-tender and tomatoes are hot (do not turn).

Per serving: 245 cal., 14 g total fat (4 g sat. fat), 65 mg chol., 322 mg sodium, 6 g carbo., 2 g fiber, 24 g pro.

Herbed Tenderloin Steaks and Vegetables

Deviled Steak ♥

The term "deviled" means added spiciness—mustard, hot sauce, cayenne pepper, or chopped chile peppers.

Prep: 5 minutes **Grill:** 10 minutes **Makes:** 4 servings

- 1 **tablespoon ketchup**
- 1 **tablespoon water**
- 1 **tablespoon Worcestershire sauce**
- 1 **teaspoon dry mustard**
- ¼ **teaspoon salt**
  Dash ground black pepper
- 1 **pound boneless beef tenderloin or sirloin steak, cut 1 inch thick**

1. For sauce, in a small bowl, combine ketchup, water, Worcestershire sauce, dry mustard, salt, and pepper.

2. Trim fat from steaks. Place steaks on the rack of an uncovered grill directly over medium-high heat. Grill for 6 minutes. Brush steaks with sauce. Turn and grill to desired doneness. Allow 4 to 6 minutes more for medium rare (145°F) or 6 to 9 minutes more for medium (145°F), brushing frequently with sauce. Brush any remaining sauce meat before serving.

Per serving: 186 cal., 9 g total fat (3 g sat. fat), 70 mg chol., 288 mg sodium, 2 g carbo., 0 g fiber, 24 g pro.

Southwest-Style Steak ♥

Serve this savory steak with Spanish rice, refried beans, and warmed tortillas.

Prep: 10 minutes **Grill:** 17 minutes **Stand:** 5 minutes **Makes:** 6 servings

- 2 **cloves garlic, peeled**
- ¾ **teaspoon salt**
- 1½ **pounds top round or flank steak, cut 1 inch thick**
- 1½ **teaspoons ground cumin**
- 1 **teaspoon chili powder**
- ½ **teaspoon dried oregano, crushed**
- ⅛ **teaspoon cayenne pepper**
  Lime wedges (optional)

1. Chop garlic and salt together on cutting board; press with side of large knife to form a paste. Trim fat from steak. Rub paste on both sides of steak.

2. For the spice rub, in a small bowl, combine cumin, chili powder, oregano, and cayenne pepper. Pat spice rub on both sides of steak.

3. Place steak on the oiled rack of an uncovered grill over medium heat for 17 to 21 minutes for medium (160°F), turning once halfway through grilling. Transfer to cutting board. Let stand for 5 minutes. Thinly slice steak diagonally across the grain. If desired, garnish with lime wedges.

Per serving: 180 cal., 8 g total fat (3 g sat. fat), 69 mg chol., 345 mg sodium, 1 g carbo., 0 g fiber, 25 g pro.

Rosemary Beef with Sweet Pepper Relish ♥

If you like, use balsamic vinegar in place of the red wine vinegar.

Prep: 22 minutes **Grill:** 8 minutes **Makes:** 4 servings

- 1 **medium red onion, thinly sliced**
- 1 **cup red, yellow, and/or orange sweet pepper strips**
- 1 **tablespoon red wine vinegar**
- 3 **teaspoons olive oil**
- ⅛ **teaspoon ground black pepper**
- 2 **teaspoons snipped fresh rosemary**
- 4 **cloves garlic, minced**
- 4 **4- to 5-ounce boneless beef top loin steaks, cut 1 inch thick**
- 1 **tablespoon prepared horseradish**

1. For relish, fold a 24×18-inch piece of heavy foil in half to measure 12×18 inches. Place onion and sweet pepper in center of foil. Drizzle vinegar and 2 teaspoons of the olive oil over vegetables; sprinkle with black pepper. Bring up 2 opposite edges of foil; seal with a double fold. Fold remaining ends to completely enclose vegetables, leaving space for steam to build. Set aside.

2. Combine the remaining 1 teaspoon olive oil, the rosemary, and garlic. Trim fat from steaks. Rub steaks with rosemary mixture. Spread 1 side of the steaks with horseradish.

3. Place steaks and relish packet on the rack of an uncovered grill directly over medium heat. Grill until desired doneness, turning steaks and relish packet halfway through grilling. Allow 8 to 12 minutes for medium rare (145°F) and 12 to 15 minutes for medium (160°F). Spoon relish over steaks to serve.

Per serving: 198 cal., 9 g total fat (2 g sat. fat), 65 mg chol., 92 mg sodium, 7 g carbo., 1 g fiber, 23 g pro.

Quick Tip Herbs such as rosemary and thyme have inedible woody stems. To strip the leaves from the stems, hold the stems over a bowl. Hold tightly onto the stem tip with one hand, and with the other hand, pull down the stem, stripping leaves to fall into the bowl.

Rosemary Beef with Sweet Pepper Relish

Flank Steak with Spanish Rice

You can enjoy steak even when you're watching fat intake. Flank steak is one of the leanest cuts of beef. At 7 grams of fat per serving, this dish is a guilt-free pleasure.

Start to Finish: 30 minutes **Makes:** 4 to 6 servings

- **1** **14.5-ounce can Mexican-style stewed tomatoes, undrained**
- **1³/₄** **cups water**
  Several dashes bottled hot pepper sauce
- **1¹/₄** **cups uncooked long grain rice**
- **1** **teaspoon chili powder**
- **¹/₂** **teaspoon salt**
- **¹/₄** **teaspoon ground cumin**
- **¹/₄** **teaspoon ground black pepper**
  Dash ground cinnamon
- **1** **1- to 1¹/₄-pound beef flank steak**

1. In a medium saucepan, combine undrained tomatoes, water, and hot pepper sauce. Bring to boiling. Stir in rice. Return to boiling; reduce heat. Simmer, covered, about 20 minutes or until rice is tender. Remove from heat; let stand for 5 minutes.

2. Meanwhile, in a small bowl, combine chili powder, salt, cumin, black pepper, and cinnamon. Trim fat from steak. Rub spice mixture onto both sides of steak.

3. Place steak on the rack of an uncovered grill directly over medium heat. Grill for 17 to 21 minutes or until medium doneness (160°F), turning once halfway through grilling.

4. To serve, thinly slice steak diagonally across the grain. Fluff rice with a fork. Serve steak slices with rice.

Per serving: 409 cal., 7 g total fat (3 g sat. fat), 47 mg chol., 709 mg sodium, 54 g carbo., 1 g fiber, 30 g pro.

Grilled Steak Salad with Blue Cheese Croutons and Red Onion Vinaigrette

Arrange steak, romaine wedges, and blue cheese toasts steakhouse-style on each plate. Drizzle it all with yummy sweet onion dressing.

Prep: 20 minutes **Grill:** 7 minutes **Makes:** 4 servings

- **4** **1-inch slices crusty bread or Texas toast**
- **1** **2- to 3-ounce chunk blue cheese, cut in 4 wedges**
- **2** **small red onions, cut in wedges**
- **6** **tablespoons olive oil**
- **1** **pound boneless beef breakfast steak, thinly cut**
  Salt and ground black pepper
- **2** **hearts of romaine, cut in half lengthwise**
- **¹/₄** **cup cider vinegar**
- **1** **teaspoon sugar**
- **¹/₂** **teaspoon salt**
- **¹/₂** **teaspoon ground black pepper**
  Fresh basil leaves (optional)

1. Place bread slices on the rack of an uncovered grill directly over medium heat. Grill for 1 to 2 minutes or until lightly toasted, turning once halfway through grilling. Top each slice with a wedge of cheese; set aside.

2. Brush onion wedges with 2 tablespoons of the olive oil. Place on the grill. Grill for 1 to 2 minutes on each side or until lightly browned; move to side of grill. Trim fat from steaks. Lightly sprinkle steaks with salt and pepper; add to grill. Grill about 4 minutes or until desired doneness, turning once. Remove steak and onions from grill.

3. On 4 serving plates, arrange bread slices, steak, about two-thirds of the onion, and romaine halves.

4. For dressing, place the remaining one-third of the onion in a blender or a small food processor. Add vinegar, sugar, salt, and pepper; blend or process to combine. With blender or processor running, gradually add the remaining 4 tablespoons olive oil. Pass dressing. If desired, garnish with fresh basil.

Per serving: 506 cal., 30 g total fat (7 g sat. fat), 58 mg chol., 883 mg sodium, 25 g carbo., 4 g fiber, 32 g pro.

Blue Cheese Burgers

These burgers are doubly blue—and that's a good thing. Stir crumbled blue cheese into the meat mixture and serve the grilled burgers with blue cheese dressing.

Prep: 5 minutes **Grill:** 14 minutes **Makes:** 6 burgers

- **1¹/₂** **pounds lean ground beef**
- **4** **ounces blue cheese, crumbled**
- **¹/₄** **cup water**
  Salt and ground black pepper
- **¹/₄** **cup blue cheese salad dressing**

1. In a medium bowl, lightly mix beef, blue cheese, water, and salt and pepper to taste. Shape beef mixture into six ³/₄-inch-thick patties.

2. Place patties on the rack of an uncovered grill directly over medium heat. Grill for 14 to 18 minutes or until done (160°F), turning once halfway through grilling. Serve with salad dressing.

Per burger: 358 cal., 28 g total fat (11 g sat. fat), 94 mg chol., 529 mg sodium, 1 g carbo., 0 g fiber, 25 g pro.

Quick Tip When making meatballs or burgers, prevent the ground meat mixture from sticking to your hands by wetting your hands. Keep a small bowl of cold water close by, dipping your hands into it occassionally as you work. Be sure to thoroughly wash the bowl, your hands, and the work surface when you finish.

Texas-Style Burgers

Two chiles and hearty Texas toast give these burgers a Lone Star State-style twist.

Prep: 15 minutes **Grill:** 14 minutes **Makes:** 4 burgers

½	**cup chopped green onions (4) or finely chopped onion (1 medium)**
2	**tablespoons fine dry bread crumbs**
3	**canned chipotle chile peppers in adobo sauce, chopped**
2	**fresh red serrano chiles, seeded and finely chopped**
½	**teaspoon salt**
1	**pound lean ground beef**
8	**1-inch slices bread, toasted, or 4 whole wheat hamburger buns, split and toasted**
	Sliced pickled green tomatoes (optional)
	Sliced red onion (optional)

1. In a large bowl, combine onion, bread crumbs, chipotle pepper, serrano chile, and salt. Add ground beef; mix well. Shape meat mixture into four ¾-inch-thick patties.

2. Place patties on the rack of an uncovered grill directly over medium coals. Grill for 14 to 18 minutes or until done (160 °F), turning once halfway through grilling.

3. To serve, place a patty on 4 of the bread slices. If desired, top with green tomato slices, red onion, and additional serrano peppers. Top with remaining bread.

Per burger: 352 cal., 13 g total fat (5 g sat. fat), 71 mg chol., 756 mg sodium, 32 g carbo., 1 g fiber, 25 g pro.

Quick Tip Serrano peppers are very hot. As with all peppers, the hottest parts of the chile are the seeds and membrane. Control the heat level of any dish by using the seeds—or not.

Texas-Style Burgers

Cheesy Sour Cream and Onion Burgers

Make these sour cream-Dijon mustard-flavored burgers with any ground meat you prefer—beef, pork, turkey, or chicken.

Prep: 17 minutes **Grill:** 15 minutes **Makes:** 2 burgers

- 1 tablespoon butter or margarine
- ¾ cup sliced fresh mushrooms
- 1 small onion, thinly sliced and separated in rings
- ¼ cup sour cream
- 2 tablespoons fine dry bread crumbs
- 1 teaspoon Dijon-style or yellow mustard
- ⅛ teaspoon salt
- ⅛ teaspoon ground black pepper
- 8 ounces ground beef, pork, uncooked turkey, or uncooked chicken
- 2 slices Monterey Jack, Swiss, or provolone cheese (1½ to 2 ounces)
- 2 kaiser rolls or hamburger buns, split and toasted
  Dijon-style or prepared mustard (optional)

1. In a small saucepan, melt butter over medium heat. Add mushrooms and onion; cook over medium-low heat for 10 to 15 minutes or until onion is tender, stirring occasionally. Set aside.

2. Meanwhile, in a medium bowl, stir together sour cream, bread crumbs, the 1 teaspoon mustard, the salt, and pepper. Stir in ground meat. Shape meat mixture into two ¾-inch-thick patties.

3. Place meat patties on the rack of an uncovered grill directly over medium coals. Grill for 14 to 18 minutes or until done (160°F), turning once halfway through grilling. Place a slice of cheese on each patty. Grill about 1 minute more or until cheese begins to melt.

4. To serve, place each patty on the bottom half of a toasted bun. Top with mushrooms and onion, then a bun top. If desired, serve with mustard.

Per burger: 684 cal., 43 g total fat (20 g sat. fat), 127 mg chol., 818 mg sodium, 40 g carbo., 3 g fiber, 33 g pro.

Quick Tip As they grill, patties shrink and get a raised top, which can cause toppings and bun tops to slide off the patties. To avoid this, when you're forming the patties, make a slight indentation in the center of each patty. After grilling, the patty will remain flat—a perfect surface for holding toppings and bun tops.

Cajun Beer Burgers

After grilling, dollop these zippy burgers with a Cajun-spiced sauce spiked with beer, onion, and sweet pepper. An ice-cold beer is the perfect beverage to sip alongside.

Prep: 10 minutes **Grill:** 14 minutes **Makes:** 6 burgers

- 1 egg, lightly beaten
- ½ cup finely chopped onion (1 medium)
- ¼ cup fine dry bread crumbs
- ¼ cup beer
- 1 tablespoon Worcestershire sauce
- ½ teaspoon dried thyme, crushed
- ¼ teaspoon dry mustard
- ¼ teaspoon cayenne pepper
- 1 pound lean ground beef
- 6 hamburger buns, split and toasted
  Romaine leaves (optional)
  Tomato slices (optional)
  Cajun Beer Sauce

1. In a large bowl, combine egg, onion, bread crumbs, beer, Worcestershire sauce, thyme, mustard, and cayenne pepper. Add ground beef; mix well. Shape meat mixture into six ¾-inch-thick patties.

2. Place patties on the rack of an uncovered grill directly over medium heat. Grill for 14 to 18 minutes or until done (160°F), turning once halfway through grilling. Meanwhile, prepare Cajun Beer Sauce.

3. Serve patties on toasted buns. If desired, serve with romaine and tomato slices. Top each burger with Cajun Beer Sauce.

Cajun Beer Sauce: In a small saucepan, heat 1 tablespoon vegetable oil over medium heat. Add ¼ cup chopped onion and ¼ cup chopped green or red sweet pepper; cook until tender. In a small bowl, stir together ½ cup beer, ½ cup water, 1 tablespoon cornstarch, and 1 teaspoon Cajun seasoning. Add to saucepan. Cook and stir over medium heat until thickened and bubbly. Cook and stir for 2 minutes more. Serve over burgers.

Per burger: 349 cal., 16 g total fat (5 g sat. fat), 82 mg chol., 390 mg sodium, 30 g carbo., 1 g fiber, 19 g pro.

Pizza Burgers

Ground beef and Italian sausage give these burgers their name and savory flavor.

Prep: 25 minutes **Grill:** 10 minutes **Makes:** 8 burgers

- 1 egg, lightly beaten
- 1¼ cups bottled meatless pasta sauce
- ½ cup fine dry bread crumbs
- ⅓ cup chopped onion (1 small)
- 1 teaspoon dried basil or oregano, crushed
- 2 cloves garlic, minced

1 **pound lean ground beef**

1 **pound bulk Italian sausage**

2 **medium green, yellow, and/or red sweet peppers, seeded, cut in rings, and halved**

1 **tablespoon olive oil or vegetable oil**

8 **kaiser rolls, split and toasted**

1 **6-ounce package sliced mozzarella cheese (8 slices)**

1. In a large bowl, combine egg and ¼ cup of the pasta sauce. Stir in bread crumbs, onion, basil, and garlic. Add ground beef and sausage; mix well. Shape meat mixture into eight ½-inch-thick patties.

2. Place sweet peppers in center of an 18×12-inch piece of heavy foil; drizzle with oil. Bring up opposite edges of foil; seal with a double fold. Fold remaining ends to completely enclose sweet peppers, leaving space for steam to build.

3. Place patties and foil packet on the rack of an uncovered grill directly over medium heat. Grill for 10 to 13 minutes or until patties are done (160°F) and sweet peppers are tender, turning patties and foil packet once halfway through grilling.

4. Meanwhile, in a small saucepan, heat the remaining 1 cup pasta sauce until bubbly. Serve patties in rolls with sweet peppers and cheese. Spoon some of the warm pasta sauce over burgers; pass any remaining sauce.

Per burger: 583 cal., 29 g total fat (11 g sat. fat), 117 mg chol., 1,146 mg sodium, 44 g carbo., 3 g fiber, 31 g pro.

Pizza Burgers

Indian Beef Patties with Cucumber Yogurt Sauce ♥

The cucumber-yogurt sauce is essentially a raita—an Indian condiment eaten with spicy foods to help cool the fire.

Prep: 15 minutes **Grill:** 14 minutes **Makes:** 2 servings

- ½ **cup plain low-fat yogurt**
- ⅓ **cup chopped, seeded cucumber**
- ¼ **cup finely chopped onion**
- 2 **tablespoons finely chopped, seeded fresh jalapeño chile (see tip, page 22)**
- 1 **tablespoon snipped fresh mint or 1 teaspoon dried mint, crushed**
- ½ **teaspoon ground cumin**
- ½ **teaspoon bottled minced garlic (1 clove) or ⅛ teaspoon garlic powder**
- ¼ **teaspoon salt**
- 8 **ounces lean ground beef**
  Indian flatbread (optional)

1. For sauce, in a small bowl, stir together yogurt and cucumber. Cover and chill until ready to serve.

2. In a medium bowl, combine onion, jalapeño chile, mint, cumin, garlic, and salt. Add ground beef; mix well. Shape beef mixture into two ¾-inch-thick patties.

3. Place patties on the rack of an uncovered grill directly over medium heat. Grill for 14 to 18 minutes or until patties are done (160°F), turning once halfway through grilling. If desired, serve the patties on flatbread. Spoon sauce over patties.

Per serving: 241 cal., 12 g total fat (5 g sat. fat), 75 mg chol., 377 mg sodium, 8 g carbo., 1 g fiber, 24 g pro.

Indian Beef Patties with Cucumber Yogurt Sauce

Stuffed Veal Chops with Gorgonzola

Serve these chops—stuffed with leek, onion, walnuts, and sage and topped with melty blue cheese—at an early fall cookout. Serve the chops with saffron rice.

Prep: 25 minutes **Grill:** 30 minutes **Makes:** 4 servings

- 2 **tablespoons olive oil**
- ½ **cup chopped onion (1 medium)**
- ½ **cup finely chopped leek (1 large)**
- 2 **tablespoons finely chopped shallot (1 medium)**
- ½ **cup chopped walnuts, toasted**
- 1 **teaspoon snipped fresh sage or ¼ teaspoon ground sage**
- ¼ **teaspoon kosher salt**
- ¼ **teaspoon ground black pepper**
- 4 **veal loin chops, cut 1 inch thick (about 1¾ pounds)**
  Kosher salt and ground black pepper
- ½ **cup crumbled blue cheese (2 ounces)**

1. For stuffing, in a medium skillet, heat 1 tablespoon of the olive oil over medium heat. Add onion, leek, and shallot; cook just until tender. Remove from heat. Stir in walnuts, sage, the ¼ teaspoon salt, and the ¼ teaspoon pepper. Set aside to cool.

2. Trim fat from chops. Make a pocket in each chop by cutting horizontally from the fat side almost to the opposite side. Spoon about 1 tablespoon of the stuffing into each pocket. If necessary, secure with wooden toothpicks. Brush chops with the remaining 1 tablespoon olive oil; sprinkle lightly with additional salt and pepper.

3. For a charcoal grill, arrange medium-hot coals around a drip pan. Test for medium heat above the pan. Place chops on the grill rack over drip pan. Cover and grill for 30 to 40 minutes or until done (160°F), turning once halfway through grilling. (For a gas grill, preheat grill. Reduce heat to medium. Adjust for indirect cooking. Grill as above.)

4. If using toothpicks, remove them. To serve, sprinkle crumbled blue cheese on chops.

Per serving: 269 cal., 15 g total fat (5 g sat. fat), 103 mg chol., 545 mg sodium, 5 g carbo., 1 g fiber, 27 g pro.

Quick Tip Leeks collect grit and dirt between layers as they grow. To thoroughly clean before using, cut off the root end and the dark green leaves. Cut the leek horizontally through the center. Lay the flat side of each half on a cutting board and slice it. Put the sliced leek in a bowl of cool water, swishing it to loosen the grit. Move the sliced leek to a salad spinner and spin dry. Or drain in a fine-mesh colander. Shake dry, then blot with paper towels before using.

Stuffed Veal Chops with Gorgonzola

Currant-Glazed
Pork Burgers

Currant-Glazed
Pork Burgers 💗

Currant jelly and cloves—favorites for flavoring Christmas hams—season these savory pork burgers.

Prep: 15 minutes **Grill:** 14 minutes **Makes:** 4 burgers

¼	**cup currant jelly**
3	**tablespoons ketchup**
1	**tablespoon vinegar**
⅛	**teaspoon ground cinnamon**
	Dash ground cloves
1	**egg, lightly beaten**
3	**tablespoons fine dry bread crumbs**
2	**tablespoons chopped onion**
2	**tablespoons milk**
¼	**teaspoon salt**
¼	**teaspoon dried thyme, crushed**
⅛	**teaspoon ground black pepper**
1	**pound lean ground pork**
4	**whole wheat hamburger buns, split**
4	**lettuce leaves**

1. For sauce, in a small saucepan, combine currant jelly, ketchup, vinegar, cinnamon, and cloves. Cook and stir just until boiling. Remove from heat and keep warm.

2. In a medium bowl, combine egg, bread crumbs, onion, milk, salt, thyme, and pepper. Add the ground pork; mix well. Shape pork mixture into four ¾-inch-thick patties.

3. Place patties on the rack of an uncovered grill directly over medium heat. Grill for 14 to 18 minutes or until meat done (160F), turning once halfway through grilling. Toast the hamburger buns on the grill.

4. Place lettuce on top of bottoms; top with patties. Spoon the sauce evenly over burgers.

Per burger: 347 cal., 11 g total fat (4 g sat. fat), 107 mg chol., 612 mg sodium, 43 g carbo., 3 g fiber, 21 g pro.

Chicago-Style Hot Dogs

Authentic Chicago dogs are dressed with yellow mustard, tomatoes, cucumber, sweet pickle relish, dill pickles, celery salt, and sometimes hot peppers—never ketchup! All the veggies on a dog is referred to as being "dragged through the garden."

Prep: 4 minutes **Grill:** 8 minutes **Makes:** 8 hot dogs

1	**1-pound package hot dogs (8)**
8	**hot dog buns**
	Yellow mustard
3	**plum tomatoes, halved through stems, thinly sliced in half-moons**
1	**small cucumber, peeled, halved lengthwise, seeded, and thinly sliced crosswise in half-moons**
	Celery salt
⅓	**cup sweet pickle relish**
4	**dill pickle spears, halved lengthwise**

1. Place hot dogs on grill rack directly over medium-high heat. Grill about 8 minutes or until heated through, turning several times. If desired, toast buns on grill rack.

2. Spread each bun with mustard. Arrange tomato on one side of bun, cucumber on the other side. Place a hot dog in each bun. Sprinkle with celery salt. Top each with mustard, 2 teaspoons relish, and a piece of pickle.

Per hot dog: 336 cal., 20 g total fat (7 g sat. fat), 29 mg chol., 1,181 mg sodium, 29 g carbo., 2 g fiber, 11 g pro.

Sage-Marinated Chops with Sweet Potatoes ♥

Cooking meat on the bone—as these pork chops are—increases the cooking time slightly but makes the meat juicy and flavorful.

Prep: 25 minutes **Marinate:** 8 to 24 hours
Grill: 25 minutes **Makes:** 4 servings

4	pork rib or loin chops, cut 1¼ inches thick
²/₃	cup cider vinegar
¹/₃	cup balsamic vinegar
2	tablespoons olive oil
2	teaspoons dried sage, crushed
¹/₂	teaspoon salt
¹/₄	teaspoon ground black pepper
2	sweet potatoes, quartered lengthwise (about 1 pound)
1	medium sweet onion (such as Vidalia), cut in ³/₄-inch slices

1. Trim fat from chops. Place chops in a resealable plastic bag set in a shallow dish. For marinade, in a small saucepan, combine cider vinegar and balsamic vinegar. Bring to boiling; reduce heat. Boil gently, uncovered, about 8 minutes or until reduced to about ²/₃ cup. Cool slightly. Stir in olive oil, sage, salt, and pepper. Remove ¹/₄ cup marinade; set aside.

Sage-Marinated Chops with Sweet Potatoes

2. Pour the remaining marinade over chops; seal bag. Marinate in the refrigerator for 8 to 24 hours, turning bag occasionally.

3. Drain chops, discarding marinade. Brush sweet potatoes and onion with the ¹/₄ cup reserved marinade.

4. Place chops, sweet potatoes, and onion on the rack of a grill directly over medium heat. Cover and grill for 25 to 30 minutes or until chops are slightly pink in center and juices run clear (160°F) and vegetables are tender, turning chops once and vegetables occasionally.

Per serving: 354 cal., 16 g total fat (4 g sat. fat), 77 mg chol., 249 mg sodium, 28 g carbo., 4 g fiber, 26 g pro.

Mojo Pork ♥

The word "mojo" (MOE-hoe) comes from the Spanish word "mojado," which means "wet." Found predominantly in Spanish and Cuban cuisines, mojos are used as sauces or marinades.

Prep: 20 minutes **Marinate:** 2 hours **Grill:** 40 minutes
Stand: 10 minutes **Makes:** 6 servings

2	12- to 16-ounce pork tenderloins
4	canned chipotle chile peppers in adobo sauce
¹/₂	cup fresh orange juice
¹/₄	cup coarsely chopped onion
2	tablespoons snipped fresh oregano or 2 teaspoons dried oregano, crushed
2	tablespoons fresh lime juice
1	tablespoon honey
1	tablespoon vegetable oil
¹/₂	teaspoon salt
3	cloves garlic, minced

1. Trim fat from meat. Place meat in a resealable plastic bag set in a shallow dish. For marinade, remove any stems from chipotle peppers. In a food processor or blender, combine chipotle peppers and adobo sauce, orange juice, onion, oregano, lime juice, honey, oil, salt, and garlic. Cover and process or blend until nearly smooth. Pour over meat; seal bag. Marinate in the refrigerator for 2 hours, turning bag occasionally. (Do not marinate more than 2 hours because the citrus juices cause the meat to become mushy.) Drain meat, discarding marinade.

2. For a charcoal grill, arrange hot coals around a drip pan. Test for medium-hot heat above pan. Place pork on grill rack over drip pan. Cover and grill for 40 to 50 minutes or until an instant-read thermometer inserted in center of the pork registers 155°F. Remove pork from grill. Cover with foil and let stand for 10 minutes. (For a gas grill, preheat grill. Reduce heat to medium-high. Adjust for indirect cooking. Place meat on a rack in a roasting pan, place on grill rack, and grill as above.)

Per serving: 157 cal., 4 g total fat (1 g sat. fat), 73 mg chol., 154 mg sodium, 3 g carbo., 0 g fiber, 24 g pro.

Chops and Pineapple with Chili Slaw ♥

Look for cored fresh pineapple in the produce section of supermarkets to make prep time extra quick.

Prep: 15 minutes **Grill:** 6 minutes **Makes:** 4 servings

- 8 boneless top loin pork chops, cut ½ inch thick (about 1½ pounds)
  Salt
- 1½ teaspoons chili powder
- ½ a cored fresh pineapple, sliced
- 3 tablespoons cider vinegar
- 2 tablespoons fresh orange juice
- 2 tablespoons olive oil
- 1 tablespoon sugar
- ⅓ small green cabbage, cored and sliced (about 5 cups)
- ½ a red onion, thinly sliced
- 1 small red sweet pepper, cut in strips
  Ground black pepper

1. Trim fat from chops. Sprinkle chops with salt and 1 teaspoon of the chili powder.

2. Place chops and pineapple on the rack of an uncovered grill directly over medium heat. Grill for 6 to 8 minutes or until chops are done (160°F), turning once halfway through grilling.

3. Meanwhile, for chili slaw, in a large bowl, whisk together vinegar, orange juice, oil, sugar, and the remaining ½ teaspoon chili powder. Add cabbage, onion, and sweet pepper; toss to mix. Season with salt and black pepper. Serve chops with pineapple pieces and slaw.

Per serving: 357 cal., 12 g total fat (3 g sat. fat), 112 mg chol., 392 mg sodium, 20 g carbo., 4 g fiber, 40 g pro.

Cheese-Stuffed Knockwurst

Knockwurst is a short, plump German sausage generously flavored with zesty seasonings and garlic. If you can't find it, bratwurst is a good substitute.

Prep: 15 minutes **Grill:** 8 minutes **Makes:** 5 servings

- 5 cooked knockwurst or cooked bratwurst
- 2 ounces Monterey Jack cheese or Havarti cheese with caraway, cut in five 2½×½×¼-inch strips
- ¼ cup thinly sliced green onions (2)
- 5 slices bacon
- 5 frankfurter buns, split and toasted
  Assorted condiments, such as ketchup, yellow mustard, and/or pickle relish (optional)

1. Cut a lengthwise slit in each knockwurst about ½ inch deep. Insert a cheese strip and some of the green onions into each knockwurst. Wrap a slice of bacon around each knockwurst; secure bacon with wooden toothpicks.

2. For a charcoal grill, arrange medium-hot coals around a drip pan. Test for medium heat above pan. Place knockwurst, cheese sides up, on grill rack over drip pan. Cover and grill for 8 to 10 minutes or until bacon is crisp. (For a gas grill, preheat grill. Reduce heat to medium. Adjust for indirect cooking. Grill as above.)

3. Serve knockwurst in buns with assorted condiments.

Per serving: 473 cal., 34 g total fat (13 g sat. fat), 77 mg chol., 1,129 mg sodium, 21 g carbo., 1 g fiber, 19 g pro.

Cheese-Stuffed Knockwurst

Lemon-and-Herb-Rubbed Pork Chops ♥

Lemon and orange complement the flavor of pork. If you like, substitute about 2 teaspoons of finely shredded orange peel for the lemon peel.

Prep: 15 minutes **Grill:** 35 minutes **Makes:** 4 servings

- 1½ **teaspoons finely shredded lemon peel**
- 1 **teaspoon dried rosemary, crushed**
- ½ **teaspoon salt**
- ½ **teaspoon dried sage, crushed**
- ½ **teaspoon ground black pepper**
- 8 **cloves garlic, minced**
- 4 **pork loin chops, cut 1¼ inches thick**

1. For rub, in a small bowl, combine lemon peel, rosemary, salt, sage, pepper, and garlic. Trim fat from chops. Sprinkle rub evenly on both sides of chops; rub in with your fingers.

2. For a charcoal grill, arrange medium-hot coals around a drip pan. Test for medium heat above pan. Place chops on grill rack over pan. Cover and grill for 35 to 40 minutes or until chops are slightly pink in center and juices run clear (160°F), turning once halfway through grilling. (For a gas grill, preheat grill. Reduce heat to medium. Adjust for indirect cooking. Grill as above.)

Per serving: 292 cal., 10 g total fat (4 g sat. fat), 105 mg chol., 371 mg sodium, 3 g carbo., 1 g fiber, 43 g pro.

Chinese Ribs

Spareribs have long been a favorite appetizer served at Chinese restaurants. This succulent recipe brings that goodness to the main course.

Prep: 25 minutes **Chill:** 6 to 24 hours **Grill:** 1½ hours
Makes: 4 to 5 servings

- 4 **pounds pork loin back ribs or meaty pork spareribs**
- 2 **tablespoons granulated sugar**
- ½ **teaspoon salt**
- ¼ **teaspoon paprika**
- ¼ **teaspoon ground turmeric**
- ¼ **teaspoon celery seeds**
- ¼ **teaspoon dry mustard**
- ¼ **cup ketchup**
- ¼ **cup soy sauce**
- 2 **tablespoons packed brown sugar**
- 2 **tablespoons water**
- 1 **teaspoon grated fresh ginger or 1 teaspoon ground ginger**
- 2 **cups alder or oak wood chips**

1. Trim fat from ribs. For rub, in a small bowl, combine granulated sugar, salt, paprika, turmeric, celery seeds, and dry mustard. Sprinkle rub evenly over both sides of ribs; rub in with your fingers. Cover and refrigerate for 6 to 24 hours.

2. For sauce, in a small bowl, combine ketchup, soy sauce, brown sugar, water, and ginger. Cover and refrigerate for 6 to 24 hours.

3. At least 1 hour before grilling, soak wood chips in enough water to cover.

4. Drain wood chips. For a charcoal grill, arrange medium-hot coals around a drip pan. Test for medium heat above pan. Sprinkle drained wood chips over coals. Place ribs, bone sides down, on grill rack over drip pan. (Or place ribs in a rib rack; place on grill rack.) Cover and grill for 1½ to 1¾ hours or until ribs are tender, brushing once with sauce during the last 15 minutes of grilling. (For a gas grill, preheat grill. Reduce heat to medium. Adjust for indirect cooking. Grill as above, except place ribs in a roasting pan and follow manufacturer's directions for using wood chips.) Before serving, brush ribs with remaining sauce.

Per serving: 527 cal., 20 g total fat (7 g sat. fat), 135 mg chol., 1,484 mg sodium, 17 g carbo., 0 g fiber, 65 g pro.

Lamb Chops with Tomatoes ♥

Lamb takes especially well to grilling. It gets a beautiful crust on the outside, and the smokiness complements the flavor of the meat.

Prep: 15 minutes **Grill:** 12 minutes **Makes:** 4 servings

- 8 **lamb loin chops, cut 1 inch thick**
  Salt and ground black pepper
- 1 **8.8-ounce pouch cooked long grain rice**
- 4 **medium plum tomatoes, cut up**
- 4 **green onions, cut in 1-inch pieces**
- 1 **tablespoon snipped fresh oregano**
- 1 **tablespoon balsamic vinegar**

1. Trim fat from chops. Sprinkle chops with salt and pepper. Place chops on the rack of an uncovered grill directly over medium heat. Grill until desired doneness, turning once halfway through grilling. Allow 12 to 14 minutes for medium rare (145°F) or 15 to 17 minutes for medium (160°F).

2. Meanwhile, microwave rice following package directions. In food processor or blender, combine tomatoes, green onions, and oregano; pulse to process or blend until coarsely chopped. Transfer to a medium bowl; stir in vinegar. Season with salt and pepper. Arrange chops on rice; top with tomato mixture.

Per serving: 273 cal., 7 g total fat (2 g sat. fat), 70 mg chol., 153 mg sodium, 26 g carbo., 3 g fiber, 25 g pro.

Lamb Chops with Tomatoes

Mediterranean Lamb Burgers

Mediterranean Lamb Burgers

Serve these Greek-style burgers with oven-roasted potatoes.

Prep: 15 minutes **Grill:** 14 minutes **Makes:** 4 burgers

- 1 **pound lean ground lamb or beef**
- ½ **to 1 teaspoon ground black pepper**
- 2 **pita bread rounds, halved crosswise, or kaiser rolls, split and toasted**
- 4 **lettuce leaves**
- 2 **ounces feta cheese, crumbled**
- 1 **tablespoon snipped fresh mint**
  Chopped tomato (optional)

1. Shape meat into four ¾-inch-thick patties. Sprinkle pepper evenly on patties; press into patties with your fingers.

2. Place patties on the rack of an uncovered grill directly over medium coals. Grill for 14 to 18 minutes or until done (160°F), turning once halfway through grilling.

3. Serve patties in pitas with lettuce, feta cheese, mint, and, if desired, tomato.

Per burger: 428 cal., 21 g total fat (9 g sat. fat), 88 mg chol., 533 mg sodium, 31 g carbo., 1 g fiber, 27 g pro.

Apricot-Stuffed Lamb Chops ♥

If you grill during winter, these fruit-stuffed lamb chops are a delicious and elegant main course for a holiday dinner.

Prep: 15 minutes **Grill:** 12 minutes **Makes:** 4 servings

- ⅓ **cup snipped dried apricots**
- 3 **tablespoons raisins**
- 1 **tablespoon finely chopped onion**
- 1 **teaspoon finely shredded orange peel**
- 8 **lamb rib chops, cut 1 inch thick (about 2 pounds)**
- 2 **teaspoons ground coriander**
- ½ **teaspoon salt**
- ¼ **teaspoon ground black pepper**

1. For stuffing, in a small bowl, combine apricots, raisins, onion, and orange peel.

2. Trim fat from chops. Make a pocket in each chop by cutting horizontally from the fat side almost to the bone. Divide stuffing among pockets in chops. If necessary, secure openings with wooden toothpicks.

3. For rub, in a small bowl, combine coriander, salt, and pepper. Sprinkle rub on chops; rub in with fingers.

4. Place chops on rack of an uncovered grill over medium coals. Grill, turning once halfway through grilling. Allow 12 to 14 minutes for medium rare (145°F) or 15 to 17 minutes for medium (160°F). Remove toothpicks.

Per serving: 210 cal., 9 g total fat (3 g sat. fat), 64 mg chol., 353 mg sodium, 13 g carbo., 2 g fiber, 20 g pro.

Grilled Chicken Breasts with Artichoke Salsa

Marinated artichokes add flavor and texture to purchased salsa, which is spooned on a chicken paillard (a fancy name for a thin piece of chicken).

Prep: 15 minutes **Grill:** 5 minutes **Makes:** 4 servings

- 1 **6-ounce jar marinated artichoke hearts**
- ½ **cup bottled salsa**
  Salt and ground black pepper
- 4 **skinless, boneless chicken breast halves (about 1¼ pounds)**

1. For artichoke salsa, drain artichoke hearts, reserving marinade. Finely chop artichoke hearts. Transfer to a small bowl. Add salsa and 1 tablespoon of the reserved marinade. Season to taste with salt and pepper.

2. Place each chicken breast half between 2 pieces of plastic wrap. Pound lightly with the flat side of a meat mallet to ½-inch thickness. Discard plastic wrap. Lightly sprinkle chicken with salt and pepper.

3. Place chicken on a grill rack directly over medium-high heat. Grill for 5 to 6 minutes or until chicken is no longer pink, turning once halfway through grilling. Serve chicken with artichoke salsa.

Per serving: 245 cal., 8 g total fat (2 g sat. fat), 82 mg chol., 576 mg sodium, 5 g carbo., 1 g fiber, 33 g pro.

Grilled Cajun Chicken Sandwich

Serve these spicy sandwiches with the potato chips or sweet potato fries from the freezer section of the supermarket.

Prep: 10 minutes **Grill:** 12 minutes **Makes:** 4 servings

- 4 **small skinless, boneless chicken breast halves (about 1 pound)**
  Olive oil or vegetable oil
- ½ **to 1 teaspoon Cajun seasoning**
- ¼ **cup Thousand Island salad dressing**
  Dash bottled hot pepper sauce
- 4 **kaiser or whole wheat buns, split and toasted**
- ½ **a small red sweet pepper, cut in strips**
- ½ **cup shredded Monterey Jack cheese with jalapeño peppers (2 ounces)**
- 4 **lettuce leaves**

1. Place each chicken breast half between plastic wrap. Pound lightly to ½-inch thickness. Discard plastic wrap. Brush chicken with oil; sprinkle with seasoning.

2. Place chicken on grill rack directly over medium heat. Grill for 12 to 15 minutes or until chicken is no longer pink (170°F), turning once halfway through grilling.

3. In a small bowl, stir together salad dressing and bottled hot pepper sauce. Spread buns with dressing mixture. Cut chicken into ½-inch thick slices. Top with chicken, sweet peppers, cheese, lettuce, and bun tops.

Per serving: 429 cal., 17 g total fat (5 g sat. fat), 101 mg chol., 544 mg sodium, 26 g carbo., 2 g fiber, 40 g pro.

Grilled Cajun Chicken Sandwich

Pear and Chicken Salad ♥

The blue cheese dressing for this salad is made with fat-free yogurt instead of mayonnaise or sour cream—which makes it light and healthful.

Prep: 20 minutes **Grill:** 12 minutes **Makes:** 4 servings

- **12 ounces fresh asparagus spears**
- **2 small pears, halved lengthwise and cored (remove stems, if desired)**
  Fresh lemon juice
- **4 skinless, boneless chicken breast halves (about 1¼ pounds)**
  Salt and ground black pepper
- **6 cups torn mixed salad greens**
  Milk (optional)
  Blue Cheese Dressing

1. Snap off and discard woody bases from asparagus. If desired, scrape off scales. In a large saucepan, cook asparagus, covered, in a small amount of boiling lightly salted water for 3 to 5 minutes or until crisp-tender. Drain; set aside.

2. Meanwhile, brush cut sides of pears with lemon juice; set aside. Sprinkle chicken with salt and pepper.

3. Place chicken on the grill rack directly over medium heat. Grill for 5 minutes. Turn chicken. Add pears to the grill rack, cut sides down. Grill chicken and pears for 7 to 10 minutes more or until chicken is no longer pink (170°F) and pears are tender. If desired, add asparagus the last 3 minutes of grilling.

4. Transfer chicken to a cutting board; slice chicken. Cut pear halves in half, forming 8 quarters.

5. On 4 plates, arrange greens, chicken, and asparagus. If necessary, stir milk into Blue Cheese Dressing to reach desired consistency. Spoon dressing on salad. Add pear pieces.

Blue Cheese Dressing: In a small bowl, combine ½ cup plain fat-free yogurt, ¼ cup chopped red onion, 2 tablespoons crumbled blue cheese, 1 tablespoon snipped fresh chives, and ⅛ teaspoon ground white pepper. Cover and chill until ready to serve. Makes ⅔ cup.

Per serving: 243 cal., 3 g total fat (1 g sat. fat), 86 mg chol., 314 mg sodium, 16 g carbo., 4 g fiber, 38 g pro.

Balsamic Barbecued Chicken Breasts ♥

Make a double batch of this supereasy, all-around-tasty sauce and refrigerate the rest to try later with pork chops or ribs.

Prep: 15 minutes **Grill:** 12 minutes **Makes:** 4 servings

- **½ cup ketchup**
- **¼ cup light-color corn syrup**
- **3 tablespoons balsamic vinegar or cider vinegar**
- **2 tablespoons thinly sliced green onion (1)**
  Several dashes bottled hot pepper sauce (optional)
- **4 skinless, boneless chicken breast halves (about 1¼ pounds)**

1. For sauce, in a small saucepan, combine ketchup, corn syrup, vinegar, green onion, and, if desired, hot pepper sauce. Bring to boiling; reduce heat. Simmer, uncovered, for 5 to 10 minutes or until desired consistency, stirring sauce occasionally.

2. Place chicken on the rack of an uncovered grill directly over medium heat. Grill for 12 to 15 minutes or until chicken is no longer pink (170°F), turning once halfway through grilling and brushing often with sauce during the last 10 minutes of grilling.

3. To serve, reheat any remaining sauce until bubbly; serve with chicken.

Per serving: 267 cal., 2 g total fat (1 g sat. fat), 82 mg chol., 432 mg sodium, 27 g carbo., 0 g fiber, 33 g pro.

Grilled Lime Chicken with Pineapple Salsa ♥

The salsa can be made up to 24 hours ahead of serving time, so all you have to do when you get home is fire up the grill.

Prep: 20 minutes **Grill:** 12 minutes **Makes:** 6 servings

- **½ teaspoon finely shredded lime peel**
- **¼ cup fresh lime juice**
- **1 tablespoon vegetable oil**
- **¼ teaspoon salt**
- **¼ teaspoon coarsely ground black pepper**

Pear and Chicken Salad

Grilled Lime Chicken with Pineapple Salsa

6 **skinless, boneless chicken breast halves (about 1 3/4 pounds)**
3 **cups fresh pineapple chunks (1 pound)**
1 **cup chopped, seeded tomato (1 large)**
1/2 **cup chopped red onion (1 medium)**
1/2 **cup chopped green or red sweet pepper**
1 **4-ounce can diced green chiles, drained**
2 **tablespoons snipped fresh cilantro**
1/2 **teaspoon finely shredded lime peel**
2 **tablespoons fresh lime juice**
1 **clove garlic, minced**

1. In a small bowl, stir together 1/2 teaspoon lime peel, the 1/4 cup lime juice, the oil, salt, and black pepper. Brush chicken with lime mixture.

2. Place chicken on the rack of an uncovered grill directly over medium coals. Grill for 12 to 15 minutes or until chicken is no longer pink (170°F), turning and brushing once with lime mixture halfway through grilling. Discard any remaining lime mixture.

3. Meanwhile, for salsa, place pineapple chunks in a food processor or blender. Cover and process or blend until coarsely chopped. Transfer pineapple to a large bowl. Stir in tomato, red onion, sweet pepper, green chiles, cilantro, 1/2 teaspoon lime peel, the 2 tablespoons lime juice, and the garlic. Cover and refrigerate until serving time. Serve with chicken.

Per serving: 226 cal., 4 g total fat (1 g sat. fat), 77 mg chol., 240 mg sodium, 15 g carbo., 2 g fiber, 32 g pro.

BBQ Chicken Burgers

BBQ Chicken Burgers

For additional flavor, grill the onion slices. Brush with a little cooking oil and season lightly with salt and pepper. If you have one, use a vegetable basket specifically made for the grill.

Prep: 15 minutes **Grill:** 10 minutes **Makes:** 6 burgers

1	**teaspoon canola oil**
1/3	**cup chopped onion (1 small)**
7	**hamburger buns**
1	**egg, lightly beaten**
3	**tablespoons bottled barbecue sauce**
1/2	**teaspoon salt**
1/4	**teaspoon ground black pepper**
1	**pound uncooked ground chicken or turkey**
1	**cup fresh corn kernels or frozen whole kernel corn, thawed**
	Nonstick cooking spray
	Sliced red onion (optional)
	Bottled barbecue sauce (optional)

1. In a small nonstick skillet, heat canola oil over medium heat. Add onion; cook until tender but not browned.

2. Tear 1 hamburger bun into pieces; place in food processor or blender. Process or blend for fine crumbs.

3. In a large bowl, combine egg, the 3 tablespoons barbecue sauce, salt, pepper, cooked onion, and bread crumbs. Add chicken and corn; mix well. Shape chicken mixture into six 1/2-inch-thick patties.

4. Lightly coat a grill rack with nonstick cooking spray. Place patties on the grill rack of an uncovered grill directly over medium heat. Grill for 10 to 13 minutes or until done (170°F). Serve on hamburger buns. If desired, top with red onion slices and additional barbecue sauce.

Per burger: 287 cal., 6 g total fat (1 g sat. fat), 77 mg chol., 583 mg sodium, 35 g carbo., 2 g fiber, 22 g pro.

Middle Eastern Grilled Chicken ♥

Ground turmeric makes curry bright yellow. Here it gives spiced yogurt sauce distinctively Middle Eastern flavor as well as a gorgeous golden hue.

Prep: 15 minutes **Grill:** 15 minutes **Makes:** 4 servings

- ½ **cup plain low-fat yogurt**
- 3 **tablespoons finely chopped onion**
- 2 **teaspoons chopped fresh oregano or savory or**
  ½ **teaspoon dried oregano or savory, crushed**
- 1 **teaspoon chopped fresh mint**
- 2 **cloves garlic, minced**
- ½ **teaspoon sesame seeds, toasted**
- ¼ **teaspoon ground cumin**
- ⅛ **teaspoon ground turmeric (optional)**
  Dash kosher salt
  Dash cayenne pepper
  Dash ground black pepper
- 4 **skinless, boneless chicken breast halves (about 1¼ pounds)**

1. In a medium bowl, combine yogurt, onion, oregano, mint, garlic, sesame seeds, cumin, turmeric (if desired), the dash salt, and the dash cayenne pepper. Set aside. Sprinkle chicken breasts with additional salt and black pepper. Spoon yogurt mixture on chicken.

2. For a charcoal grill, arrange medium-hot coals around a drip pan. Test for medium heat above the pan. Place chicken on grill rack over drip pan. Cover and grill for 15 to 18 minutes or until chicken is no longer pink (170°F), turning once halfway through grilling. (For a gas grill, preheat grill. Reduce heat to medium. Adjust heat for indirect cooking. Grill as above.)

Per serving: 169 cal., 4 g total fat (1 g sat. fat), 60 mg chol., 166 mg sodium, 7 g carbo., 0 g fiber, 26 g pro.

Chicken Caribbean with Coconut-Orange Sauce ♥

Boost the flavor of the rice by stirring in a little shredded orange peel and freshly snipped basil.

Start to Finish: 25 minutes **Makes:** 4 servings

- ½ **teaspoon Jamaican jerk seasoning**
- 4 **skinless, boneless chicken breast halves (about 1¼ pounds)**
- ½ **cup canned unsweeteend coconut milk**
- ½ **teaspoon finely shredded orange peel (optional)**
- ¼ **cup fresh orange juice**
- 1 **tablespoon snipped fresh basil**
- 2 **cups hot cooked rice**
- 1 **tablespoon thinly sliced basil**
  Orange slices (optional)

1. Rub jerk seasoning evenly on both sides of chicken. Place chicken on the rack of an uncovered grill directly over medium heat. Grill for 12 to 15 minutes or until no longer pink (170°F), turning once halfway through grilling.

2. Meanwhile, for sauce, in a small saucepan, combine coconut milk, orange peel (if desired), orange juice, and the snipped basil. Bring to boiling; reduce heat. Simmer, uncovered, about 5 minutes or until sauce is reduced to ½ cup.

3. Serve chicken with sauce and rice; sprinkle with sliced basil. If desired, garnish with orange slices.

Per serving: 294 cal., 8 g total fat (6 g sat. fat), 66 mg chol., 108 mg sodium, 25 g carbo., 0 g fiber, 29 g pro.

Chicken Caribbean with
Coconut-Orange Sauce

Honey-Dijon Barbecued Chicken

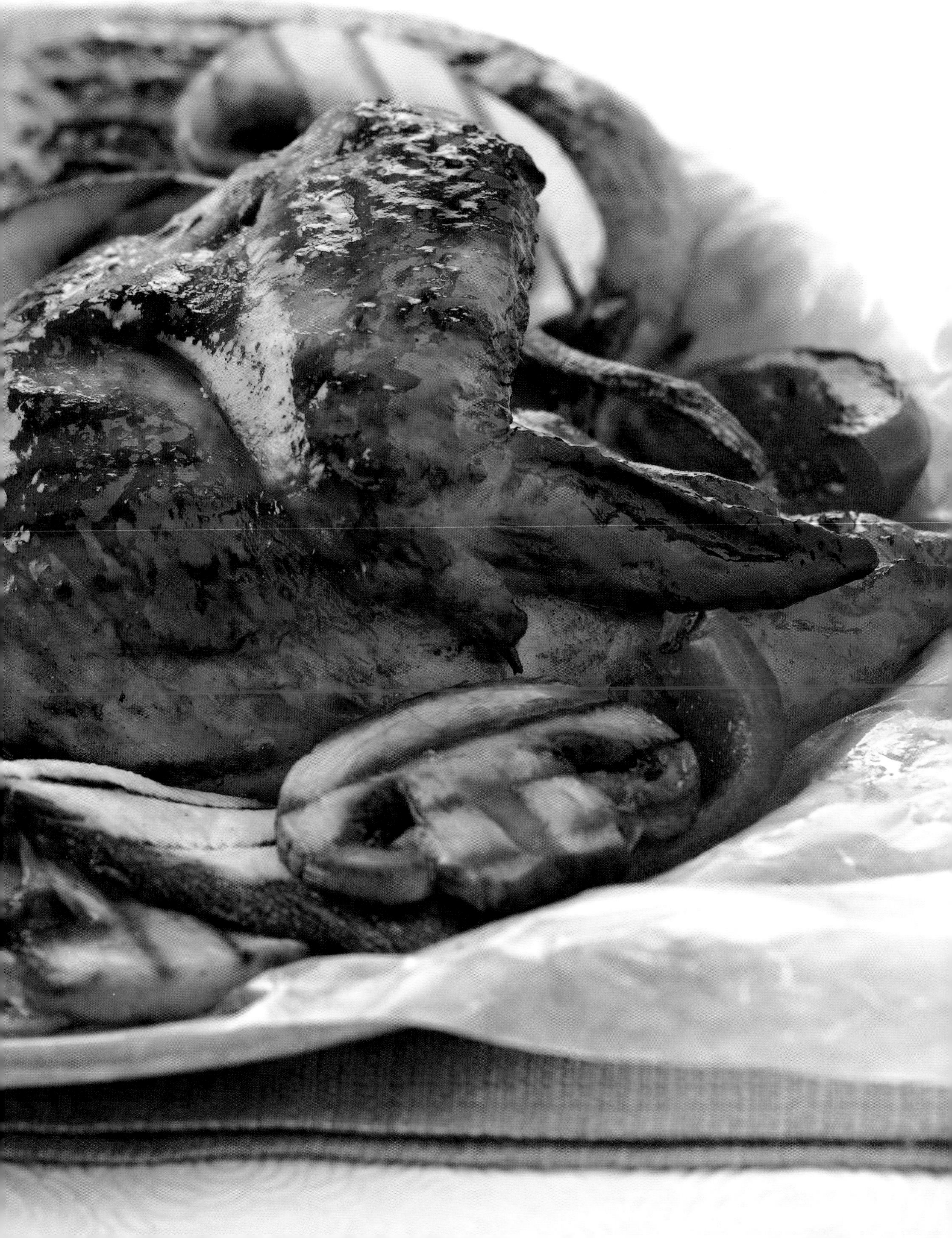

Honey-Dijon Barbecued Chicken

Chilled rosé is a popular summer beverage in the South of France. Look for those made in Provence, which are fairly dry. It's good in the marinade and as something to sip with the chicken.

Prep: 15 minutes **Marinate:** 8 to 24 hours
Grill: 50 minutes **Makes:** 4 servings

- 1 **3- to 3½-pound broiler-fryer chicken, quartered**
- ½ **cup white or rosé wine, apple juice, or apple cider**
- ¼ **cup olive oil or vegetable oil**
- ¼ **cup honey**
- ¼ **cup Dijon-style mustard**
- ½ **teaspoon ground black pepper**
- ¼ **teaspoon salt**
- 4 **cloves garlic, minced**
  Grilled vegetables (optional)

1. Place chicken in a resealable plastic bag set in a dish. For marinade, combine wine, oil, honey, mustard, pepper, salt, and garlic. Pour over chicken; seal bag. Marinate in refrigerator 8 to 24 hours, turning bag occasionally.

2. Drain chicken, reserving marinade. For a charcoal grill, arrange medium-hot coals around a drip pan. Test for medium heat above pan. Place chicken, bone sides up, on grill rack over drip pan. Cover and grill for 50 to 60 minutes or until chicken is no longer pink (170°F for breast portions; 180°F for thigh portions), brushing once with reserved marinade after 30 minutes. (For a gas grill, preheat grill. Reduce heat to medium. Adjust for indirect cooking. Grill as above.) Discard any remaining marinade.

3. If desired, serve with grilled vegetables.

Per serving: 597 cal., 40 g total fat (10 g sat. fat), 172 mg chol., 384 mg sodium, 11 g carbo., 0 g fiber, 45 g pro.

Sesame Chicken Kabobs with Wasabi-Soy Dipping Sauce

Find black sesame seeds at Asian markets or health food stores. It's OK to use white sesame seeds. The kabobs won't look quite as fetching, but they'll taste every bit as good.

Prep: 20 minutes **Grill:** 10 minutes **Makes:** 4 servings

- 1 **pound boneless, skinless chicken breast halves, cut in 1-inch strips**
  Salt and freshly ground black pepper
- 3 **tablespoons white sesame seeds**
- 3 **tablespoons black sesame seeds**
- 4 **baby bok choy, halved lengthwise**
- 2 **yellow or red sweet peppers, trimmed, seeded, and quartered lengthwise**
- 1 **tablespoon vegetable oil**
  Wasabi-Soy Dipping Sauce

1. Lightly sprinkle chicken with salt and pepper. In a shallow dish, combine the white and black sesame seeds. Thoroughly coat the chicken strips in the sesame seeds. Thread the chicken, accordian-style, onto skewers. (If you use wooden skewers, soak them in water for 30 minutes before using to keep them from burning on the grill.)

2. Brush bok choy and sweet peppers with the oil; lightly sprinkle with salt and black pepper.

3. Place kabobs and sweet pepper on the rack of an uncovered grill directly over medium heat. Grill for 10 to 12 minutes or until chicken is no longer pink, turning to cook evenly. Add bok choy the last 6 minutes of grilling, turning once, or until heated through.

4. Cut vegetables in bite-size pieces. Serve vegetables with chicken kabobs and Wasabi-Soy Dipping Sauce.

Wasabi-Soy Dipping Sauce In a small saucepan, combine ¼ cup plum jelly, 3 tablespoons soy sauce, 1 tablespoon rice vinegar, ½ teaspoon dark sesame oil, and ½ to 1 teaspoon wasabi powder. Cook over medium heat until jelly is melted.

Per serving: 355 cal., 13 g total fat (2 g sat. fat), 66 mg chol., 1,126 mg sodium, 30 g carbo., 5 g fiber, 34 g pro.

Grilled Chicken Caesar

Watercress is a tender green with a peppery bite. Baby arugula, similar in taste and shape, is a good substitute.

Prep: 20 minutes **Grill:** 8 minutes **Makes:** 4 servings

- 1 **tablespoon fresh lemon juice**
- 1 **teaspoon anchovy paste**
- ¼ **teaspoon freshly ground black pepper**
- 2 **tablespoons olive oil**
- 1 **tablespoon finely chopped shallot**
- 4 **skinless, boneless chicken breast halves (1¼ pounds)**
  4 **cups trimmed watercress**
  Lemon wedges (optional)

1. For dressing, in a small bowl, whisk together lemon juice, anchovy paste, and the ¼ teaspoon pepper; whisk in olive oil and shallot. Set aside.

2. Place each chicken breast half between 2 pieces of plastic wrap. Pound lightly with the flat side of a meat mallet to ¼-inch thickness. Discard plastic wrap. Lightly sprinkle chicken with salt and pepper.

3. Place chicken on the rack of an uncovered grill directly over medium heat. Grill for 8 to 10 minutes or until chicken is no longer pink, turning once halfway through grilling.

4. Meanwhile, toss watercress with dressing; arrange on 4 plates. Top with chicken. If desired, garnish with lemon wedges.

Per serving: 225 cal., 9 g total fat (1 g sat. fat), 87 mg chol., 185 mg sodium, 1 g carbo., 0 g fiber, 34 g pro.

Chicken Breasts with Red Wine Sauce ♥

Any fruity, dry wine works in the sauce—a Merlot or Beaujolais is especially nice.

Prep: 15 minutes **Grill:** 12 minutes **Makes:** 4 servings

- ¼ **cup orange marmalade**
- ½ **teaspoon cornstarch**
- ¼ **teaspoon salt**
- ¼ **cup dry red wine**
- 4 **skinless, boneless chicken breast halves (about 1¼ pounds)**
  Hot cooked pasta (optional)
  Orange slices (optional)
  Fresh thyme (optional)

1. For sauce, in a small saucepan, combine orange marmalade, cornstarch, and salt. Stir in wine. Cook and stir until mixture is thickened and bubbly. Cook and stir for 2 minutes more.

2. Place chicken on the rack of an uncovered grill directly over medium heat. Grill for 5 minutes. Turn chicken and brush with sauce; grill for 7 to 10 minutes more or until chicken is no longer pink (170°F). Brush with remaining sauce before serving. If desired, serve over hot cooked pasta and garnish with orange slices and thyme.

Per serving: 184 cal., 3 g total fat (1 g sat. fat), 59 mg chol., 199 mg sodium, 15 g carbo., 1 g fiber, 22 g pro.

Chicken with New Mexican-Style Rub ♥

The seasoning rub makes about 7 tablespoons. Store the leftover mixture, covered, in a cool, dry place and use within 6 months.

Prep: 15 minutes **Grill:** 12 minutes **Makes:** 4 servings

- 1 **tablespoon dried oregano**
- 1 **tablespoon dried thyme**
- 1 **teaspoon coriander seeds**
- 1 **teaspoon anise seeds**
- ¼ **cup chili powder**
- 1 **teaspoon paprika**
- ½ **teaspoon cracked black pepper**
- ¼ **teaspoon salt**
- 4 **skinless, boneless chicken breast halves (about 1¼ pounds)**

1. For seasoning rub, using a mortar and pestle, grind together the oregano, thyme, coriander seeds, and anise seeds. Stir in chili powder, paprika, cracked black pepper, and salt.

2. With your fingers, gently rub some of the seasoning rub on both sides of chicken.

3. Place chicken on the rack of an uncovered grill directly over medium heat. Grill for 12 to 15 minutes or until chicken is no longer pink (170°F), turning once halfway through grilling.

Per serving: 123 cal., 3 g total fat (1 g sat. fat), 59 mg chol., 88 mg sodium, 0 g carbo., 0 g fiber, 22 g pro.

Turkey Tenderloins with Cilantro Pesto ♥

This grilled turkey can go Mexican or Italian, depending on whether you use cilantro or basil for the pesto. If you use cilantro, serve with lime; if you go with basil, serve with lemon.

Prep: 15 minutes **Grill:** 12 minutes **Makes:** 8 servings

- 4 **turkey breast tenderloins (about 2 pounds)**
- 1½ **cups lightly packed fresh cilantro or basil leaves**
- ⅓ **cup broken walnuts**
- 3 **tablespoons olive oil**
- 3 **tablespoons fresh lime juice**
- 2 **cloves garlic, minced**
- ¼ **teaspoon salt**
  Salt and ground black pepper
  Lime or lemon wedges (optional)

1. Cut each turkey tenderloin in half horizontally to make 8 steaks; set aside. For the cilantro pesto, in a blender or food processor, place cilantro, walnuts, olive oil, lime juice, garlic, and salt. Cover and blend or process until nearly smooth.

2. Lightly sprinkle turkey with salt and pepper.

3. Place turkey on the rack of an uncovered grill directly over medium heat. Grill for 12 to 15 minutes or until no longer pink (170°F), turning once and brushing lightly with cilantro pesto halfway through grilling. Serve turkey with remaining pesto. If desired, serve with lime wedges.

Per serving: 213 cal., 10 g total fat (2 g sat. fat), 68 mg chol., 134 mg sodium, 2 g carbo., 1 g fiber, 28 g pro.

Quick Tip When you use a sauce or marinade to brush on during grilling as well as to pass at the table, first remove the amount you want to use during grilling to a separate bowl. Don't dip a grilling brush that has had contact with partially cooked meat into a sauce to serve at the table. To serve a marinade that has had raw meat, poultry, or fish soaking in it, put it in a small saucepan and bring it to a rolling boil to make it safe to eat. When recipes specify to discard marinade, never use it beyond the marinade step.

Turkey Tenderloins with Cilantro Pesto

Thai Curried Turkey with Green Onion Slaw

Serve this spicy coconut curried turkey with hot cooked basmati or jasmine rice.

Prep: 15 minutes **Grill:** 6 minutes **Makes:** 4 servings

- **6 green onions**
- **2 cups finely shredded savoy cabbage, napa cabbage, or bok choy**
- **3 tablespoons dry-roasted cashew halves**
- **¼ cup rice vinegar**
- **½ teaspoon sugar**
- **1 pound turkey tenderloins**
- **2 to 3 tablespoons Thai green curry paste**
- **¼ cup dry white wine**
- **½ cup canned unsweetened coconut milk**

1. Using a sharp knife, cut green onions lengthwise in thin slivers. In a large bowl, toss onions with cabbage and cashews; set aside. In a small bowl, stir together vinegar and sugar until sugar is dissolved; set aside.

2. Cut tenderloins crosswise in 1-inch slices. Place each turkey piece between 2 pieces of plastic wrap. Pound lightly with the flat side of a mallet to ½-inch thickness. Lightly spread half the green curry paste on turkey.

3. Lightly oil grill rack. Place turkey on the rack of the uncovered grill directly over medium heat. Grill about 6 minutes or until no longer pink, turning once halfway through cooking. Set aside; keep warm.

4. For sauce, in a small skillet, stir together wine and the remaining green curry paste. Cook, uncovered, over medium-high heat for 1 to 2 minutes or until liquid is nearly evaporated, stirring often. Carefully stir in coconut milk. Bring to boiling; reduce heat. Cook, uncovered, for 1 to 2 minutes or until thickened to desired consistency.

5. To serve, toss cabbage mixture with vinegar mixture; arrange on 4 plates. Top with warm turkey and drizzle with sauce.

Per serving: 297 cal., 14 g total fat (6 g sat. fat), 68 mg chol., 637 mg sodium, 10 g carbo., 2 g fiber, 29 g pro.

Herb-Crusted Salmon

For a slightly different flavor, substitute Italian (flat-leaf) parsley or basil for the cilantro.

Prep: 15 minutes **Grill:** 6 minutes **Makes:** 4 servings

- **1 12-ounce fresh or frozen salmon fillet, ¾ inch thick**
- **⅓ cup coarsely chopped fresh oregano**
- **⅓ cup coarsely chopped fresh cilantro**
- **¼ cup sliced green onions (2)**
- **1 clove garlic**
- **1 tablespoon fresh lemon juice**
- **2 teaspoons olive oil**
- **¼ teaspoon salt**
- **⅛ teaspoon ground black pepper**
  Cherry tomatoes, halved (optional)
  Fresh oregano sprigs (optional)

1. Thaw salmon, if frozen. Cut fish in 2 pieces; set aside.

2. In a food processor or a mini chopper, combine the ⅓ cup oregano, the cilantro, green onions, garlic, lemon juice, oil, salt, and pepper. Cover and process until evenly chopped. (Or use a knife to finely chop oregano, cilantro, green onions, and garlic. Transfer herb mixture to a shallow bowl. Stir in lemon juice, olive oil, salt, and pepper.) Generously coat top of salmon with the herb mixture.

3. Place fish, skin sides down, on the greased rack of an uncovered grill directly over medium heat. Grill for 6 to 8 minutes or until fish begins to flake when tested with a fork. To serve, cut each salmon piece in 2 serving-size pieces. If desired, garnish with cherry tomato halves and oregano sprigs.

Per serving: 126 cal., 5 g total fat (1 g sat. fat), 44 mg chol., 207 mg sodium, 2 g carbo., 0 g fiber, 17 g pro.

Quick Tip Thin ends of salmon fillet will cook much more quickly than the thick center, which makes them vulnerable to drying out. When grilling over charcoal, position the salmon on the grill with thin ends close to the cooler edge of the grill or tuck thin edges under the fillet.

Thai Curried Turkey with Green Onion Slaw

Salmon Burgers

Process the salmon only until it is finely chopped. Overprocessing can toughen the burgers.

Prep: 20 minutes **Grill:** 10 minutes **Makes:** 4 burgers

1/4	**cup light mayonnaise or salad dressing**
2	**tablespoons chopped fresh dill**
1	**pound salmon fillet, skinned and cut up**
1/3	**cup fine dry bread crumbs**
1/4	**cup thinly sliced green onions (2)**
1/4	**teaspoon salt**
1/4	**teaspoon ground black pepper**
	Nonstick cooking spray
4	**whole wheat hamburger buns, split and toasted**

1. In a small bowl, combine mayonnaise and 1 tablespoon of the dill; set aside. In a food processor or blender, combine remaining 1 tablespoon dill, the salmon, bread crumbs, green onions, salt, and pepper. Process or blend until combined and salmon is finely chopped. Shape salmon mixture in four 3-inch-diameter patties; lightly coat both sides of patties with nonstick cooking spray.

2. Place patties on rack of an uncovered grill directly over medium-high heat. Grill about 10 minutes or until done (160°F), carefully turning once halfway through grilling.

3. Place patties on buns and spread each with some of the dill mayonnaise.

Per burger: 406 cal., 19 g total fat (3 g sat. fat), 72 mg chol., 609 mg sodium, 29 g carbo., 3 g fiber, 28 g pro.

Basil-Grilled Salmon with Spicy Corn Relish ♥

Pour yourself a cold margarita or lemonade to sip while you grill this Mexican-inspired salmon. Serve it with lime wedges.

Prep: 20 minutes **Marinate:** 30 minutes **Grill:** 4 to 6 minutes per 1/2-inch thickness **Makes:** 4 servings

4	**6-ounce fresh or frozen salmon fillets or steaks**
1	**bunch fresh basil, washed and stemmed**
2	**teaspoons finely shredded lemon peel**
1/4	**cup fresh lemon juice**
4	**cloves garlic, peeled**
1	**teaspoon olive oil**
1/2	**teaspoon salt**
1/2	**teaspoon black pepper**
	Spicy Corn Relish (optional)

1. Thaw fish, if frozen. Measure thickness. Place in a dish.

2. In food processor or blender, combine basil, lemon peel, lemon juice, garlic, olive oil, salt, and pepper. Process or blend until smooth. Spread half the basil mixture on fish; reserve remaining half for basting. Turn fish over to coat. Place fish in a resealable plastic bag; seal bag. Marinate in the refrigerator for 30 minutes, turning after 15 minutes.

3. Place fish on the greased rack of an uncovered grill directly over medium heat. Grill until fish begins to flake when tested with a fork, turning once and brushing with reserved marinade halfway through grilling. Allow 4 to 6 minutes per 1/2-inch thickness of fish. Transfer fish to plates. If desired, serve with Spicy Corn Relish.

Per serving: 197 cal., 6 g total fat (1 g sat. fat), 83 mg chol., 241 mg sodium, 2 g carbo., 0 g fiber, 32 g pro.

Spicy Corn Relish: In a medium bowl, combine 1 cup cooked fresh or frozen corn kernels; 1 ripe avocado, peeled, pitted, and diced; 1/2 cup chopped fresh cilantro; 1/3 cup chopped, seeded tomato; 2 tablespoons fresh lime juice; 2 jalapeño chiles seeded and finely chopped (see tip, page 22); 1/4 teaspoon salt; and 1/4 teaspoon ground black pepper. Stir gently to avoid mashing avocado.

Dilly Salmon Fillets

The mayo-mustard-dill sauce grills right on the fish to keep it moist.

Prep: 15 minutes **Marinate:** 10 minutes **Grill:** 5 minutes **Makes:** 4 servings

4	**5- to 6-ounce fresh or frozen skinless salmon fillets, 1/2 to 3/4 inch thick**
3	**tablespoons fresh lemon juice**
2	**tablespoons snipped fresh dill**
2	**tablespoons mayonnaise or salad dressing**
2	**teaspoons Dijon-style mustard)**

1. Thaw fish, if frozen. For marinade, in a shallow dish, combine lemon juice and 1 tablespoon of the dill. Add fish; turn to coat with marinade. Marinate at room temperature for 10 minutes. Meanwhile, in a small bowl, stir together the remaining 1 tablespoon dill, the mayonnaise, and mustard; set aside.

2. For a charcoal grill, arrange medium-hot coals around a drip pan. Test for medium heat above the pan. Place fish on greased grill rack over drip pan. Cover and grill for 3 minutes. Turn fish; spread with mayonnaise mixture. Cover and grill for 2 to 6 minutes more or until fish begins to flake when tested with a fork. (For a gas grill, preheat grill. Reduce heat to medium. Adjust for indirect cooking. Grill as above.)

Per serving: 211 cal., 11 g total fat (2 g sat. fat), 35 mg chol., 204 mg sodium, 1 g carbo., 0 g fiber, 25 g pro.

Quick Tip Marinating times for meat, poultry, and fish vary drastically, from minutes to hours, because each reacts differently to acids in the marinades. Acids—citrus juice, wine, and vinegar—start to cook the delicate fish when marinated too long. A brief time imparts plenty of flavor—and leaves the cooking to the grill.

Dilly Salmon Fillets

Minty Grilled Halibut
with Summer Squash

Asian Grilled Tuna Sandwich

Head-clearing, bright green wasabi paste—available at some supermarkets and Asian grocery stores—is a type of prepared horseradish. Combined with mayonnaise, it makes a zesty spread for these sandwiches.

Prep: 20 minutes **Grill:** 8 minutes **Makes:** 4 servings

- 4   5- to 6-ounce fresh or frozen tuna steaks, cut 1 inch thick
- 3   tablespoons rice wine vinegar
- 2   teaspoons sugar
- 1½ teaspoons minced shallot
- ¾   teaspoon grated fresh ginger
- 1   tablespoon vegetable oil
- ¼   teaspoon salt
- ¼   cup mayonnaise or salad dressing
- 1   teaspoon soy sauce
- ¾   teaspoon prepared wasabi paste
- 1   clove garlic, minced
- 8   slices Tuscan bread, lightly toasted
- 3   cups packed mesclun, watercress, or other mixed salad greens (4 ounces)
       Sesame noodles (optional)

1. Thaw fish, if frozen. For vinaigrette, in a small bowl, combine rice wine vinegar, sugar, shallot, and ginger; set aside.

2. Brush fish with oil; sprinkle with salt. Place fish on the greased rack of an uncovered grill directly over medium heat. Grill for 8 to 12 minutes or until fish is slightly pink in center. Set aside; keep warm.

3. For Asian mayonnaise, in another small bowl, combine mayonnaise, soy sauce, wasabi paste, and garlic. Spread evenly on 4 slices of the bread; set aside.

4. In a medium bowl, toss salad greens with vinaigrette; divide evenly on the remaining 4 bread slices. Arrange tuna steaks on greens. Top with bread spread with mayonnaise, mayonnaise sides down. Cut sandwiches in half. If desired, serve with sesame noodles.

Per serving: 519 cal., 23 g total fat (4 g sat. fat), 59 mg chol., 720 mg sodium, 35 g carbo., 2 g fiber, 39 g pro.

Minty Grilled Halibut with Summer Squash ♥

Generally you can get about ¼ cup of lemon juice from one lemon. To maximize the juice from a lemon, microwave it for 8 to 10 seconds, then roll it on the counter under your palm before juicing.

Prep: 15 minutes **Grill:** 8 minutes **Makes:** 4 servings

- 4   5- to 6-ounce fresh or frozen halibut or salmon steaks, 1 inch thick
- ¼   cup fresh lemon juice
- 2   tablespoons olive oil
- 3   cloves garlic, minced
- 2   medium yellow summer squash or zucchini, halved lengthwise
       Salt and ground black pepper
- 2   tablespoons snipped fresh basil
- 1   tablespoon snipped fresh mint

1. Thaw fish, if frozen. In a small bowl, whisk together lemon juice, olive oil, and garlic. Set aside 3 tablespoons of the lemon mixture. Brush remaining lemon juice mixture on fish and the cut sides of the squash. Lightly sprinkle fish and squash with salt and pepper.

2. Place fish on the greased rack of an uncovered grill directly over medium heat. Grill for 8 to 12 minutes or until fish begins to flake when tested with a fork, turning once halfway through grilling. During the last 5 to 6 minutes of grilling, grill the squash just until tender, turning once.

3. Meanwhile, stir basil and mint into the reserved lemon juice mixture.

4. Transfer the squash to a cutting board; cool slightly and cut into 1/4-inch slices. Place squash on a serving platter; drizzle with some of the basil mixture. Top with fish; drizzle with the remaining basil mixture.

Per serving: 233 cal., 10 g total fat (1 g sat. fat), 46 mg chol., 112 mg sodium, 5 g carbo., 1 g fiber, 30 g pro.

Halibut Steaks with Fresh Tomato Sauce

When the temperature soars and the tomatoes are ripe on the vine, fix this fresh-tasting fish dish.

Prep: 10 minutes **Grill:** 8 minutes **Makes:** 4 servings

- **4** **5- to 6-ounce fresh or frozen tuna, halibut, or salmon steaks, cut 1 inch thick**
- **1/2** **cup chopped tomato (1 medium)**
- **2** **tablespoons finely chopped red onion**
- **1** **tablespoon snipped fresh basil or 1 teaspoon dried basil, crushed**
- **1** **tablespoon mayonnaise or salad dressing**
- **1** **clove garlic, minced**
- **1/4** **teaspoon salt**
- **1** **tablespoon olive oil or vegetable oil**

1. Thaw fish, if frozen. For fresh tomato sauce, in a small bowl, combine tomato, onion, basil, mayonnaise, garlic, and salt. Cover and chill until serving time.

2. Brush both sides of fish with oil. Place fish on the greased rack of an uncovered grill directly over medium heat. Grill for 8 to 12 minutes or just until fish begins to flake easily when tested with a fork, turning once and brushing occasionally with oil. Serve with fresh tomato sauce.

Per serving: 330 cal., 15 g total fat (3 g sat. fat), 73 mg chol., 228 mg sodium, 2 g carbo., 1 g fiber, 44 g pro.

Grilled Blackened Redfish ♥

Smoky, spicy-hot blackened fish is ideal for outdoor cooking. This crisp blackened fish is delicious with corn bread and cooling creamy coleslaw.

Prep: 10 minutes **Grill:** 4 minutes **Makes:** 4 servings

- **1** **pound fresh or frozen skinless redfish or red snapper fillets**
- **1/2** **teaspoon onion powder**
- **1/2** **teaspoon garlic powder**
- **1/2** **teaspoon ground white pepper**
- **1/2** **teaspoon cayenne pepper**
- **1/2** **teaspoon ground black pepper**
- **1/2** **teaspoon dried thyme, crushed**
- **1/4** **teaspoon salt**
- **3** **tablespoons butter, melted**

1. Thaw fish, if frozen. Measure thickness of fish. Cut fish in 4 serving-size pieces, if necessary. In a small bowl, combine onion powder, garlic powder, white pepper, cayenne pepper, black pepper, thyme, and salt. Brush fish with some of the melted butter. Coat fish evenly on both sides with pepper mixture.

2. Remove grill rack from charcoal grill. Place a 12-inch cast-iron skillet directly on hot coals. Heat about 5 minutes or until a drop of water sizzles in the skillet. Add fish to skillet; drizzle with remaining melted butter. Cook, uncovered, until fish begins to flake when tested with a fork, turning once halfway through grilling. Allow 2 to 3 minutes each side for 1/2- to 3/4-inch fillets (3 to 4 minutes per side for 1-inch fillets).

Per serving: 194 cal., 10 g total fat (2 g sat. fat), 42 mg chol., 151 mg sodium, 1 g carbo., 0 g fiber, 24 g pro.

Quick Tip Cast-iron requires a little bit of special treatment. Most new cast-iron cookware comes preseasoned—which means it has had a hard, shiny, nonstick surface baked on at the factory. It's the same effect your grandmother's cast-iron skillet achieved after years of use—and proper cleaning. Wash cast-iron only with hot water (no soap) and a stiff brush. Soap can destroy the seasoning.

Thai-Spiced Scallops ♥

Although Thai cooks use a variety of basil called (no surprise) Thai basil, sweet basil contributes the same peppery, clovelike flavor.

Prep: 15 minutes **Grill:** 15 minutes **Makes:** 4 servings

- 1 **pound fresh or frozen sea scallops**
- 2 **medium yellow summer squash and/or zucchini, quartered lengthwise and sliced ½ inch thick**
- 1½ **cups packaged peeled baby carrots**
- ⅔ **cup bottled sweet-and-sour sauce**
- 2 **tablespoons snipped fresh basil**
- 1 **teaspoon Thai seasoning or five-spice powder**
- ½ **teaspoon bottled minced garlic**

1. Thaw scallops, if frozen. Fold a 36×18-inch piece of heavy foil in half to a 18-inch square. Place squash and carrots in center of foil. Sprinkle lightly with salt and pepper. Bring up opposite edges of foil; seal with a double fold. Fold remaining ends to completely enclose the vegetables, leaving space for steam to build.

2. Meanwhile, for the sauce, in a small bowl, combine the sweet-and-sour sauce, basil, Thai seasoning, and garlic. Transfer ¼ cup of the sauce to another bowl for basting. Set aside remaining sauce until ready to serve.

3. Rinse scallops; pat dry with paper towels. Halve any large scallops. Thread scallops onto four 8- to 10-inch skewers.

4. Place vegetable packet on rack of an uncovered grill over medium heat. Grill for 10 minutes, turning packet occasionally. Place skewers on rack next to packet. Grill for 5 to 8 minutes more or until vegetables are crisp-tender and scallops are opaque, turning packet occasionally and turning scallops and brushing with basting sauce once. Serve scallops and vegetables with the reserved sauce.

Per serving: 168 cal., 1 g total fat (0 g sat. fat), 34 mg chol., 370 mg sodium, 25 g carbo., 3 g fiber, 16 g pro.

Thai-Spiced Scallops

Provençal Shrimp

To make this in the oven, bake packets on a large baking sheet at 450°F for 12 to 15 minutes or until shrimp are opaque.

Prep: 15 minutes **Grill:** 12 minutes **Makes:** 4 servings

- 1 **pound fresh or frozen peeled and deveined medium shrimp (tails on)**
  Nonstick cooking spray
- 4 **teaspoons olive oil**
- ½ **teaspoon salt**
- ½ **teaspoon ground black pepper**
- 3 **cups cherry tomatoes, halved**
- ⅓ **cup pitted kalamata olives, coarsely chopped**
- 4 **cloves garlic, minced**
- 2 **teaspoons finely shredded lemon peel**
- ¼ **cup snipped Italian (flat-leaf) parsley**
  Hot cooked brown rice (optional)

1. Thaw shrimp, if frozen. Rinse shrimp; pat dry with clean paper towels.

2. Cut four 32×18-inch pieces heavy foil. Fold each in half to 16×18-inch rectangles. Coat foil pieces with nonstick cooking spray.

3. In a large bowl, stir together 2 teaspoons of the olive oil, ¼ teaspoon of the salt, and ¼ teaspoon of the pepper. Add tomatoes and olives; toss to coat. Divide tomato mixture among the foil rectangles.

4. In the same bowl, combine garlic, lemon peel, the remaining 2 teaspoons olive oil, ¼ teaspoon salt, and ¼ teaspoon pepper; mix well. Add shrimp; toss to coat. Divide shrimp evenly among foil rectangles on tomato mixture. Bring up opposite edges of foil; seal with a double fold. Fold remaining ends to completely enclose shrimp and vegetables, leaving space for steam to build.

5. Place packets on grill rack directly over medium heat. Grill for 12 to 15 minutes or until shrimp are opaque. Carefully open packets; transfer contents to 4 plates. Sprinkle with parsley. If desired, serve with brown rice.

Per serving: 209 cal., 8 g total fat (1 g sat fat), 172 mg chol., 567 mg sodium, 9 g carbo., 2 g fiber, 25 g pro.

Grilled California-Style Pizza

If you can't find pitted kalamata olives, pit them yourself. With the tip of a paring knife, make an X in one end of each olive, then firmly press down on the other end. The pit should pop right out.

Prep: 20 minutes **Grill:** 8 minutes **Makes:** 4 servings

- 1 **tablespoon olive oil**
- 1 **clove garlic, minced**
- ¼ **teaspoon crushed red pepper**
- 1 **12-inch packaged prebaked pizza crust or Italian bread shell (such as Boboli)**
- 1 **cup chopped yellow or red tomato (1 large)**

Grilled California-Style Pizza

³/₄ **cup bottled roasted red sweet peppers, cut in thin strips**

¼ **cup thinly sliced red onion wedges**

2 **ounces semisoft goat cheese or feta cheese, crumbled or cut up**

10 **pitted kalamata olives, quartered lengthwise**

1¼ **cups shredded mozzarella cheese or shredded Italian-blend cheese (5 ounces)**

3 **tablespoons fresh oregano leaves or snipped fresh basil**

1. In a small bowl, combine olive oil, garlic, and crushed red pepper; brush onto pizza crust. Top with tomato, roasted red peppers, onion, goat cheese, and olives. Sprinkle with mozzarella cheese. Fold a 24×18-inch piece of heavy foil in half crosswise. Place pizza on foil, turning edges of foil up to edge of pizza.

2. For a charcoal grill, arrange medium-hot coals around outside edge of grill. Test for medium heat in center of grill. Place pizza on center of rack. Cover and grill for 8 minutes or until pizza is heated and cheese is melted. (For a gas grill, preheat grill. Reduce heat to medium. Adjust for indirect cooking. Place pizza on grill rack. Grill as above.) Before serving, sprinkle with oregano leaves.

Per serving: 519 cal., 24 g total fat (8 g sat. fat), 35 mg chol., 1,065 mg sodium, 56 g carbo., 4 g fiber, 26 g pro.

Grilled Shrimp and Pesto Pizza: Omit olive oil, garlic, crushed red pepper, chopped tomato, roasted red peppers, and goat cheese. Instead, spread crust with ¼ cup purchased pesto. Cut 8 ounces cooked and peeled shrimp in half lengthwise. Thinly slice 3 plum tomatoes. Top crust with tomato slices, cooked shrimp, onion, and olives. Sprinkle with mozzarella cheese. Grill as directed. Before serving, sprinkle with oregano leaves.

Artichoke-Lover's Cheese Bread

This vegetable-laden cheese bread is wrapped in foil and heated to its yummy, gooey melting point on the grill.

Prep: 15 minutes **Grill:** 15 minutes **Makes:** 4 servings

2 **hoagie buns**

2 **tablespoons olive oil**
   Nonstick cooking spray

4 **ounces thinly sliced mozzarella cheese**

1 **medium tomato, sliced**

1 **6-ounce jar marinated artichoke hearts, drained and chopped**

¼ **cup sliced, pitted ripe olives**

2 **tablespoons grated Parmesan cheese**

2 **tablespoons snipped fresh basil or 1 teaspoon dried basil, crushed**

¼ **teaspoon ground black pepper**

1. Split the buns horizontally. Brush the cut sides of buns with olive oil. Tear off a 24×18-inch piece of heavy foil. Fold in half to make a 12×18-inch rectangle. Lightly coat foil with nonstick cooking spray.

2. Place the bottom halves of buns in center of foil. Top with mozzarella cheese, tomato, and artichokes. Sprinkle with olives, Parmesan cheese, basil, and pepper. Place tops of buns. Bring up the opposite edges of foil; seal with a double fold. Fold in the remaining ends to completely enclose bread.

3. Place packets on the rack of uncovered grill directly over medium heat. Grill about 15 minutes or until heated, turning once halfway through grilling. To serve, cut each bun in half crosswise.

Per serving: 377 cal., 23 g total fat (7 g sat. fat), 17 mg chol., 707 mg sodium, 31 g carbo., 2 g fiber, 12 g pro.

Pumpkin, Chickpea,
and Red Lentil Stew, **page 255**

Shredded Pork Sandwiches
with Vinegar Slaw, **page 239**

Herbed Apricot Pork
Loin Roast, **page 240**

Buffalo Chicken Drumsticks with
Blue Cheese Dip, **page 248**

Slow and Simple

Come home to delicious
aromas—and homecooked
dinners ready to eat. All
it takes is a few minutes
in the morning to combine
fresh ingredients in the
slow cooker, then turn
it on. For busy families,
these recipes are
time-saving wonders.

Boeuf à la Bourguignonne

Fork-tender beef and a superbly seasoned wine gravy are the hallmarks of this famous French dish, as popular in bistros as it is in home kitchens.

Prep: 45 minutes **Cook:** 10 to 12 hours (low) or 5 to 6 hours (high) **Makes:** 6 servings

- 3 **slices bacon, coarsely chopped**
- 2 **pounds boneless beef chuck roast, cut in 1-inch pieces**
- 1½ **cups chopped onions**
- 2 **cloves garlic, minced**
- 4 **stems fresh Italian (flat-leaf) parsley**
- 3 **sprigs fresh thyme**
- 1 **sprig fresh rosemary**
- 2 **bay leaves**
- ¼ **teaspoon whole black peppercorns**
- 4 **medium carrots, cut in ¾-inch pieces**
- 2 **cups frozen whole pearl onions**
- 3 **tablespoons quick-cooking tapioca, crushed**
- 1 **cup Burgundy (or red table wine)**
- ½ **cup beef broth**
- ¼ **cup brandy**
- 1 **tablespoon tomato paste**
- 1 **tablespoon olive oil**
- 1 **cup quartered fresh cremini mushrooms**
   Skins-On Garlic Mashed Potatoes
   Snipped fresh Italian (flat-leaf) parsley

1. In a large skillet, cook bacon over medium heat until crisp. Remove bacon from skillet, reserving drippings. Drain bacon on paper towels. Cover and chill cooked bacon until serving time. In the drippings, cook half the beef over medium heat until browned; remove from skillet. Add remaining beef, chopped onions, and garlic to drippings; cook until meat is browned and onions are tender. Remove from heat; combine all meat in skillet.

2. For the bouquet garni, place parsley stems, thyme sprigs, rosemary sprig, bay leaves, and peppercorns in the center of an 8-inch square of 100%-cotton cheesecloth. Gather corners together and tie closed with 100%-cotton kitchen string.

3. In a 3½- or 4-quart slow cooker, combine carrots and whole pearl onions. Sprinkle with tapioca. Place meat mixture on vegetables. Add bouquet garni. In a medium bowl, whisk together Burgundy, beef broth, brandy, and tomato paste. Pour over meat and vegetables in cooker.

4. Cover and cook on low-heat setting for 10 to 12 hours or on high-heat setting for 5 to 6 hours. Remove and discard bouquet garni.

5. In a large skillet, heat olive oil over medium-high heat. Add mushrooms; cook until browned. Serve beef with Skins-On Garlic Mashed Potatoes. Top each serving with bacon, mushrooms, and snipped parsley.

Skins-On Garlic Mashed Potatoes: Cut 1⅓ pounds red-skin, Yukon gold, or russet potatoes in quarters. In a large covered saucepan, cook potatoes and 4 garlic cloves, peeled and halved, in enough boiling salted water to cover for 20 to 25 minutes or until tender; drain. Mash with potato masher or beat with an electric mixer on low speed. Add 3 tablespoons butter or margarine. Season to taste with salt and ground black pepper. Slowly beat in milk (3 to 5 tablespoons) until potato mixture is light and fluffy.

Per serving: 616 cal., 30 g total fat (12 g sat. fat), 127 mg chol., 556 mg sodium, 37 g carbo., 5 g fiber, 36 g pro.

Tex-Mex Mac and Cheese

Please kids at a potluck. Macaroni and cheese with taco seasoning combines two favorite foods in one yummy dish.

Prep: 20 minutes **Cook:** 5½ to 6 hours (low) **Makes:** 10 servings

- 2 **pounds lean ground beef**
- 1 **cup chopped onion (1 large)**
- 3 **cups shredded Mexican-blend cheese (12 ounces)**
- 1 **16-ounce jar salsa**
- 1 **15-ounce jar cheese dip**
- 1 **4-ounce can diced green chiles, undrained**
- 1 **2.25-ounce can sliced, pitted ripe olives, drained**
- 12 **ounces dried elbow macaroni**

1. In a large skillet, cook ground beef and onion over medium heat until meat is browned and onion is tender. Drain off fat. Transfer meat mixture to a 4½- to 6-quart slow cooker. Add cheese, salsa, cheese dip, undrained chiles, and olives; stir to combine.

2. Cover and cook on low-heat setting for 5½ to 6 hours (do not use high-heat setting).

3. Cook macaroni following package directions; drain. Stir macaroni into beef mixture in cooker.

Per serving: 577 cal., 32 g total fat (17 g sat. fat), 113 mg chol., 1,337 mg sodium, 36 g carbo., 2 g fiber, 35 g pro.

Tex-Mex Mac and Cheese

Classic Beef Stroganoff ♥

Beef stroganoff usually calls for expensive meat, such as tenderloin or sirloin steak. This recipe calls for stew meat, which is less expensive and lets the slow cooker work its slow-simmering magic for rich and tender results.

Prep: 30 minutes **Cook:** 8 to 10 hours (low) or 4 to 5 hours (high) + 30 minutes **Makes:** 6 servings

1½	pounds beef stew meat
1	tablespoon vegetable oil
2	cups sliced fresh mushrooms
½	cup sliced green onions (4) or chopped onion (1 medium)
2	cloves garlic, minced
½	teaspoon dried oregano, crushed
½	teaspoon salt
¼	teaspoon dried thyme, crushed
¼	teaspoon ground black pepper
1	bay leaf
1½	cups lower-sodium beef broth
⅓	cup dry sherry
1	8-ounce carton light sour cream
¼	cup cold water
2	tablespoons cornstarch
	Snipped fresh parsley (optional)

1. Trim fat from meat. Cut meat into 1-inch pieces. In a large skillet, heat oil over medium heat. Cook meat, half at a time, in the hot oil until browned. Drain off fat. Set aside.

2. In a 3½- or 4-quart slow cooker, place mushrooms, onions, garlic, oregano, salt, thyme, pepper, and bay leaf. Add meat. Pour beef broth and sherry over meat and vegetables in cooker.

3. Cover and cook on low-heat setting for 8 to 10 hours or on high-heat setting for 4 to 5 hours. Discard bay leaf.

4. If using low-heat setting, turn to high-heat setting. In a medium bowl, combine sour cream, the water, and cornstarch. Stir about 1 cup of the hot cooking liquid into sour cream mixture. Stir sour cream mixture into cooker. Cover and cook about 30 minutes more or until thickened. If desired, sprinkle each serving with parsley.

Per serving: 248 cal., 9 g total fat (4 g sat. fat), 79 mg chol., 408 mg sodium, 8 g carbo., 1 g fiber, 28 g pro.

Mediterranean Beef Ragout ♥

Gremolata, a blend of fresh parsley, lemon peel, and garlic, brightens the flavor and appearance of this rich stew.

Prep: 25 minutes **Cook:** 7 to 9 hours (low) or 3½ to 4½ hours (high) + 30 minutes (high) **Makes:** 6 servings

1½	pounds beef stew meat
1	tablespoon olive oil
2	medium onions, cut in thin wedges (1 cup)
3	medium carrots, cut in ½-inch slices
2	cloves garlic, minced
1	teaspoon dried thyme, crushed
¼	teaspoon salt
¼	teaspoon ground black pepper
1	14.5-ounce can diced tomatoes, undrained
½	cup beef broth
1	medium zucchini, halved lengthwise and cut in ¼-inch slices
6	ounces fresh green beans, cut in 2-inch pieces
	Hot cooked whole wheat couscous or brown rice (optional)
	Gremolata

1. Trim fat from meat. Cut meat in 1-inch pieces. In a large skillet, heat olive oil over medium-high heat. Cook meat, half at a time, in hot oil until browned. Drain off fat. Transfer meat to a 3½- or 4-quart slow cooker. Add onions and carrots. Sprinkle with garlic, thyme, salt, and pepper. Pour undrained tomatoes and beef broth over meat and vegetables in cooker.

2. Cover and cook on low-heat setting for 7 to 9 hours or on high-heat setting for 3½ to 4½ hours.

3. If using low-heat setting, turn cooker to high-heat setting. Stir in zucchini and green beans. Cover and cook for 30 minutes more. If desired, serve over couscous. Top each serving with Gremolata.

Gremolata: In a small bowl, stir together ¼ cup snipped fresh parsley; 1 tablespoon finely shredded lemon peel; and 2 cloves garlic, minced.

Per serving: 260 cal., 11 g total fat (3 g sat. fat), 55 mg chol., 405 mg sodium, 14 g carbo., 4 g fiber, 28 g pro.

Mediterranean Beef Ragout

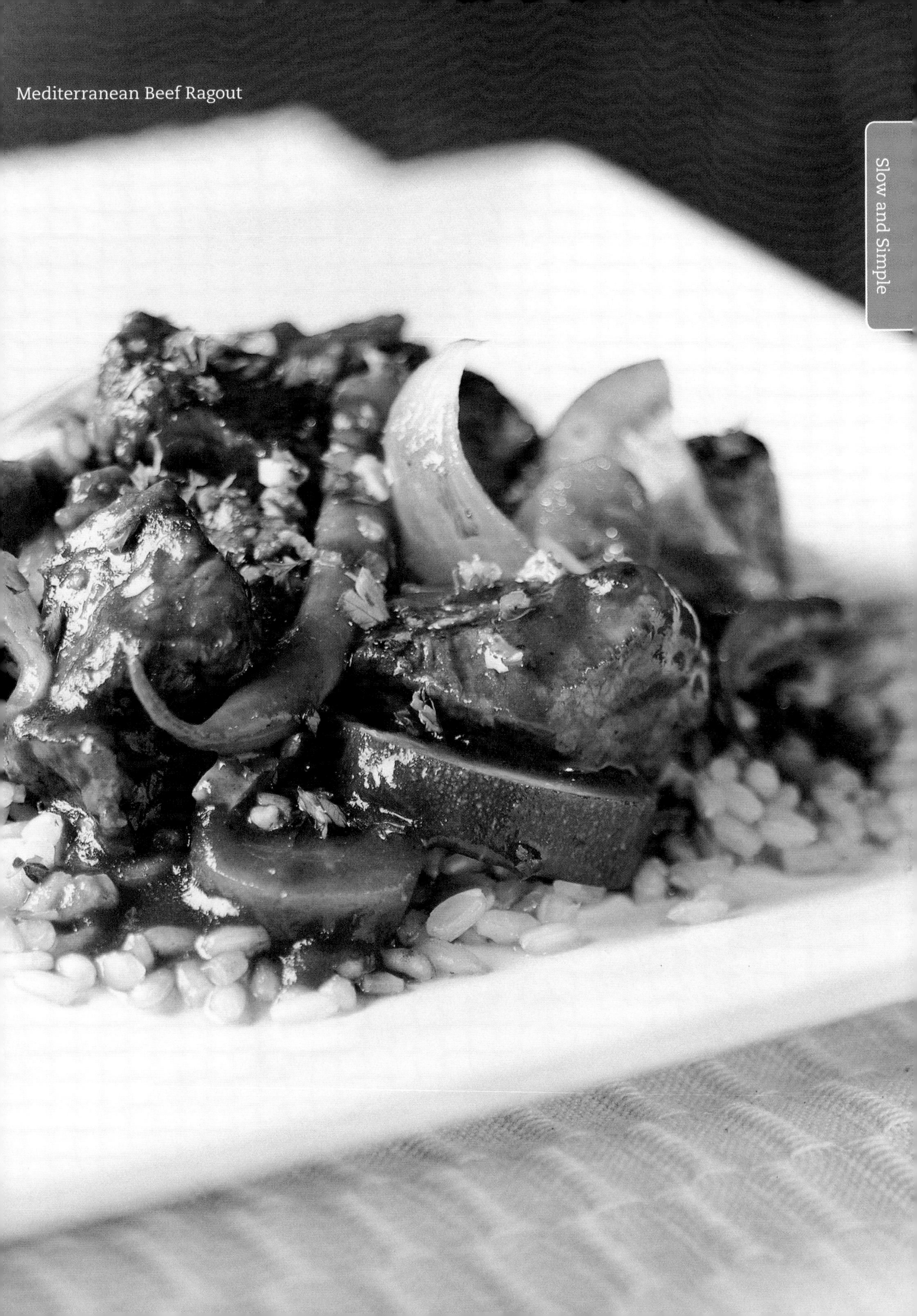

In-Your-Sleep Chili

Cook the meat and onions the night before, cool, then store in a covered container in the refrigerator. The next day, stir the ingredients into the slow cooker.

Prep: 15 minutes **Cook:** 4 to 6 hours (low) or 2 to 3 hours (high) **Makes:** 6 servings

- 1 **pound lean ground beef**
- 1 **cup chopped onion (1 large)**
- 2 **15-ounce cans chili beans in chili gravy**
- 1 **14.5-ounce can diced tomatoes and green chiles, undrained**
- 1 **11.5-ounce can hot-style vegetable juice**
  Sliced green onions, sour cream, and/or shredded cheddar cheese (optional)

1. In a large skillet, cook ground beef and onion over medium heat until meat is browned; drain off fat.

2. In a 3¹/₂- or 4-quart slow cooker, combine meat mixture, undrained beans, tomatoes, and vegetable juice.

3. Cover and cook on low-heat setting for 4 to 6 hours or high-heat setting for 2 to 3 hours. If desired, top with green onions, sour cream, and/or cheddar cheese.

Per serving: 332 cal., 12 g total fat (4 g sat. fat), 51 mg chol., 873 mg sodium, 31 g carbo., 9 g fiber, 23 g pro.

Korean Beef Short Ribs

Look for the chile bean paste at an Asian grocery. Because it contains a hefty dose of chile peppers, wear plastic or rubber gloves when rubbing it onto the ribs.

Prep: 20 minutes **Cook:** 6 to 7 hours (low) or 3 to 3¹/₂ hours (high) **Makes:** 6 to 8 servings

- 3 **pounds boneless beef short ribs**
- 1 **tablespoon vegetable oil**
- 2 **teaspoons gochujang (chile bean paste)**
- 4 **cloves garlic**
- 2 **teaspoons grated fresh ginger**
- ¹/₂ **teaspoon paprika**
- ¹/₄ **teaspoon ground black pepper**
- 1 **cup lower-sodium beef broth**
- ¹/₄ **cup reduced-sodium soy sauce**
- 2 **tablespoons vermouth or apple juice**
- 1 **tablespoon rice vinegar**
- 1 **tablespoon packed brown sugar**
- 1 **teaspoon dark sesame oil**
- 6 **to 8 cups finely shredded napa cabbage**
- 2 **tablespoons shredded carrot**
- 2 **tablespoons sliced green onion (1)**
- ¹/₂ **teaspoon toasted sesame seeds**

1. Trim fat from ribs. In a large skillet, heat oil over medium-high heat. Cook ribs on all sides, half at a time if necessary, in hot oil until browned. In a small bowl, combine

gochujang, garlic, ginger, paprika, and pepper. Wearing plastic gloves, rub mixture onto meat.

2. Place meat in a 3¹/₂- or 4-quart slow cooker. Add broth, soy sauce, vermouth, vinegar, brown sugar, and sesame oil.

3. Cover and cook on low-heat setting for 6 to 7 hours or on high-heat setting for 3 to 3¹/₂ hours. To serve, line a platter with napa cabbage. Place meat on cabbage. Skim fat from cooking liquid. Stir carrot, green onion, and sesame seeds into cooking liquid. Serve with beef.

Per serving: 457 cal., 26 g total fat (10 g sat. fat), 134 mg chol., 695 mg sodium, 5 g carbo., 1 g fiber, 45 g pro.

Chile Verde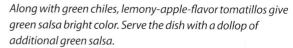

Along with green chiles, lemony-apple-flavor tomatillos give green salsa bright color. Serve the dish with a dollop of additional green salsa.

Prep: 40 minutes **Cook:** 6 to 8 hours (low) or 3 to 4 hours (high) + 15 minutes (high) **Makes:** 6 servings

- 1 **teaspoon ground cumin**
- ¹/₂ **teaspoon salt**
- ¹/₄ **teaspoon ground black pepper**
- 1¹/₂ **pounds boneless pork shoulder**
  Nonstick cooking spray
- 1 **tablespoon olive oil**
- 1 **pound fresh tomatillos, husks removed and chopped (about 4 cups)**
- 1 **cup chopped onion (1 large)**
- 3 **teaspoons finely shredded lime peel**
- 2 **tablespoons fresh lime juice**
- 4 **cloves garlic, minced**
- ³/₄ **cup chopped yellow or red sweet pepper (1 medium)**
- 12 **6-inch corn tortillas, warmed**
- 2 **tablespoons snipped fresh cilantro**
  Purchased green salsa (optional)

1. In a small bowl, combine cumin, salt, and black pepper; set aside. Trim fat from meat. Cut meat in 1-inch pieces. Sprinkle cumin mixture on meat. Coat a large skillet with cooking spray. Cook half the meat in hot skillet over medium heat until browned. Remove meat from skillet. Add oil to skillet. Cook remaining meat in hot oil until browned. Drain off fat. Place meat in a 3¹/₂- or 4-quart slow cooker. Add tomatillos, onion, 1 teaspoon of the lime peel, the lime juice, and garlic. Stir to combine.

2. Cover and cook on low-heat setting for 6 to 8 hours or on high-heat setting for 3 to 4 hours.

3. If using low-heat setting, turn to high-heat setting. Add sweet pepper to cooker. Cover and cook for 15 minutes more. To serve, fill tortillas with meat; sprinkle with cilantro and remaining lime peel. If desired, serve with green salsa.

Per serving: 333 cal., 11 g total fat (3 g sat. fat), 73 mg chol., 314 mg sodium, 32 g carbo., 4 g fiber, 27 g pro.

Barbecued Country-Style Ribs

This big-batch recipe creates succulent, meaty, fall-off-the-bone ribs. Use leftovers for Shredded Pork Sandwiches and Vinegar Slaw on page 239.

Prep: 30 minutes **Cook:** 10 to 11 hours (low) or 5 to 5½ hours (high) **Makes:** 8 servings

4½	**to 5 pounds boneless pork country-style ribs**
1½	**cups bottled barbecue sauce**
½	**cup chopped onion (1 medium)**
½	**cup chopped celery (1 stalk)**
2	**tablespoons yellow mustard**
1	**tablespoon packed brown sugar**
1	**tablespoon Worcestershire sauce**
2	**cloves garlic, minced**
1	**teaspoon dried thyme, crushed**
2	**cups hot cooked noodles**
	Fresh thyme sprigs (optional)

1. Trim fat from ribs. Place ribs in a 4- to 5-quart slow cooker. In a medium bowl, combine barbecue sauce, onion, celery, mustard, brown sugar, Worcestershire sauce, garlic, and thyme. Pour sauce over ribs in cooker.

2. Cover and cook on low-heat setting for 10 to 11 hours or on high-heat setting for 5 to 5½ hours.

3. Using a slotted spoon, remove ribs from sauce. Strain sauce; if necessary, skim fat from sauce. Serve half the ribs and half the sauce with hot cooked noodles. If desired, garnish with thyme sprigs.

4. Using two forks, shred remaining rib meat, trimming fat.

Per serving: 554 cal., 22 g total fat (7 g sat. fat), 189 mg chol., 632 mg sodium, 30 g carbo., 2 g fiber, 54 g pro.

To store ribs and sauce: Place shredded pork (about 3 cups) and 1 cup of the sauce in an airtight container; stir to combine. Place remaining sauce (about 2 cups) in a second airtight container. Seal and refrigerate for up to 3 days. (Or freeze for up to 3 months. Thaw in refrigerator overnight before using.) Use in Shredded Pork Sandwiches and Vinegar Slaw on page 239.

Shredded Pork Sandwiches with Vinegar Slaw

Shredded Pork Sandwiches with Vinegar Slaw

Getting messy never tasted so good! These satisfying sandwiches start with leftover meat and sauce from the Barbecued Country-Style Ribs on page 237. For a quick version of slaw, just pick up some from the deli—you'll need about 1½ cups.

Prep: 25 minutes **Chill:** 2 to 24 hours
Makes: 4 sandwiches

- 2   **cups packaged shredded cabbage with carrot (coleslaw mix)**
- ¼   **cup cider vinegar**
- 3   **tablespoons honey**
- ¼   **teaspoon salt**
- ⅛   **teaspoon ground black pepper**
       Meat and sauce from Barbecued Country-Style Ribs* (see recipe, page 237)
- 4   **kaiser rolls or hoagie buns, split and toasted**
       Bottled hot pepper sauce (optional)

1. In a medium bowl, combine coleslaw mix, vinegar, honey, salt, and pepper. Toss to combine. Cover and refrigerate for 2 to 24 hours, stirring occasionally.

2. In a medium saucepan, heat reserved meat mixture, covered, over medium heat about 10 minutes or until heated through, stirring occasionally. If desired, add some of the reserved sauce to moisten meat. In a small saucepan, heat any remaining sauce over medium-low heat until heated through.

3. To serve, strain cabbage mixture, discarding liquid. Divide meat mixture among roll bottoms. Top with cabbage and roll tops. Pass reserved sauce and, if desired, bottled hot pepper sauce.

Per sandwich: 673 cal., 23 g total fat (7 g sat. fat), 162 mg chol., 1,089 mg sodium, 56 g carbo., 3 g fiber, 57 g pro.

*3 cups reserved shredded pork mixed with 1 cup sauce and about 2 cups additional reserved sauce

Choucroute

"Choucroute" (shoo-KROOT) is a French word that refers to sauerkraut garnished with potatoes and meats—in this recipe, smoked pork and sausage. Serve it with Dijon mustard and rye bread.

Prep: 10 minutes **Cook:** 8 to 9 hours (low) or 4 to 4½ hours (high) **Makes:** 8 servings

- 1   **14- to 15-ounce can Bavarian-style sauerkraut (with caraway seeds), rinsed and drained**
- 1   **pound Yukon gold potatoes, quartered**
- 1   **pound cooked smoked boneless pork chops, halved crosswise**
- 1   **pound cooked bratwurst, halved crosswise, or cooked smoked Polish sausage, cut in 3-inch lengths**
- 1   **12-ounce bottle or can of beer**

1. In a 4½- to 6-quart slow cooker, place sauerkraut and potatoes. Top with pork chops and bratwurst. Pour beer over all.

2. Cover and cook on low-heat setting for 8 to 9 hours or on high-heat setting for 4 to 4½ hours.

Per serving: 311 cal., 17 g total fat (6 g sat. fat), 64 mg chol., 2,158 mg sodium, 16 g carbo., 1 g fiber, 19 g pro.

Pork and Edamame Soup

Nutty-tasting green soybeans, edamame, are classic bar food at sushi restaurants—and they're healthful. Soy is associated with a reduced risk of some types of cancer and the maintenance or improvement of bone health.

Prep: 25 minutes **Cook:** 7 to 8 hours (low) or 3½ to 4 hours (high) + 5 minutes **Makes:** 6 servings

- 2   **pounds boneless pork shoulder**
- 1   **tablespoon vegetable oil**
- 2   **14-ounce cans chicken broth**
- 1   **12-ounce package frozen sweet soybeans (edamame)**
- 1   **8-ounce can sliced water chestnuts, drained**
- 1   **cup chopped red sweet pepper (1 large)**
- 2   **tablespoons reduced-sodium soy sauce**
- 1   **tablespoon bottled hoisin sauce**
- 2   **teaspoons grated fresh ginger**
- ¼   **to ½ teaspoon crushed red pepper**
- 6   **cloves garlic, minced (1 tablespoon)**
- 1   **3-ounce package ramen noodles, broken**
       Sliced green onions (optional)

1. Trim fat from meat. Cut meat in 1-inch pieces. In a large skillet, heat oil over medium-high heat. Cook meat, half at a time, in hot oil until browned. Drain off fat.

2. Transfer to a 3½- to 4½-quart slow cooker. Stir in broth, soybeans, water chestnuts, sweet pepper, soy sauce, hoisin sauce, ginger, crushed red pepper, and garlic.

3. Cover and cook on low-heat setting for 7 to 8 hours or on high-heat setting for 3½ to 4 hours. Skim off fat. Stir in ramen noodles (reserve seasoning packet for another use). Cover and cook for 5 minutes more. If desired, top each serving with sliced green onions.

Per serving: 400 cal., 15 g total fat (4 g sat. fat), 111 mg chol., 906 mg sodium, 22 g carbo., 7 g fiber, 41 g pro.

Herbed Apricot Pork Loin Roast ♥

Pork pairs well with fruit—pineapple, apples, plums or prunes, peaches, and, of course, apricots.

Prep: 20 minutes **Cook:** 6 to 7 hours (low) or 3 to 3½ hours (high) **Stand:** 15 minutes **Makes:** 8 servings

- 1 **3-pound boneless pork top loin roast (double loin, tied)**
   Salt and ground black pepper
- 1 **10-ounce jar apricot spreadable fruit**
- ⅓ **cup finely chopped onion (1 small)**
- 2 **tablespoons Dijon-style mustard**
- 1 **tablespoon brandy**
- 1 **teaspoon finely shredded lemon peel**
- 1 **teaspoon snipped fresh rosemary**
- 1 **teaspoon snipped fresh sage**
- 1 **teaspoon snipped fresh thyme**
- ¼ **teaspoon ground black pepper**
- 2 **tablespoons water**
- 4 **teaspoons cornstarch**
   Fresh apricots (optional)
   Fresh thyme, sage, and/or rosemary (optional)

1. Sprinkle pork roast with salt and pepper. In a medium bowl, combine spreadable fruit, onion, mustard, brandy, lemon peel, rosemary, sage, thyme, and pepper.

2. Place roast in a 4- to 5-quart slow cooker. Pour fruit mixture over roast.

3. Cover and cook on low-heat setting for 6 to 7 hours or on high-heat setting for 3 to 3½ hours.

4. Remove roast from cooker. Cover loosely with foil and let stand for 15 minutes before carving. Meanwhile, for sauce, in a medium saucepan, combine the water and cornstarch; carefully stir in liquid from slow cooker. Cook and stir sauce until thickened and bubbly; cook and stir for 2 minutes more. Serve sauce with pork. If desired, garnish with fresh apricots and herbs.

Per serving: 314 cal., 7 g total fat (2 g sat. fat), 107 mg chol., 247 mg sodium, 21 g carbo., 0 g fiber, 38 g pro.

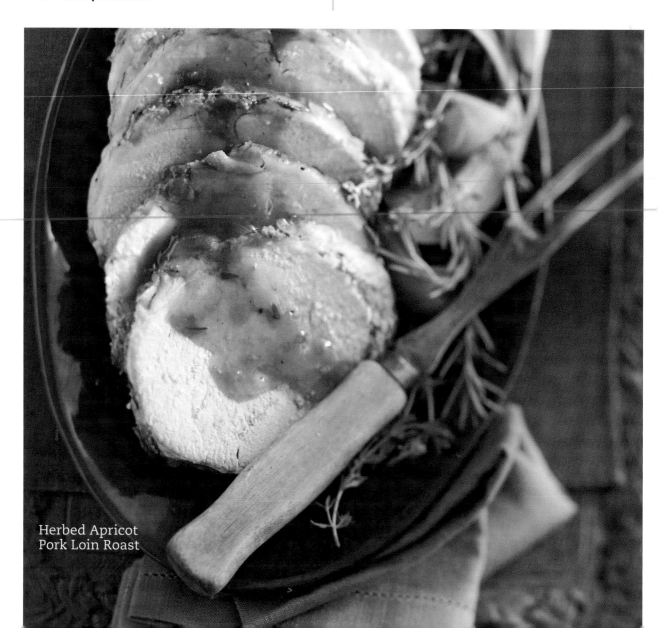

Herbed Apricot
Pork Loin Roast

Sage-Scented Pork Chops ♥

This hearty dish is ideal for fall evenings. Reserve four chops to make Pork and Potato Gratin with Gruyère Cheese (right)—and you're more than halfway prepared for another dinner.

Prep: 30 minutes **Cook:** 4 to 5 hours (low) or 2 to 2½ hours (high) **Makes:** 6 servings

- 10 boneless pork loin chops, cut ¾ inch thick (about 3½ pounds)
- 2 teaspoons dried sage, crushed
- 1 teaspoon ground black pepper
- ½ teaspoon salt
- 2 tablespoons vegetable oil
- 1 medium onion, thinly sliced
- ½ cup chicken broth
- ⅓ cup dry white wine or apple juice
- 3 tablespoons quick-cooking tapioca, crushed
- ½ a medium head green cabbage, cut in ½-inch strips
- 1 tablespoon Dijon-style mustard
- 1 teaspoon caraway seeds
  Salt and ground black pepper

1. Trim fat from chops. In a small bowl, stir together sage, the 1 teaspoon pepper, and ½ teaspoon salt. Rub sage mixture onto one side of each chop. In an extra-large skillet, heat oil over medium heat. Brown both sides of chops, half at a time, in hot oil over medium heat.

2. In a 6- to 7-quart slow cooker, place onion, chicken broth, wine, and tapioca. Add the chops to cooker. Top with cabbage.

3. Cover and cook on low-heat setting for 4 to 5 hours or on high-heat setting for 2 to 2½ hours.

4. Reserve and store* 4 chops. Use for Pork and Potato Gratin with Gruyère Cheese. Transfer remaining 6 chops to a platter; cover and keep warm. Using a slotted spoon, transfer cabbage and onion to a serving bowl. Stir mustard and caraway seeds into remaining juices in cooker. Season sauce to taste with salt and pepper. Spoon sauce over pork and cabbage.

Per serving: 300 cal., 12 g total fat (4 g sat. fat), 87 mg chol., 351 mg sodium, 9 g carbo., 1 g fiber, 37 g pro.

*To store: Place chops in an airtight container; seal. Refrigerate up to 3 days or freeze up to 3 months. Thaw in refrigerator overnight before using.

Pork and Potato Gratin with Gruyère Cheese

Serve this creamy casserole with steamed green beans and rolls.

Prep: 30 minutes **Bake:** 45 minutes **Stand:** 10 minutes **Oven:** 375°F **Makes:** 6 servings

- 3 tablespoons butter or margarine
- ½ cup chopped onion (1 medium)
- 3 tablespoons all-purpose flour
- ¾ teaspoon salt
- ½ teaspoon ground black pepper
- ¼ teaspoon ground nutmeg
- 1¾ cups milk
- 1¼ cups shredded Gruyère cheese (5 ounces)
- 2 pounds round red or white potatoes, peeled and thinly sliced (5 to 6 potatoes)
  Reserved Sage-Scented Pork Chops (see recipe, left), chopped

1. Preheat oven to 375°F. For sauce, in a medium saucepan, melt butter over medium heat. Add onion; cook until tender. Stir in flour, salt, pepper, and nutmeg. Cook and stir 1 minute. Add milk. Cook and stir until thickened and bubbly. Add cheese; cook and stir until melted.

2. Spread half the potatoes in a greased 2½- to 3-quart rectangular baking dish or au gratin dish. Top with meat. Cover with half the sauce. Repeat layers.

3. Bake, covered, about 45 minutes or until potatoes are tender. Let stand for 10 minutes before serving.

Per serving: 488 cal., 24 g total fat (12 g sat. fat), 109 mg chol., 618 mg sodium, 29 g carbo., 2 g fiber, 37 g pro.

Quick Tip Varieties of potatoes have different uses. Russet potatoes, for baking and french fries, have a dry and grainy texture that gives fries crispy exteriors and light, fluffy interiors. In this gratin, russets would fall apart and get mushy. The firm, waxy texture of round red or white potatoes, however, holds up when boiled or cooked in a gratin.

Sage-Scented Pork Chops

Italian Sausage Soup

Depending on how spicy you like food, use either sweet or hot Italian sausage in this soup. Adding the orzo at the end of the cooking time keeps it al dente.

Prep: 25 minutes **Cook:** 8 to 10 hours (low) or 4 to 5 high (high) + 20 minutes (high) **Makes:** 8 servings

- 1 **pound Italian sausage, casings removed if present**
- 1 **cup chopped onion (1 large)**
- 1 **clove garlic, minced**
- 1 **cup chopped carrots (2 medium)**
- ½ **cup chopped celery (1 stalk)**
- 1 **14.5-ounce can diced tomatoes, undrained**
- 1 **8-ounce can tomato sauce**
- 1 **teaspoon dried oregano, crushed**
- ½ **teaspoon dried rosemary, crushed**
- ½ **teaspoon dried basil, crushed**
- ¼ **teaspoon dried thyme, crushed**
- ¼ **teaspoon fennel seeds, crushed**
- 1 **bay leaf**
- 3 **14-ounce cans reduced-sodium chicken broth**
- ½ **cup dried orzo or finely broken capellini pasta**
  Finely shredded Parmesan cheese (optional)

1. In a large skillet, combine Italian sausage, onion, and garlic. Cook over medium heat until sausage is browned. Drain off fat.

2. In a 4½- to 6-quart slow cooker, combine carrots and celery. Place sausage mixture on vegetables. In a medium bowl, combine undrained tomatoes, tomato sauce, oregano, rosemary, basil, thyme, fennel seeds, and bay leaf. Pour over sausage mixture. Pour broth over all.

3. Cover and cook on low-heat setting for 8 to 10 hours or on high-heat setting for 4 to 5 hours.

4. If using low-heat setting, turn to high-heat setting. Add orzo. Cover and cook for 20 minutes more. Discard bay leaf. If desired, sprinkle servings with Parmesan cheese.

Per serving: 250 cal., 13 g total fat (5 g sat. fat), 38 mg chol., 923 mg sodium, 17 g carbo., 2 g fiber, 12 g pro.

Italian Sausage Soup

Cider-Braised Pork Roast and Apples ♥

This recipe makes a mountain of meat. To store leftovers, place meat in an airtight container; cover. Refrigerate 3 days or freeze up to 3 months. Thaw in refrigerator overnight before using.

Prep: 30 minutes **Cook:** 8 to 10 hours (low) or 4 to 5 hours (high) **Makes:** 6 servings

- 1 **3-pound boneless pork top loin roast**
- ½ **teaspoon salt**
- ½ **teaspoon dried thyme, crushed**
- ½ **teaspoon dried sage, crushed**
- ¼ **teaspoon ground black pepper**
- 2 **tablespoons vegetable oil**
- 4 **red, yellow, and/or green apples, cored and each cut in 6 wedges**
- ⅓ **cup chopped shallot**
- 1 **tablespoon bottled minced garlic or 6 cloves garlic, minced**
- 3 **tablespoons quick-cooking tapioca, crushed**
- ¾ **cup chicken broth**
- ¾ **cup apple cider or juice**
- 3 **cups hot cooked rice**

1. Trim fat from meat. In a small bowl, stir together salt, thyme, sage, and pepper. Sprinkle spice mixture on meat; rub in with your fingers. In a large skillet, heat oil over medium heat. Brown meat on all sides in hot oil.

2. In a 6- to 7-quart slow cooker, place apple wedges, shallot, and garlic; sprinkle with tapioca. Place meat on apple mixture. Pour chicken broth and apple cider over meat.

3. Cover and cook on low-heat setting for 8 to 10 hours or on high-heat setting for 4 to 5 hours.

4. Slice pork; serve with apples and hot cooked rice. Spoon some of the cooking liquid over all. Reserve and store leftover meat; use for sandwiches and salads.

Per serving: 407 cal., 12 g total fat (3 g sat. fat), 67 mg chol., 303 mg sodium, 43 g carbo., 2 g fiber, 30 g pro.

Cider-Braised Pork Roast and Apples

German Sausages and Sauerkraut in Beer

For an authentic German dining experience, add a little polka music and an Oktoberfest beer.

Prep: 20 minutes **Cook:** 7 to 9 hours (low) or 3$\frac{1}{2}$ to 4$\frac{1}{2}$ hours (high) **Makes:** 6 servings

- 1 **large sweet onion, cut in thin wedges (1 cup)**
- 8 **ounces tiny new potatoes, halved**
- 3 **medium carrots, cut in $\frac{1}{2}$-inch pieces**
- 1 **pound smoked cooked bratwurst, knockwurst, and/or kielbasa, cut in 2-inch pieces**
- 1 **12-ounce bottle Oktoberfest beer or other amber lager beer or nonalcoholic beer**
- 1 **cup chicken broth**
- $\frac{1}{2}$ **teaspoon paprika**
- $\frac{1}{2}$ **teaspoon caraway seeds**
- $\frac{1}{2}$ **teaspoon cracked black pepper**
- 1 **14- to 16-ounce can sauerkraut, rinsed and drained**
- 3 **cups hot cooked spaetzle or noodles**
  Coarse-grain mustard (optional)

1. In a 4-quart slow cooker, place onion, potatoes, and carrots. Top with sausages. Add beer, chicken broth, paprika, caraway seeds, and pepper. Top with sauerkraut.

2. Cover and cook on low-heat setting for 7 to 9 hours or on high-heat setting for 3$\frac{1}{2}$ to 4$\frac{1}{2}$ hours.

3. Using a slotted spoon, transfer sausages and vegetable mixture to a serving dish. Serve with spaetzle drizzled with cooking liquid and, if desired, mustard.

Per serving: 550 cal., 22 g total fat (5 g sat. fat), 103 mg chol., 1,837 mg sodium, 62 g carbo., 7 g fiber, 21 g pro.

Italian Sausage Grinders

For a taste of fair and festival food at home, serve these zesty sandwiches. (Have lots of napkins handy!)

Prep: 25 minutes **Bake:** 5 minutes
Cook: 7 to 8 hours (low) or 3$\frac{1}{2}$ to 4 hours (high)
Oven: 350°F **Makes:** 8 sandwiches

- 3 **large green and/or red sweet peppers, cut into bite-size strips**
- 4 **4.5-ounce jars (drained weight) sliced mushrooms, drained**
- 1 **26-ounce jar marinara sauce**
- 1 **15-ounce can tomato sauce with garlic and onion**
- 1 **to 2 teaspoons crushed red pepper**
- 8 **uncooked Italian sausage links (about 1$\frac{1}{2}$ pounds)**
- 8 **hoagie buns or french-style rolls, split and toasted**
- 2 **cups shredded mozzarella cheese (8 ounces)**

1. In a 5- to 6-quart slow cooker, place sweet peppers and mushrooms. Stir in sauce, tomato sauce, and crushed red pepper. Add sausage.

2. Cover and cook on low-heat setting for 7 to 8 hours or on high-heat setting for 3$\frac{1}{2}$ to 4 hours.

3. To serve, preheat oven to 350°F. Place a sausage on each hoagie bun. Using a slotted spoon, spoon vegetable mixture over the sausages. Sprinkle with mozzarella cheese. Arrange sandwiches on a baking sheet. Bake, uncovered, for 5 to 10 minutes or until cheese melts. Serve any remaining sauce for dipping.

Per sandwich: 762 cal., 39 g total fat (15 g sat. fat), 81 mg chol., 2,170 mg sodium, 73 g carbo., 7 g fiber, 30 g pro.

Greek Lamb with Spinach and Orzo ♥

The bed of spinach wilts slightly when the hot lamb and pasta mixture is spooned on this Mediterranean-style dish.

Prep: 20 minutes **Cook:** 8 to 10 hours (low) or 4 to 5 hours (high) **Makes:** 8 servings

- 1 **tablespoon dried oregano, crushed**
- 1 **tablespoon finely shredded lemon peel**
- 4 **cloves garlic, minced**
- $\frac{1}{2}$ **teaspoon salt**
- 3 **pounds lamb stew meat**
- $\frac{1}{4}$ **cup lemon juice**
- 12 **ounces dried orzo**
- 1 **10-ounce bag prewashed fresh spinach, chopped**
- 1 **cup crumbled feta cheese (4 ounces)**
  Lemon wedges (optional)

1. In a small bowl, stir together oregano, lemon peel, garlic, and salt. Sprinkle oregano mixture evenly on meat; rub in with your fingers. Place meat in a 3$\frac{1}{2}$- or 4-quart slow cooker. Sprinkle meat with lemon juice.

2. Cover and cook on low-heat setting for 8 to 10 hours or on high-heat setting for 4 to 5 hours.

3. Prepare orzo following package directions. Stir cooked orzo into meat mixture in cooker. Place spinach on a large platter. Spoon lamb mixture on the spinach. Sprinkle with feta cheese. If desired, serve with lemon wedges.

Per serving: 437 cal., 13 g total fat (5 g sat. fat), 123 mg chol., 445 mg sodium, 35 g carbo., 2 g fiber, 43 g pro.

Moroccan Lamb Tagine

Tagine (tay-JEAN) is a type of long-simmered Moroccan meat or poultry stew—as well as the ceramic vessel in which it is cooked. Look for orange flower water in specialty food shops.

Prep: 40 minutes **Cook:** 8 to 10 hours (low) or 4 to 5 hours (high) **Makes:** 6 servings

- 1/2 **teaspoon ground ginger**
- 1/2 **teaspoon ground cumin**
- 1/2 **teaspoon salt**
- 1/4 **teaspoon ground turmeric**
- 1/4 **teaspoon ground cinnamon**
- 1 1/2 **to 2 pounds boneless lamb shoulder or lamb stew meat, cut in 1-inch pieces**
- 1 1/2 **cups coarsely chopped, peeled sweet potato**
- 2 **medium carrots, cut in 1-inch pieces**
- 1/2 **cup chopped onion (1 medium)**
- 1 **medium plum tomato, chopped**
- 1/3 **cup pitted dates, quartered**
- 1/4 **cup green olives, halved**
- 2 **tablespoons quick-cooking tapioca, crushed**
- 1/2 **teaspoon finely shredded lemon peel**
- 1 **tablespoon lemon juice**
- 1 **tablespoon honey**
- 2 **cloves garlic, minced**
- 1 **14-ounce can chicken broth**
- 1 **teaspoon orange-flower water (optional)**
- 3 **cups hot cooked couscous**
- 1/3 **cup sliced almonds, toasted**

1. In a large bowl, combine ginger, cumin, salt, turmeric, and cinnamon. Add lamb to bowl; toss to coat lamb with spices.

2. In a 3 1/2- to 4-quart slow cooker, place lamb, sweet potato, carrots, onion, tomato, dates, olives, tapioca, lemon peel, lemon juice, honey, and garlic. Pour chicken broth over all.

3. Cover and cook on low-heat setting for 8 to 10 hours or on high-heat setting for 4 to 5 hours. If desired, stir in orange-flower water.

4. Serve with couscous sprinkled with almonds.

Per serving: 368 cal., 8 g total fat (2 g sat. fat), 70 mg chol., 674 mg sodium, 45 g carbo., 5 g fiber, 28 g pro.

Irish Stew

Try something new this St. Patrick's Day. Have this hearty stew bubbling and ready to eat when you walk in the door. Serve it with Irish soda bread.

Prep: 25 minutes **Cook:** 10 to 11 hours (low) or 5 to 5 1/2 hours (high) **Makes:** 6 servings

- 1 **pound lean boneless lamb**
- 2 **tablespoons vegetable oil**
- 2 **medium turnips, peeled and cut into 1/2-inch pieces**
- 3 **medium carrots, cut in 1/2-inch pieces**
- 2 **medium potatoes, peeled and cut in 1/2-inch pieces**
- 2 **medium onions, cut in thin wedges**
- 1/4 **cup quick-cooking tapioca**
- 1/2 **teaspoon salt**
- 1/4 **teaspoon ground black pepper**
- 1/4 **teaspoon dried thyme, crushed**
- 2 **14-ounce cans beef broth**

1. Trim fat from lamb. Cut lamb in 1-inch pieces. In a large skillet, heat oil over medium heat. Cook lamb, half at a time, in hot oil until browned. Drain off fat.

2. In a 3 1/2- or 4-quart slow cooker, combine lamb, turnips, carrots, potatoes, onions, tapioca, salt, pepper, and thyme. Pour beef broth over lamb and vegetables in cooker.

3. Cover and cook on low-heat setting for 10 to 11 hours or on high-heat setting for 5 to 5 1/2 hours.

Per serving: 234 cal., 8 g total fat (2 g sat. fat), 49 mg chol., 784 mg sodium, 21 g carbo., 3 g fiber, 19 g pro.

Quick Tip Tapioca may seem like a strange ingredient to stir into a savory dish, but it becomes nearly invisible and acts as a thickener when cooked. To crush it, use a mortar and pestle or put it in a plastic bag and crush it with a rolling pin.

Moroccan Lamb Tagine

Hot-and-Spicy Braised Peanut Chicken

Hot-and-Spicy Braised Peanut Chicken

For additional Thai flavor, serve this rich-tasting dish over hot cooked jasmine rice—an aromatic rice with delicate, nutty flavor.

Prep: 30 minutes **Cook:** 5 to 6 hours (low) or 2½ to 3 hours (high) **Stand:** 5 minutes **Makes:** 6 servings

- 2 **medium onions, cut in thin wedges**
- 1½ **cups sliced carrots (3 medium)**
- 1 **small red sweet pepper, cut in bite-size strips**
- 2 **pounds skinless, boneless chicken thighs, cut in 1-inch pieces**
- ¾ **cup chicken broth**
- 3 **tablespoons creamy peanut butter**
- ½ **teaspoon finely shredded lime peel**
- 2 **tablespoons fresh lime juice**
- 2 **tablespoons soy sauce**
- 2 **tablespoons quick-cooking tapioca, crushed**
- 1 **tablespoon grated fresh ginger**
- 2 **to 3 teaspoons red curry paste**
- 4 **cloves garlic, minced**
- ½ **cup canned unsweetened coconut milk**
- 1 **cup frozen peas**
- 2 **cups hot cooked rice**
  Chopped peanuts (optional)
  Snipped fresh cilantro (optional)

1. In a 3½- or 4-quart slow cooker, place onions, carrots, and sweet pepper. Top with chicken. In a medium bowl, whisk together chicken broth, peanut butter, lime peel, lime juice, soy sauce, tapioca, ginger, curry paste, and garlic until smooth. Pour over chicken and vegetables in cooker.

2. Cover and cook on low-heat setting for 5 to 6 hours or on high-heat setting for 2½ to 3 hours. Stir in coconut milk and peas. Let stand, covered, for 5 minutes.

3. Serve chicken mixture on hot cooked rice. If desired, sprinkle with chopped peanuts and cilantro.

Per serving: 444 cal., 15 g total fat (7 g sat. fat), 126 mg chol., 708 mg sodium, 39 g carbo., 4 g fiber, 37 g pro.

Buffalo Chicken Drumsticks
with Blue Cheese Dip

Buffalo Chicken Drumsticks with Blue Cheese Dip

If you love the flavors of buffalo wings as appetizers, try them as an entrée. Steamed rice and peas on the side would help cut the heat. Pass plenty of blue cheese dip too!

Prep: 30 minutes **Cook:** 6 to 8 hours (low) or 3 to 4 hours (high) **Makes:** 8 servings

16	chicken drumsticks (about 4 pounds), skinned, if desired
1	16-ounce bottle buffalo wing hot sauce (2 cups)
1/4	cup tomato paste
2	tablespoons white or cider vinegar
2	tablespoons Worcestershire sauce
1	8-ounce container sour cream
1/2	cup mayonnaise or salad dressing
1/2	cup crumbled blue cheese (2 ounces)
1/4	to 1/2 teaspoon cayenne pepper or bottled hot pepper sauce
	Celery sticks

1. Place drumsticks in a 4- to 5-quart slow cooker. In a medium bowl, combine hot sauce, tomato paste, vinegar, and Worcestershire sauce. Pour over chicken in cooker.

2. Cover and cook on low-heat setting for 6 to 8 hours or on high-heat setting for 3 to 4 hours.

3. Meanwhile, for blue cheese dip, in a small bowl, combine sour cream, mayonnaise, blue cheese, and cayenne pepper. Cover and refrigerate until ready to serve.

4. Using a slotted spoon, remove drumsticks from cooker. Skim fat from cooking juices. Serve drumsticks with cooking juices, the blue cheese dip, and celery sticks.

Per serving: 454 cal., 33 g total fat (11 g sat. fat), 141 mg chol., 2,084 mg sodium, 6 g carbo., 1 g fiber, 31 g pro.

Cheesy Garlic Chicken ♥

A double dose of cheese—luscious cream cheese and oozy melted mozzarella—provides richness to this chicken. In spite of that, it's still healthful at fewer than 300 calories and 8 grams of fat per serving. Serve it with hot cooked pasta or rice.

Prep: 20 minutes **Cook:** 3½ to 4½ hours (low) or 1½ to 2 hours (high) + 30 minutes (high) **Stand:** 10 minutes **Makes:** 6 servings

2	pounds skinless, boneless chicken breast halves
1½	cups cauliflower florets
4	cloves garlic, minced
¾	cup reduced-sodium chicken broth
2	tablespoons quick-cooking tapioca, crushed
¼	teaspoon salt
1½	cups frozen cut green beans
½	of an 8-ounce package reduced-fat cream cheese (Neufchâtel), cubed
½	cup shredded part-skim mozzarella cheese (2 ounces)
⅔	cup chopped plum tomatoes (2 medium)

1. Cut chicken in 1½-inch pieces. In a 3½- or 4-quart slow cooker, combine chicken, cauliflower, garlic, chicken broth, tapioca, and salt.

2. Cover and cook on low-heat setting for 3½ to 4½ hours or on high-heat setting for 1½ to 2 hours.

3. If using low-heat setting, turn to high-heat setting. Add beans to cooker. Cover and cook for 30 minutes more. Turn off cooker.

4. Stir cream cheese into mixture in cooker. Cover and let stand for 10 minutes. Uncover and gently stir until cream cheese is melted and sauce is smooth. Sprinkle each serving with mozzarella cheese and tomatoes.

Per serving: 283 cal., 8 g total fat (4 g sat. fat), 108 mg chol., 393 mg sodium, 10 g carbo., 2 g fiber, 41 g pro.

Chicken and White Bean Stew

Green chiles and a generous amount of cumin add Tex-Mex flavor to this creamy chicken and bean stew.

Prep: 35 minutes **Cook:** 4 to 5 hours (low) or 2 to 2½ hours (high) **Makes:** 8 servings

2	pounds skinless, boneless chicken thighs
2	teaspoons ground cumin
⅛	teaspoon ground black pepper
1	tablespoon olive oil
2	10-ounce packages refrigerated light Alfredo pasta sauce
1	15-ounce can Great Northern or white kidney (cannellini) beans, rinsed and drained
1	cup reduced-sodium chicken broth
½	cup chopped red onion (1 medium)
1	4-ounce can diced green chiles, undrained
4	cloves garlic, minced
¼	cup shredded sharp cheddar or Monterey Jack cheese (1 ounce) (optional)

1. Cut chicken in 1-inch pieces. Sprinkle chicken with cumin and black pepper. In a large skillet, heat oil over medium heat. Cook chicken, half at a time, in hot oil over medium heat until browned. Place chicken in a 3½- or 4-quart slow cooker. Stir in Alfredo sauce, beans, chicken broth, onion, undrained chiles, and garlic.

2. Cover and cook on low-heat setting for 4 to 5 hours or on high-heat setting for 2 to 2½ hours. If desired, sprinkle servings with cheese.

Per serving: 360 cal., 16 g total fat (8 g sat. fat), 122 mg chol., 918 mg sodium, 20 g carbo., 3 g fiber, 31 g pro.

Easy Chicken Tetrazzini

Legend says this dish was created in San Francisco in the early 1900s for Luisa Tetrazzini, a renowned Italian opera singer and gourmand. Despite its high-minded origins, it is decidedly comforting fare.

Prep: 20 minutes **Cook:** 5 to 6 hours (low) or 2½ to 3 hours (high) **Makes:** 8 servings

2½	pounds skinless, boneless chicken breast halves and/or thighs, cut in 1-inch pieces
2	4.5-ounce jars (drained weight) sliced mushrooms, drained
1	16-ounce jar Alfredo pasta sauce
¼	cup chicken broth or water
2	tablespoons dry sherry (optional)
¼	teaspoon ground black pepper
¼	teaspoon ground nutmeg
10	ounces dried spaghetti or linguini
⅔	cup grated Parmesan cheese
¾	cup thinly sliced green onions (6)
	French bread slices, toasted (optional)

1. In a 3½- or 4-quart slow cooker, combine chicken and drained mushrooms. In a medium bowl, stir together Alfredo sauce, chicken broth, sherry (if desired), pepper, and nutmeg. Pour over chicken mixture in cooker.

2. Cover and cook on low-heat setting for 5 to 6 hours or on high-heat setting for 2½ to 3 hours.

3. Meanwhile, cook pasta following package directions; drain. Stir Parmesan cheese into chicken mixture in cooker. Serve chicken over pasta; top with green onions. If desired, serve with toasted French bread.

Per serving: 430 cal., 14 g total fat (6 g sat. fat), 121 mg chol., 753 mg sodium, 32 g carbo., 2 g fiber, 42 g pro.

Nacho Cheese
Chicken Chowder

Nacho Cheese Chicken Chowder ♥

Mac 'n' cheese lovers will love this soup.

Prep: 10 minutes **Cook:** 4 to 5 hours (low) or 2 to 2½ hours (high) **Makes:** 6 servings

- 1 **pound skinless, boneless chicken breast halves, cut into ½-inch pieces**
- 2 **14.5-ounce cans Mexican-style stewed tomatoes, undrained**
- 1 **10.75-ounce can condensed nacho cheese soup**
- 1 **10-ounce package frozen whole kernel corn (2 cups)**
  Shredded taco or cheddar cheese (optional)

1. In a 3½- or 4-quart slow cooker, stir together chicken, undrained tomatoes, soup, and corn.
2. Cover and cook on low-heat setting for 4 to 5 hours or on high-heat setting for 2 to 2½ hours. If desired, sprinkle servings with cheese.

Per serving: 244 cal., 6 g total fat (3 g sat. fat), 55 mg chol., 347 mg sodium, 24 g carbo., 2 g fiber, 23 g pro.

Alfredo Chicken

Italian green beans are broader and flatter than most other green beans—which you could also use if you prefer.

Prep: 20 minutes **Cook:** 6 to 7 hours (low) or 3 to 3½ hours (high) **Makes:** 6 servings

- 3 **pounds meaty chicken pieces (breast halves, thighs, and drumsticks), skinned**
  Salt and ground black pepper
- 1 **16-ounce jar light Parmesan Alfredo pasta sauce**
- 1 **9-ounce package frozen Italian green beans, thawed**

- 3 **cups hot cooked whole wheat pasta**
  Finely shredded Parmesan cheese (optional)

1. Place chicken in a 3½- or 4-quart slow cooker. Sprinkle lightly with salt and pepper. Pour sauce over chicken.
2. Cover and cook on low-heat setting for 6 to 7 hours or on high-heat setting for 3 to 3½ hours, adding green beans during the last 30 minutes of cooking.
3. Using a slotted spoon, transfer chicken and green beans to a platter. Stir cooked pasta into sauce in cooker; serve with the chicken and beans. If desired, sprinkle servings with Parmesan cheese.

Per serving: 392 cal., 15 g total fat (7 g sat. fat), 123 mg chol., 680 mg sodium, 26 g carbo., 3 g fiber, 36 g pro.

Turkey Chablis ♥

The crisp, dry flavor of Chablis is ideal for simmering turkey. Chardonnay or Sauvignon Blanc would work equally well. Serve with mashed potatoes to take advantage of the delicious wine gravy.

Prep: 15 minutes **Cook:** 9 hours (low) or 4½ hours (high) + 10 minutes **Makes:** 8 servings

- ¾ **cup dry white wine (such as Chablis) or apple juice**
- ½ **cup chopped onion (1 medium)**
- 1 **clove garlic, minced**
- 1 **bay leaf**
- 1 **teaspoon dried rosemary, crushed**
- ¼ **teaspoon ground black pepper**
- 1 **3-pound frozen boneless turkey roast, thawed**
- ⅓ **cup half-and-half, light cream, or milk**
- 2 **tablespoons cornstarch**
  Dinner rolls, split (optional)

1. In a 4- to 5-quart slow cooker, combine wine, onion, garlic, bay leaf, rosemary, and pepper. If gravy packet is present with turkey, remove and discard or refrigerate for another use. Place turkey roast in cooker.
2. Cover; cook on low-heat setting for 9 hours or on high-heat setting for 4½ hours. Transfer turkey to a platter; cover and keep warm.
3. For gravy, strain cooking juices; discard solids. Skim off fat from cooking juices. Measure 1⅓ cups of the cooking juices (add water if necessary); pour into a small saucepan. In a small bowl, stir together half-and-half and cornstarch; stir into cooking juices in saucepan. Cook and stir until thickened and bubbly. Cook and stir for 2 minutes more.
4. If turkey is wrapped in netting, remove and discard. Slice turkey. If desired, serve on split rolls. Spoon some of the gravy over turkey. Pass remaining gravy.

Per serving: 365 cal., 9 g total fat (3 g sat. fat), 176 mg chol., 193 mg sodium, 5 g carbo., 0 g fiber, 58 g pro.

Turkey Chablis

4. To assemble, place some of the turkey mixture on each warmed tortilla. If desired, top with some of the sauce from the cooker. Sprinkle with green onions.

Per wrap: 207 cal., 5 g total fat (1 g sat. fat), 67 mg chol., 422 mg sodium, 20 g carbo., 2 g fiber, 20 g pro.

Oriental Hot-and-Sour Soup

Slowly stir in the beaten egg to get even strands. Not stirring results in clumps; stirring too vigorously makes the soup cloudy.

Prep: 20 minutes **Cook:** 9 to 11 hours (low) or 3 to 4 hours (high) + 50 minutes **Makes:** 8 servings

4	**cups chicken broth**
1	**8-ounce can bamboo shoots, drained**
1	**8-ounce can sliced water chestnuts, drained**
1	**4-ounce can (drained weight) sliced mushrooms, drained**
3	**tablespoons quick-cooking tapioca, crushed**
3	**tablespoons rice wine vinegar or vinegar**
1	**tablespoon soy sauce**
1	**teaspoon sugar**
½	**teaspoon ground black pepper**
1	**8-ounce package frozen peeled and deveined shrimp**
4	**ounces firm tofu (fresh bean curd), drained and cubed**
1	**egg, lightly beaten**
2	**tablespoons snipped parsley or fresh coriander**

1. In a 3-½- or 4-quart slow cooker, combine chicken broth, bamboo shoots, water chestnuts, mushrooms, tapioca, vinegar, soy sauce, sugar, and pepper.

2. Cover and cook on low-heat setting for 9 to 11 hours or on high-heat setting for 3 to 4 hours. Add shrimp and tofu. Cover and cook on low- or high-heat setting for 50 minutes more.

3. Pour the beaten egg slowly into the soup in a thin stream. Stir the soup gently so the egg forms fine strands rather than clumps. Sprinkle servings with parsley.

Per serving: 114 cal., 2 g total fat (1 g sat. fat), 83 mg chol., 664 mg sodium, 9 g carbo., 1 g fiber, 13 g pro.

Quick Tip Shrimp cooks quickly and is easy to overcook —which makes it tough and rubbery. Add it at the end of the cooking time to ensure that it stays tender. When shrimp turns pink and is slightly opaque, it's done cooking.

Sesame-Ginger Turkey Wraps

Sesame-Ginger Turkey Wraps ♥

If you're not cooking for a crowd, refrigerate or freeze some of the leftover turkey to reheat for another meal. Cooked turkey and chicken are convenient to have on hand.

Prep: 20 minutes **Cook:** 6 to 7 hours (low) or 3 to 3½ hours (high) **Stand:** 5 minutes **Makes:** 12 wraps

	Nonstick cooking spray
3	**turkey thighs, skinned (3½ to 4 pounds)**
1	**cup bottled sesame-ginger stir-fry sauce**
¼	**cup water**
1	**16-ounce package shredded broccoli (broccoli slaw mix)**
12	**8-inch flour tortillas, warmed**
¾	**cup sliced green onions (6)**

1. Lightly coat a 3½- or 4-quart slow cooker with cooking spray. Place turkey in prepared cooker. In a small bowl, stir together stir-fry sauce and the water. Pour over turkey in cooker.

2. Cover and cook on low-heat setting for 6 to 7 hours or on high-heat setting for 3 to 3½ hours.

3. Remove turkey from cooker; cool slightly. Remove turkey from bones; discard bones. Using two forks, shred turkey in bite-size pieces. Return to cooker. Add shredded broccoli to slow cooker. Stir to coat; cover and let stand for 5 minutes. Using a slotted spoon, remove turkey and broccoli from cooker.

Pumpkin, Chickpea,
and Red Lentil Stew

Pumpkin, Chickpea, and Red Lentil Stew

Serve this Indian-style stew with crispy lentil crackers, pappadum, available at Indian markets and specialty food shops. Toast them over an open flame or in a dry skillet to make them crispy.

Prep: 25 minutes **Cook:** 8 to 10 hours (low) or 4 to 5 hours (high) **Makes:** 6 servings

- 1 **pound pie pumpkin or winter squash, peeled, seeded, and cut in 1-inch cubes**
- 1 **15-ounce can garbanzo beans (chickpeas), rinsed and drained**
- 3 **medium carrots, sliced ¹⁄₂ inch thick**
- 1 **cup chopped onion (1 large)**
- 1 **cup dry red lentils, rinsed and drained**
- 2 **tablespoons tomato paste**
- 1 **tablespoon grated fresh ginger**
- 1 **tablespoon fresh lime juice**
- 1 **teaspoon ground cumin**
- ¹⁄₄ **teaspoon salt**
- ¹⁄₄ **teaspoon ground turmeric**
- ¹⁄₄ **teaspoon ground black pepper**
- 4 **cups chicken or vegetable broth**
- ¹⁄₄ **cup chopped peanuts**
- 2 **tablespoons chopped fresh cilantro**
  Plain nonfat yogurt (optional)

1. In a 3¹⁄₂- or 4-quart slow cooker, combine pumpkin, chickpeas, carrots, onion, lentils, tomato paste, ginger, lime juice, cumin, salt, turmeric, and pepper. Pour broth over all in cooker.

2. Cover and cook on low-heat setting for 8 to 10 hours or on high-heat setting for 4 to 5 hours. Top each serving with peanuts, cilantro, and, if desired, yogurt.

Per serving: 275 cal., 4 g total fat (1 g sat. fat), 2 mg chol., 1,027 mg sodium, 46 g carbo., 10 g fiber, 14 g pro.

Red Beans Creole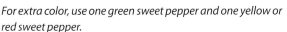

For extra color, use one green sweet pepper and one yellow or red sweet pepper.

Prep: 25 minutes **Stand:** 1 hour **Cook:** 11 to 13 hours (low) or 5¹⁄₂ to 6¹⁄₂ hours (high) + 30 minutes (high) **Makes:** 4 or 5 servings

- 3¹⁄₂ **cups dry red beans (1¹⁄₂ pounds), rinsed and drained**
- 5 **cups water**
- 3 **cups chopped onions (3 large)**
- 2 **4-ounce cans (drained weight) sliced mushrooms, drained**
- 6 **cloves garlic, minced**
- 2 **tablespoons Creole seasoning**

- 1 **14.5-ounce can diced tomatoes with basil, garlic, and oregano, undrained**
- 2 **cups instant brown rice**
- 2 **medium green sweet peppers, cut in strips**
  Bottled hot pepper sauce (optional)

1. Place beans in a large saucepan. Add enough water to cover beans by 2 inches. Bring to boiling; reduce heat. Simmer, uncovered, for 10 minutes. Remove from heat. Cover and let stand for 1 hour. Drain and rinse beans.

2. In a 3¹⁄₂- or 4-quart slow cooker, combine beans, the 5 cups water, onions, mushrooms, garlic, and Creole seasoning.

3. Cover and cook on low-heat setting for 11 to 13 hours or on high-heat setting for 5¹⁄₂ to 6¹⁄₂ hours.

4. If using low-heat setting, turn to high-heat setting. Stir in undrained tomatoes, uncooked rice, and sweet peppers. Cover and cook for 30 minutes more. If desired, pass bottled hot pepper sauce.

Per serving: 415 cal., 2 g total fat (0 g sat. fat), 0 mg chol., 541 mg sodium, 81 g carbo., 16 g fiber, 23 g pro.

Bean-and-Rice-Stuffed Peppers

With only five ingredients, these hearty stuffed peppers are assembled in a snap. Team them with corn bread or whole wheat rolls and dinner is done!

Prep: 15 minutes **Cook:** 6 to 6¹⁄₂ hours (low) or 3 to 3¹⁄₂ hours (high) **Makes:** 4 servings

- 4 **medium green, red, and/or yellow sweet peppers**
- 1 **15-ounce can chili beans with chili gravy**
- 1 **cup cooked converted rice**
- 1 **cup shredded Monterey Jack cheese (4 ounces)**
- 1 **15-ounce can tomato sauce**

1. Remove tops, membranes, and seeds from peppers. In a medium bowl, stir together chili beans with chili gravy, cooked rice, and ¹⁄₂ cup of the cheese; spoon into peppers. Pour tomato sauce into a 5- to 6-quart slow cooker. Place peppers, filled sides up, in slow cooker.

2. Cover and cook on low-heat setting for 6 to 6¹⁄₂ hours or on high-heat setting for 3 to 3¹⁄₂ hours.

3. Transfer peppers to serving plates. Spoon tomato sauce from cooker over peppers. Sprinkle with the remaining ¹⁄₂ cup cheese.

Per serving: 332 cal., 12 g total fat (5 g sat. fat), 25 mg chol., 918 mg sodium, 42 g carbo., 10 g fiber, 16 g pro.

Peppered Turkey Panini, **page 268**

Meatballs and Greens on Ciabatta, **page 262**

Catfish Po'Boys, **page 270**

Steak and Cheese Melt Pizza, **page 275**

Sandwiches and Pizzas

Breads and spreads—stacked and layered with a savory array of fillings and toppings—offer casual, utensils-free meals and snacks. For something to munch while watching the game or a quick weeknight dinner, begin with bread.

Beef and Red Onion Sandwiches

No side dish needed when you serve these veggie-rich sandwiches—the salad is built right in.

Start to Finish: 20 minutes **Makes:** 4 sandwiches

8	sliced dried tomatoes or dried tomato halves (not oil packed)
12	ounces beef sirloin steak, about ¾ inch thick
1	small red onion, thinly sliced
2	tablespoons olive oil
	Salt and ground black pepper
4	square bagels or ciabatta rolls, split
¼	cup mayonnaise or salad dressing
1	cup mixed salad greens

1. Preheat broiler. Place dried tomatoes in a small bowl; cover with water. Microwave on 100% power (high) for 1 minute. Meanwhile, brush olive oil on steak and onion; arrange on the unheated rack of a broiler pan. Broil 3 to 4 inches from heat for 12 to 16 minutes or until desired doneness, turning once halfway through broiling. Thinly slice steak across the grain into bite-size pieces.

2. Meanwhile drain tomatoes. Lightly spread split sides of rolls with mayonnaise. Layer rolls with steak, onion, drained tomatoes, and salad greens.

Per sandwich: 451 cal., 22 g total fat (4 g sat. fat), 51 mg chol., 681 mg sodium, 40 g carbo., 3 g fiber, 26 g pro.

Beef and Tapenade Open-Face Sandwiches

These hearty sandwiches feature deli roast beef—a fast meal for a no-cook night.

Start to Finish: 10 minutes **Makes:** 4 sandwiches

⅓	cup light mayonnaise or salad dressing
1	teaspoon Dijon-style or yellow mustard
4	slices crusty Italian country or sourdough bread
¼	cup purchased olive tapenade
12	ounces thinly sliced deli roast beef
2	small tomatoes, thinly sliced
1	cup fresh baby spinach

1. In small bowl, combine mayonnaise and mustard. Lightly spread on one side of each bread slice. Spread with tapenade. Top with roast beef, tomato slices, and spinach.

Per sandwich: 362 cal., 19 g total fat (4 g sat. fat), 46 mg chol., 1,681 mg sodium, 21 g carbo., 2 g fiber, 21 g pro.

Garlic-Mustard Steak Sandwiches

Honey mustard gives these sandwiches a sweeter, lighter flavor than classic Dijon-style mustard.

Prep: 15 minutes **Broil:** 16 minutes
Makes: 4 to 6 sandwiches

4	to 6 hoagie rolls, split
2	tablespoons honey mustard
½	teaspoon dried marjoram or thyme, crushed
1	clove garlic, minced
¼	teaspoon coarsely ground black pepper
1	1- to 1½-pound beef flank steak
1	large red onion, sliced ½ inch thick
4	to 6 slices Swiss cheese
	Honey mustard (optional)

1. Preheat broiler. Place rolls, cut sides up, on the unheated rack of a broiler pan. Broil 4 to 5 inches from heat for 1 to 2 minutes or until toasted. Set aside.

2. In a small mixing bowl, stir together the 2 tablespoons mustard, the marjoram, garlic, and pepper; set aside. Trim fat from the steak. Score steak on both sides by making shallow diagonal cuts at 1-inch intervals in a diamond pattern. Brush both sides of steak with mustard mixture.

3. Place steak on the unheated rack of a broiler pan. Place onion slices beside steak. Broil 4 to 5 inches from heat for 15 to 18 minutes or until steak is medium doneness (160°F) and onion is tender, turning steak and onion slices once halfway through broiling.

4. Thinly slice steak at an angle across the grain. Separate onion slices into rings. Arrange steak strips, onion rings, and cheese on roll bottoms. Broil about 1 minute or until cheese begins to melt. Add roll tops. If desired, pass additional mustard.

Per sandwich: 685 cal., 22 g total fat (9 g sat. fat), 65 mg chol., 844 mg sodium, 78 g carbo., 4 g fiber, 43 g pro.

Garlic-Mustard Steak Sandwiches

Beef and Blue Cheese Wraps

Meatloaf Open-Facers

Meatloaf sandwiches are usually made with leftovers—these fun open-face sandwiches call for prepared meatloaf.

Start to Finish: 18 minutes **Makes:** 4 sandwiches

4	½-inch slices eggplant
2	tablespoons olive oil
	Salt and ground black pepper
1	17-ounce package refrigerated meatloaf with tomato sauce
½	cup no-salt-added tomato sauce
4	1-inch diagonal slices Italian bread, toasted
¼	cup finely shredded Parmesan cheese (1 ounce) (optional)

1. Preheat broiler. Brush oil on both sides eggplant. Sprinkle with salt and pepper. Place eggplant slices on the unheated rack of broiler pan. Broil 3 to 4 inches from heat for 2 to 3 minutes per side or until browned.

2. Meanwhile, slice meatloaf; place slices in a large skillet. Pour sauce from package and tomato sauce over slices. Cook over medium-high heat about 6 minutes or until heated through.

3. Place meatloaf slices on toast; top with eggplant, any remaining sauce, and cheese.

Per sandwich: 327 cal., 16 g total fat (5 g sat. fat), 64 mg chol., 707 mg sodium, 21 g carbo., 2 g fiber, 27 g pro.

Beef and Blue Cheese Wraps 🔲

These wraps offer the wonderful flavors of a blue cheese-topped steak and roasted pepeprs.

Start to Finish: 20 minutes **Makes:** 4 wraps

3	tablespoons mayonnaise or salad dressing
1	teaspoon dried thyme, crushed
2	tablespoons yellow mustard
4	8-inch flour tortillas
12	ounces thinly sliced deli roast beef
1	12-ounce jar roasted red sweet peppers, drained
⅓	cup crumbled blue cheese
4	cups mixed salad greens
	Olive oil (optional)
	Additional crumbled blue cheese (optional)

1. In a small bowl, combine mayonnaise and thyme; remove and set aside 1 tablespoon. Stir mustard into the remaining mayonnaise mixture.

2. Spread one side of each tortilla with mayonnaise-mustard mixture. Evenly divide roast beef, roasted peppers, and the ⅓ cup blue cheese among tortillas. Roll up; brush with reserved mayonnaise-thyme mixture.

3. In an extra-large skillet, cook tortilla wraps over medium heat about 2 minutes per side or until lightly browned. Cut each wrap in half. Divide greens among 4 plates. If desired, drizzle greens with olive oil and sprinkle with additional blue cheese; top with halved wraps.

Per wrap: 395 cal., 23 g total fat (7 g sat. fat), 50 mg chol., 1,145 mg sodium, 22 g carbo., 3 g fiber, 21 g pro.

Beef and Cabbage Wraps 🔲

Call all hands on deck to get dinner on the table: Set out tortillas and fillings and let everyone assemble the wraps.

Start to Finish: 20 minutes **Oven:** 350°F
Makes: 4 servings (2 wraps per serving)

8	8-inch flour tortillas
12	ounces lean ground beef
½	cup chopped onion (1 medium)
1	cup frozen whole kernel corn
½	to ⅔ cup bottled barbecue sauce
2	cups packaged shredded cabbage with carrots (coleslaw mix)

1. Preheat oven to 350°F. Wrap tortillas tightly in foil; place on baking sheet. Heat in oven about 10 minutes or until heated through.

2. Meanwhile, in large skillet, cook beef and onion over medium heat until beef is browned and onion is tender. Drain off fat. Stir in corn and ⅓ cup of the barbecue sauce. Cook and stir until heated through.

3. To serve, spread one side of tortillas with the remaining barbecue sauce. Spoon about ½ cup beef mixture on each tortilla. Add shredded cabbage. Roll up.

Per serving (2 wraps): 391 cal., 14 g total fat (4 g sat. fat), 54 mg chol., 535 mg sodium, 46 g carbo., 3 g fiber, 21 g pro.

Beef and Cabbage Wraps

Meatballs and Greens on Ciabatta

Meatballs and Greens on Ciabatta 🔲

To speed up heating the meatballs with the parsley mixture, heat frozen meatballs first following package directions. Then combine cooked meatballs and parsley mixture.

Start to Finish: 15 minutes **Makes:** 6 sandwiches

- ⅓ **cup olive oil**
- ¼ **cup fresh lemon juice**
- 1 **bunch Italian (flat-leaf) parsley, large stems removed**
- 2 **cloves garlic**
  Salt and ground black pepper
- 1 **16- to 18-ounce package frozen cooked Italian-style meatballs, thawed**
- 6 **ciabatta rolls, split and toasted**
- ½ **a small head romaine, cut up or torn**

1. In a food processor or blender, combine olive oil, lemon juice, parsley, and garlic. Cover and process or blend until finely chopped. Season to taste with salt and pepper.

2. Transfer parsley mixture to a large skillet; add meatballs. Cook, covered, over medium heat, until heated through, stirring and spooning sauce over meatballs occasionally.

3. Place one ciabatta roll, toasted side up, on each plate. Top with romaine. Remove meatballs from skillet with a slotted spoon; place on romaine. Drizzle with warm parsley mixture.

Per sandwich: 534 cal., 31 g total fat (10 g sat. fat), 49 mg chol., 1,002 mg sodium, 43 g carbo., 6 g fiber, 20 g pro.

Meatball and Pineapple Hoagies

Meatball and Pineapple Hoagies [one]

Mango chutney is delicious in this fruit-filled sandwich. Choose mild or spicy, depending on your taste buds.

Start to Finish: 20 minutes **Makes:** 4 sandwiches

- 2 **tablespoons olive oil**
- 1 **large sweet onion, halved and sliced**
- 1 **16-ounce package frozen cooked meatballs, thawed**
- 1 **cup peeled, cored pineapple, chopped (about one-fourth of a pineapple)**
- 1 **cup desired chutney**
- ¼ **teaspoon crushed red pepper**
- 4 **hoagie buns, split and toasted**

1. In a large skillet, heat olive oil over medium heat. Add onion; cook about 8 minutes or until tender, stirring frequently. Stir in meatballs, pineapple, chutney, and crushed red pepper. Cover skillet; cook about 3 minutes more or until heated through, stirring once. Serve in buns.

Per sandwich: 878 cal., 40 g total fat (13 g sat. fat), 40 mg chol., 1,403 mg sodium, 109 g carbo., 6 g fiber, 24 g pro.

Philly Cheese Steak Calzones [one]

This recipe puts a favorite American sandwich in a pocket.

Prep: 40 minutes **Bake:** 13 minutes **Oven:** 425°F
Makes: 8 calzones

- 6 **ounces thinly sliced deli roast beef or cooked beef steak**
- 1 **cup shredded provolone or mozzarella cheese (4 ounces)**
- 1 **cup shredded sharp white cheddar cheese (4 ounces)**
- 1 **small banana pepper, cut in ¼-inch rings**
- 1 **16-ounce loaf frozen white bread dough, thawed**
- 1 **tablespoon butter or margarine, melted**
- 2 **tablespoons grated Romano or Parmesan cheese**
- 1 **teaspoon dried Italian seasoning or ½ teaspoon dried oregano, crushed**
- 1 **cup bottled ranch salad dressing**

1. Line a large baking sheet with foil; lightly grease foil. Set aside. For filling, cut beef into bite-size pieces. In a medium bowl, toss together beef, provolone cheese, cheddar cheese, and banana pepper. Set aside.

2. Preheat oven to 425°F. Divide thawed bread dough in 8 portions. On a lightly floured surface, roll each portion in a 7-inch round. Divide beef mixture among the 8 dough circles, leaving a 1-inch border around edges. Lightly brush edges of dough with water.

3. For each calzone, fold dough over filling to opposite edge, stretching slightly. Fold over edges, making a 1-inch fold. Press dough with tines of a fork to seal. Arrange calzones on baking sheet. Prick tops to allow steam to escape. Lightly brush tops with melted butter. Sprinkle with Romano cheese and Italian seasoning.

4. Bake for 13 to 15 minutes or until golden. Serve warm calzones with ranch dressing for dipping.

Per calzone: 386 cal., 21 g total fat (9 g sat. fat), 50 mg chol., 374 mg sodium, 26 g carbo., 0 g fiber, 18 g pro.

Pork and Veggie Rolls [one]

Creamy avocado and peppery pork provide savory contrasts in these supersimple hot sandwiches.

Start to Finish: 15 minutes
Makes: 4 servings (2 pieces each)

- 1 **18.4-ounce peppercorn-seasoned pork tenderloin**
- 1 **ripe avocado**
- ¼ **teaspoon salt**
- ⅛ **teaspoon ground black pepper**
- 1 **10-inch focaccia, cut in quarters and split horizontally**
- ½ **a medium red onion, thinly sliced**
- 1 **large tomato, cored and sliced**

1. Preheat broiler. Cut tenderloin in ½-inch slices; flatten slightly with palm of hand. Arrange slices on the unheated rack of a broiler pan. Broil 4 inches from the heat for 4 to 6 minutes or just until slightly pink in center, turning once halfway through broiling.

2. Meanwhile, halve, seed, and peel avocado. Place avocado in a small bowl; mash with a fork. Stir in salt and pepper.

3. Spread bottoms of bread quarters with avocado mixture. Layer red onion, pork, and tomato on top of avocado mixture. Add bread tops. Cut each in half to serve.

Per serving: 476 cal., 14 g total fat (4 g sat. fat), 61 mg chol., 925 mg sodium, 57 g carbo., 7 g fiber, 35 g pro.

Bacon and Egg Salad Sandwiches

Bacon and Egg Salad Sandwiches

Bacon and eggs also make a terrific dinner. Serve with a glass of chilled white or rosé wine.

Start to Finish: 20 minutes **Makes:** 4 sandwiches

6	**eggs**
8	**slices applewood-smoked bacon**
8	**slices challah bread**
1/2	**cup mayonnaise or salad dressing**
2	**teaspoons yellow mustard**
12	**to 16 basil leaves**
1/2	**an English cucumber, chopped**

1. Place eggs in a medium saucepan; cover with water. Bring to boiling over high heat; cover and remove from heat. After 6 minutes, remove 2 eggs. Rinse with cold water; peel and set aside. Let remaining eggs stand in hot water for 4 minutes more. Drain; rinse with cold water. Peel and coarsely chop the 10-minute eggs.

2. Meanwhile, in an extra-large skillet, cook bacon until crisp; drain. Discard drippings; wipe skillet with a paper towel. Lightly toast both sides of bread slices in skillet. In a small bowl, combine mayonnaise and mustard.

3. Top 4 of the bread slices with basil leaves, chopped egg, and cucumber. Halve the remaining 2 eggs and place one half on each sandwich. Top with mayonnaise mixture, bacon, and remaining bread slices.

Per sandwich: 614 cal., 40 g total fat (10 g sat. fat), 391 mg chol., 765 mg sodium, 38 g carbo., 2 g fiber, 22 g pro.

Pecan-Crusted Sliders [one]

These sweet and savory little sandwiches depart from traditional sliders. They're made with slices of pork tenderloin rather than with ground meat.

Start to Finish: 25 minutes
Makes: 4 servings (2 sliders each)

12	**ounces pork tenderloin, sliced crosswise in 8 pieces**
1	**egg**
2	**tablespoons honey**
1	**cup finely chopped pecans**
1	**teaspoon salt**
1/2	**teaspoon ground black pepper**
2	**tablespoons vegetable oil**
1	**small green apple**

1½ **cups packaged shredded broccoli (broccoli slaw mix)**

¼ **cup mayonnaise or salad dressing**

8 **small buns or dinner rolls, split**
Dijon-style mustard (optional)

1. With palm of hand, flatten pork slices to ¼-inch thickness. In a shallow dish, whisk together egg and 1 tablespoon of the honey. In another shallow dish, combine pecans, salt, and pepper. Dip pork into egg mixture, then into nut mixture, pressing to coat.

2. In an extra-large skillet, heat oil over medium-high heat. Cook pork in hot oil for 2 to 3 minutes per side or until golden and slightly pink in center.

3. Meanwhile, for slaw, quarter apple; remove core and seeds. Thinly slice apple. In a medium bowl, combine apple, shredded broccoli, mayonnaise, and the remaining 1 tablespoon honey. Season to taste with salt and pepper. For sliders, place pork in buns; top with slaw. If desired, pass mustard.

Per serving (2 sliders): 694 cal., 44 g total fat (6 g sat. fat), 115 mg chol., 1,029 mg sodium, 49 g carbo., 5 g fiber, 29 g pro.

Caprese Chicken Sandwiches

Tomato, fresh mozzarella, and fresh basil—the trio known as insalata caprese—is layered with grilled chicken between mayo-slathered rolls in these summer-fresh sandwiches.

Start to Finish: 20 minutes **Makes:** 4 sandwiches

4 **skinless, boneless chicken breast halves**

1 **tablespoon vegetable oil**
Salt and ground black pepper

4 **French rolls, split**

¼ **cup mayonnaise or salad dressing**

4 **ounces fresh mozzarella cheese, sliced**

1 **large tomato, sliced**

8 **fresh basil leaves**

1. Brush chicken breasts with oil; sprinkle with salt and pepper.

2. Place chicken on the rack of an uncovered grill directly over medium heat. Grill for 12 to 15 minutes or until no longer pink (170°F), turning once halfway through grilling. If desired, grill rolls for 1 to 2 minutes to toast.

3. Cut chicken breast halves diagonally in half to fit rolls. Spread rolls with mayonnaise. Layer chicken on roll bottoms. Top with mozzarella cheese, tomato slices, and basil leaves. Add roll tops.

Per serving: 478 cal., 24 g total fat (7 g sat. fat), 107 mg chol., 634 mg sodium, 21 g carbo., 2 g fiber, 42 g pro.

Fajita-Ranch Chicken Wraps [one]

To warm the tortillas, wrap them tightly in foil, then heat in a 350°F oven for about 10 minutes or until heated through and soft.

Start to Finish: 30 minutes **Oven:** 350°F
Makes: 4 servings (½ wrap each)

12 **ounces chicken breast strips for stir-fry**

½ **teaspoon chili powder**

¼ **teaspoon garlic powder**
Nonstick cooking spray

2 **small red, yellow, and/or green sweet peppers, seeded and cut in thin strips**

2 **tablespoons bottled reduced-calorie ranch salad dressing**

2 **10-inch whole wheat, tomato, or jalapeño flour tortillas, warmed**

½ **cup purchased deli-style fresh salsa**

⅓ **cup reduced-fat shredded cheddar cheese**

1. Sprinkle chicken with chili powder and garlic powder. Coat a large unheated nonstick skillet with cooking spray. Preheat over medium-high heat. Cook chicken in hot skillet over medium heat for 4 to 6 minutes or until chicken is no longer pink. Remove chicken from skillet. Add sweet peppers to skillet; cook about 5 minutes or until tender. Return chicken to skillet. Add salad dressing; toss to coat.

2. Divide chicken mixture among warmed tortillas, placing it to one side of each tortilla. Top with salsa and cheese. Fold tortillas over; cut each into 2 pieces.

Per serving (½ wrap): 267 cal., 7 g total fat (2 g sat. fat), 57 mg chol., 706 mg sodium, 24 g carbo., 5 g fiber, 26 g pro.

Fajita-Ranch Chicken Wraps

Thai Chicken-Broccoli Wraps ♥ [one]

When short on time, make these wraps with bottled peanut sauce instead of mixing it.

Start to Finish: 25 minutes **Makes:** 6 servings (½ wrap each)

- **12 ounces chicken breast strips for stir-fry**
- **¼ teaspoon garlic salt**
- **⅛ teaspoon ground black pepper**
  Nonstick cooking spray
- **2 cups packaged shredded broccoli (broccoli slaw mix)**
- **¼ teaspoon ground ginger**
- **3 10-inch whole wheat flour tortillas (wrap in foil and warm in 350°F oven for 10 minutes)**
  Peanut Sauce

1. Sprinkle chicken with garlic salt and pepper. Coat a large unheated nonstick skillet with cooking spray. Preheat skillet over medium-high heat. Add chicken; cook and stir for 2 to 3 minutes or until chicken is no longer pink. Remove chicken from skillet; keep warm. Add broccoli and ginger to skillet. Cook and stir for 2 to 3 minutes or until vegetables are crisp-tender.

2. Spread tortillas with Peanut Sauce. Top with chicken mixture. Roll up and cut in half. Serve immediately.

Peanut Sauce: In a small saucepan, combine 3 tablespoons creamy peanut butter; 2 tablespoons water; 1 tablespoon reduced-sodium soy sauce; 1 clove garlic, minced; and ¼ teaspoon ground ginger. Heat over low heat until melted.

Per serving (½ wrap): 191 cal., 6 g total fat (1 g sat. fat), 33 mg chol., 460 mg sodium, 16 g carbo., 2 g fiber, 18 g pro.

Thai Chicken-Broccoli Wraps

Spicy Chicken and Pepper Hoagies

If you can find it, 1 to 2 teaspoons of chipotle pepper paste works as a substitute for the canned chipotle peppers.

Start to Finish: 20 minutes **Makes:** 4 sandwiches

- **4 hoagie buns**
- **⅓ cup light mayonnaise or salad dressing**
- **2 to 3 teaspoons finely chopped canned chipotle pepper in adobo sauce**
- **1¼ cups packaged shredded cabbage with carrots (coleslaw mix)**
- **1 small red or yellow sweet pepper, cut in matchstick-size strips**
- **1 2¼- to 2½-pound whole roasted chicken**

1. Halve hoagie buns; hollow out bun bottoms, leaving a ½-inch shell. In a medium bowl, combine mayonnaise and chipotle pepper; spread lightly in the bottom of each bread shell. Stir shredded cabbage and sweet pepper into the remaining mayonnaise mixture.

2. Remove and discard skin and bones from chicken; coarsely chop chicken. Divide chicken among the bun shells. Top with cabbage mixture and bun tops.

Per sandwich: 749 cal., 25 g total fat (6 g sat. fat), 133 mg chol., 1,247 mg sodium, 77 g carbo., 5 g fiber, 53 g pro.

Grilled Chicken and Gouda Melt

Save time by buying grilled chicken at the supermarket. Just warm it before making the sandwiches.

Prep: 15 minutes **Cook:** 8 minutes **Bake:** 4 minutes **Oven:** 375°F **Makes:** 4 sandwiches

- **4 skinless, boneless chicken breast halves (about 1¼ pounds)**
- **1 tablespoon olive oil**
  Salt and ground black pepper
- **½ cup apricot preserves**
- **4½ teaspoons red wine vinegar**
- **1 tablespoon Dijon-style mustard**
- **4 slices crusty whole-grain bread or raisin-nut bread, toasted**
- **6 ounces Gouda cheese, sliced**
- **4 cups arugula (3 ounces)**
- **½ a red onion, thinly sliced**

1. Brush chicken with olive oil. Sprinkle chicken with salt and pepper. Heat a nonstick grill pan over medium-high heat. Cook chicken on hot pan for 8 to 12 minutes or until chicken is no longer pink (170°F).

2. Meanwhile, preheat oven to 375°F. For dressing, in a small bowl, stir together preserves, vinegar, and mustard; season with salt and pepper.

Make-Your-Own Garden Tacos

3. Place toasted bread on baking sheet. Layer cheese and chicken. Bake about 4 minutes or until cheese begins to melt. In a medium bowl, combine arugula and onion; drizzle with some of the dressing and toss to coat. Place sandwiches on plates, top with salad, and drizzle with remaining dressing.

Per sandwich: 495 cal., 15 g total fat (8 g sat. fat), 114 mg chol., 641 mg sodium, 46 g carbo., 5 g fiber, 43 g pro.

Make-Your-Own Garden Tacos

Some of the fun of eating these tacos is in making them— exactly how you like them.

Start to Finish: 15 minutes **Makes:** 4 servings

- ½ **cup mayonnaise or salad dressing**
- 3 **to 4 tablespoons purchased dried-tomato pesto**
- 8 **to 12 6-inch corn or 7- to 8-inch flour tortillas**
- 2 **6-ounce packages refrigerated grilled chicken breast strips**
- 2 **small yellow summer squash or zucchini (8 ounces), cut in matchstick-sizestrips**
- 1 **medium sweet pepper, cut in strips**
  Cilantro sprigs (optional)

1. In a bowl, stir together mayonnaise and pesto; divide among 4 small bowls. Place tortillas on a microwave-safe plate, cover with paper towels. Microwave on 100% power (high) for 30 to 45 seconds or until tortillas are warm.

2. Divide chicken, squash, sweet pepper, and warm tortillas among 4 shallow bowls. Place a bowl of pesto mixture with each bowl. If desired, garnish with cilantro.

Per serving: 481 cal., 30 g total fat (6 g sat. fat), 66 mg chol., 1,021 mg sodium, 30 g carbo., 5 g fiber, 24 g pro.

Peppered Turkey Panini 🔲

If you have a panini maker, use it for these sandwiches. Or use the grill-pan-and-spatula method described in Smoked Turkey Reuben with Green Apple on page 269.

Start to Finish: 20 minutes **Makes:** 4 sandwiches

- ⅓ **cup broken walnuts (optional)**
- 8 **½-inch slices country Italian bread**
- ½ **cup refrigerated classic bruschetta topper**
- 2 **tablespoons mayonnaise or salad dressing**
- 12 **ounces sliced cooked peppered or smoked turkey breast**
- 1 **cup large spinach leaves**
  Olive oil

1. Preheat an extra-large skillet over medium heat. Add walnuts (if using) to skillet; cook and stir for 2 minutes or until toasted. Remove nuts from skillet and set aside.

2. To assemble sandwiches, spread one side of 4 bread slices with bruschetta topper; spread the slices with mayonnaise. Layer walnuts, turkey, and spinach on top of the bruschetta-spread slices. Top with mayonnaise-spread slices, mayonnaise sides down. Brush sandwiches lightly with olive oil.

3. Place the sandwiches in panini maker or heated skillet. Weigh sandwiches down by placing a large skillet on top of sandwiches and a few cans of food in skillet. Grill about 2 minutes; turn. Replace weight and cook about 2 minutes more or until golden and heated through.

Per sandwich: 448 cal., 23 g total fat (4 g sat. fat), 43 mg chol., 1,522 mg sodium, 35 g carbo., 2 g fiber, 26 g pro.

Turkey Burgers and Home Fries

Curry mayonnaise flavors and adds color to these burgers.

Prep: 10 minutes **Cook:** 12 minutes
Broil: 11 minutes **Makes:** 4 burgers

- ½ **cup mayonnaise or salad dressing**
- 2 **teaspoons curry powder**
- 2 **tablespoons olive oil**
- 2 **cups refrigerated sliced potatoes**
  Salt and ground black pepper
- 1 **pound uncooked ground turkey breast**
- 2 **ounces feta cheese with basil and tomato, crumbled**
- ¼ **teaspoon salt**
- 4 **Greek pita flatbreads**
  Red onion slices (optional)
  Fresh spinach (optional)
  Feta cheese, crumbled (optional)

1. Preheat broiler. In a small bowl, stir together mayonnaise and curry powder; set aside. In an extra-large skillet, heat olive oil over medium-high heat. Add potatoes; sprinkle with salt and pepper. Cook for 6 minutes; turn potatoes. Cook about 6 minutes more or until crisp.

2. Meanwhile, in a medium bowl, combine turkey, 2 tablespoons of the curry-mayonnaise, the 2 ounces feta cheese, and ¼ teaspoon salt. Shape turkey mixture in four ½-inch-thick patties. Place patties on the unheated rack of a broiler pan. Broil 4 inches from heat for 11 to 13 minutes or until done (165°F), turning once halfway through broiling.

3. Spread the remaining curry-mayonnaise on bread; place patties on bread. If desired, layer with onion, spinach, and feta. Serve with potatoes.

Per burger: 658 cal., 33 g total fat (6 g sat. fat), 91 mg chol., 1,033 mg sodium, 51 g carbo., 3 g fiber, 38 g pro.

Quick Tip Greek pita bread comes in two types—pocket bread and flatbread. The pocket bread is great when it's fresh, soft, and pliable, and you fill it with something fairly light, such as chicken salad. But it can crack or tear easily stuffed with a burger and fixings. This recipes calls for Greek pita flatbread, which is pocketless. Wrap the bread around the fillings and tuck in.

Turkey Burgers and Home Fries

Smoked Turkey Reuben with Green Apple one

In place of a panini machine, use a grill pan and press down the sandwiches with a sturdy spatula.

Start to Finish: 30 minutes **Makes:** 4 sandwiches

- ½ **cup mayonnaise or salad dressing**
- 2 **tablespoons ketchup**
- 2 **tablespoons finely chopped shallot**
- 2 **tablespoons sweet pickle relish**
- 1 **teaspoon Dijon-style mustard**
  Salt and ground black pepper
- 8 **slices pumpernickel bread**
- 1 **Granny Smith apple, cored and thinly sliced**
- 8 **ounces thinly sliced smoked turkey**
- 1 **cup drained sauerkraut, rinsed**
- 6 **ounces thinly sliced Gruyère or Jarlsberg cheese**

1. In a small bowl, whisk together mayonnaise, ketchup, shallot, relish, and mustard; season with salt and pepper. Spread mayonnaise mixture on one side of each bread slice. Layer apple and turkey slices on half of the bread slices, mayonnaise sides up. Top with sauerkraut, cheese, and remaining bread, mayonnaise sides down.

2. Preheat a panini machine until hot. Grill sandwiches, in batches, until cheese is melted and bread is golden brown.

Per sandwich: 645 cal., 40 g total fat (13 g sat. fat), 93 mg chol., 1,613 mg sodium, 44 g carbo., 5 g fiber, 30 g pro.

Catfish Po'Boys

Throw in a little Cajun music and a cold beer, and these spicy sandwiches take you to the bayou and back, just for dinner.

Start to Finish: 20 minutes **Makes:** 4 sandwiches

1   to 1¼ **pounds fresh or frozen farm-raised catfish fillets**
       Salt and ground black pepper
½   **cup fine dry bread crumbs**
2   **tablespoons olive oil**
2   **medium red and/or yellow sweet peppers, cored and sliced in rings**
1   **cup shredded Monterey Jack cheese with jalapeño peppers (4 ounces)**
1   **cup deli coleslaw**
4   **hoagie buns, split and, if desired, toasted**
       Bottled hot pepper sauce (optional)
       Small hot peppers (optional)

1. Thaw fish, if frozen. Cut fish fillets in 3-inch pieces. Lightly sprinkle fish with salt and pepper. Coat fish with the bread crumbs.

2. In an extra-large skillet, heat olive oil over medium-high heat. Add fish; cook for 6 to 8 minutes or until golden brown and fish begins to flake when tested with a fork, turning once halfway through cooking.

3. Layer fish, sweet peppers, cheese, and coleslaw in buns. If desired, pass hot pepper sauce and hot peppers.

Per sandwich: 675 cal., 30 g total fat (10 g sat. fat), 86 mg chol., 1,004 mg sodium, 67 g carbo., 4 g fiber, 35 g pro.

Fish Sandwiches with Basil Mayonnaise

Baking these fillets at high heat makes the crumb coating crispy—and keeps the fish moist and juicy.

Prep: 15 minutes **Bake:** 4 minutes **Oven:** 500°F
Makes: 4 sandwiches

1   **pound fresh or frozen skinless fish fillets, about ½ inch thick**
¼   **cup milk**
½   **cup fine dry bread crumbs**
¼   **teaspoon paprika**

¹⁄₈ **teaspoon salt**

¹⁄₈ **teaspoon ground black pepper**

2 **tablespoons butter or margarine, melted**

4 **hamburger buns or kaiser rolls, split and toasted**

4 **lettuce leaves**

   Basil Mayonnaise

1. Thaw fish, if frozen. Cut fish in 4 serving-size portions; set aside. Grease a shallow baking pan; set aside.

2. Preheat oven to 500°F. Pour milk into a shallow dish. In another shallow dish, combine bread crumbs, paprika, salt, and pepper. Dip fish into milk, then roll in crumb mixture to coat. Place fish in the prepared baking pan, tucking under any thin edges for uniform thickness. Drizzle with melted butter.

3. Bake for 4 to 6 minutes or until fish begins to flake when tested with a fork and coating is golden. Serve fish in buns with lettuce and Basil Mayonnaise.

Basil Mayonnaise: In a small bowl, stir together 3 tablespoons mayonnaise or salad dressing; 2 tablespoons sour cream; 2 tablespoons snipped fresh basil or ¹⁄₂ teaspoon dried basil, crushed; and ¹⁄₂ teaspoon finely shredded lemon peel.

Per sandwich: 399 cal., 22 g total fat (5 g sat. fat), 30 mg chol., 529 mg sodium, 29 g carbo., 1 g fiber, 21 g pro.

Salmon Salad Sandwiches

Tired of tuna salad? For lunch or dinner try this twist on a traditional fish salad sandwich.

Start to Finish: 20 minutes **Makes:** 4 sandwiches

4 **sandwich rolls**

¹⁄₂ **cup bottled ranch salad dressing**

2 **6-ounces cans skinless, boneless salmon**

2 **small tomatoes**

¹⁄₂ **a medium cucumber**

1 **cup coarsely shredded carrots (2) or shredded, peeled jicama (¹⁄₄ of a jicama)**

1. Split sandwich rolls. Lightly spread sliced rolls with some of the salad dressing. Drain salmon. Place salmon in a medium bowl and flake with a fork. Add remaining salad dressing to salmon; mix to combine.

2. Thinly slice tomatoes and cucumber. Layer tomato slices on rolls. Top with salmon mixture, cucumber slices, shredded carrots, and roll tops.

Per sandwich: 575 cal., 25 g total fat (4 g sat. fat), 64 mg chol., 1,094 mg sodium, 57 g carbo., 4 g fiber, 32 g pro.

Salmon Salad Sandwiches

Shrimp-Avocado Hoagies

Shrimp-Avocado Hoagies

These creamy, cool, no-cook sandwiches are perfect for a simple dinner on a warm summer evening.

Start to Finish: 15 minutes **Makes:** 4 servings

- 1 **10-to 12-ounce package frozen peeled, cooked shrimp, thawed and coarsely chopped**
- 2 **large avocados, seeded, peeled, and chopped**
- ½ **cup shredded carrot (1)**
- ⅓ **cup bottled coleslaw salad dressing**
- 4 **hoagie buns**
  Lemon wedges (optional)

1. In large mixing bowl, combine shrimp, avocado, carrot, and salad dressing.

2. Halve hoagie buns. Using a spoon, slightly hollow bottoms and tops of hoagie buns, leaving ½-inch shells. Reserve excess bread for another use. Toast buns.

3. Spoon shrimp mixture into buns. If desired, serve with lemon wedges.

Per serving: 560 cal., 24 g total fat (4 g sat. fat), 144 mg chol., 825 mg sodium, 63 g carbo., 8 g fiber, 25 g pro.

Strawberry, Goat Cheese, and Arugula Toasts

These sandwiches have a delicious flavor combination—tangy goat cheese, sweet strawberries, and peppery arugula.

Prep: 15 minutes **Broil:** 3½ minutes
Makes: 4 sandwiches

- 1 **8-ounce baguette, halved crosswise, then each halved lengthwise**
- 1 **tablespoon olive oil**
- 1 **4-ounce log goat cheese (chèvre)**
- 1½ **cups sliced strawberries**
- ½ **cup arugula**
  Olive oil
  Sea salt or coarse salt
  Freshly ground black pepper
  Snipped fresh oregano, thyme, rosemary, and/or basil

1. Preheat broiler. Place baguette quarters, cut sides up, on a large baking sheet. Brush with 1 tablespoon olive oil. Broil 3 to 4 inches from heat for 1½ to 2 minutes or until bread is lightly toasted.

2. Slice goat cheese and divide evenly among bread quarters; top with sliced strawberries. Return to broiler; broil for 2 to 3 minutes or until cheese is softened and berries begin to juice out. Remove from broiler; top with arugula. Drizzle with additional olive oil; sprinkle with salt, pepper, and fresh herb.

Per sandwich: 346 cal., 16 g total fat (7 g sat. fat), 22 mg chol., 616 mg sodium, 37 g carbo., 2 g fiber, 13 g pro.

Nutty Hummus Open-Face Sandwiches

Look for hummus flavors such as three-pepper, roasted pepper, scallion, roasted garlic, and more. Use any flavor you like in these meatless sandwiches.

Start to Finish: 15 minutes **Makes:** 4 sandwiches

- 1 **tablespoon olive oil**
- ½ **cup coarsely chopped walnuts**
- ¾ **cup coarsely chopped bottled roasted red sweet peppers**
- ½ **a 7- to 8-ounce container hummus**
- 4 **½-inch slices round country Italian bread, toasted**
- 1 **small cucumber (8 ounces), thinly sliced**

1. In a large skillet, heat olive oil over medium heat. Add walnuts; cook until toasted. Stir in roasted peppers. Cook and stir until heated through; set aside.

2. Spread hummus on toasted bread slices; arrange on serving plates. Top with cucumber slices and walnut mixture.

Per sandwich: 264 cal., 17 g total fat (2 g sat. fat), 0 mg chol., 343 mg sodium, 25 g carbo., 4 g fiber, 7 g pro.

Summer-Fresh Quesadillas

To grill these, place the quesadillas on a grill over medium heat for about 2 minutes or until the cheese begins to melt and the tortillas start to brown, turning once.

Start to Finish: 20 minutes **Makes:** 4 quesadillas

- 4 **9- to 10-inch flour tortillas**
- 1 **tablespoon vegetable oil**
- 2 **large plum tomatoes, thinly sliced**
- 8 **ounces thin asparagus, trimmed and cut in 1-inch lengths**
- ½ **cup shredded fresh basil**
- 1½ **cups shredded mozzarella cheese (6 ounces)**
  Purchased refrigerated salsa or marinara sauce or bottled fruit salsa (optional)

1. Brush 1 side of each tortilla with oil. Place tortillas, oiled sides down, on a baking sheet. Top half of each tortilla with tomato, asparagus, basil, and cheese. Fold in half.

2. Preheat an extra-large nonstick skillet over medium-high heat. Cook quesadillas, two at a time, in hot skillet for 2 to 3 minutes or until cheese begins to melt and tortillas start to brown, turning once halfway through cooking. Cut quesadillas in wedges. If desired, serve with salsa.

Per quesadilla: 289 cal., 14 g total fat (6 g sat. fat), 27 mg chol., 446 mg sodium, 27 g carbo., 2 g fiber, 15 g pro.

Beef and Blue Pizza

Beef and Blue Pizza

Partially baking the bread shell before adding toppings ensures that it stays crisp.

Start to Finish: 18 minutes **Oven:** 450°F/Broil
Makes: 4 servings

- 2 **tablespoons olive oil**
- ½ **a medium red onion, cut in thin slivers**
- 1 **12-inch Italian bread shell (such as Boboli)**
- 8 **ounces thinly sliced deli roast beef**
- 1 **small red, green, or yellow sweet pepper, seeded and chopped**
- 4 **ounces crumbled blue cheese**
- ¼ **teaspoon pizza seasoning (optional)**

1. Position oven rack in the center of the oven. Preheat oven to 425°F. In a large skillet, heat 1 tablespoon of the olive oil over medium-high heat. Add onion; cook for 3 to 5 minutes or just until onion is just until onion is tender.

2. Meanwhile, place bread shell on a large baking sheet; brush with the remaining 1 tablespoon olive oil. Bake for 5 minutes. Change oven setting to broil.

3. Meanwhile, place beef on a cutting board, layering slices to stack if necessary. Slice beef crosswise in strips. Top partially baked bread shell with beef, sweet pepper, cooked onion, blue cheese, and pizza seasoning.

4. Broil pizza for 4 to 5 minutes or until toppings are heated through and crust is lightly browned. Cut into wedges.

Per serving: 553 cal., 23 g total fat (7 g sat. fat), 56 mg chol., 1,637 mg sodium, 54 g carbo., 1 g fiber, 31 g pro.,

Steak and Cheese Melt Pizza

Make this pizza with smoked provolone for another version.

Start to Finish: 25 minutes **Makes:** 6 servings

- 1 **tablespoon vegetable oil**
- 2 **large onions, thinly sliced (about 1 pound)**
  Nonstick cooking spray
- 1¼ **teaspoons steak seasoning**
- 2 **8-ounce boneless strip steaks, cut ½ to ¾ inch thick**
- 1 **12-inch Italian bread shell (such as Boboli)**
- 2 **tablespoons deli-style mustard**
- 1 **cup shredded mild cheddar cheese (4 ounces)**
- 1 **cup shredded provolone cheese (4 ounces)**

1. Preheat broiler. In a large skillet, heat oil over medium heat. Add onions and ½ teaspoon of the steak seasoning. Cook about 10 minutes or until onions are lightly browned, stirring occasionally,

2. Meanwhile, coat the rack of an unheated broiler pan with cooking spray. Sprinkle steaks with remaining ¾ teaspoon steak seasoning; place on broiler pan. Broil 3 to 4 inches from heat 4 minutes or until desired doneness, turning once. Transfer to cutting board; thinly slice across the grain.

Steak and Cheese Melt Pizza

3. Place bread shell on the broiler pan; spread with mustard. Sprinkle half the cheddar and half the provolone cheese. Top with steak and cooked onion. Sprinkle the remaining cheddar and provolone cheese on steak and onion. Broil about 1 minute or until cheese is melted and steak is heated. Transfer pizza to a cutting board; cut in 6 wedges.

Per serving: 490 cal., 23 g total fat (10 g sat. fat), 79 mg chol., 849 mg sodium, 35 g carbo., 3 g fiber, 34 g pro.

Creamy Pepperoni Pizza

The creamy in this pizza is from ricotta cheese stirred together with pesto and Parmesan.

Prep: 10 minutes **Bake:** 10 minutes **Cool:** 5 minutes
Oven: 450°F **Makes:** 4 servings

- 1 **1-pound loaf Italian bread**
- 1¼ **cups ricotta cheese**
- 3 **tablespoons purchased pesto**
- 2 **tablespoons grated Parmesan cheese**
- ½ **teaspoon salt**
- ¼ **teaspoon ground black pepper**
- 1 **3.5-ounce package sliced pepperoni**
- 1 **cup shredded mozzarella cheese (4 ounces)**

1. Preheat oven to 450°F. Cut bread in half lengthwise, then crosswise to make 4 pizza crusts.

2. In a medium bowl, combine ricotta cheese, pesto, Parmesan cheese, salt, and pepper. Spread cheese mixture on crusts. Top with pepperoni; sprinkle with mozzarella cheese. Place pizzas on a baking sheet.

3. Bake about 10 minutes or until cheese is melted. Cool for 5 minutes before serving.

Per serving: 757 cal., 39 g total fat (18 g sat. fat), 90 mg chol., 1,854 mg sodium, 67 g carbo., 4 g fiber, 34 g pro.

Buffalo Chicken Pizzas

Buffalo Chicken Pizzas

These spicy pizzas bring sports-bar food home. Make them the next time the game-watching party is at your house.

Prep: 10 minutes **Bake:** 10 minutes **Oven:** 450°F
Makes: 4 pizzas

- 4 pita bread rounds
- ¼ cup bottled blue cheese salad dressing
- 1 9-ounce package refrigerated Southwest-flavor cooked chicken breast strips
- ¾ cup thinly sliced celery
  Blue cheese crumbles (optional)
  Bottled hot pepper sauce or buffalo wing sauce (optional)

1. Preheat oven to 450°F. Place pita rounds on baking sheet. Brush with blue cheese dressing. Scatter chicken strips and celery on dressing. Bake, uncovered, for 10 minutes or until heated through and pitas are crisp.

2. Transfer to plates. If desired, sprinkle with blue cheese and pass hot pepper sauce.

Per pizza: 353 cal., 14 g total fat (3 g sat. fat), 45 mg chol., 1,084 mg sodium, 36 g carbo., 2 g fiber, 21 g pro.

Individual Pita Pizzas

Forget having a piece of the pie—have the whole pie! Sharing may be a virtue, but having a pizza all to yourself can be a very good thing too.

Prep: 10 minutes **Bake:** 8 minutes **Cook:** 7 minutes
Oven: 475°F **Makes:** 6 pizzas

- 6 pita bread rounds
  Nonstick cooking spray
- 4 ounces cremini or white mushrooms, sliced
- 1 small red onion, thinly sliced
- 1 8-ounce package diced ham
- ½ teaspoon dried Italian seasoning, crushed
  Salt and ground black pepper
- 1 14-ounce jar pizza sauce
- 1½ cups shredded Monterey Jack cheese with jalapeño peppers (6 ounces)

1. Position oven rack in top third of oven. Preheat oven to 475°F. Place pita rounds directly on oven rack; toast for 4 minutes. Use tongs to remove pitas from oven; place on a large baking sheet.

2. Meanwhile, coat a medium nonstick skillet with cooking spray; heat over medium heat. Add mushrooms and onion; cook for 5 minutes. Add ham and Italian seasoning. Cook for 2 minutes; remove from heat. Season to taste with salt and pepper.

3. Spread each toasted pita round with ¼ cup of the pizza sauce. Top each with ⅓ cup of the ham mixture and

¼ cup shredded cheese. Bake about 4 minutes or until cheese is melted.

Per pizza: 383 cal., 14 g total fat (8 g sat. fat), 54 mg chol., 1,225 mg sodium, 43 g carbo., 3 g fiber, 21 g pro.

Focaccia-Camembert Pizzas

These simple pizzas make sophisticated appetizers.

Start to Finish: 20 minutes **Makes:** 4 pizzas

- 4 6-inch Italian flatbreads (focaccia)
- 2 large tomatoes, sliced
  Salt and ground black pepper
- 1 8-ounce round Camembert cheese, chilled
- ⅓ cup chopped walnuts
- 2 tablespoons snipped fresh chives

1. Preheat broiler. Place flatbreads on the unheated rack of a broiler pan. Top with tomato slices; sprinkle with salt and pepper. Cut cheese in thin slices. Place cheese slices on tomato slices.

2. Broil 4 to 5 inches from heat about 2 minutes or until cheese begins to melt. Sprinkle with walnuts; broil 1 minute more. Sprinkle with fresh chives.

Per pizza: 449 cal., 24 g total fat (11 g sat. fat), 41 mg chol., 1,027 mg sodium, 41 g carbo., 6 g fiber, 21 g pro.

Focaccia-Camembert Pizzas

Smoky Pizza Margherita 🔲one

Margherita pizza always features red tomatoes, white mozzarella, and green basil—the colors of the Italian flag. The smoky flavor in this version comes from smoked mozzarella.

Prep: 15 minutes **Bake:** 14 to 16 minutes
Oven: 500°F **Makes:** 4 servings

Nonstick cooking spray
1 **purchased pizza dough (about 2 pounds)**
1 **cup bottled or canned pizza sauce**
2 **cups shredded smoked mozzarella cheese (8 ounces)**
1 **cup grape tomatoes, quartered**
1/2 **teaspoon dried oregano, crushed**
1/4 **teaspoon salt**
1 **tablespoon olive oil**
1/2 **cup packed fresh basil leaves**

1. Preheat oven to 500°F. Coat a 14-inch round pizza pan with cooking spray.

2. On a well-floured work surface, roll out dough to a 14-inch circle. Place on prepared pizza pan.

3. Spread pizza sauce on dough, leaving 1/2 inch around the edge. Sprinkle cheese on the sauce. Scatter the tomatoes on the cheese. Sprinkle with dried oregano and salt. Drizzle olive oil.

4. Bake for 14 to 16 minutes or until crust is golden brown. Remove pizza from oven; arrange basil on top. Let stand for 5 to 10 minutes. To serve, cut into 8 wedges.

Per serving (2 wedges): 715 cal., 27 g total fat (12 g sat. fat), 47 mg chol., 1,869 mg sodium, 93 g carbo., 6 g fiber, 24 g pro.

Canadian Bacon and Pineapple Calzone 🔲one

The toppings for Hawaiian-style pizza are stuffed into a calzone. Rather than indiviudal calzones, this recipe makes a large one.

Prep: 25 minutes **Bake:** 20 minutes **Oven:** 425°F
Makes: 4 servings

1 **8-ounce can crushed pineapple (juice pack)**
4 **ounces sliced Canadian-style bacon or turkey ham, cut in bite-size pieces (about 1 cup)**
1/2 **cup chunky meatless pasta sauce**
1 **13.8-ounce package refrigerated pizza dough**
1 **8-ounce package shredded mozzarella cheese (2 cups)**
1 **tablespoon milk**
2 **tablespoons grated Parmesan cheese**

1. Preheat oven to 425°F. Drain pineapple, pressing out as much liquid as possible. In a medium bowl, stir together drained pineapple, bacon, and pasta sauce.

2. Grease a 12-inch pizza pan; press pizza dough into pan. Sprinkle half the mozzarella cheese on one-half of the dough to within 1/2 inch of the edge. Spoon meat mixture cheese. Sprinkle with remaining cheese.

3. Fold the pizza dough over the filling, making a half circle. Seal the edges with the tines of a fork. Make slits in the top to allow steam to escape. Brush top with milk and sprinkle with Parmesan cheese.

4. Bake about 20 minutes or until golden. Cool for about 5 minutes. Cut in 8 wedges.

Per serving (2 wedges): 431 cal., 16 g total fat (9 g sat. fat), 61 mg chol., 1,128 mg sodium, 46 g carbo., 1 g fiber, 24 g pro.

Italian Hero Calzones 🔲one

Brushing the calzone with reserved oil from oil-packed dried tomatoes helps the crust get crispy and provides flavor. These mini calzones make great party food. Served in multiples with fruit, they are a fun, kid-friendly dinner.

Prep: 35 minutes **Bake:** 12 minutes **Oven:** 425°F
Makes: 20 mini calzones

2 **tablespoons cornmeal**
1/4 **cup snipped oil-packed dried tomatoes**
3 **ounces thinly sliced smoked turkey and/or sliced pepperoni, chopped**
1/4 **cup chopped pitted ripe olives**
3/4 **cup shredded mozzarella cheese (3 ounces)**
2 **13.8-ounce packages refrigerated pizza dough**
Finely shredded or grated Parmesan cheese
Cayenne pepper (optional)

1. Preheat oven to 425°F. Lightly grease a very large baking sheet and sprinkle with cornmeal; set aside. Drain tomatoes well, reserving oil. In a medium bowl, combine the drained tomatoes, turkey, and olives. Stir in mozzarella cheese.

2. On a lightly floured surface, roll pizza dough, one package at a time, to a 12×9-inch rectangle. Using a 3-inch round cutter, cut each rectangle into ten 3-inch circles. Place about 1 tablespoon of the turkey mixture slightly off-center on each dough circle. Fold dough over turkey-cheese mixture, forming half-circles. Seal edges with fork tines.

3. Place calzones on prepared baking sheet. Brush tops with reserved oil from dried tomatoes. Sprinkle with Parmesan cheese and, if desired, cayenne pepper.

4. Bake for 12 to 15 minutes or until golden brown. Serve warm.

Per mini calzone: 110 cal., 3 g total fat (1 g sat. fat), 5 mg chol., 232 mg sodium, 16 g carbo., 1 g fiber, 5 g pro.

Italian Hero Calzones

Chicken-Olive Calzones

Chicken-Olive Calzones

Whether served warm with spaghetti sauce or at room temperature from a lunch bag, these pizza-flavor sandwiches will be a family favorite.

Prep: 25 minutes **Bake:** 10 minutes **Stand:** 5 minutes
Oven: 425°F **Makes:** 6 calzones

1½	**cups chopped cooked chicken (8 ounces)**
½	**cup shredded Monterey Jack cheese (2 ounces)**
¼	**cup chopped celery**
¼	**cup chopped pitted ripe olives**
½	**teaspoon dried basil, crushed**
¼	**teaspoon dried oregano, crushed**
⅛	**teaspoon garlic powder**
⅛	**teaspoon ground black pepper**
⅓	**cup tub-style cream cheese with chives and onion**
1	**13.8-ounce package refrigerated pizza dough**
1	**egg, lightly beaten**
1	**tablespoon water**
	Grated Parmesan cheese (optional)
	Spaghetti sauce, warmed (optional)

1. Preheat oven to 425°F. For filling, in a medium bowl, combine chicken, Monterey Jack cheese, celery, olives, basil, oregano, garlic powder, and pepper. Stir in cream cheese. Set aside.

2. For calzones, unroll pizza dough. On lightly floured surface, roll dough into a 15×10-inch rectangle. Cut into six 5-inch squares. Divide chicken-olive filling among the squares. Brush edges with water. Lift one corner and stretch dough over to the opposite corner, forming triangles. Seal edges of dough well with fork tines. Arrange calzones on a greased baking sheet. Prick tops with a fork. In a small bowl, combine egg and 1 tablespoon water; brush on the calzones. If desired, sprinkle with Parmesan cheese.

3. Bake for 10 to 12 minutes or until golden. Let stand for 5 minutes before serving. If desired, serve with warm spaghetti sauce.

Per calzone: 306 cal., 14 g total fat (6 g sat. fat), 88 mg chol., 413 mg sodium, 26 g carbo., 1 g fiber, 18 g pro.

Ham and Cheese Calzones

However you like ham and cheese—with melted Swiss, provolone, or Cheddar—works well for this recipe. For Reuben versions, add a little sauerkraut to each calzone before sprinkling the last bit of cheese.

Prep: 15 minutes **Bake:** 15 minutes **Stand:** 5 minutes
Oven: 400°F **Makes:** 4 calzones

1	**13.8-ounce package refrigerated pizza dough**
¼	**cup coarse-grain mustard**
6	**ounces sliced Swiss or provolone cheese**
1½	**cups cubed cooked ham (8 ounces)**
½	**teaspoon caraway seeds**

1. Preheat oven to 400°F. Line a baking sheet with foil; lightly grease foil. Set aside.

2. Unroll pizza dough. On a lightly floured surface, roll or pat dough in a 15×10-inch rectangle. Cut dough in half crosswise and lengthwise to make four rectangles. Spread mustard on rectangles. Divide half the cheese among rectangles, placing cheese on half of each rectangle and cutting or tearing to fit as necessary. Top with ham; sprinkle with caraway seeds. Top with remaining cheese. Brush edges with water. For each calzone, fold dough over filling to opposite edge, stretching slightly if necessary. Seal edges with fork tines. Place calzones on the prepared baking sheet. Prick tops to allow steam to escape.

3. Bake about 15 minutes or until golden. Let stand for 5 minutes before serving.

Per calzone: 421 cal., 21 g total fat (10 g sat. fat), 72 mg chol., 1,390 mg sodium, 28 g carbo., 1 g fiber, 30 g pro.

Spinach Calzones

These cheesy pocket pizzas may entice picky eaters to eat their vegetables.

Prep: 30 minutes **Bake:** 10 minutes **Oven:** 450°F
Makes: 4 calzones

1	**10-ounce package frozen chopped spinach**
2	**eggs**
1	**8-ounce can pizza sauce**
¼	**cup grated Parmesan cheese**
1	**teaspoon dried basil, crushed**
⅛	**teaspoon garlic powder**
1	**13.8-ounce package refrigerated pizza dough**
1	**cup shredded mozzarella cheese (4 ounces)**
	Vegetable oil
1	**tablespoon grated Parmesan cheese**

1. Cook spinach following package directions. Drain, squeezing out excess liquid. In a medium bowl, beat eggs with a fork. Stir in spinach, ¼ cup of the pizza sauce, the ¼ cup Parmesan cheese, the basil, and garlic powder.

2. Preheat oven to 450°F. Grease a large baking sheet; set aside. Unroll refrigerated pizza dough. On a lightly floured surface, press or roll dough in a 15×10-inch rectangle. Cut dough in half crosswise and lengthwise to make 4 rectangles. Divide mozzarella cheese among rectangles, sprinkling on one-half of each rectangle. Spoon spinach mixture evenly on cheese. Fold dough over mixture. Seal edges. Place on prepared baking sheet. Brush calzones with oil. Sprinkle with the 1 tablespoon Parmesan cheese. Cut small slits in top of each calzone to allow steam to escape.

3. Bake for 10 to 15 minutes or until golden. In a small saucepan, cook and stir remaining pizza sauce until heated through. Serve warmed pizza sauce with calzones.

Per calzone: 378 cal., 16 g total fat (6 g sat. fat), 136 mg chol., 1,120 mg sodium, 35 g carbo., 3 g fiber, 22 g pro.

Spinach Calzones

Green Beans with Basil and Mint, **page 289**

Nutty Broccoli,
page 293

Creamy Brussels Sprouts with
Peppered Bacon, **page 297**

Checkerboard Rolls,
page 307

Tasty Side Dishes

Although main
dishes get most of the
attention, side dishes
often complete the
meals. These salads,
vegetables, potatoes, rice
medleys, pastas, and
breads deliciously round
out dinner.

Napa Cabbage Slaw

Napa Cabbage Slaw

Dark sesame oil is made with toasted sesame seeds. It's very rich in flavor, so a little goes a long way.

Start to Finish: 15 minutes **Makes:** 6 servings

- 3 **cups finely shredded napa cabbage**
- 1 **cup finely shredded bok choy**
- ¼ **a small red sweet pepper, cut in thin strips (about ¼ cup)**
- ¼ **cup rice vinegar or white wine vinegar**
- 1 **tablespoon salad oil**
- ½ **teaspoon dark sesame oil**

1. In a large bowl, combine cabbage, bok choy, and sweet pepper strips.

2. For dressing, in a small bowl, stir together vinegar, salad oil, and sesame oil. Pour dressing over cabbage mixture; toss gently to coat. If desired, cover and refrigerate up to 2 hours.

Per serving: 40 cal., 3 g total fat (0 g sat. fat), 0 mg chol., 81 mg sodium, 2 g carbo., 2 g fiber, 1 g pro.

Herb Salad with Creamy Lemon Dressing

With sweet and tender butterhead lettuce, a melange of fresh herbs, and brightly flavored lemon dressing, this salad is the essence of spring.

Start to Finish: 20 minutes **Makes:** 6 to 8 servings

- 4 **teaspoons finely shredded lemon peel**
- ⅓ **cup fresh lemon juice**
- 3 **cloves garlic, minced**
- 2 **teaspoon Dijon-style mustard**
- ¼ **teaspoon salt**
- ¼ **teaspoon ground black pepper**
- ½ **cup olive oil**
- ½ **cup dairy sour cream**
- 2 **to 3 medium heads butterhead lettuce, torn, or 6 to 8 cups mixed baby salad greens**
- 1½ **cups assorted fresh herbs, such as chives, basil, parley, or mint; torn**
- 12 **to 16 radishes, thinly sliced**

1. For dressing, in a small bowl, combine lemon peel, lemon juice, garlic, mustard, salt, and pepper. Slowly whisk in olive oil until thickened. Whisk in sour cream.

2. In a large bowl, toss together lettuce and herbs; transfer to a platter. Top with sliced radishes; pass dressing.

Per serving: 215 cal., 22 g total fat (5 g sat. fat), 7 mg chol., 161 mg sodium, 5 g carbo., 1 g fiber, 2 g pro.

Caesar Salad

Add grilled chicken, steak, or shrimp to this favorite salad to make it a meal.

Start to Finish: 18 minutes **Makes:** 4 to 6 servings

- 1 **whole clove garlic, peeled**
- 2 **tablespoons refrigerated or frozen egg product**
- 3 **anchovy fillets (optional)**
- ½ **teaspoon Dijon-style mustard**
- 2 **tablespoons grated Parmesan cheese**
- 1 **tablespoon fresh lemon juice**
- ½ **cup olive oil**
- 2 **tablespoons olive oil**
- 1 **tablespoon butter**
- 1 **clove garlic, minced**
- 2 **cups ¾-inch cubes Italian bread**
- 1 **tablespoon chopped fresh parsley**
- 1 **tablespoon grated Parmesan cheese**
- 1 **head romaine, torn in 1½-inch pieces**

1. For dressing, in a small saucepan, cook the whole garlic clove in boiling water for 5 minutes. Drain. Place garlic in a food processor or blender. Add egg product, anchovies (if desired), mustard, the 2 tablespoons Parmesan cheese, and the lemon juice. Process or blend for 1 minute. With machine running, add the ½ cup olive oil in a stream until blended.

2. For croutons, in a large nonstick skillet, heat the 2 tablespoons olive oil and butter over medium-low heat. Add minced garlic; cook for 2 minutes. Add bread cubes. Increase heat to medium-high; cook for 7 to 8 minutes or until bread is evenly browned, stirring frequently. Stir in parsley and the 1 tablespoon Parmesan cheese; toss to coat.

3. To assemble, in a large bowl, toss together romaine, dressing, and croutons. Divide equally among 4 to 6 plates.

Per serving: 292 cal., 26 g total fat (5 g sat. fat), 8 mg chol., 176 mg sodium, 10 g carbo., 1 g fiber, 5 g pro.

Quick Tip To make the Caesar dressing for this salad, emulsify the oil. Add the oil in a stream as other liquids blend at high speed for a thick, creamy texture. If the oil is simply stirred in, it separates from the other ingredients and the dressing becomes runny. Apply the same method to other homemade dressings.

Heirloom Tomato Salad 🔲

Find heirloom tomatoes—old varieties that are far superior in flavor and texture than standard grocery-store varieties—at farmers' markets and some specialty stores.

Start to Finish: 30 minutes **Makes:** 4 servings

- 4   **eggs**
- 1/3 **cup olive oil**
- 4   **tablespoons sherry vinegar**
- 1/2 **teaspoon salt**
- 1/8 **teaspoon ground black pepper**
- 4   **cups mâche or mixed salad greens**
- 2   **shallots, peeled and thinly sliced**
- 4   **to 5 heirloom tomatoes, cored, seeded, and cut in wedges**
- 2   **cups purchased or homemade croutons***

1. Place eggs in a medium saucepan; add enough cold water to cover eggs by at least 1 inch. Bring to a rapid boil. Remove from heat. Cover saucepan and let stand for 15 minutes; drain. Run cold water over eggs or place them in ice water until cool enough to handle; drain. Peel eggs and cut lengthwise into quarters.

2. For dressing, in a small bowl, whisk together olive oil, sherry vinegar, 1/4 teaspoon of the salt, and the pepper.

3. On individual plates or a large platter, arrange salad greens and shallots. Drizzle with 1/4 cup of the dressing. Sprinkle tomato wedges with the remaining 1/4 teaspoon salt. Arrange tomatoes, egg quarters, and croutons on greens. Drizzle with remaining dressing.

Per serving: 383 cal., 27 g total fat (5 g sat. fat), 213 mg chol., 635 mg sodium, 26 g carbo., 5 g fiber, 11 g pro.

Sugar Snap, Tomato, and Feta Salad

*Note: To make croutons, cut bread slices in cubes to equal 2 cups. Place bread cubes in a single layer on a baking sheet. Preheat oven to 350°F. Coat bread cubes with nonstick cooking spray; sprinkle with salt and ground black pepper to taste. Bake about 10 minutes or until golden; cool.

Spinach Salad

Add a grilled steak and a baked potato to this classic steakhouse salad and stay in for a special dinner. You only need half the dressing for the salad. Store the rest in the refrigerator up to 3 days. Use it on tossed salad greens.

Start to Finish: 30 minutes **Makes:** 6 to 8 servings

- 8   **to 10 cups torn fresh spinach**
- 3/4 **cup sliced radishes**
- 1/2 **cup sliced red onion**
- 1/2 **cup shredded cheddar cheese (2 ounces)**
- 1/4 **cup salad oil**
- 1   **tablespoon sugar**
- 1   **tablespoon fresh lemon juice**
- 1   **tablespoon mayonnaise or salad dressing**
- 2   **teaspoons cider vinegar**
- 1   **teaspoon yellow mustard**
- 1/2 **teaspoon seasoned salt**
- 1/2 **teaspoon bottled minced garlic (1 clove)**
- 6   **slices bacon, crisp-cooked, drained, and crumbled**

1. In a large bowl, combine spinach, radishes, red onion, and cheese.

2. For dressing, in a screw-top jar, combine oil, sugar, lemon juice, mayonnaise, vinegar, mustard, seasoned salt, and garlic. Cover and shake well. Pour about half the dressing over salad; toss to coat evenly. Top with bacon.

Per serving: 192 cal., 17 g total fat (5 g sat. fat), 17 mg chol., 364 mg sodium, 4 g carbo., 4 g fiber, 6 g pro.

Sugar Snap, Tomato, and Feta Salad 🔲

The success of this simple warm salad relies on the best ingredients. Look for young, tender sugar snap or snow peas. Avoid any pea pods that look overgrown or bruised—they can be tough.

Start to Finish: 15 minutes **Makes:** 4 to 6 servings

- 1   **tablespoon olive oil**
- 8   **ounces sugar snap peas or snow peas, strings removed (about 2 cups)**
- 1   **cup grape tomatoes, halved**
- 1/4 **cup fresh mint leaves, coarsely chopped**
       Salt and ground black pepper
- 1/2 **cup coarsely crumbled feta cheese (2 ounces)**

1. In a large skillet, heat olive oil over medium-high heat. Add peas; cook for 2 to 4 minutes or until crisp-tender. Stir in tomatoes and mint. Sprinkle with salt and pepper. Heat through. Add feta cheese and toss to combine.

Per serving: 111 cal., 8 g total fat (3 g sat. fat), 17 mg chol., 359 mg sodium, 7 g carbo., 2 g fiber, 5 g pro.

Green Bean and Blue Cheese Salad

Make the salad and dressing up to 2 hours ahead of serving time. Add the dressing right before serving.

Start to Finish: 20 minutes **Cook:** 10 minutes
Makes: 8 servings

- 2   **16-ounce packages frozen cut green beans**
- 1   **cup crumbled blue cheese (4 ounces)**
- 1   **cup halved and thinly sliced red onion**
- ¼   **cup olive oil**
- 3   **tablespoons white wine vinegar or white balsamic vinegar**
- 2   **teaspoons Dijon-style mustard**
- ¼   **teaspoon salt**
- ¼   **teaspoon ground black pepper**

1. Cook beans following package directions. Place cooked beans in a colander; rinse with cold water until cool. Drain well. In a large salad bowl, combine beans, blue cheese, and onion. (If desired, cover and chill up to 2 hours.)

2. For dressing, in a screw-top jar, combine olive oil, vinegar, mustard, salt, and pepper. Cover and shake well. (If desired, chill, covered, up 2 hours; shake before serving.) To serve, drizzle dressing over salad mixture; toss to coat.

Per serving: 154 cal., 11 g total fat (4 g sat. fat), 11 mg chol., 315 mg sodium, 7 g carbo., 3 g fiber, 5 g pro.

Heidelberg German Potato Salad

Sweet-and-sour German potato salad is usually served warm. Make this when you have bratwrust or pork chops on the grill.

Prep: 15 minutes **Cook:** 15 minutes
Makes: 12 servings

- 5   **pounds red-skin potatoes**
- 8   **ounces bacon, chopped**
- 2   **cups beef broth**
- 1   **cup chopped sweet onion (1 large)**
- ½   **cup salad oil**
- ⅓   **cup apple cider vinegar**
- 1   **tablespoon sugar**
- ¾   **teaspoon salt**
- ¼   **teaspoon ground black pepper**

1. In a large pot, cook potatoes in lightly salted boiling water for 15 to 20 minutes or until fork-tender. Drain and cool slightly.

2. Meanwhile, in a large skillet, cook bacon until crisp. Drain bacon on paper towels; reserve 1 tablespoon of the drippings.

3. Peel and slice the warm potatoes. Place potatoes in a large bowl. Spoon bacon and the reserved drippings over potatoes. Add beef broth, onion, oil, vinegar, sugar, salt, and pepper. Mix gently. Serve warm.

Per serving: 350 cal., 18 g total fat (4 g sat. fat), 22 mg chol., 744 mg sodium, 36 g carbo., 4 g fiber, 11 g pro.

Garden Macaroni Salad

How can you improve on a great macaroni salad? This one has dill, spicy radishes, and cucumbers for crisp texture and fresh flavor. It's the perfect side for a grilled steak or kabobs.

Start to Finish: 35 minutes **Makes:** 8 servings

- 8   **ounces dried elbow macaroni (2⅓ cups)**
- 1   **cup buttermilk or sour milk (see Quick Tip, below)**
- ½   **cup mayonnaise or salad dressing**
- 1   **tablespoon fresh lemon juice**
- 2   **teaspoons Dijon-style mustard**
- 1   **teaspoon salt**
- ¾   **teaspoon freshly ground black pepper**
- ⅛   **teaspoon bottled hot pepper sauce**
- 1   **bunch radishes, halved and sliced**
- 1   **cucumber, peeled, quartered, seeded, and sliced**
- 1   **cup shredded carrots (2)**
- ¼   **cup sliced green onions (2)**
- ¼   **cup chopped fresh parsley**
- 3   **tablespoons chopped fresh dill or 1½ teaspoons dried dill**

1. In a large saucepan, cook macaroni following package directions; drain. Rinse under cold water and drain again.

2. In a large bowl, whisk together buttermilk, mayonnaise, lemon juice, mustard, salt, black pepper, and bottled hot pepper sauce. Add macaroni; toss to coat. Stir in radishes, cucumber, carrots, green onions, parsley, and dill. Toss gently to mix.

Per serving: 236 cal., 12 g total fat (2 g sat. fat), 6 mg chol., 454 mg sodium, 26 g carbo., 2 g fiber, 5 g pro.

Quick Tip To make 1 cup sour milk, place 1 tablespoon fresh lemon juice or vinegar in a glass measuring cup. Add milk to equal 1 cup of liquid; stir to combine. Let the mixture stand for 5 minutes before using it in a recipe.

Green Beans with Basil and Mint

Green Beans with Basil and Mint ♥ one

Red sweet pepper brightens the look of these tasty beans, while a generous amount of shredded fresh herbs piques the flavor. For best taste and texture, cook beans al dente.

Start to Finish: 15 minutes **Makes:** 8 servings

6	cups water
2	pounds fresh green beans, trimmed if desired
2	cloves garlic, minced
1/2	cup chopped red sweet pepper (1 small)
1/2	cup shredded fresh basil
1/3	cup shredded fresh mint
2	tablespoons olive oil
1/2	teaspoon salt

1. In a 4-quart Dutch oven, bring water to boiling. Add green beans and return to boiling; reduce heat. Simmer, uncovered, for 7 to 8 minutes or until beans are crisp-tender, adding garlic the last 1 minute of cooking. Drain.

2. Meanwhile, in a large bowl, combine sweet pepper, basil, mint, olive oil, and salt. Add drained green beans and garlic. Toss gently to combine.

Per serving: 71 cal., 4 g total fat (1 g sat. fat), 0 mg chol., 154 mg sodium, 9 g carbo., 4 g fiber, 2 g pro.

Sesame Green Beans one

These soy-and-sesame-infused green beans are just the thing to serve when the main course has Asian flavors.

Start to Finish: 15 minutes **Makes:** 6 servings

2	tablespoons olive oil
2	cloves garlic, minced
1 1/2	pounds green beans, trimmed
1/4	cup water
3	tablespoons reduced-sodium soy sauce
1	teaspoon sesame seeds

1. In a large skillet, heat oil over medium-high heat. Add garlic; cook and stir for 30 seconds. Add green beans; cook and stir for 2 minutes.

2. Add water and soy sauce to skillet. Sprinkle with sesame seeds. Reduce heat to medium. Cook, covered, for 8 to 10 minutes or until beans are crisp-tender, shaking pan occasionally. Stir beans to coat. Serve warm.

Per serving: 84 cal., 5 g total fat (1 g sat. fat), 0 mg chol., 295 mg sodium, 9 g carbo., 4 g fiber, 3 g pro.

Quick Tip To intensify the sesame flavor of these green beans, substitute 1/2 teaspoon of the olive oil for 1/2 teaspoon of toasted sesame oil. Just add both oils to the pan at once before adding the garlic.

Lemony Green Beans

Lemony Green Beans ♥ one

This dish can be made ahead of serving time. Two hours ahead, cook beans as directed in Step 1; cover and refrigerate. Thirty minutes ahead, finish the recipe as directed in Step 2.

Start to Finish: 20 minutes **Makes:** 8 servings

1 1/2	pounds green beans, trimmed, or three 9-ounce packages frozen whole green beans
3	tablespoons olive oil
3	large shallots, cut in thin wedges
6	cloves garlic, thinly sliced
1	tablespoon finely shredded lemon peel
1/2	teaspoon salt
1/8	teaspoon ground black pepper
	Lemon wedges (optional)

1. In an extra-large skillet, cook beans in lightly salted boiling water for 2 to 5 minutes or until barely crisp-tender. Drain; rinse beans with cold water. Set aside.

2. In the same skillet, heat olive oil over medium-high heat. Add shallots and garlic. Cook for 2 to 3 minutes or until beginning to brown, stirring occasionally. Add green beans. Toss for 1 to 2 minutes or until heated through. Remove from heat. Stir in lemon peel, salt, and pepper. If desired, serve with lemon wedges.

Per serving: 80 cal., 5 g total fat (1 g sat. fat), 0 mg chol., 152 mg sodium, 9 g carbo., 3 g fiber, 2 g pro.

Roasted Asparagus with Gruyère

Roasted Asparagus with Gruyère ♥

Gruyère is an aromatic Swiss cheese with nutty flavor and slightly grainy texture. It is a good melting cheese, similar to mozzarella, but it doesn't get as stringy as mozzarella.

Prep: 15 minutes **Roast:** 20 minutes **Stand:** 2 minutes
Oven: 400°F **Makes:** 6 servings

- 2 **pounds fresh asparagus spears**
- 1 **small onion, cut in thin wedges**
- 1 **small red or yellow sweet pepper, cut in thin strips**
- 1 **tablespoon canola oil**
- ¼ **teaspoon salt**
- ¼ **teaspoon ground black pepper**
- ¼ **cup shredded Gruyère or Swiss cheese (1 ounce)**

1. Preheat oven to 400°F. Snap off and discard woody bases from asparagus spears. If desired, scrape off scales. In a 15×10×1-inch baking pan, place asparagus, onion, and sweet pepper. Drizzle with oil; toss gently to coat. Spread in a single layer. Sprinkle with salt and black pepper.

2. Roast, uncovered, about 20 minutes or until asparagus is crisp-tender. Transfer to a platter; sprinkle with cheese. Let stand about 2 minutes or until cheese is melted.

Per serving: 73 cal., 4 g total fat (1 g sat. fat), 5 mg chol., 127 mg sodium, 4 g carbo., 2 g fiber, 4 g pro.

Quick Tip When you oven-roast vegetables or potatoes, make cleanup a snap by lining the roasting pan or baking sheet with foil or parchment paper before adding the food. When dinner is done, discard the foil or paper. The pan should need only a quick rinse in hot soapy water—no scrubbing required.

Prosciutto with Asparagus and New Potatoes

To make Parmesan cheese ribbons, draw a vegetable peeler along a narrow edge of a wedge of Parmesan cheese.

Prep: 15 minutes **Cook:** 15 minutes **Makes:** 8 servings

- 1½ **pounds fresh asparagus spears**
- 1 **20-ounce package refrigerated red potato wedges**
- ¼ **cup bottled Italian salad dressing**
- 1 **teaspoon finely shredded lemon peel**
- 6 **ounces thinly sliced prosciutto slices**
  Parmesan cheese ribbons (optional)

1. Snap off and discard woody bases from the asparagus spears. If desired, scrape off scales. Cut in 2-inch pieces. Set aside.

2. In a large saucepan, cook the potatoes, covered, in a small amount of lightly salted boiling water for 11 minutes. Add asparagus. Cook, covered, about 4 minutes more or until asparagus is crisp-tender and potatoes are tender; drain. Transfer to a platter.

3. Meanwhile, in a small bowl, combine salad dressing and lemon peel. Drizzle salad dressing mixture over potatoes and asparagus. Arrange prosciutto beside vegetables. If desired, top with Parmesan cheese ribbons. Serve warm.

Per serving: 116 cal., 4 g total fat (1 g sat. fat), 15 mg chol., 770 mg sodium, 11 g carbo., 3 g fiber, 9 g pro.

Peas with Mint and Cashews

These minty peas are also delicious sprinkled with chopped dry-roasted pistachios in place of the cashews.

Start to Finish: 12 minutes **Makes:** 4 servings

- 1 **10-ounce package frozen peas**
- ¼ **cup chopped onion**
- 1 **tablespoon butter or margarine**
- 1 **tablespoon snipped fresh mint or 1 teaspoon dried mint, crushed**
- ⅛ **teaspoon salt**
- ¼ **cup chopped dry-roasted cashews**

1. In a medium saucepan, cook peas and onion, covered, in a small amount of boiling lightly salted water about 5 minutes or until tender; drain. Add butter, mint, and salt to peas in saucepan; gently stir until butter is melted. Sprinkle with cashews.

Per serving: 139 cal., 7 g total fat (3 g sat. fat), 8 mg chol., 109 mg sodium, 14 g carbo., 4 g fiber, 5 g pro.

Prosciutto with Asparagus and New Potatoes

Basil Peas and Mushrooms ♥

Mushrooms and fresh basil infuse an old standby—peas and carrots—with new flavors.

Start to Finish: 25 minutes **Makes:** 6 servings

- ½ **cup sliced carrot (1 medium)**
- 1 **10-ounce package frozen peas**
- 1 **tablespoon butter or margarine**
- 2 **cups sliced fresh mushrooms**
- 2 **green onions, cut in ½-inch pieces**
- 1 **tablespoon snipped fresh basil or ½ teaspoon dried basil, crushed**
- ¼ **teaspoon salt**
  Dash ground black pepper

1. In a medium saucepan, cook carrot, covered, in a small amount of boiling lightly salted water for 3 minutes. Add peas. Return to boiling; reduce heat. Cook, covered, about 5 minutes more or until carrot and peas are tender. Drain well. Remove vegetables from saucepan; set aside.

2. In the same saucepan, melt butter over medium heat. Add mushrooms and green onions; cook until tender. Stir in basil, salt, and pepper. Return carrot and peas to saucepan; stir gently to mix. Heat through.

Per ⅔ cup: 69 cal., 3 g total fat (1 g sat. fat), 5 mg chol., 171 mg sodium, 9 g carbo., 3 g fiber, 4 g pro.

Honey-Glazed Carrots and Green Onions ♥

Crinkle-cut carrot coins in ginger-spiked honey glaze and green onions contrast sweet with savory.

Start to Finish: 20 minutes **Makes:** 4 servings

- 3 **cups packaged sliced or crinkle-cut fresh carrots**
- 4 **green onions, bias-sliced in 1 inch pieces (½ cup)**
- 2 **tablespoons honey**
- 2 **tablespoons butter or margarine**
- ⅛ **teaspoon ground ginger**
  Ground black pepper

1. In a medium saucepan, cook carrots, covered, in a small amount of boiling lightly salted water for 7 to 9 minutes or until nearly tender. Drain; remove from saucepan.

2. For glaze, in the same saucepan, combine green onions, honey, butter, and ginger. Cook and stir over medium heat until combined. Stir in carrots. Cook, uncovered, about 2 minutes or until glazed, stirring frequently. Season to taste with pepper.

Per serving: 130 cal., 6 g total fat (4 g sat. fat), 16 mg chol., 95 mg sodium, 19 g carbo., 3 g fiber, 1 g pro.

Glazed Baby Carrots

Glazed Baby Carrots ♥

Baby carrots aren't just for munching raw. Serve this side dish with ham, pork chops, or chicken.

Prep: 2 minutes **Cook:** 8 minutes **Makes:** 6 servings

- 1 **1-pound package peeled fresh baby carrots**
- 1 **tablespoon butter or margarine**
- 1 **tablespoon packed brown sugar**
- ⅛ **teaspoon ground cinnamon**
- ⅛ **teaspoon salt**

1. In a medium saucepan, cook carrots, covered, in a small amount of boiling salted water for 8 to 10 minutes or until carrots are crisp-tender.

2. Drain carrots. Add butter, sugar, cinnamon, and salt to carrots in saucepan; stir to coat.

Per serving: 52 cal., 2 g total fat (1 g sat. fat), 5 mg chol., 72 mg sodium, 8 g carbo., 2 g fiber, 1 g pro.

Savory Apples and Carrots ♥

Granny Smith apples are the tartest; Braeburn are sweet-tart. Use either one alone or a combination of the two.

Start to Finish: 25 minutes **Makes:** 4 servings

- 1 **tablespoon vegetable oil**
- 1 **cup packaged sliced or crinkle-cut carrots**
- 1 **medium onion, cut into wedges and halved crosswise**
- 3 **cups sliced Granny Smith and/or Braeburn apples (3 medium)**
- 1 **tablespoon sugar**
- ¼ **teaspoon salt**

3   tablespoons apple juice

½   teaspoon snipped fresh sage

1. In a large skillet, heat oil over medium heat. Add carrots; cook and stir for 2 minutes. Add onion; cook and stir for 2 to 3 minutes more or until carrots and onion are crisp-tender. (If necessary, add more oil during cooking.)

2. Add apples to skillet; cook and stir for 2 minutes. Sprinkle with sugar and salt. Carefully add apple juice. Cook, covered, for 2 to 3 minutes more or until apples and carrots are tender. Gently stir in sage.

Per serving: 117 cal., 4 g total fat (1 g sat. fat), 0 mg chol., 157 mg sodium, 22 g carbo., 4 g fiber, 1 g pro.

Nutty Broccoli ♥

Quick orange glaze adds sweetness to this beautiful, bright green broccoli dish—toasted nuts add crunch. It all adds up to great taste and great nutrition.

Start to Finish: 25 minutes   Makes: 6 servings

1   pound broccoli, trimmed and cut in 2-inch pieces

3   tablespoons butter or margarine

2   tablespoons fresh orange juice

½   teaspoon finely shredded orange peel (set aside)

¼   teaspoon salt

3   tablespoons chopped walnuts or pecans, sliced almonds, or pine nuts, toasted
    Orange wedges (optional)

1. If desired, halve stem pieces of broccoli lengthwise. Place a steamer basket in a 3-quart saucepan. Add water to reach just below the bottom of the basket. Bring to boiling. Add broccoli to steamer basket. Cover and reduce heat. Steam for 8 to 10 minutes or just until stems are tender. Transfer broccoli to a serving dish.

2. Meanwhile, in a medium skillet, melt butter over medium-high heat; cook and stir for 3 to 4 minutes or until medium brown in color. Add orange juice and cook for 10 seconds. Remove from heat; stir in orange peel and salt. Pour over broccoli; sprinkle with walnuts. If desired, garnish with orange wedges.

Per serving: 94 cal., 8 g total fat (4 g sat. fat), 15 mg chol., 153 mg sodium, 4 g carbo., 1 g fiber, 2 g pro.

Quick Tip   When shredding orange peel (or any citrus), shred only the top layer and not the white pith beneath it, which will make food taste bitter.

Nutty Broccoli

Creamy Succotash

Serve this rich vegetable dish with grilled chicken or pork.

Start to Finish: 30 minutes **Makes:** 8 servings

- **1** **10-ounce package frozen lima beans**
- **2** **tablespoons butter or margarine**
- **4** **strips bacon, cut in 1/4-inch pieces**
- **1** **cup chopped green sweet pepper (1 large)**
- **1/2** **cup chopped red onion (1 medium)**
- **4** **cups fresh corn kernels (from 6 large ears)**
- **1/2** **cup chicken broth**
- **3/4** **teaspoon salt**
- **1/2** **teaspoon ground black pepper**
- **1/2** **cup whipping cream**
- **1** **cup cherry tomatoes, halved**
- **1/2** **cup Italian (flat-leaf) parsley, chopped**

1. Cook lima beans following package directions. Drain and set aside.

2. In a large skillet, cook butter and bacon over medium heat about 3 minutes or until bacon starts to brown. Stir in green pepper and onion; cook for 10 minutes, stirring occasionally.

3. Add corn, chicken broth, salt, black pepper, and the cooked lima beans. Bring to boiling; reduce heat. Simmer, uncovered, for 5 minutes, stirring occasionally. Stir in whipping cream, tomatoes, and parsley. Heat through.

Per serving: 245 cal., 11 g total fat (6 g sat. fat), 31 mg chol., 402 mg sodium, 33 g carbo., 4 g fiber, 8 g pro.

Spring Succotash

Succotash usually consists of lima beans and corn, and sometimes peppers, and is cooked slowly on the stovetop. In this updated version, the vegetables are sautéed to preserve texture—and edamame (green soybeans) steps in for the limas.

Start to Finish: 20 minutes **Makes:** 8 servings

- **2** **tablespoons olive oil**
- **1** **tablespoons butter or margarine**
- **1** **12-ounce package shelled frozen sweet soybeans (edamame), thawed**
- **4** **cups fresh or frozen corn kernels, thawed**
- **1** **cup chopped red onion (1 large)**
- **1** **tablespoon sherry or red wine vinegar**
  Salt and pepper
- **1/2** **cup snipped fresh basil**

1. In a large skillet, heat olive oil and butter over medium-high heat. Add edamame; cook and stir about 2 minutes or until almost tender. Add corn and onion; cook and stir about 3 minutes more or until vegetables are tender.

2. Remove skillet from heat. Stir in vinegar. Add salt, pepper, and additional vinegar to taste. Cool slightly; stir in basil. Serve warm or at room temperature.

Per serving: 185 cal., 9 g total fat (3 g sat. fat), 6 mg chol., 20 mg sodium, 21 g carbo., 6 g fiber, 9 g pro.

Roasted Root Vegetables

Roasting condenses and caramelizes the sugars in the vegetables, giving them wonderful sweetness. Textures become soft and tender—punctuated by crisp, flavorful edges.

Prep: 25 minutes **Roast:** 35 minutes **Oven:** 425°F **Makes:** 8 servings

- **4** **medium parsnips, peeled, halved lengthwise, and cut in 1-inch pieces**
- **4** **medium turnips, peeled and cut into 1-inch pieces, or 1 medium rutabaga, peeled and cut into 1-inch pieces**
- **2** **small Yukon gold potatoes, peeled and cut in quarters, or 1 medium sweet potato, peeled and cut into 1-inch pieces**
- **3** **medium carrots, halved lengthwise and cut in 1-inch pieces**
- **2** **medium onions, cut in 1-inch wedges**
- **8** **fresh sage leaves, slivered**
- **3** **tablespoons olive oil**
- **1 1/2** **teaspoons sea salt or kosher salt**
- **1/2** **teaspoon freshly ground black pepper**
- **1/4** **cup honey**
  Snipped fresh sage

1. Preheat oven to 425°F. In a large greased roasting pan, combine parsnips, turnips, potatoes, carrots, onions, and the 8 leaves of slivered sage. Combine oil, salt, and pepper; drizzle over vegetables in pan. Toss lightly.

2. Roast, uncovered, for 30 to 35 minutes until vegetables are lightly browned and tender, stirring occasionally. Drizzle honey over vegetables. Stir gently to coat. Roast for 5 minutes more. Sprinkle with the snipped sage.

Per serving: 168 cal., 5 g total fat (1 g sat. fat), 0 mg chol., 354 mg sodium, 30 g carbo., 5 g fiber, 2 g pro.

Quick Tip Though names are used interchangeably and both work equally well in most recipes, sweet potatoes and yams are different. Sweet potatoes have pale yellow flesh and a somewhat dry, mealy texture—similar to a baking potato. Yams have fairly dense, dark orange flesh and are generally sweeter than sweet potatoes. Either one works here.

Creamy Brussels Sprouts with Peppered Bacon

Creamy Brussels Sprouts with Peppered Bacon 🄾

This side dish is a crowd-pleaser and proof that everything is better with bacon.

Prep: 20 minutes **Cook:** 15 minutes **Makes:** 8 servings

- 4 slices peppered bacon
- 2 pounds Brussels sprouts, trimmed and halved through stem ends
- ³/₄ cup reduced-sodium chicken broth
- ¹/₂ teaspoon kosher salt
- ¹/₄ teaspoon freshly ground black pepper
- ³/₄ cup whipping cream
  Cracked black pepper

1. In an extra-large skillet, cook bacon over medium heat until browned and crisp. Drain on paper towels, reserving 2 tablespoons drippings in skillet.

2. Add Brussels sprouts to drippings in skillet; cook and stir over medium heat for 4 minutes. Add chicken broth, salt, and pepper. Heat to boiling. Reduce heat. Simmer, covered, for 5 minutes. Uncover; cook for 2 to 4 minutes or until liquid is nearly evaporated. Add whipping cream. Cook about 4 minutes or until thickened.

3. Transfer sprouts to a serving dish. Sprinkle with crumbled bacon and cracked pepper.

Per serving: 174 cal., 14 g total fat (7 g sat. fat), 38 mg chol., 305 mg sodium, 10 g carbo., 4 g fiber, 6 g pro.

Skillet Tomatoes and Okra 🄾

Caribbean cooking features an abundance of okra dishes, a result of its African influence. Although frozen (and thawed) okra can be substituted for this dish, fresh okra produces slightly better texture and flavor.

Start to Finish: 30 minutes **Makes:** 4 servings

- 2 slices bacon
- 1 tablespoon butter or margarine
- 1 small onion, cut into thin wedges
- 2 cloves garlic, minced
- 8 ounces whole okra, cut in ¹/₂-inch pieces (2 cups)
- ¹/₂ teaspoon salt
- ¹/₄ teaspoon freshly ground black pepper
- 4 small tomatoes, cut in thin wedges
- 2 teaspoons fresh lime juice
- 2 tablespoons snipped fresh basil

1. In a large skillet, cook bacon over medium heat until crisp. Drain bacon on paper towels, reserving 1 tablespoon drippings in skillet. Crumble bacon; set aside.

2. Add butter to drippings in skillet. Cook onion and garlic in hot bacon drippings and butter until onion is tender.

3. Stir in okra, salt, and pepper. Cook, covered, over low heat about 15 minutes or until okra is almost tender. Add tomato wedges to skillet. Cook and stir about 3 minutes or until heated through. Drizzle with lime juice. Sprinkle with crumbled bacon and basil.

Per serving: 126 cal., 8 g total fat (3 g sat. fat), 14 mg chol., 400 mg sodium, 11 g carbo., 3 g fiber, 3 g pro.

Sautéed Spinach with Bacon and Mustard 🄾

This quick and savory spinach sauté is delicious with steak.

Start to Finish: 15 minutes **Makes:** 4 to 6 servings

- 4 slices bacon, cut in 1-inch pieces
- 2 10-ounce packages fresh spinach
- 1 tablespoon butter or margarine
- 1 tablespoon Dijon-style mustard
- ¹/₄ teaspoon crushed red pepper

1. In an extra-large skillet, cook bacon over medium heat until crisp. Drain bacon on paper towels, reserving 1 tablespoon drippings in skillet.

2. Gradually add spinach to skillet, stirring frequently with metal tongs. Cook for 2 to 3 minutes or just until spinach is wilted. Remove spinach from skillet to a colander; hold over sink and press lightly to drain. (If using large-leaf spinach, use kitchen scissors to snip.)

3. In the same skillet, melt butter over medium heat; stir in mustard and crushed red pepper. Add drained spinach; toss to coat and, if necessary, reheat spinach. Top with cooked bacon. Serve immediately.

Per serving: 135 cal., 11 g total fat (4 g sat. fat), 18 mg chol., 340 mg sodium, 5 g carbo., 3 g fiber, 7 g pro.

Sautéed Spinach with Bacon and Mustard

Creamed Spinach

Can't get the kids to try spinach? Add butter, onion, garlic, and cream to the equation and try again.

Start to Finish: 30 minutes **Makes:** 4 servings

- 2 **10-ounces packages fresh spinach (large stems removed) or two 10-ounce packages frozen chopped spinach, thawed**
- 2 **tablespoons butter or margarine**
- 1/2 **cup chopped onion (1 medium)**
- 2 **to 3 cloves garlic, minced**
- 1 **cup whipping cream**
- 1/2 **teaspoon freshly ground black pepper**
- 1/4 **teaspoon salt**
- 1/4 **teaspoon ground nutmeg**

1. In a large pot of rapidly boiling salted water, cook fresh spinach (if using) for 1 minute. Drain well, squeezing out excess liquid. Pat dry with paper towels. Snip spinach with kitchen scissors to coarsely chop; set aside. If using frozen spinach, drain well, squeezing out excess liquid.

2. In a large skillet, melt butter over medium heat. Add onion and garlic; cook about 5 minutes or until onion is tender. Stir in whipping cream, pepper, salt, and nutmeg. Bring to boiling; cook, uncovered, until cream begins to thicken. Add spinach. Simmer, uncovered, about 2 minutes or until thickened. Season to taste with additional salt and pepper.

Per serving: 312 cal., 29 g total fat (17 g sat. fat), 98 mg chol., 347 mg sodium, 11 g carbo., 4 g fiber, 6 g pro.

Greek Spinach and Rice

To use half a package of the frozen spinach, microwave the unwrapped package on 30% power (medium-low) for 2 to 4 minutes or until soft enough to cut in half. Rewrap one half and return to the freezer.

Prep: 10 minutes **Cook:** 15 minutes **Makes:** 4 servings

- 1 **cup water**
- 1/2 **cup finely chopped onion (1 medium)**
- 2 **cloves garlic, minced**
- 1 **teaspoon dried oregano, crushed**
- 1 **teaspoon instant chicken bouillon granules**
- 1/2 **teaspoon finely shredded lemon peel or 1 tablespoon fresh lemon juice**
- 1/8 **teaspoon ground black pepper**
- 1/2 **cup uncooked long grain rice**
- 1/2 **a 10-ounce package frozen chopped spinach, thawed and drained**
  Lemon peel strips (optional)

1. In a medium saucepan, combine water, onion, garlic, oregano, bouillon granules, lemon peel, and pepper. Bring to boiling. Stir in rice; reduce heat. Simmer, covered, for 10 minutes.

2. Stir in spinach. Cook, covered, for 5 to 10 minutes more or until rice is tender and liquid is absorbed. Stir lightly with a fork before serving. If desired, garnish with lemon peel strips.

Per serving: 113 cal., 0 g total fat, 0 mg chol., 251 mg sodium, 24 g carbo., 2 g fiber, 3 g pro.

Pesto Potatoes ♥

These lightened mashed potatoes use no-fat cream cheese, fat-free milk, and homemade low-fat basil and spinach pesto. Freeze any leftover pesto and use it on baked potatoes or toss with pasta.

Start to Finish: 35 minutes **Makes:** 8 servings

- 2 **pounds medium Yukon gold potatoes**
- 1/2 **an 8-ounce package fat-free cream cheese**
  Salt and ground black pepper
- 2 **to 3 tablespoons fat-free milk**
  Pesto

1. Peel and quarter potatoes. In a large saucepan, cook potatoes, covered, in a small amount of boiling lightly salted water for 15 to 20 minutes or until tender. Drain; return to pan.

2. Using a potato masher or an electric mixer on low speed, mash potatoes. Add cream cheese. Season to taste with salt and pepper. Gradually beat in enough milk to make potatoes light and fluffy. Top each serving with 1 teaspoon Pesto.

Per serving: 134 cal., 2 g total fat (1 g sat. fat), 3 mg chol., 45 mg sodium, 24 g carbo., 2 g fiber, 5 g pro.

Pesto: In a food processor or blender, combine 1 cup firmly packed fresh basil leaves; 1/2 cup torn fresh spinach; 1/4 cup grated Parmesan cheese; 1/4 cup pine nuts or almonds; 2 cloves garlic, quartered; and, if desired, 1/4 teaspoon salt. Cover and process or blend with pulses until a paste forms, stopping the machine several times and scraping down the sides. With machine running, gradually add 2 tablespoons olive oil or vegetable oil and 2 tablespoons water. Process to the consistency of soft butter. Cover and refrigerate for up to 2 days or freeze for up to 1 month. Makes about 1/2 cup.

Garlic-Herb Smashed Potatoes

These lightly smashed (not fully mashed) potatoes are flavored with fresh herbs and topped with bacon and green onions.

Start to Finish: 30 minutes **Makes:** 6 to 8 servings

- 1 1/2 **pounds tiny new potatoes, quartered**
- 4 **cloves garlic, peeled**
- 1/2 **of an 8-ounce package cream cheese, cubed and softened**
- 1/2 **an 8-ounce container sour cream**

Roasted Cheddar Potatoes

2 tablespoons butter or margarine, softened
¼ teaspoon salt
¼ teaspoon ground black pepper
1 tablespoon snipped fresh dill, rosemary, and basil
2 tablespoons crumbled crisp-cooked bacon (optional)
1 tablespoon sliced green onion (optional)

1. In a large saucepan, cook potatoes and garlic in lightly salted boiling water for 12 to 15 minutes or until tender. Drain; return to pan.

2. Add cream cheese, sour cream, butter, salt, and pepper to potatoes. Using a potato masher or electric mixer on low speed, mash potatoes lightly to combine. Stir in fresh herbs. Spoon into serving bowl. If desired, top with bacon and green onion.

Per serving: 231 cal., 14 g total fat (9 g sat. fat), 39 mg chol., 221 mg sodium, 22 g carbo., 3 g fiber, 5 g pro.

Roasted Cheddar Potatoes 🍴

Smoked paprika—also called pimenton—is made from a type of Spanish pepper that is dried in a wood-fired oven. Find it in both sweet and hot varieties at specialty food stores.

Prep: 10 minutes **Bake:** 25 minutes **Makes:** 8 servings

1 24-ounce package frozen potato wedges (skins on)
2 tablespoons vegetable oil

4 cloves garlic, minced
1 teaspoon smoked paprika or paprika
¼ teaspoon salt
  Nonstick cooking spray
1 cup shredded white or other cheddar cheese (4 ounces)
⅔ cup crushed croutons (about 1 cup croutons)
  Sour cream (optional)

1. Preheat oven following package directions for potatoes. Place frozen potatoes in a large resealable plastic bag. In a small bowl, combine oil, garlic, paprika, and salt. Drizzle on potato wedges. Seal bag and shake to coat potatoes.

2. Lightly coat a 15×10×1-inch baking pan with cooking spray. Spread potatoes in a single layer on prepared pan. Bake potato wedges following package directions, turning once.

3. In a small bowl, combine the cheese and crushed croutons. Sprinkle on the potatoes during the last 3 minutes of baking. Use a large spatula to transfer potato wedges to a platter or large plate, keeping potatoes in a single layer. If desired, serve with sour cream.

Per serving: 165 cal., 8 g total fat (4 g sat. fat), 15 mg chol., 217 mg sodium, 19 g carbo., 1 g fiber, 5 g pro.

Balsamic-Roasted Potatoes and Vegetables

Lemon Hollandaise on New Potatoes

Real hollandaise takes time and can be challenging to make. This version with sour cream and mayo is a close second .

Start to Finish: 30 minutes **Makes:** 4 servings

- 12   ounces tiny new potatoes, halved
- 1   medium carrot, cut in thin strips
- ¼   cup sour cream
- ¼   cup mayonnaise or salad dressing
- ½   teaspoon finely shredded lemon peel
- 1   teaspoon lemon juice
       Milk
- ¼   cup thinly sliced green onions (2)
       Cherry tomatoes (optional)

1. In a large saucepan, cook potatoes, covered, in a small amount of lightly salted boiling water for 12 minutes. Add carrot; cook for 5 to 6 minutes more or just until vegetables are tender. Drain vegetables; transfer to a serving bowl. Keep warm.

2. Meanwhile, for sauce, in a small saucepan, combine sour cream, mayonnaise, lemon peel, and lemon juice. Cook and stir over low heat just until heated through; do not boil. If necessary, stir enough milk into the sour cream mixture for drizzling consistency. Drizzle sauce over cooked vegetables. Sprinkle with green onions . If desired, garnish with tomatoes.

Per serving: 197 cal., 14 g total fat (3 g sat. fat), 13 mg chol., 97 mg sodium, 17 g carbo., 2 g fiber, 3 g pro.

Balsamic-Roasted Potatoes and Vegetables ⬚one

If you don't have fresh rosemary, substitute dried rosemary. Use 1 teaspoon dried for the 3 teaspoons fresh.

Prep: 10 minutes **Bake:** 30 minutes **Oven:** 425°F
Makes: 6 servings

- 1½   pounds tiny new potatoes, halved
- ½   a 16-ounce package peeled fresh baby carrots
- 1   medium red onion, cut in wedges
- 3   tablespoons olive oil or vegetable oil
- 3   teaspoon fresh snipped rosemary
- ¾   teaspoon salt
- ¼   teaspoon ground black pepper
- 3   tablespoons balsamic vinegar

1. Preheat oven to 425°F. In a lightly greased shallow baking pan, combine potatoes, carrots, and onion. In a small bowl, stir together oil, rosemary, salt, and pepper. Drizzle over vegetables; toss to coat.

2. Roast, uncovered, for 30 to 35 minutes or until potatoes and onion are tender, stirring once or twice. Drizzle with balsamic vinegar and toss to coat; serve immediately.

Per serving: 179 cal., 7 g total fat (1 g sat. fat), 0 mg chol., 327 mg sodium, 27 g carbo., 3 g fiber, 3 g pro.

Rosemary-Roasted Potatoes and Tomatoes

Roasting potatoes makes them crisp; roasting tomatoes makes them soft and sweet. Combined with fresh rosemary, kalamata olives, and a dusting of Parmesan cheese, these vegetables taste and smell wonderful.

Prep: 10 minutes **Bake:** 25minutes **Oven:** 450°F
Makes: 8 servings

- **1** **pound tiny new potatoes, quartered (10 to 12)**
- **2** **tablespoons olive oil**
- **1** **teaspoon snipped fresh rosemary**
- **¼** **teaspoon salt**
- **¼** **teaspoon ground black pepper**
- **4** **plum tomatoes, quartered lengthwise**
- **½** **cup pitted kalamata olives, halved**
- **3** **cloves garlic, minced**
- **¼** **cup grated Parmesan cheese**

1. Preheat oven to 450°F. Lightly grease a 15×10×1-inch baking pan; place potatoes in pan. In a small bowl, combine olive oil, rosemary, salt, and pepper; drizzle over potatoes, tossing to coat.

2. Bake for 20 minutes, stirring once. Add tomatoes, olives, and garlic, tossing to combine. Bake for 5 to 10 minutes more or until potatoes are tender and brown on the edges and tomatoes are soft. Transfer to a serving dish. Sprinkle with Parmesan cheese.

Per serving: 102 cal., 5 g total fat (1 g sat. fat), 2 mg chol., 208 mg sodium, 11 g carbo., 2 g fiber, 3 g pro.

Rosemary-Roasted
Potatoes and Tomatoes

Oven Sweet-Potato Fries

These oven-fried potatoes are healthful in more than one way. Most obviously, they're roasted instead of fried—which cuts down on the fat. Sweet potatoes are also sources of vitamins A and C.

Prep: 10 minutes **Bake:** 30 minutes
Oven: 350°F **Makes:** 6 servings

- **2** **pounds sweet potatoes, peeled and cut in strips**
- **2** **tablespoons vegetable oil**
- **¼** **teaspoon salt**
- **⅛** **teaspoon freshly ground black pepper**

1. Preheat oven to 350°F. Place sweet potato strips in a 15×10×1-inch baking pan. Drizzle with oil and sprinkle with salt and pepper; toss to coat. Spread potatoes in a single layer.

2. Bake about 30 minutes or until tender.

Per serving: 134 cal., 5 g total fat (0 g sat. fat), 0 mg chol., 157 mg sodium, 22 g carbo., 3 g fiber, 2 g pro.

Caramelized Sweet Potatoes

This simple side dish to serve with a pork, beef, or poultry holiday dinner is quick and doesn't take up oven space.

Start to Finish: 30 minutes **Makes:** 4 servings

- **1** **tablespoon butter**
- **1** **medium red or white onion, cut in ¾-inch pieces**
- **2** **large sweet potatoes, peeled and cut in ½-inch slices (about 1 pound)**
- **¼** **cup water**
- **2** **tablespoons packed brown sugar**
- **¾** **teaspoon snipped fresh rosemary**
  Snipped fresh rosemary (optional)

1. In a large skillet, melt butter over medium-high heat. Add onion; cook for 3 to 4 minutes or until onion is nearly tender, stirring frequently. Stir in sweet potatoes and water. Cook, covered, over medium heat for 10 to 12 minutes or until potatoes are nearly tender when tested with a fork, stirring occasionally.

2. Add brown sugar and the ¾ teaspoon fresh rosemary. Cook, stirring gently, over medium-low heat for 1 to 2 minutes or until onion and sweet potatoes are glazed. If desired, garnish with additional fresh rosemary.

Per serving: 173 cal., 4 g total fat (1 g sat. fat), 0 mg chol., 57 mg sodium, 33 g carbo., 4 g fiber, 2 g pro.

Parsley-Herb Rice 🔲

Dried cranberries and walnuts dress up this basic herbed rice pilaf for the holidays.

Prep: 15 minutes **Cook:** 15 minutes **Stand:** 5 minutes **Makes:** 8 servings

- 2²/₃ **cups water**
- 1¹/₃ **cup uncooked long grain or regular brown rice**
- ¹/₄ **cup butter or margarine**
- 1¹/₂ **teaspoons dried basil, crushed, or 2 tablespoons snipped fresh basil**
- ³/₄ **teaspoon salt or 1 tablespoon instant chicken bouillon granules**
- ¹/₂ **cup dried cranberries**
- ¹/₂ **cup snipped fresh Italian (flat-leaf) parsley**
- ¹/₂ **cup walnut pieces**

1. In a medium saucepan, combine water, rice, butter, dried basil (if using), and salt. Bring to boiling; reduce heat. Simmer, covered, about 15 minutes for long grain rice (about 40 minutes for brown rice) or until rice is tender and liquid is absorbed. Remove from heat. Stir in cranberries. Let stand, covered, for 5 minutes.

2. Just before serving, stir fresh basil (if using), parsley, and walnuts into the cooked rice.

Per serving: 240 cal., 11 g total fat (4 g sat. fat), 16 mg chol., 267 mg sodium, 32 g carbo., 2 g fiber, 4 g pro.

Chile Rice 🔲

Serve this 15-minute version of Spanish rice with Mexican dishes and grilled or roasted meats. Or stir in pinto or black beans, sprinkle it with shredded cheese, add salsa, and use it as a tortilla filling for a quick burrito-style meal.

Prep: 10 minutes **Stand:** 5 minutes **Makes:** 6 servings

- 1 **14.5-ounce can diced tomatoes with onion and garlic, undrained**
- 1 **cup water**
- 1 **4-ounce can diced green chiles, undrained**
- 1 **teaspoon chili powder**
- ¹/₄ **teaspoon salt**
- 2 **cups instant white rice**

1. In a medium saucepan, combine undrained tomatoes, water, undrained chiles, chili powder, and salt. Bring to boiling; stir in uncooked rice.

2. Remove from heat; cover and let stand for 5 minutes. Stir before serving.

Per serving: 147 cal., 1 g total fat (0 g sat. fat), 0 mg chol., 488 mg sodium, 32 g carbo., 0 g fiber, 4 g pro.

Parsley-Herb Rice

Basmati Rice Pilaf with
Toasted Pecans

Basmati Rice Pilaf with Toasted Pecans

Try this with chopped dry-roasted pistachios in place of the pecans. Stir nuts in right before serving to keep them crunchy.

Start to Finish: 30 minutes **Makes:** 6 servings

2	teaspoons olive oil or vegetable oil
2	cloves garlic, minced
2½	cups water
1	cup uncooked basmati rice
2	teaspoons instant chicken bouillon granules
1½	cups sliced fresh mushrooms
½	cup thinly sliced green onions (4)
¼	cup chopped red sweet pepper
2	teaspoons finely shredded lemon peel
¼	teaspoon salt
⅛	teaspoon ground black pepper
¼	cup chopped pecans, toasted

1. In a medium saucepan, heat oil over medium heat. Add garlic; cook for 30 seconds. Carefully add water, rice, and bouillon granules. Bring to boiling; reduce heat. Simmer, covered, for 10 minutes. Add mushrooms, green onions, sweet pepper, lemon peel, salt, and black pepper to saucepan. Cook, covered, for 10 to 15 minutes more or until rice is tender and liquid is absorbed. Stir in pecans.

Per serving: 159 cal., 6 g total fat (1 g sat. fat), 0 mg chol., 396 mg sodium, 25 g carbo., 2 g fiber, 4 g pro.

Quick Tip Basmati rice is used widely in India. Along with jasmine rice—used widely in Thailand—it is considered to be one of the aromatic rices. Both basmati and jasmine rice have a nutty fragrance and flavor that sets them apart from long grain rice—which you can use if you don't have basmati.

Grits Gruyère

A Southern favorite gets a European twist with the addition of Gruyère and Parmesan cheeses.

Prep: 15 minutes **Bake:** 20 minutes **Oven:** 350°F
Makes: 8 servings

4	cups milk
¼	cup butter or margarine, cut up
½	teaspoon salt
1	cup quick-cooking grits
1	cup shredded Gruyère cheese or Swiss cheese (4 ounces)
	Several dashes bottled hot pepper sauce or
¼	teaspoon cayenne pepper (optional)
¼	cup grated Parmesan cheese

1. Preheat oven 350°F. Grease a 2-quart square baking dish; set aside.

2. In a large saucepan, combine milk, butter, and salt. Cook over medium heat until almost boiling, stirring occasionally. (Watch carefully to prevent boiling over.) Gradually stir in grits; cook and stir with a long-handled wooden spoon just until boiling. Stir 2 minutes more or until thickened. (Reduce heat, if necessary.) Remove from heat; stir in Gruyère cheese and, if desired, hot pepper sauce. Spread grits mixture evenly in prepared dish. Sprinkle with Parmesan cheese.

3. Bake, uncovered, for 20 to 25 minutes or until golden.

Per serving: 246 cal., 14 g total fat (8 g sat. fat), 43 mg chol., 363 mg sodium, 20 g carbo., 1 g fiber, 11 g pro.

Curried Garbanzo Couscous

Try this pretty yellow dish with grilled chicken.

Start to Finish: 15 minutes **Makes:** 4 servings

1½	cups couscous
1	tablespoon olive oil
1	cup chopped green sweet pepper (1 large)
⅔	cup canned garbanzo beans (chickpeas), rinsed and drained
¼	cup chopped onion
1	teaspoon curry powder

1. Prepare couscous following package directions. Set aside.

2. Meanwhile, in a small skillet, heat olive oil over medium heat. Add sweet pepper, garbanzo beans, onion, and curry powder. Cook for 5 minutes, adding a little water if necessary. Serve bean mixture over couscous.

Per serving: 350 cal., 4 g total fat (1 g sat. fat), 0 mg chol., 128 mg sodium, 65 g carbo., 5 g fiber, 11 g pro.

Zucchini-Olive Couscous

Zucchini-Olive Couscous 🔲

Make this large-yield side dish for a party or potluck.

Start to Finish: 30 minutes **Makes:** 8 servings

- 1 **tablespoon olive oil**
- 2 **cloves garlic, minced**
- 3 **cups chicken broth**
- 1 **cup pimiento-stuffed green olives, pitted green olives, and/or pitted ripe olives, cut up**
- 1 **10-ounce package couscous**
- 3 **medium zucchini, halved lengthwise and thinly sliced (about 3¾ cups)**
- 2 **teaspoons finely shredded lemon peel**
- ¼ **teaspoon freshly ground black pepper**
- ½ **cup sliced green onion (4)**
- 2 **tablespoons snipped fresh parsley**
  Thin strips of lemon peel (optional)
  Lemon wedges (optional)

1. In a large saucepan, heat olive oil over medium heat. Add garlic; cook and stir for 1 minute. Add chicken broth and olives; bring to boiling. Stir in couscous, zucchini, shredded lemon peel, and pepper. Cover; remove from heat. Let stand for 5 minutes.

2. To serve, gently stir in green onions and parsley. If desired, top with thin strips of lemon peel and serve with lemon wedges.

Per serving: 190 cal., 5 g total fat (1 g sat. fat), 0 mg chol., 762 mg sodium, 31 g carbo., 3 g fiber, 6 g pro.

Fennel and Carrot Pasta

Colorful and flavorful fennel, carrots, and radicchio brighten this pasta dish. To save on prep and cleanup time, the vegetables are cooked along with the pasta.

Start to Finish: 25 minutes **Makes:** 4 servings

- 1 **bulb fennel (about 1 pound)**
- 4 **ounces dried bow tie, gemelli, or corkscrew pasta**
- 2 **large carrots, cut in thin strips (1 cup)**
- 2 **teaspoons olive oil**
- ½ **cup chopped onion (1 medium)**
- 2 **cloves garlic, minced**
- ¼ **teaspoon ground black pepper**
- ⅛ **teaspoon salt**
- 1½ **cups shredded radicchio or fresh spinach**
- 2 **tablespoons grated Parmesan cheese**

1. Remove upper stalks from fennel, including feathery leaves. Discard any wilted outer layers on fennel bulb; cut off a thin slice from the base. Wash fennel and pat dry. Quarter fennel bulb lengthwise and discard core; cut quarters in thin strips.

2. Cook pasta in a large pot of lightly salted boiling water for 5 minutes. Add fennel and carrots; cook about 5 minutes more or until pasta is al dente (tender yet firm); drain.

3. Meanwhile, in a small skillet, heat olive oil over medium heat. Add onion and garlic; cook about 3 minutes or until onion is tender. Stir in pepper and salt. Transfer pasta mixture to a serving dish. Add onion mixture, radicchio, and Parmesan cheese to pasta mixture. Toss well to mix.

Per serving: 247 cal., 4 g total fat (1 g sat. fat), 2 mg chol., 242 mg sodium, 44 g carbo., 2 g fiber, 10 g pro.

Rosemary and Swiss Buns

Dress up hot roll mix with cheese, onions, and herbs. The buns are delicious with beef or pork.

Prep: 25 minutes **Rise:** 30 minutes **Bake:** 12 minutes
Oven: 375°F **Makes:** 12 buns

- 1 **16-ounce package hot roll mix**
- ¾ **cup shredded Swiss cheese (3 ounces)**
- 1 **tablespoon vegetable oil**
- 2 **small onions, thinly sliced and separated into rings (²/₃ cup)**
- 1 **tablespoon snipped fresh rosemary or 1 teaspoon dried rosemary, crushed**

1. Grease 2 large baking sheets; set aside. Prepare hot roll mix following package directions, except stir in Swiss cheese with the liquid. Continue with package directions through the kneading and resting steps. After dough rests, divide in 12 equal portions and shape in balls.

2. On a lightly floured surface, roll each ball in a 4-inch round. Place on prepared baking sheets. Cover the rolls and set aside.

3. In a medium skillet, heat oil over medium heat. Add onion and rosemary; cook until onion is tender. Using your fingertips, make ½-inch-deep indentations on the surface of the dough rounds. Divide the onion mixture among the rounds. Cover and let rise in a warm place until nearly double (30 to 40 minutes).

4. Preheat oven to 375°F. Bake buns for 12 to 15 minutes or until golden. Transfer buns to a wire rack and cool completely.

Per bun: 200 cal., 6 g total fat (1 g sat. fat), 23 mg chol., 265 mg sodium, 30 g carbo., 0 g fiber, 7 g pro.

Chive Batter Rolls

These savory yeast rolls are easy to make. Try them with soups and stews.

Prep: 30 minutes **Rise:** 20 minutes **Bake:** 18 minutes
Stand: 5 minutes **Oven:** 350°F **Makes:** 12 rolls

- 1 **tablespoon yellow cornmeal**
- 2 **cups all-purpose flour**
- 1 **package fast-rising active dry yeast**
- ¼ **teaspoon ground black pepper**
- 1 **cup milk**
- 2 **tablespoons sugar**
- 3 **tablespoons butter or margarine**
- ½ **teaspoon salt**
- 1 **egg**
- ½ **cup snipped fresh chives or ¼ cup finely chopped green onions (green tops only)**
- ⅓ **cup yellow cornmeal**

1. Grease the bottoms and sides of twelve 2½-inch muffin cups. Sprinkle bottoms with the 1 tablespoon cornmeal; set aside. In a large mixing bowl, stir together 1¼ cups of the flour, the yeast, and the pepper; set aside.

2. In a small saucepan, combine milk, sugar, butter, and salt; heat and stir over medium heat just until mixture is warm (120°F to 130°F) and butter is almost melted. Add milk mixture and egg to flour mixture. Beat with an electric mixer on low to medium speed for 30 seconds, scraping bowl constantly. Beat on high speed for 3 minutes. Stir in the chives and the ⅓ cup cornmeal. Stir in remaining flour. (The batter will be soft and sticky.) Cover and let rest in a warm place for 10 minutes.

3. Preheat oven to 350°F. Spoon batter into prepared muffin cups. Cover loosely. Let rise in a warm place for 20 minutes.

4. Bake, uncovered, about 18 minutes or until rolls sound hollow when tapped. Cool in muffin cups for 5 minutes; loosen edges and remove from muffin cups. Serve warm.

Per roll: 140 cal., 4 g total fat (2 g sat. fat), 28 mg chol., 144 mg sodium, 21 g carbo., 1 g fiber, 4 g pro.

Chive Batter Rolls

Checkerboard Rolls ♥

Try a garlic-herb variation too: Prepare the rolls according to the method below, except in Step 1 omit the lemon-pepper seasoning. Substitute 1 teaspoon dried Italian seasoning, crushed, and ¹⁄₂ teaspoon garlic powder.

Prep: 20 minutes **Chill:** 8 to 24 hours
Stand: 45 minutes **Bake:** 20 minutes **Oven:** 375°F
Makes: 16 rolls

- 2 **tablespoons poppy seeds**
- 2 **tablespoons sesame seeds**
- 1 **teaspoon lemon-pepper seasoning**
- 2 **tablespoons yellow cornmeal**
- 2 **tablespoons grated or finely shredded Parmesan cheese**
- 3 **tablespoons butter or margarine, melted**
- 16 **pieces (1.3 ounces each) frozen white roll dough**

1. Grease a 9×9×2-inch square pan; set aside. In a shallow dish, combine poppy seeds, sesame seeds, and lemon-pepper seasoning. In another shallow dish, combine cornmeal and Parmesan cheese. Place butter in a third dish. Working quickly, roll dough pieces in butter, then in one of the seasoning mixtures to lightly coat. (Coat half of the rolls with one seasoning mixture and the remaining rolls with the other seasoning mixture.) Alternate rolls in prepared pan. Cover rolls with greased plastic wrap. Let thaw in refrigerator for at least 8 hours or up to 24 hours.

2. Remove pan from refrigerator; uncover and let stand at room temperature for 45 minutes. After 35 minutes, preheat oven to 375°F.

3. Bake rolls for 20 to 25 minutes or until golden. Remove rolls from pan to wire rack. Cool slightly.

Per roll: 136 cal., 5 g total fat (2 g sat. fat), 6 mg chol., 189 mg sodium, 19 g carbo., 1 g fiber, 4 g pro.

Garlic Dinner Rolls

Transform refrigerated breadsticks into pretty fleur-de-lis shapes, then brush with garlic butter and a blend of grated Asiago, parsley, and cayenne pepper.

Prep: 15 minutes **Bake:** 13 minutes **Oven:** 375°F
Makes: 12 rolls

- 1 **11-ounce package (12) refrigerated breadsticks**
- 2 **tablespoons purchased garlic butter spread, melted**
- ¹⁄₂ **cup finely shredded or grated Asiago or Romano cheese (2 ounces)**
- 1 **teaspoon dried parsley flakes**
- ¹⁄₈ **teaspoon cayenne pepper**

1. Preheat oven to 375°F. Line a large baking sheet with foil; set aside. On a lightly floured surface, separate dough in 12 breadsticks. Cut each piece lengthwise into three strips, leaving ³⁄₄ inch uncut at one end. For each fleur-de-lis roll, coil strips from cut end toward uncut base, coiling outside strips away from center and coiling the center strip in either direction. If necessary, pinch slightly to hold shape. Transfer to prepared baking sheet.

2. Brush rolls with melted garlic butter spread. In a small bowl, combine cheese, parsley flakes, and cayenne pepper; sprinkle generously on rolls.

3. Bake for 13 to 15 minutes or until golden. Serve warm.

Per roll: 112 cal., 5 g total fat (2 g sat. fat), 8 mg chol., 263 mg sodium, 12 g carbo., 0 g fiber, 3 g pro.

Cracked Pepper Breadsticks ♥

These biscuit-style breadsticks bite back. Gauge your tolerance for heat as you decide how much pepper to use.

Prep: 25 minutes **Bake:** 10 minutes **Oven:** 450°F
Makes: 32 breadsticks

- 2 **cups all-purpose flour**
- 1 **tablespoon baking powder**
- 1 **to 1¹⁄₂ teaspoons cracked black pepper**
- ¹⁄₄ **teaspoon salt**
- ¹⁄₃ **cup butter**
- ²⁄₃ **cup beef or chicken broth**

1. Preheat oven to 450°F. In a medium bowl, stir together flour, baking powder, pepper, and salt. Cut in butter until mixture resembles coarse crumbs. Make a well in the center. Add broth; stir just until dough clings together.

2. Turn dough out onto a lightly floured surface. Knead gently for 10 to 12 strokes. Divide dough in 8 equal portions; divide each portion into fourths. Roll each piece to a 10-inch-long rope. Fold each rope in half; twist two or three times. Arrange twists on an ungreased baking sheet.

3. Bake for 5 minutes; turn and bake for 5 to 6 minutes more or until brown. Serve warm or cool completely on a wire rack before serving.

Per breadstick: 44 cal., 2 g total fat (1 g sat. fat), 5 mg chol., 54 mg sodium, 6 g carbo., 0 g fiber, 1 g pro.

Quick Tip Buy cracked black pepper bottled. Or make it by placing whole black peppercorns in a sealed plastic bag. Crush them lightly with a rolling pin or meat mallet.

Tasty Side Dishes

Fresh Strawberry Fool,
page 323

Butterscotch Marble
Cake, **page 311**

Shortcut Chocolate
Revel Bars, **page 315**

Pistachio-Lemon Gelato,
page 320

Sweet Tooth Desserts

You may not indulge in dessert every night, but when you do, you want it to be easy to make and satisfying to eat. These recipes—built on no-fuss ingredients— make dessert sweet and simple.

Butterscotch Marble Cake

Butterscotch Marble Cake

One cake mix divided and flavored two ways—with butterscotch pudding and chocolate syrup—makes for an eye-catching yet easy-to-make cake.

Prep: 20 minutes **Bake:** 55 minutes **Cool:** 2 hours
Oven: 350°F **Makes:** 12 servings

- 1 **package 2-layer-size white cake mix**
- 1 **4-serving-size package instant butterscotch pudding mix**
- 1 **cup water**
- ¼ **cup vegetable oil**
- 4 **eggs**
- ½ **cup chocolate-flavored syrup**
- 2 **ounces sweet baking chocolate, cut up**
- 2 **tablespoons butter or margarine**
- ¾ **cup powdered sugar**
- 1 **tablespoon hot water**

1. Preheat oven to 350°F. Grease and flour a 10-inch fluted tube pan; set aside.

2. In a large mixing bowl, combine cake mix, pudding mix, water, oil, and eggs. Beat with an electric mixer on low speed until combined. Beat on medium speed for 2 minutes, scraping side of bowl often.

3. Transfer 1½ cups of batter to another bowl; stir in the chocolate-flavored syrup. Pour light batter into the prepared pan. Spoon chocolate batter over top. Using a knife, gently cut through batters to marble.

4. Bake for 55 to 60 minutes or until a toothpick inserted near the center comes out clean. Cool cake in pan on a wire rack for 15 minutes. Remove cake from pan and cool completely on wire rack.

5. For icing, in a medium saucepan, melt chocolate and butter over low heat, stirring frequently. Remove from heat. Stir in powdered sugar and 1 tablespoon hot water. Stir in additional hot water, if needed, to reach drizzling consistency. Drizzle cake with icing.

Per serving: 372 cal., 13 g total fat (4 g sat. fat), 76 mg chol., 388 mg sodium, 62 g carbo., 1 g fiber, 5 g pro.

Quick Tip When you melt chocolate, take care not to drip or splash any water into the pan. Even the smallest drop of water can cause the chocolate to seize up, get grainy, and form lumps.

New Year's Champagne Cake

The Champagne and pretty pink color make this a romantic choice for Valentine's Day or a bridal shower.

Prep: 20 minutes **Bake:** following package directions
Cool: 1 hour **Oven:** 350°F **Makes:** 10 servings

- 1 **package 2-layer-size white cake mix**
  Champagne or sparkling wine
- 1 **16-ounce can vanilla frosting**
  Few drops red food coloring
  Sliced or whole strawberries (optional)

1. Preheat oven to 350°F. Grease and flour two 8×1½-inch round cake pans; set aside.

2. Prepare cake mix following package directions, except replace water with an equal amount of Champagne or sparkling wine. Divide batter evenly among the prepared pans. Bake following package directions. Cool layers in pans on wire racks for 10 minutes. Remove layers from pans and cool completely on wire racks.

3. Place frosting in a medium bowl. Stir in a few drops of red food coloring to make light pink. Fill and frost cake with tinted frosting. If desired, garnish with strawberries.

Per serving: 465 cal., 17 g total fat (4 g sat. fat), 0 mg chol., 423 mg sodium, 72 g carbo., 1 g fiber, 3 g pro.

Angel Food Cake with Peaches, Whipped Cream, and Raspberries

For a pretty presentation, spoon some of the raspberry purée on on the plate around the slice of cake.

Prep: 15 minutes **Makes:** 12 servings

- 1 **cup whipping cream**
- 2 **tablespoons powdered sugar**
- ½ **teaspoon almond extract**
- 1 **10-ounce package frozen red raspberries, thawed**
- 12 **slices angel food cake**
- 1 **16-ounce can peach slices in light syrup, drained**
- 12 **fresh mint leaves (optional)**

1. In a chilled medium mixing bowl, combine whipping cream, powdered sugar, and almond extract. Beat with an electric mixer on medium speed until soft peaks form.

2. Place raspberries in food processor or blender. Process or blend until smooth. Press purée through a sieve.

3. Arrange cake slices on 12 dessert plates. Spoon a few tablespoons seedless raspberry purée over each slice. Garnish with peach slices, whipped cream, remaining raspberry purée, and, if desired, mint.

Per serving: 180 cal., 8 g total fat (5 g sat. fat), 27 mg chol., 222 mg sodium, 27 g carbo., 2 g fiber, 3 g pro.

Almond Cake with Fresh Fruit

This supersimple cake is whipped together in a blender.

Prep: 10 minutes **Bake:** 20 minutes **Cool:** 2 hours
Oven: 350°F **Makes:** 6 servings

- **1**   **tablespoon all-purpose flour**
- **½**   **teaspoon baking powder**
- **½**   **teaspoon finely shredded orange peel**
- **2**   **eggs**
- **⅓**   **cup sugar**
- **6**   **ounces unblanched whole almonds**
- **3**   **pears, peeled, cored, and halved, or 2 cups assorted fresh fruit, cut up**
- **½**   **cup snipped dried pears or other dried fruit**

1. Preheat oven to 350°F. Grease and lightly flour an 8×1½-inch round cake pan; set aside. In a large bowl, stir together flour, baking powder, and orange peel; set aside.

2. In a food processor or blender, combine eggs and sugar. Cover and process or blend until smooth. Add almonds. Cover and process or blend about 1 minute or until nearly smooth. Add egg mixture to the flour mixture; stir just until smooth. Spread the batter into the prepared pan.

3. Bake about 20 minutes or until lightly browned. Cool cake in pan on a wire rack for 10 minutes. Remove from pan; cool completely on wire rack.

4. To serve, cut cake in wedges. Arrange the cake and fruit in dessert bowls.

Per serving: 272 cal., 17 g total fat (2 g sat. fat), 71 mg chol., 65 mg sodium, 26 g carbo., 4 g fiber, 8 g pro.

Gingerbread Deluxe

Layers of sweet-tart lemon curd turn a start-with-a-mix gingerbread cake into an elegant dessert. Look for lemon curd in the jams and jellies section of the supermarket. If you can't find it there, look for it at a specialty food shop.

Prep: 20 minutes **Bake:** 35 minutes **Cool:** 1 hour
Oven: 350°F **Makes:** 12 servings

- **2**   **14.5-ounce packages gingerbread mix**
- **2**   **10-ounce jars lemon curd**
-      **Powdered sugar**

1. Preheat oven to 350°F. Grease and lightly flour two 8×8×2-inch cake pans; set aside. Prepare gingerbread mixes and bake following package directions using one prepared mix for each pan. Cool cake layers in pans on wire racks for 10 minutes. Loosen and remove from pans. Cool completely on wire racks.

2. Split each cake layer in half horizontally. Place one layer, flat side up, on serving platter. Spread with one-third of the lemon curd; top with second layer, flat side down. Spread with another one-third of lemon curd. Top with third cake layer and spread with remaining lemon curd. Top with remaining cake layer. Sift powdered sugar over top of cake. Cover and store cake in the refrigerator up to 24 hours.

Per serving: 463 cal., 10 g total fat (3 g sat. fat), 71 mg chol., 504 mg sodium, 90 g carbo., 5 g fiber, 5 g pro.

Gingerbread Deluxe

Orange-Chocolate Cake

Orange-Chocolate Cake

A splash of orange liqueur infuses this rich cake with flavor.

Bake: following package directions **Cool:** 1 hour
Oven: 350°F **Makes:** 12 servings

- 1 **package 2-layer-size devil's food cake mix**
- ¼ **cup orange liqueur (such as Cointreau)**
- 1 **16-ounce can chocolate frosting**
  Candied orange slices (optional)

1. Preheat oven to 350°F. Prepare cake following directions, except replace ¼ cup water with the orange liqueur. Use desired pan size.

2. Frost cooled cake with chocolate frosting. If desired, garnish with candied orange slices.

Per serving: 475 cal., 24 g total fat (6 g sat. fat), 55 mg chol., 469 mg sodium, 56 g carbo., 1 g fiber, 4 g pro.

Quick Tip Create the swirled icing effect on this cake with a dinner fork. Place the iced cake on a lazy Susan. As you turn the cake, drag a fork through the icing, moving it in and out slightly in a scalloped pattern.

Chocolate-Coconut Cheesecake

Dress up a purchased plain frozen cheesecake in minutes with decadent fudge topping, crispy macaroon cookies, and golden toasted almonds. Family or guests will think you've been busy in the kitchen all day!

Start to Finish: 10 minutes **Makes:** 12 servings

- 1 **30-ounce package frozen New York-style cheesecake**
- 1 **12-ounce jar fudge ice cream topping**
- 4 **soft coconut macaroon cookies, crumbled**
- ¼ **cup sliced almonds, toasted**

1. Thaw cheesecake following package directions for microwave thawing. Spread top of cheesecake with fudge topping, allowing some to drip down side of cheesecake. Sprinkle with crumbled cookies and almonds.

Per serving: 371 cal., 17 g total fat (9 g sat. fat), 45 mg chol., 305 mg sodium, 48 g carbo., 0 g fiber, 6 g pro.

Gingerbread Cupcakes

Gingerbread Cupcakes

The crackly tops and flavor of these cupcakes will remind you of gingersnap cookies. They're delicious for dessert—or as an extra-special after-school snack with a glass of cold milk!

Prep: 10 minutes **Bake:** 15 minutes **Cool:** 10 minutes
Oven: 350°F **Makes:** 8 cupcakes

- 1 **cup all-purpose flour**
- 1/2 **teaspoon baking powder**
- 1/2 **teaspoon ground ginger**
- 1/2 **teaspoon ground cinnamon**
- 1/4 **teaspoon baking soda**
  Dash salt
- 1 **egg white, lightly beaten**
- 1/3 **cup molasses**
- 1/3 **cup water**
- 3 **tablespoons vegetable oil**
  Powdered sugar (optional)

1. Preheat oven to 350°F. Line eight 2½-inch muffin cups with paper bake cups; set aside. In a medium bowl, stir together flour, baking powder, ginger, cinnamon, soda, and salt; set aside.

2. In a small bowl, stir together egg white, molasses, water, and oil. Stir molasses mixture into flour mixture just until blended. Spoon batter into prepared muffin cups.

3. Bake for 15 to 20 minutes or until cupcakes spring back when pressed lightly in centers. Cool in pans on wire racks for 10 minutes. Remove cupcakes from pans. Serve warm or cool. If desired, sift powdered sugar over cupcakes before serving.

Per cupcake: 137 cal., 5 g total fat (0 g sat. fat), 0 mg chol., 82 mg sodium, 20 g carbo., 1 g fiber, 2 g pro.

Shortcut Chocolate Revel Bars

These all-time favorite bars can be made with a fraction of the effort using refrigerated oatmeal chocolate chip cookie dough.

Prep: 20 minutes **Bake:** 25 minutes **Cool:** 1 hour
Oven: 350°F **Makes:** 30 bars

- 1½ cups semisweet chocolate pieces
- 1 14-ounce can sweetened condensed milk (1¼ cups)
- 2 tablespoons butter or margarine
- ½ cup chopped walnuts or pecans
- 2 teaspoons vanilla
- 2 18-ounce rolls refrigerated oatmeal chocolate chip cookie dough

1. Preheat oven to 350°F. In a small saucepan, combine chocolate pieces, condensed milk, and butter. Cook and stir over low heat until chocolate is melted. Remove from heat. Stir in nuts and vanilla.

2. Press two-thirds (1⅓ rolls) of the cookie dough into the bottom of an ungreased 15×10×1-inch baking pan. Spread the chocolate mixture evenly over the cookie dough. Dot the remaining cookie dough on top of chocolate mixture.

3. Bake about 25 minutes or until top is lightly browned (chocolate will still look moist). Cool on a wire rack. Cut into bars. To store, cover and refrigerate up to 3 days or freeze up to 1 month.

Per bar: 255 cal., 13 g total fat (5 g sat. fat), 13 mg chol., 136 mg sodium, 33 g carbo., 1 g fiber, 3 g pro.

Shortcut Chocolate Revel Bars

Easy Gingerbread Bars

For a quick holiday treat, these bars are made with packaged gingerbread mix that's studded with dried fruit and nuts.

Prep: 10 minutes **Bake:** 20 minutes **Cool:** 1 hour
Oven: 350°F **Makes:** 24 bars

- 1 14.5-ounce package gingerbread mix
- ¾ cup water
- 1 egg
- 1 7-ounce package tropical blend mixed dried fruit bits
- 1 cup chopped pecans
- 1 cup powdered sugar
- ⅛ teaspoon ground ginger
- 3 to 4 teaspoons milk

1. Preheat oven to 350°F. Grease a 13×9×2-inch baking pan; set aside.

2. In a medium bowl, stir together gingerbread mix, water, egg, fruit bits, and pecans just until blended. Spread batter in prepared pan.

3. Bake for 15 to 20 minutes or until a toothpick inserted near the center comes out clean. Cool completely on a wire rack.

4. For glaze, in a small bowl, stir together powdered sugar, ginger, and enough milk to make a drizzling consistency. Drizzle glaze over top. Cut into bars.

Per bar: 148 cal., 6 g total fat (1 g sat. fat), 9 mg chol., 123 mg sodium, 24 g carbo., 0 g fiber, 2 g pro.

Salted Peanut Bars

These are for fans of sweet-and-salty flavors—particularly those who are fond of a certain popular candy bar.

Prep: 20 minutes **Chill:** 2 hours **Makes:** 48 bars

- Nonstick cooking spray
- 4 cups dry-roasted or honey-roasted peanuts
- 1 10.5-ounce package tiny marshmallows
- ½ cup butter or margarine
- 1 12-ounce package peanut butter-flavored pieces (2 cups)
- 1 14-ounce can sweetened condensed milk (1¼ cups)
- ½ cup creamy peanut butter

1. Line a 13×9×2-inch baking pan with heavy foil. Coat foil with cooking spray. Spread half the peanuts in the pan.

2. In a 3-quart saucepan, melt marshmallows and butter over low heat. Stir in peanut butter pieces, condensed milk, and peanut butter until smooth. Quickly pour over the peanuts in pan. Sprinkle remaining peanuts on top.

3. Chill until firm; cut into bars. Store in refrigerator.

Per bar: 93 cal., 6 g total fat (2 g sat. fat), 4 mg chol., 82 mg sodium, 8 g carbo., 1 g fiber, 3 g pro.

Cranberry-Almond Wedges

Take a sugar cookie mix, stir in some dried cranberries and nuts, pat, sprinkle with sugar, and bake. The result: superquick shortbread bars.

Prep: 20 minutes **Bake:** 18 minutes **Cool:** 1 hour
Oven: 350°F **Makes:** 32 cookies

- 1   **17.5-ounce package sugar cookie mix**
- 1/4 **teaspoon almond extract**
- 1/2 **cup butter**
- 1   **cup dried cranberries**
- 1   **tablespoon milk**
- 3/4 **cup sliced almonds**
       Coarse or granulated sugar

1. Preheat oven to 350°F. Line two 9×1 1/2-inch round cake pans with foil, extending foil over the pan edges. Set aside.

2. Place sugar cookie mix in a large bowl. Sprinkle almond extract over mix. Using a pastry blender, cut in butter until mixture resembles coarse crumbs. Stir in dried cranberries. (Dough will be crumbly.) Divide mixture between the two prepared pans. Press mixture firmly onto bottoms of pans. Brush tops lightly with milk. Top with almonds. Sprinkle with sugar.

3. Bake for 18 to 20 minutes or until centers are set and tops are lightly browned. Cool in pans on wire racks. Using the edges of the foil, lift cookie rounds out of the pans. Cut each round in 16 wedges. To store, layer cookies between sheets of waxed paper in an airtight container; cover. Store at room temperature up to 2 days or freeze for up to 3 months.

Per cookie: 120 cal., 5 g total fat (2 g sat. fat), 8 mg chol., 57 mg sodium, 17 g carbo., 0 g fiber, 1 g pro.

Spiced Brownies with Cream Cheese Swirl

These rich chocolate brownies from a mix have cinnamon, cloves, ginger, and a swirl of cream cheese for stunning showstoppers.

Prep: 20 minutes **Bake:** 25 minutes **Cool:** 1 hour
Oven: 350°F **Makes:** 32 brownies

- 1   **3-ounce package cream cheese, softened**
- 1/4 **cup sugar**
- 1   **egg yolk**
- 1   **tablespoon all-purpose flour**
- 1   **18.3-ounce package traditional fudge brownie mix**
- 1/2 **teaspoon ground cinnamon**
- 1/2 **teaspoon ground ginger**
- 1/4 **teaspoon ground nutmeg**
- 1/8 **teaspoon ground cloves**
       Melted butter

1. Preheat oven to 350°F. Line a 13×9×2-inch baking pan with heavy foil, extending foil over the pan edges. Lightly grease foil. Set pan aside. In a small mixing bowl, combine cream cheese and sugar. Beat with an electric mixer on medium to high speed until combined. Beat in egg yolk and flour; set aside.

2. In a large bowl, combine the brownie mix, cinnamon, ginger, nutmeg, and cloves. Prepare batter following package directions, except use melted butter in place of the oil. Spoon batter into prepared pan, spreading evenly. Spoon cream cheese mixture in small mounds on brownie batter. Using a table knife, swirl cream cheese mixture into brownie batter.

3. Bake for 25 to 30 minutes or until center is set (cream cheese swirl will be lightly browned). Cool in pan on a wire rack for 1 hour. Cover and refrigerate until serving time. Using the foil, lift the uncut brownies out of the pan. Cut into bars. To store, place bars in a single layer in an airtight container; cover. Store in the refrigerator up to 4 days or freeze up to 3 months.

Per brownie: 128 cal., 7 g total fat (4 g sat. fat), 33 mg chol., 88 mg sodium, 15 g carbo., 0 g fiber, 1 g pro.

Uncovered Blueberry Pie

Showcase summer fruit in this fast dessert. This one-crust, no-bake blueberry pie can be ready for the table in less than an hour. Or make it ahead of time and served chilled.

Prep: 15 minutes **Cook:** 10 minutes **Cool:** 30 minutes
Makes: 8 servings

- 3/4 **cup sugar**
- 3   **tablespoons cornstarch**
- 1/8 **teaspoon salt**
- 1   **cup water**
- 3   **cups fresh blueberries**
- 1   **tablespoon butter or margarine**
- 1   **9-inch baked pie shell**
       Sweetened whipped cream

1. For filling, in a medium saucepan, combine sugar, cornstarch, and salt. Stir in water and 1 cup of the blueberries. Cook and stir over medium heat until thickened and bubbly. Cook and stir for 2 minutes more. Remove from heat. Stir in the remaining 2 cups blueberries and the butter until butter is melted. Cool completely.

2. Pour filling into shell. If desired, cover and refrigerate until ready to serve. Serve with whipped cream.

Per serving: 261 cal., 10 g total fat (3 g sat. fat), 4 mg chol., 122 mg sodium, 40 g carbo., 3 g fiber, 2 g pro.

Uncovered Blueberry Pie

Easy, Pleasing Peppermint-Stick Pie

Easy, Pleasing Peppermint-Stick Pie

Whether your serve it at holiday time or as a refreshing cold treat at a summer party, this three-ingredient pie is a crowd-pleaser.

Prep: 10 minutes **Freeze:** 4 hours **Stand:** 5 minutes
Makes: 8 servings

1 half-gallon peppermint ice cream, softened
1 chocolate-flavored crumb pie shell
1 12-ounce jar fudge ice cream topping
  Crushed peppermint candies (optional)

1. In a chilled large bowl, stir the ice cream until softened.

2. Spoon ice cream into pie shell, spreading evenly. Return to freezer; freeze at least 4 hours or until serving time.

3. To serve, let pie stand at room temperature for 5 minutes before cutting. Meanwhile, warm the fudge topping following microwave directions on jar. Serve pie with warmed topping and, if desired, peppermint candies.

Per serving: 554 cal., 24 g total fat (13 g sat. fat), 63 mg chol., 474 mg sodium, 72 g carbo., 1 g fiber, 8 g pro.

Cherry and Chocolate Pastry Hearts

Though these pastry hearts make a sweet dessert any time of year, they're especially suited to a Valentine's dinner at home.

Prep: 15 minutes **Bake:** 15 minutes **Cool:** 1 hour
Oven: 375°F **Makes:** 8 servings

½ a 17.25-ounce package frozen puff pastry sheets (1 sheet), thawed
¾ cup canned cherry pie filling
8 teaspoons fudge ice cream topping
2 tablespoons chopped nuts

1. Preheat oven to 375°F. On a lightly floured surface, unfold pastry sheet. Using a 3½- to 4-inch heart-shape cookie cutter, cut out pastry, discarding scraps or reserving for another use. Place pastry hearts on an ungreased baking sheet.

2. Bake for 15 to 18 minutes or until puffed and golden. Cool completely on a wire rack. Split pastry hearts horizontally; fill with pie filling. Drizzle with fudge topping; sprinkle with nuts.

Per serving: 193 cal., 11 g total fat (0 g sat. fat), 0 mg chol., 144 mg sodium, 22 g carbo., 0 g fiber, 2 g pro.

Quick Tip Serve these filled pastry hearts immediately so they stay crisp. If they sit too long, they get soggy.

Today's French Silk Pie

This simple recipe brings a favorite restaurant dessert home. For a quicker version, purchase a frozen pie shell.

Prep: 35 minutes **Bake:** 13 minutes **Chill:** 5 hours
Oven: 450°F **Makes:** 10 servings

  Baked Pastry Shell
¾ cup butter, softened
¾ cup sugar
1 cup semisweet chocolate pieces, melted and cooled
1 teaspoon vanilla
¾ cup refrigerated or frozen egg product, thawed
  Whipped cream (optional)
  Chocolate curls (optional)

1. Prepare Baked Pastry Shell; set aside.

2. For filling, in a large bowl, beat butter and sugar with an electric mixer on medium speed about 4 minutes or until fluffy. Stir in chocolate and vanilla. Gradually add egg product, beating on high speed and scraping side of bowl constantly until light and fluffy.

3. Pour filling into pastry shell. Cover and chill for 5 hours. If desired, garnish with whipped cream and chocolate curls.

Baked Pastry Shell: Preheat oven to 450°F. In a large bowl, stir together 1¼ cups all-purpose flour and ¼ teaspoon salt. Using a pastry blender, cut in ⅓ cup shortening until pieces are pea size. Sprinkle 1 tablespoon cold water over part of the mixture; gently toss with a fork. Push moistened dough to the side of the bowl. Repeat moistening dough, using 1 tablespoon cold water at a time, until all the dough is moistened (4 to 5 tablespoons cold water total). Form dough into a ball. On a lightly floured surface, use your hands to slightly flatten dough. Roll dough from center to edge into a circle about 12 inches in diameter. To transfer pastry, wrap it around the rolling pin. Unroll pastry into a 9-inch pie plate. Ease into pie plate, being careful not to stretch pastry. Trim pastry to ½ inch beyond edge of pie plate. Fold under extra pastry. Crimp edge as desired. Generously prick bottom and all around where bottom and side meet in pie plate with a fork. Line pastry with a double thickness of foil. Bake for 8 minutes. Remove foil. Bake for 5 to 6 minutes more or until golden. Cool on a wire rack. Makes one 9-inch pie shell.

Per serving: 378 cal., 24 g total fat (10 g sat. fat), 37 mg chol., 229 mg sodium, 38 g carbo., 0 g fiber, 4 g pro.

Easy Lemon Tarts

To make one large cake, substitute one large spongecake shell for the six small shells.

Start to Finish: 15 minutes **Makes:** 6 tarts

- 1 **cup powdered sugar**
- 4 **to 5 teaspoons milk**
- 6 **purchased small spongecake shells**
- 6 **tablespoons purchased lemon curd**
  Fresh raspberries (optional)
  Fresh mint sprig (optional)

1. For icing, in a small bowl, stir together powdered sugar and milk until drizzling consistency. Pour icing into a small plastic bag; snip off a small corner. Drizzle icing over spongecake shells. Place 1 rounded tablespoon of lemon curd into each center. If desired, garnish with fresh raspberries and mint sprigs.

Per tart: 255 cal., 4 g total fat (1 g sat. fat), 30 mg chol., 16 mg sodium, 55 g carbo., 2 g fiber, 1 g pro.

Double-Chocolate-Mousse Tarts

How does a chocolate mousse mix become double-chocolate? When it's made with chocolate milk!t

Prep: 15 minutes **Freeze:** 5 minutes **Makes:** 6 tarts

- 1 **4-serving-size package chocolate mousse mix**
- 1 **cup chocolate milk or milk**
- 1 **tablespoon amaretto**
- 3 **tablespoons sliced almonds or chopped pecans**
- 6 **graham cracker tart shells or baked pastry tart shells**
  Sliced almonds or chopped pecans
  Chocolate wafers (optional)

1. In a small mixing bowl, beat together mousse mix, milk, and amaretto with an electric mixer on low speed until combined. Beat on high speed for 3 minutes. Fold in the 3 tablespoons nuts. Divide mixture among tart shells.

2. Chill tarts in the freezer for 5 minutes. If desired, garnish with chocolate wafers and additional nuts.

Per tart: 254 cal., 10 g total fat (3 g sat. fat), 3 mg chol., 173 mg sodium, 33 g carbo., 3 g fiber, 3 g pro.

Quick Tip Make the filling for these tarts ahead of serving time and refrigerate it. Right before serving, fill the shells.

Chocolate Mousse Shake

Here's a cool and creamy dessert for a hot summer night.

Prep: 10 minutes **Stand:** 5 minutes
Makes: 4 (8-ounce) servings

- 1½ **cups fat-free milk**
- 1 **4-serving size package instant chocolate pudding mix**
- 3 **tablespoons unsweetened cocoa powder**
- 1 **teaspoon vanilla**
- 3 **cups chocolate ice cream**
  Sweetened Whipped Cream (optional)
  Shaved semisweet or milk chocolate (optional)

1. In a blender, combine milk, pudding mix, cocoa powder, and vanilla. Cover and blend for 1 minute. Gradually add ice cream, blending after each addition until smooth.

2. Divide among 4 glasses. Let stand for 5 minutes for mixture to thicken slightly. If desired, top with Sweetened Whipped Cream and shaved chocolate.

Per serving: 368 cal., 14 g total fat (8 g sat. fat), 41 mg chol., 478 mg sodium, 56 g carbo., 2 g fiber, 8 g pro.

Sweetened Whipped Cream: In a chilled small bowl, whisk ¼ cup whipping cream, 2 teaspoons sugar, and ¼ teaspoon vanilla until soft peaks form.

Pistachio-Lemon Gelato

Gelato is an Italian custardlike version of ice cream. Frozen lemonade concentrate gives it a refreshing citrus flavor without the need to squeeze and strain lemons.

Prep: 30 minutes **Chill:** several hours
Freeze: following manufacturer's directions
Makes: 14 (½-cup) servings

- 1 **medium lemon**
- 12 **egg yolks, lightly beaten**
- 4 **cups whole milk**
- 1⅓ **cups sugar**
- ½ **cup frozen lemonade concentrate, thawed**
- ⅓ **cup chopped pistachios or almonds, toasted**

1. Using a vegetable peeler, cut long strips of peel from the lemon. In a large saucepan, combine egg yolks, milk, sugar, and the lemon peel strips. Cook and stir over medium heat just until the mixture coats a metal spoon. Remove from heat. Remove peel and discard.

2. Transfer the cooked egg mixture to a large bowl. Cover surface with plastic wrap. Refrigerate several hours or overnight until completely chilled.

3. Stir lemonade concentrate and nuts into cooled egg mixture. Freeze mixture in a 4- or 5-quart ice cream freezer following manufacturer's directions.

Per serving: 204 cal., 8 g total fat (3 g sat. fat), 192 mg chol., 41 mg sodium, 27 g carbo., 0 g fiber, 5 g pro.

Pistachio-Lemon Gelato

Fresh Strawberry Fool

Fresh Strawberry Fool

A fool, in dessert terms, is related to another fruit-based dessert—the trifle. A trifle is a bit of foolishness. Make sense?

Start to Finish: 10 minutes **Makes:** 4 servings

- ½ **cup whipping cream**
- ⅓ **cup powdered sugar**
- ½ **teaspoon vanilla**
- 1 **6-ounce container lemon yogurt**
- 3 **cups sliced fresh strawberries or 2 cups fresh blueberries**
- ½ **cup coarsely crumbled shortbread cookies (5 cookies)**

1. In a chilled medium mixing bowl, beat whipping cream, powdered sugar, and vanilla with an electric mixer on medium speed until soft peaks form. By hand, fold in the yogurt and half the berries.

2. Spoon some whipped cream mixture in four 10-ounce glasses. Top each with some berries, the rest of the whipped cream mixture, and remaining berries. Serve immediately or cover and refrigerate up to 2 hours. Before serving, sprinkle with crumbled cookies.

Per serving: 272 cal., 15 g total fat (8 g sat. fat), 47 mg chol., 98 mg sodium, 32 g carbo., 3 g fiber, 4 g pro.

Caramel Oranges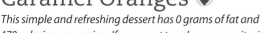

This simple and refreshing dessert has 0 grams of fat and 170 calories per serving. If you want to splurge, serve it with a butter cookie or shortbread on the side.

Start to Finish: 20 minutes **Makes:** 6 servings

- 1 **cup sugar**
- ½ **cup hot orange-flavored tea**
- 1 **or 2 drops oil of orange or ¼ teaspoon vanilla**
- 4 **medium oranges, peeled and sliced crosswise**
- 4 **teaspoons finely snipped crystallized ginger (optional)**
  Orange peel curl (optional)

1. For syrup, in a small heavy saucepan, heat sugar, without stirring, over medium-high heat just until it begins to melt. Reduce heat to medium-low; cook and stir with a wooden spoon about 4 minutes or until sugar is melted and turns a deep golden brown. Do not overcook. Remove from heat. Very slowly and carefully stir hot tea into caramelized sugar. If necessary, return to heat; cook until any hard sugar particles dissolve. Cool to room temperature. Stir oil of orange into cooled syrup.

2. To serve, pour syrup onto 6 dessert plates. Arrange orange slices in syrup. if desired, sprinkle each serving with ginger and garnish with an orange peel curl.

Per serving: 170 cal., 0 g total fat, 0 mg chol., 1 mg sodium, 44 g carbo., 2 g fiber, 1 g pro.

Raspberry Coffee Frappe

This fun and fancy ice cream shop dessert is easy to make at home—and much less expensive. Make it prettier with a garnish of fresh mint.

Start to Finish: 10 minutes **Makes:** 6 servings

- 2 **cups strong coffee, chilled**
- ¼ **cup raspberry-flavored syrup**
- ½ **cup half-and-half or light cream**
- 18 **ice cubes (about 2½ cups)**
- 6 **scoops coffee-flavored ice cream**

1. In a blender, combine 1 cup of the coffee, the raspberry-flavor syrup, half-and-half, and ice cubes. Cover and blend until the ice is finely crushed. Add the remaining coffee. Cover and blend on the lowest speed just until combined. Pour into glasses. Top each glass with a scoop of coffee-flavored ice cream.

Per serving: 243 cal., 14 g total fat (9 g sat. fat), 87 mg chol., 69 mg sodium, 24 g carbo., 0 g fiber, 4 g pro.

Quick Tip Look for raspberry-flavored syrup wherever flavored syrups made for coffee drinks are available. This dessert would also be delicious made with strawberry-, cherry-, boysenberry-, or mandarin orange-flavored syrup.

Raspberry Coffee Frappe

Index

Note: **Boldfaced** page numbers indicate photographs.

FOR A RECIPE TO EARN THIS "HEALTHY"
ICON, IT MUST MEET CERTAIN CALORIE,
FAT, AND SODIUM REQUIREMENTS.

Maximum levels per serving include:
- **Main dish:** 400 calories, 13 grams fat, and
　480 milligrams sodium.
- **One-dish meals:** 500 calories, 17 grams fat,
　and 600 milligrams sodium.
- **Side dish:** 200 calories, 6 grams fat, and
　200 milligrams sodium.
- **Desserts:** 200 calories, 6 grams fat, and
　300 milligrams sodium.

In-a-Pinch Substitutions

It can happen to the best of us: Halfway through a recipe, you find you're completely out of a key ingredient. Here's what to do:

Recipe Calls For:	You May Substitute:
1 square unsweetened chocolate	3 Tbsp. unsweetened cocoa powder + 1 Tbsp. butter/margarine
1 cup cake flour	1 cup less 2 Tbsp. all-purpose flour
2 Tbsp. flour (for thickening)	1 Tbsp. cornstarch
1 tsp. baking powder	¼ tsp. baking soda + ½ tsp. cream of tartar + ¼ tsp. cornstarch
1 cup corn syrup	1 cup sugar + ¼ cup additional liquid used in recipe
1 cup milk	½ cup evaporated milk + ½ cup water
1 cup buttermilk or sour milk	1 Tbsp. vinegar or lemon juice + enough milk to make 1 cup
1 cup sour cream (for baking)	1 cup plain yogurt
1 cup firmly packed brown sugar	1 cup sugar + 2 Tbsp. molasses
1 tsp lemon juice	¼ tsp. vinegar (not balsamic)
¼ cup chopped onion	1 Tbsp. instant minced
1 clove garlic	¼ tsp. garlic powder
2 cups tomato sauce	¾ cup tomato paste + 1 cup water
1 Tbsp. prepared mustard	1 tsp. dry mustard + 1 Tbsp. water

How to Know What You Need

Making a shopping list based on a recipe can be tricky if you don't know how many tomatoes yields 3 cups chopped. Our handy translations:

When the Recipe Calls For:	You Need:
4 cups shredded cabbage	1 small cabbage
1 cup grated raw carrot	1 large carrot
2½ cups sliced carrots	1 pound raw carrots
4 cups cooked cut fresh green beans	1 pound beans
1 cup chopped onion	1 large onion
4 cups sliced raw potatoes	4 medium-size potatoes
1 cup chopped sweet pepper	1 large pepper
1 cup chopped tomato	1 large tomato
2 cups canned tomatoes	16 oz. can
4 cups sliced apples	4 medium-size apples
1 cup mashed banana	3 medium-size bananas
1 tsp. grated lemon rind	1 medium-size lemon
2 Tbsp. lemon juice	1 medium-size lemon
4 tsp. grated orange rind	1 medium-size orange
1 cup orange juice	3 medium-size oranges
4 cups sliced peaches	8 medium-size peaches
2 cups sliced strawberries	1 pint
1 cup soft bread crumbs	2 slices fresh bread
1 cup bread cubes	2 slices fresh bread
2 cups shredded Swiss or Cheddar cheese	8 oz. cheese
1 cup egg whites	6 or 7 large eggs
1 egg white	2 tsp. egg white powder + 2 Tbsp. water
4 cups chopped walnuts or pecans	1 pound shelled